The Washington Consensus Reconsidered

THE INITIATIVE FOR POLICY DIALOGUE SERIES

The Initiative for Policy Dialogue (IPD) brings together the top voices in development to address some of the most pressing and controversial debates in economic policy today. The IPD book series approaches topics such as capital market liberalization, macroeconomics, environmental economics, and trade policy from a balanced perspective, presenting alternatives and analyzing their consequences on the basis of the best available research. Written in a language accessible to policymakers and civil society, this series will rekindle the debate on economic policy and facilitate a more democratic discussion of development around the world.

OTHER TITLES PUBLISHED BY OXFORD UNIVERSITY PRESS IN THIS SERIES

Fair Trade for All

Joseph E. Stiglitz and Andrew Charlton

Stability with Growth

Joseph E. Stiglitz, José Antonio Ocampo, Shari Spiegel, Ricardo Ffrench-Davis, and Deepak Nayyar

Economic Development and Environmental Sustainability

Edited by Ramón López and Michael A. Toman

Capital Market Liberalization and Development

Edited by José Antonio Ocampo and Joseph E. Stiglitz

The Washington Consensus Reconsidered

Towards a New Global Governance

Edited by

Narcís Serra and Joseph E. Stiglitz

OXFORD
UNIVERSITY PRESS

Great Clarendon Street, Oxford OX2 6DP

Oxford University Press is a department of the University of Oxford. It furthers the University's objective of excellence in research, scholarship, and education by publishing worldwide in

Oxford New York

Auckland Cape Town Dar es Salaam Hong Kong Karachi Kuala Lumpur Madrid Melbourne Mexico City Nairobi New Delhi Shanghai Taipei Toronto

With offices in

Argentina Austria Brazil Chile Czech Republic France Greece Guatemala Hungary Italy Japan Poland Portugal Singapore South Korea Switzerland Thailand Turkey Ukraine Vietnam

Oxford is a registered trade mark of Oxford University Press in the UK and in certain other countries

Published in the United States by Oxford University Press Inc., New York

First published 2008

British Library Cataloguing in Publication Data
Data available

Library of Congress Cataloging in Publication Data
Data available

Typeset by SPI Publisher Services, Pondicherry, India
Printed in Great Britain
on acid-free paper by
Biddles Ltd., King's Lynn, Norfolk

ISBN 978–0–19–953408–1
ISBN 978–0–19–953409–8 (Pbk)

10 9 8 7 6 5 4 3 2 1

Acknowledgements

This book is the work of the participants of the seminar series 'From the Washington Consensus, Towards a New Global Governance', which culminated at the Universal Forum of Cultures in Barcelona in 2004.

The seminars were co-hosted by the Initiative for Policy Dialogue (IPD) at Columbia University and the Center for International Relations and Development Studies (CIDOB) in Barcelona. IPD is a global network of over 250 economists, researchers and practitioners committed to furthering understanding of the development process. The CIDOB Foundation is a research, training and documentation center devoted to international relations and development studies. Both organizations are grateful to each other for a wonderful intellectual and working relationship and for the great hospitality given when visiting each other's cities.

We would like to thank all seminar participants, whose contributions to the provocative and productive dialogues and debates on global governance alternatives informed the content of this book.

Thanks to the members of the advisory committee for their enthusiasm and energetic devotion to the project, despite their own significant responsibilities.

We would like to extend a special thank you to Joan Clos, the Mayor of Barcelona, for his encouragement and personal involvement in our endeavor. Joan attended the entire conference, including the long dinners and off-table discussions.

Special thanks to Mireia Belil and her dialogue team in particular, Lourdes and Cristina, who worked behind the scenes to ensure that the event ran smoothly. Also of invaluable help behind the scenes were Jorge Blázquez, Carlos Ocaña and Rocío Martínez-Sampere.

We would also like to thank friends Pasqual Maragall, Lionel Jospin, Antonio Guterres, Carlos Slim, Gerry Arsenis and Felipe González for responding quickly to our invitation and graciously adding a necessary political dimension to the discussion.

Special thanks goes to Shari Spiegel, who served as Executive Director of IPD over the course of this project, and to Shana Hoftsetter for organizing meetings and to Sylvia Wu for her role in editing the book.

Thank you also to IPD staff Sheila Chanani, Sarah Green, Siddhartha Gupta, Ariel Schwartz and Lauren Anderson, as well as interns Dora Beszterczey and James Giganti, for helping to manage the project and coordinate production of the book.

We thank our editors Sarah Caro and Jennifer Wilkinson and the staff of Oxford University Press for bringing this book into publication.

We are most grateful to The John D. and Catherine T. MacArthur Foundation and the Ford Foundation for supporting the seminar series and the work of IPD.

Finally, a very special thank you to the people of Barcelona, who embraced the Universal Forum of Cultures and enriched our debates through their attendance and enthusiastic participation.

Contents

List of Figures

List of Tables

List of Contributors

Alice H. Amsden is Barton L. Weller Professor of Political Economy at the Massachusetts Institute of Technology.

Olivier Blanchard is Class of 1941 Professor at the Massachusetts Institute of Technology.

Guillermo Calvo is Professor of Economics, Public and International Affairs at Columbia University, and Former Chief Economist of the Inter-American Development Bank (IADB), Washington, DC.

Daniel Cohen, Paris School of Economics, OECD Development Centre, and Center for Economic Policy Research (CEPR).

Jeffrey A. Frankel is Harpel Professor at the Kennedy School of Government, Harvard University.

Ricardo Hausmann, John F. Kennedy School of Government, Harvard University.

Martin Khor is a journalist, economist, and Director of the Third World Network, which is based in Penang, Malaysia.

Paul Krugman is Professor of Economics and International Affairs at Princeton University.

Deepak Nayyar is Professor of Economics at Jawaharlal Nehru University, New Delhi, India.

José Antonio Ocampo is Co-President of the Initiative for Policy Dialogue and Professor at Columbia University.

Dani Rodrik, John F. Kennedy School of Government, Harvard University.

Narcís Serra is President of the CIDOB Foundation, Centre for International Relations and Development Studies, Barcelona.

Shari Spiegel is Senior Portfolio Manager, New Holland Capital.

Joseph Stiglitz is Co-President of the Initiative for Policy Dialogue and University Professor at Columbia University.

Ernesto Talvi is the Executive Director of Centro de Estudios de la Realidad Económica y Social (CERES), a public policy research institution in Montevideo, Uruguay, specializing in economic analysis of Latin America.

Andrés Velasco, John F. Kennedy School of Government, Harvard University.

John Williamson is Senior Fellow at the Peterson Institute for International Economics.

Foreword

Both of us, one a policymaker and the other an academic who has worked in both government and an international financial institution, have long been reflecting on the effects that the prevailing neoliberal economic policy recipe has had on developing economies and on economic doctrine in general. The Universal Forum of Cultures, which took place in Barcelona from March to September 2004, appeared as a magnificent opportunity to organize a lively debate on the issue. The Forum was a new world event based on cultures and the arts, designed to counter the tensions of globalization through dialogue, debate, and celebration. We both hoped that something more might emerge: a new post-Washington Consensus consensus, perhaps a Barcelona Consensus, on the kinds of economic policies that would best promote development of the poorest countries of the world.

The spirit of the World Forum coincided perfectly with the spirit that underlay the founding of the Initiative for Policy Dialogue (IPD) at Columbia University, which was predicated on the belief that open dialogue is an essential part of democratic life, and is necessary to create policies that will succeed in enhancing the well-being of those in the developing world. Joan Clos, Mayor of Barcelona, not only believed in the importance of the project from the very beginning, but also encouraged us to 'use' the Forum as the most appropriate context and best atmosphere in which to put into effect an initiative such as the one we had in mind.

The first step we took was to nominate a steering committee under the coordination of both Centre for International Relations and Development Studies (CIDOB) and IPD. We want to use this opportunity to thank Mr Ramon Caminal, Professor of Economics, CSIC; Mr Antón Costas, Professor of Economics, University of Barcelona; Mr Guillermo de la Dehesa, Chairman of CEPR; Mr Jordi Galí, Director of CREI, University Pompeu Fabra; Mr Miguel Sebastián, Lecturer of Economics, Complutense University of Madrid; Mr Joan Tugores, Professor of Economics, University of Barcelona; Mr Jaume Ventura, Professor of Economics, University Pompeu Fabra; and Mr Xavier Vives, Professor of Economics and Finance, INSEAD—all members of this committee—for their invaluable help and significant work.

This committee met on several occasions throughout 2003 to shape the project. It was decided that the best organization of the two-day event would be a seminar format, which would maximize debate among participants. We combined this with an open floor discussion. The program of the September seminar 'From the Washington Consensus Towards a New Global Governance' was thus designed with this format in mind. In order to facilitate a high quality debate, we organized a preliminary seminar on January 28, 2004, at the Initiative for Policy Dialogue. In this seminar, drafts of the papers were presented and the authors had an opportunity to discuss them. Our objective was to ensure that the program would address the key issues and be balanced both politically and geographically. It would have been easy to achieve a consensus among those on the right or the left; our challenge was to see whether we could achieve a consensus on some core issues that crossed the political and geographical boundaries that divide the world. The Barcelona Development Agenda shows that our hopes were more than realized.

We thought that it would be enlightening to organize a roundtable of politicians to discuss the final document the day following the Barcelona seminar, to get their reactions to what the academics had produced. Gerry Arsenis, former Director of UNCTAD; Felipe González, former President of the Spanish government; Antonio Guterres, former President of the Portuguese government; Lionel Jospin, former President of the French government; and Carlos Slim, President of Fundación Telmex, kindly agreed to participate in this discussion.

The response of the people of Barcelona to the seminar, and the subsequent roundtable, was enormous. More than 1,000 people attended, demonstrating how compelling the issues under discussion have become. We view this volume as a magnificent opportunity to further enhance discussion and to complement the final document, the already widely-discussed Barcelona Development Agenda that came out of the seminar.

Given the nature of the issue, we understood that the seminar would be part of a larger open project, worked in a continuous manner from the very beginning and with no foreseeable end. Development is complex, and our understanding of it will necessarily change—as will the world in which we live.

This explains why we envisaged not just a one-time event to be held in Barcelona, but prior discussions and meetings and a continuing dialogue, including the publication of this book, which contains all of the contributions from the original seminars. We also planned a series of follow-up seminars. In particular, the CIDOB Foundation organized a seminar on the Barcelona agenda focusing on Latin American countries in the wake of the Ibero-American summit that the Spanish government hosted in October 2005; and, in the spirit of the Barcelona Agenda, IPD, working with the Argentinean government, organized a seminar on the Buenos Aires Consensus in August 2005.

IPD is also publishing several task force books that deal with many of the issues covered in the Barcelona Agenda as part of the Oxford University Press

IPD Book Series. In particular, *Stability with Growth*, by Joseph Stiglitz, José Antonio Ocampo, Shari Spiegel, Ricardo Ffrench-Davis, and Deepak Nayyar explores many of the macroeconomic and capital market issues discussed in Barcelona. IPD is also publishing taskforce volumes on most of the other issues covered in the Agenda, including industrial policy, environmental policy, and trade, as part of this series.

We very much hope that this book, and the subsequent CIDOB and IPD books and events, will continue to stimulate debate on these crucial topics.

Joseph E. Stiglitz
Co-President, Initiative for Policy Dialogue and University Professor, Columbia University

Narcís Serra
President, CIDOB Foundation, Centre for International Relations and Development Studies in Barcelona

Part I

The Washington Consensus: From Its Origins to Its Critics

1

Introduction: From the Washington Consensus Towards a New Global Governance

Narcís Serra, Shari Spiegel, and Joseph E. Stiglitz

The point of departure for this book is the Washington Consensus—the set of views about effective development strategies that have come to be associated with the Washington-based institutions: the IMF, the World Bank, and the US Treasury. John Williamson (1990) provided a brilliant articulation of that consensus. According to Williamson, 'The Washington Consensus was a ... response to a leading role for the state in initiating industrialization and import substitution. The Washington Consensus said that this era was over' (Williamson 1990). Proponents of the Washington Consensus argue that the original conception had three big ideas: a market economy, openness to the world, and macroeconomic discipline.[1]

Since its inception in 1990, the term Washington Consensus has come to be used in ways that are both narrower and broader than what was envisioned in the original conception. The current interpretation is narrower in that it focuses primarily on privatization, liberalization, and macro stability—meaning price stability; it is broader in that it includes some forms of liberalization not included in the original definition, such as capital market liberalization. More generally, the Washington Consensus has come to be associated with 'market fundamentalism,' the view that markets solve most, if not all, economic problems by themselves—views from which Williamson has carefully distanced himself.

As Joseph Stiglitz points out in his contribution to this volume, advances in economic theory in the 1970s showed that market failures are pervasive, especially in developing economies rife with imperfections in information, limitations in competition, and incomplete markets. Under these conditions,

[1] See Williamson (2002).

there is a presumption that markets are *not* efficient. Stiglitz argues that these advances in economic theory had already removed the intellectual foundations of market fundamentalism before the Washington Consensus became fashionable. Accordingly, it should not have come as much of a surprise that the Washington Consensus prescriptions (as broadly interpreted) failed to work as promised, and that disillusion with the Washington Consensus grew throughout the developing world.[2, 3]

In the countries that followed Washington Consensus policies, economic growth was limited at best, and disproportionately benefited those at the top. In Latin America, for example, seven years of strong growth in the early 1990s were followed by seven years of stagnation and recession, so that for the period as a whole, growth under the Washington Consensus was half of what it had been from the 1950s through the 1970s when the region followed other economic policies, such as import substitution. Even in countries where Washington Consensus policies did appear to promote growth, such growth was often not accompanied by significant reductions in poverty.

Meanwhile, the countries of East Asia followed a quite different set of policies, and had enormous successes. For instance, governments played an important role in promoting particular industries. In some cases, government enterprises (such as Korea's national steel company) became global leaders in efficiency. To be sure, governments in the region did maintain macro stability, but they were slow to liberalize trade, and some countries, such as China, still have not fully liberalized capital markets. In short, both theory and evidence weigh heavily against what has come to be called Washington Consensus policies.

[2] The first chapter of this book contains a brief discussion of the relationship between the Washington Consensus as formulated by Williamson, and how that term had come to be widely understood. We have already noted one key difference: Williamson never elevated capital market liberalization as one of the key policies that countries need to pursue, but this was at the heart of the IMF's agenda. The IMF went so far as to try (unsuccessfully) to change its charter to allow it to push capital market liberalization on wary developing countries.

[3] Williamson's Washington Consensus centered on ten reforms: (i) fiscal discipline in order to eliminate public deficits; (ii) a change in the priorities of public spending: withdrawal of subsidies and increased spending in health and education; (iii) tax reform: broadening tax bases and reducing tax rates; (iv) positive real interest rates, determined by the market; (v) exchange rates determined by the market, which must guarantee its competitiveness; (vi) liberalization of trade and opening of the economy (Williamson did not attach any priority to the liberalization of capital flows); (vii) no restrictions on foreign direct investment; (viii) privatization of public enterprises; (ix) deregulation of economic activity; (x) a solid guarantee of property rights.

We can organize Williamson's ten items into two main groups: on one hand, the promotion of economic stability through fiscal adjustment and market orthodoxy; on the other hand, a dramatic reduction of the role of the state in the economy. It was a development strategy that markedly differed from the import substitution strategy that dominated in the 1970s.

The chapters in this book can be viewed as *revisiting* the Washington Consensus through an examination of its original formulations, how it has come to be interpreted, and what has been left out. The volume is divided into three parts. Part I introduces the debate on the Washington Consensus. It includes both a short history by John Williamson—in which he traces the origin of the term and argues that the original meaning of the Washington Consensus is very different from how the term has come to be used—as well as a discussion on the later usage by Joseph Stiglitz. The chapters in this section are more informal and less academic than chapters in the rest of the book, and we hope they'll give the reader an impression of the spirit of the debate, as well as the issues involved.

The chapters in this section also set the stage for a formulation of a post-Washington Consensus consensus. John Williamson argues that the reforms listed in 1990 are no longer adequate, and proposes a set of reforms to the original consensus. Stiglitz's chapter presents ideas for a framework on what a new consensus might look like, and how it might differ from the original Washington Consensus. Although not everyone at the Barcelona meeting agreed with all of Stiglitz's recommendations, his chapter sets a frame for the ensuing discussion on a new consensus. Despite their differing perspectives, the participants were able to reach a broad consensus as to what a new development agenda might look like. The details of the agreement, the Barcelona Development Agenda, are presented in the final chapter of Part I.

Part II of the book analyzes in more detail many of the issues that were discussed at the Barcelona meeting and included in the agreed-upon set of principles. The chapters in this section look at domestic policies (such as macroeconomic and industrial policies) as well as issues surrounding the international financial architecture, a topic that was not addressed in the original Washington Consensus. One goal of this section is to examine where agreements exist, as well as the limits of those agreements—where reasonable people might disagree with each other. Because of the different perspectives of the participants, some of the chapters in this section sometimes present different interpretations of the same problems, and give different solutions. For example, while Jeffrey Frankel and Martin Khor agree that the current trading system needs reforms, they disagree on the underlying benefits of trade agreements for economic development. We present both chapters in this volume.

The final part of the book looks towards formulating new policy frameworks beyond the Washington Consensus. Dani Rodrik, Andrés Velasco, and Ricardo Hausmann outline a new framework for domestic policy designs, and Joseph Stiglitz examines how global governance must be reformed to keep pace with economic globalization.

The Barcelona Development Agenda

The Barcelona Development Agenda is made up of seven general principles. Most starkly, in contrast with the old doctrines, the Barcelona principles emphasize a balanced role for the state and markets, experimentation as a tool for development, and the use of microeconomic interventions to redress market failures and promote productivity (combined with incentives for improved performance).

Several of the principles outlined represent longstanding views on successful development, such as the need to maintain macroeconomic discipline. These remain as important today as they were more than 15 years ago, when Williamson formulated the Washington Consensus. Others represent the continual evolution of our understanding of the development process—an emphasis on institutions and the importance of orderly and sequential reforms. And several represent a major departure from the past, such as the importance of income distribution, poverty reduction, and maintaining the environment, as well as the importance of tailoring policies to country-specific situations—issues that were not included in the Washington Consensus, but that after the debacles that marked the many crises of the 1990s and the early years of this century, are perhaps now self-evident. For example, John Williamson's chapter acknowledges that one of the major failings of the original Washington Consensus (even as it was originally formulated) is that it didn't include equity. In his contribution, Paul Krugman examines the key issue of income inequality in more detail and analyzes implications for a post-Washington Consensus consensus.

In many ways, the Washington Consensus was a consensus for liberalization and globalization rather than a consensus for equitable growth and sustainable development. After all, as we've pointed out, reducing poverty, equity, and sustaining the environment were not part of the Consensus. The Washington Consensus called for the opening of countries to the outside world.[4] As a result, the fortunes of developing countries have increasingly depended on what happens outside their boundaries, such as the access of developing countries to foreign markets, foreigners' access to their markets, and instability in exchange rates and capital markets, (which affect the availability of capital and the interest rates developing countries have to pay). Yet, the Washington Consensus didn't address the international architecture necessary to govern globalization.

Participants in the Barcelona Conference agreed that, in general, international arrangements are not working well. Several of the points of the

[4] As we have noted, the extent to which this was done differed in the 'narrow' conception (of Williamson himself, who rejected capital market liberalization) and the broader conception.

Barcelona principles addressed these failures, and several of the chapters in this volume focus on the facets of economic globalization (capital flows, trade, intellectual property, and labor) in which international arrangements and global governance have not kept pace with the changing world, or in which the arrangements significantly disadvantaged developing countries. There was agreement that multilateral trade negotiations and international financial arrangements need to be reformed. There was also a consensus on the need for a set of international rules and institutions to guide cross-border movements of people. Similarly there was an agreement that the worsening of the environment, including global warming, needs to be tackled globally as well as nationally.

Central Issues in Development

The Washington Consensus took stands on issues that many economists (who were not part of the policymaking circles in Washington at the time) disagreed on how both theory and evidence should be interpreted. Even those topics that remain high on the 'agenda,' such as macroeconomic stability, are open to alternative interpretations. While no one would have advocated macroeconomic *instability*, what constitutes 'good' macroeconomic policy remains contentious. In the first chapter of Part II, José Antonio Ocampo calls for a broader view of macroeconomic stability that includes not only price stability and sound fiscal policies, but also a stable *real* economy. It was natural in 1990, for example, after the episodes of high inflation and hyperinflation that Latin America experienced in the 1980s, to emphasize price stability. But *real stability*—variability in unemployment or real growth—is as, or arguably more, important. Price stability, as we have learned, may not lead to growth or full employment, and excessive zeal in pushing for price stability may stifle growth and lead to high levels of unemployment. Ocampo emphasizes the importance of developing a macroeconomic framework that includes an active role for countercyclical government policies, together with capital management techniques (including capital account regulations and prudential regulations).

In the next chapter in this section, Alice Amsden takes a closer look at industrial policy, an issue that the Washington Consensus took a strong stand against. The term 'industrial policy' lost credibility after the Latin American economic crises in the 1980s. But the argument against these policies is based on a naive reading of economic theory and a misreading of economic history. As discussed earlier, standard economic theory is based on perfectly competitive markets, which rarely exist, especially in developing countries. Modern economic research and recent experience have shown that markets do not always produce efficient outcomes by themselves, implying that there's a role for government intervention. Standard theories of market efficiency also assume that technology is fixed.[5] Yet, it is the change in technology and the development and adoption of new modes of production and products that is at the center of economic growth. On the other hand, economic theory that recognizes the existence of asymmetric and incomplete information and markets has created a strong presumption for the role of government and industrial policies. Knowledge is a public good—in the technical sense that when another individual comes to know a particular piece of knowledge, it does not subtract from the knowledge that others have ('consumption is non-rivalrous'); and the production of knowledge, like the production of other public goods, will be below the optimal level if left to the private sector alone.[6]

Critics of industrial policy cite failures and abuses that existed in the past. However, countries in East Asia, such as Korea, were able to use forms of industrial policy to develop high technology industries, resulting in real economic growth. Amsden argues that the benefits of globalization can only be realized by developing countries that have their own nationally owned companies, which expand abroad. In her view, governments should promote private nationally owned enterprises.

The discussion of industrial policy at the Conference made it clear that the issue is still controversial and not all the participants at the Barcelona meeting agreed with this perspective, as we discuss below. There was, however, a general acknowledgement that many successful developing countries have used industrial promotion as a tool for sustained growth. The Barcelona principles included an agreement that carefully designed policies aimed at market failures can be useful tools for development.

Highlighting the alternative views at the Conference, Guillermo Calvo and Ernesto Talvi argue that the reform agenda of the 1990s had a strong beneficial effect; they agree with much of what the Washington Consensus said. In their view, the problem is with what it left out—such as an adequate recognition

[5] The rigorous formulation of Adam Smith's 'invisible hand' conjecture, that the pursuit of self-interest leads as if by an invisible hand to economic efficiency, is due to Arrow and Debreu. They showed that competitive markets are only efficient under highly restricted conditions. Greenwald and Stiglitz (1986) extended their analysis, showing that whenever markets were incomplete (e.g., there does not exist a complete set of risk markets) or information is imperfect (always the case), then markets are not efficient. This changed the presumption: while earlier, the presumption was that *unless there was a limited set of market failures,* so long as one maintained competition, markets would be efficient. Now the presumption was that *even with competition,* markets would not be efficient, and that these problems were likely to be particularly severe in areas, like financial markets, where information was at the center of the analysis. All of these analyses, however, assumed *fixed* technology. But as Stiglitz (1975) argued, changes in knowledge were very much like changes in information—they were, in fact changes in information about how to organize and conduct production—so that markets would not work well when technology was endogenous.

[6] See Stiglitz (1999, 1987). This view has since become standard in the literature on innovation.

of the imperfections in capital markets. They argue that most of the failures of the late 1990s and early 2000s came from sudden stops in international capital flows, combined with domestic financial vulnerabilities. In contrast to Ocampo, who presents a compelling argument on the need for managing capital inflows through direct controls and regulations, Calvo and Talvi believe that capital controls are not effective tools. In their view, countries need to focus on fixing key points of financial vulnerability, and the international community needs to reform the international financial architecture to mobilize a stable source of capital flows to developing countries.

Daniel Cohen's chapter examines the failures of the international financial architecture from a different perspective. He focuses on the resolution, rather than prevention, of crises. In particular, he looks at how to resolve sovereign debt crises, and introduces an innovative proposal for the use of standstills on the debtor side, collective actions clauses on the creditor side, and a lender of 'first resort' by the international financial institutions.

The sense of unhappiness with the international financial architecture was reinforced by the inequities in the global trading regime. Not only was there an agreement that the overall international economic architecture is not working, but there was also a consensus that the system of international governance is biased against developing countries. This bias is most evident in the WTO trade regime, which has allowed developed countries to retain their agricultural subsidies, but greatly curtailed the use of trade policy by developing countries to promote their own development and to protect those who might be adversely affected by unfettered liberalization.[7] Though we did not achieve a consensus on reforming the system of global governance at Barcelona, the consensus that there was a need for reform—across a broad spectrum of participants, from the left to the right—was itself significant.

As we mentioned above, we include two contributions on reforming the global trading system. Both authors argue for the need for reform. Jeffrey Frankel argues that countries can still gain considerably from opening their markets and integrating into the global trading system. He questions the significance of non-economic effects of increased trade such as increased pollution, and argues that such issues need to be addressed through other multilateral institutions. Martin Khor, on the other hand, argues more broadly that the current trading system doesn't address development needs of poor countries. He is not convinced that countries necessarily gain from opening their markets. For example, he argues that inappropriate import liberalization can have negative effects on industry and agriculture in developing countries.

[7] Unfettered liberalization would, for instance, hurt farmers in both the north and the south. The instrument of choice in the north for protecting farmers is subsidies, but developing countries do not have the resources to subsidize their farmers. Money spent on subsidizing farmers is money that cannot be spent on education or investments in infrastructure. But the alternative, tariff protection or quotas, are not allowed under the WTO regime.

Khor's chapter also addresses imbalances in the current intellectual property multilateral agreements. The debate on intellectual property in the 1990s and early 2000s tended to assume that stronger intellectual property regimes were better, for both rich and poor countries. But, as economists have long recognized, a stronger regime may not be better. Ultimately, it is not just a question of 'strong' or 'weak' intellectual property rights, but the design of the intellectual property regime that matters. Unbalanced rules can have huge implications for public health and global distribution, and can impede efforts to close the 'knowledge gap' between developed and developing countries by restricting the ability of domestic firms in developing countries to adopt modern technology. Yet, as Khor points out, the benefits of WTO's Agreement on Trade-Related Aspects of Intellectual Property Rights (TRIPS) primarily accrue to the wealthy countries while the costs (higher prices and royalties) are disproportionately borne by developing countries. His chapter concludes with proposals for making the intellectual property regime and the global trading system more development oriented.

The final facet of economic globalization covered in our volume is the flow of labor. We start by examining domestic labor policies. The Washington Consensus sent a standard message for countries to increase labor market flexibility. The reasoning behind this message was clear: *if* markets were in every other way perfect (e.g., perfect competition, perfect information, perfect capital and risk markets), then wage rigidities could give rise to unemployment—indeed, under the stated assumptions, they would presumably be *the* explanation for unemployment. The problem with this view, however, is that some of the labor market inflexibilities are *endogenous,* the response, for instance, to imperfect information and incomplete insurance.[8] When other markets are imperfect or inflexible, workers end up bearing the cost of economic adjustments through lower wages and unemployment, even when labor market problems are not the core of the problem facing the country. Private markets on their own have not done a good job of protecting workers. Olivier Blanchard's chapter examines domestic labor market institutions and explores unemployment insurance and protection schemes. He also analyzes what optimal structures of unemployment insurance would look like, and how different countries can implement these policies.

Somewhat ironically, labor market flexibility across borders—which could mitigate some of the costs associated with flexible domestic markets by allowing workers to leave when wages fall—was not addressed in the Washington Consensus. Enormous energy has been focused on facilitating the flows of

[8] This is the central point of the efficiency wage and implicit contract theories. For an overview, see, for instance, Stiglitz (1986). The classic paper on efficiency wage is that of Shapiro and Stiglitz (1984). An attempt to integrate implicit contract theory and efficiency wage theory is provided by Richard Arnott et al. (1988). Patrick Rey and J.E. Stiglitz (1993) show that more flexibiity may not result in increased welfare.

investment and capital, while movements of labor remain highly restricted. Whereas capital markets are one of the most integrated facets of economic globalization (as discussed above), labor markets are one of the least. Yet the gains to global economic efficiency from liberalizing labor flows are an order of magnitude greater than the gains from liberalizing capital flows. Indeed, liberalizing movements of short-term speculative capital has been associated with increased instability, but not enhanced economic growth.

This disparity between labor market and capital market liberalization has large distributional consequences. Capital can move easily; it can leave a country if it is taxed or if policies that threaten returns to capital are implemented. Workers, on the other hand, cannot threaten to move. This disparity is one of the reasons for the growing inequality in incomes that have marked most countries around the world, and is one of the reasons that globalization has often led to falling incomes for workers, even when it has brought increases in GDP. Deepak Nayyar's chapter explores the issue of international migration and the effects on economic development. He points out that migration has significant implications on development and that, similar to capital and trade flows, it is important to think of a multilateral framework for cross-border movement of people, one of the principles agreed to as part of the Barcelona Development Agenda.

Towards a New Global Governance

At the time the Washington Consensus was formulated, little attention was paid to the subject of governance—the behavior of public institutions. Since then it has come to the center of the stage. But it is not just governance of countries, but governance of the world economy that is of concern. In the first chapter of Part III of this volume, Joseph Stiglitz builds on the earlier discussion of global institutions to discuss the issue of global governance. He points out that economic globalization has proceeded faster than political globalization. The system of global governance is a patchwork of institutions, agreements, and arrangements that might be called global governance without global government. His chapter examines the structures of global governance, links their deficiencies (for example, their undemocratic nature) to the unsatisfactory observed outcomes, and looks to the forces that may lead to meaningful reform and change.

The final chapters in this volume then look to the next steps for formulating a framework for domestic policy design. The Barcelona Agenda emphasizes the importance of allowing countries to define their own economic policies, and the importance of experimentation for finding successful development strategies. Perhaps more important than the Barcelona Agenda itself, however, is its recognition that while there can be general principles, how these get translated into policies may differ markedly from country to country. Dani Rodrik, Andrés Velasco, and Ricardo Hausmann provide a framework for identifying the set of interrelated critical problems facing an individual country. Dani Rodrik's chapter complements this by outlining a way to think about growth strategies. He suggests that countries focus on where constraints to growth exist, devise imaginative policies to target these constraints, and then learn to institutionalize the process. As we discussed above, within this framework, participants at the meeting agreed that with individualized well-tailored policies, microeconomic tools can be useful complements for macroeconomic management.

The Barcelona Development Agenda is, in our opinion, an important starting point in the formulation of a new and better system of policies—policies that offer more flexible approaches to development, with broader concerns for *equitable* and *sustainable* development—and the creation of a better system of global governance. It provides the basis of a post-Washington Consensus consensus that is now emerging. The new consensus is different from the Washington Consensus in important ways. It emphasizes broader goals for macroeconomic policy (including long-term sustainable growth and equity), a wider range of economic policy instruments (including prudential regulations and other microeconomic tools—though the details of these tools is still being debated), and a balanced role for markets and government (as opposed to minimizing the role of the state).[9] It recognizes the importance of the international architecture and is based on a more democratic global governance with a fairer set of international agreements including better risk sharing between wealthy and poor countries. It further recognizes the need for countries to be able to define their own policies, and the importance of experimentation in policy design. But, this framework is only a starting point. Many questions remain to be answered, and many issues are still being debated. We hope that this book provides the opportunity to continue the dialogue and open up the discussion.

References

Arnott, R., Hosios, A., and Stigliltz, J. E. (1988). 'Implicit Contracts, Labor Mobility and Unemployment'. *American Economic Review*, 78/5: 1046–66 (December).

Greenwald, B. and Stiglitz, J. E. (1986). 'Externalities in Economies with Imperfect Information and Incomplete Markets'. *Quarterly Journal of Economics*, 101/2: 229–64.

Rey, P. and Stiglitz, J. E. (1993). 'Moral Hazard and Unemployment in Competitive Equilibrium'. Working Paper (October).

Shapiro, C. and Stiglitz, J. E. (1984). 'Equilibrium Unemployment as a Worker Discipline Device'. *American Economic Review*, 74/3: 433–44 (June).

[9] For more on the macroeconomic framework for development, see Stiglitz et al. (2006).

Stiglitz, J. E. (1975). 'Information and Economic Analysis', in J. M. Parkin and A. R. Nobay (eds.), *Current Economic Problems*. Cambridge: Cambridge University Press, 27–52. (Proceedings of the Association of University Teachers of Economics, Manchester, England, April 1974.)

—— (1986). 'Theories of Wage Rigidities', in J. L. Butkiewicz, K. J. Koford, and J. B. Miller (eds.), *Keynes' Economic Legacy: Contemporary Economic Theories*. New York: Praeger Publishers, 153–206.

—— (1987). 'On the Microeconomics of Technical Progress', in J. M. Katz (ed.), *Technology Generation in Latin American Manufacturing Industries*. London: Macmillan Press Ltd, 56–77. (Presented to IDB-Cepal Meetings, Buenos Aires, November 1978.)

—— (1999). 'Knowledge as a Global Public Good', in I. Kaul, I. Grunberg, and M. A. Stern (eds.), *Global Public Goods: International Cooperation in the 21st Century*. New York: Oxford University Press, 308–25.

—— Ocampo, J. A., Spiegel, S., Ffrench-Davis, R., and Nayyar, D. (2006). *Stability with Growth: Macroeconomics, Liberalization, and Development*. New York: Oxford University Press.

Williamson, J. (1990). 'What Washington Means by Policy Reform', in J. Williamson (ed.), *Latin American Adjustment: How Much Has Happened?* Washington, DC: Institute for International Economics.

—— (2002) 'Did the Washington Consensus Fail?' Outline of speech at the Center for Strategic & International Studies, Washington, DC.

2

A Short History of the Washington Consensus[1]

John Williamson

Introduction

The term 'Washington Consensus' was coined in 1989. The first written usage was in my background paper for a conference that the Institute for International Economics convened in order to examine the extent to which the old ideas of development economics that had governed Latin American economic policy since the 1950s were being swept aside by the set of ideas that had long been accepted as appropriate within the OECD. In order to try and ensure that the background papers for that conference dealt with a common set of issues, I made a list of ten policies that I thought more or less everyone in Washington would agree were needed more or less everywhere in Latin America, and labeled this the 'Washington Consensus.' Little did it occur to me that 15 years later, I would be asked to write about the history of a term that had become the center of fierce ideological controversy.

The first section of this chapter describes what I recollect about the circumstances of my background paper for the 1989 conference. The second section retraces much more familiar ground, summarizing the ten points that I included in the Washington Consensus. This is followed by an account of the reception given to the term, and the analysis. The next section tries to account for the fact that the term became used in such different ways in different quarters and thus to be at the center of ideological controversies. The last substantive section is forward-looking, and describes what I believe needs to be added to my original list in order to formulate a policy agenda for Latin America today.

[1] A paper presented to a conference 'From the Washington Consensus Towards a New Global Governance' held in Barcelona on September 24–5, 2004.

Background

The story started in the spring of 1989 when I was testifying before a Congressional committee in favor of the Brady Plan. I argued that it would be good policy to help the debtor countries overcome their debt burden, now that they were making profound changes in economic policy, along the lines advocated by Balassa et al. (1986). I encountered rank disbelief in the congressmen before who I was testifying that there were any significant changes in economic policies and attitudes in process in Latin America. After discussion with Fred Bergsten, the Director at the Institute for International Economics where I was (and am) professionally located, we decided to convene a conference to test the extent to which I was correct and to put the change in policy attitudes on the record in Washington.

A few weeks later, I gave a seminar at the Institute for Development Studies in England, where I made much the same argument. I was challenged by Hans Singer to spell out what I meant when I said that many of the countries were changing their policies for the better. This emphasized the need to be very explicit about the policy changes of which I was thinking. I decided that the conference that we were planning for the autumn, which we decided to call 'Latin American Adjustment: How Much Has Happened?' needed a background paper that would spell out the substance of the policy changes in which we were interested. That paper, which was entitled 'What Washington Means by Policy Reform,' was sent to the ten authors who had agreed to write country studies for our conference, in an attempt to ensure that they addressed a common set of issues in their papers.

That paper said, inter alia, on its opening page:

> This paper identifies and discusses 10 policy instruments about whose proper deployment Washington can muster a reasonable degree of consensus.... The paper is intended to elicit comment on both the extent to which the views identified do indeed command a consensus and on whether they deserve to command it. It is hoped that the country studies to be guided by this background paper will comment on the extent to which the Washington consensus is shared in the country in question...
>
> The Washington of this paper is both the political Washington of Congress and senior members of the administration and the technocratic Washington of the international financial institutions, the economic agencies of the U.S. government, the Federal Reserve Board, and the think tanks. The Institute for International Economics made a contribution to codifying and propagating several aspects of the Washington consensus in its publication Towards Renewed Economic Growth in Latin America.
>
> (Balassa et al. 1986)

My opinion at that time was that views had pretty much coalesced on the sort of policies that had long been advocated by the OECD. I specifically did not believe that most of the 'neoliberal' innovations[2] of the Reagan administration in the United States or the Thatcher government in Britain had survived the demise of the former (Mrs Thatcher's government was still in its death throes at the time). The exception was privatization, which was Mrs Thatcher's personal gift to the economic policy agenda of the world, and which, by 1989, had proved its worth. But I thought all the other new ideas with which Reagan and Thatcher had entered office, notably monetarism, supply-side economics, and minimal government, had by then been discarded as impractical or undesirable fads, so no trace of them can be found in what I labeled the 'Washington Consensus.' Of course, acceptance as relevant to the developing world of ideas that had long been motherhood and apple pie in the developed world was a momentous change. All through the Cold War, the world had remained frozen in the 1950s' classification of First, Second, and Third Worlds, each of which was assumed to have its own distinct set of economic laws. The year 1989 marked the end of the Second World, to the great relief of most of its subjects, and also the end of the intellectual apartheid that had so long assumed that citizens of the Third World behaved quite differently than those of the First World. But the globalization of knowledge never meant general acceptance of neoliberalism by any definition I know.

Content of the Original List

The ten reforms that constituted my list were as follows:

1. *Fiscal discipline*. This was in the context of a region where almost all countries had run large deficits that led to balance of payments crises and high inflation, which mainly affected the poor because the rich could stow their money abroad.
2. *Re-ordering public expenditure priorities*. This suggested switching towards pro-growth and pro-poor expenditures, from things like non-merit subsidies to basic health care, education, and infrastructure. It did not call for the entire burden of achieving fiscal discipline to be placed on expenditure cuts; on the contrary, the intention was to be strictly neutral about the desirable size of the public sector, an issue which even a hopeless consensus seeker like me did not imagine that the battle had been resolved with the end of history that was being promulgated at the time.
3. *Tax reform*. The aim was a tax system that would combine a broad tax base with moderate marginal tax rates.

[2] I use the word 'neoliberalism' in its original sense, to refer to the doctrines espoused by the Mont Pelerin Society. If there is another definition, I would love to hear what it is so that I can decide whether neoliberalism is more than an intellectual swear word.

4. *Liberalizing interest rates.* In retrospect, I wish I had formulated this in a broader way as financial liberalization, stressed that views differed on how fast it should be achieved, and—especially—recognized the importance of accompanying financial liberalization with prudential supervision.
5. *A competitive exchange rate.*[3] I fear I indulged in wishful thinking in asserting that there was a consensus in favor of ensuring that the exchange rate would be competitive, which essentially implies an intermediate regime; in fact, Washington was already beginning to edge towards the two corner doctrine, which holds that a country must either fix firmly or else it must float 'cleanly.'
6. *Trade liberalization.* I acknowledged that there was a difference of view about how quickly trade should be liberalized, but everyone agreed that this was the appropriate direction in which to move.
7. *Liberalization of inward foreign direct investment.* I specifically did not include comprehensive capital account liberalization, because I did not believe that it did or should command a consensus in Washington.
8. *Privatization.* As noted already, this was the one area in which what originated as a neoliberal idea had won broad acceptance. We have since been made very conscious that it matters a great deal how privatization is done: it can be a highly corrupt process that transfers assets to a privileged elite for a fraction of their true value, but the evidence is that it brings benefits (especially in terms of improved service coverage) when done properly, and the privatized enterprise either sells into a competitive market or is properly regulated.
9. *Deregulation.* This focused specifically on easing barriers to entry and exit, not on abolishing regulations designed for safety or environmental reasons, or to govern prices in a non-competitive industry.
10. *Property rights.* This was primarily about providing the informal sector with the ability to gain property rights at acceptable cost (inspired by Hernando de Soto's analysis).

First Reactions

The three American discussants whom I had invited to react to my paper were Richard Feinberg (then at the Overseas Development Council), Stanley Fischer

[3] I have seen it asserted that a competitive exchange rate is the same as an undervalued rate. Not so. A competitive rate is a rate that is not overvalued, in other words, that is either undervalued or correctly valued. My fifth point reflects a conviction that overvalued exchange rates are worse than undervalued rates, but a rate that is neither overvalued nor undervalued is better still.

(then Chief Economist at the World Bank), and Allan Meltzer (then, as now, a professor at Carnegie-Mellon University). I invited Feinberg and Meltzer to ensure that I had not represented as consensual anything that one or other side of the political spectrum would regard as rubbish, while Fischer would play the same safeguard role with regard to the international financial institutions (IFIs).

Fischer was most supportive of the basic thrust of the paper, saying that 'there are no longer two competing economic development paradigms' and that 'Williamson has captured the growing Washington consensus on what the developing countries should do.' But he pointed to some areas on which I had not commented and where sharp disagreements remained, such as the environment, military spending, a need for more comprehensive financial reform than freeing interest rates, bringing back flight capital, and freeing flows of financial capital.[4] It was not my intention to argue that controversy had ended, so I would not take issue with his contention that there remained sharp disagreements on a number of issues (including the desirability of capital account liberalization). And indeed, my initial paper did formulate the financial liberalization question too narrowly.

Meltzer expressed his pleasure at finding how much the mainstream had learned (according to my account) about the futility of things such as policy activism, exploiting the unemployment/inflation tradeoff, and development planning. The two elements of my list on which he concentrated his criticism were once again the interest rate question (though here, he focused more on my interim objective of a positive but moderate real interest rate than on the long run objective of interest rate liberalization) and a competitive exchange rate. The criticism of the interest rate objective I regard as merited. His alternative to a competitive exchange rate—namely, a currency board—certainly would not be consensual, but the fact that he raised this issue was my first warning that on the exchange rate question, I had misrepresented the degree of agreement in Washington.

Feinberg started off by suggesting that there really was not much of a consensus at all, but his comment mellowed as it progressed, and he concluded by saying that there was convergence on key concepts, though there was still plenty to argue about. His most memorable line does not appear in his written comment, but consisted of the suggestion that I should have labeled my list the 'Universal Convergence' rather than the 'Washington Consensus,' since the extent of agreement is far short of consensus but runs far wider than Washington. This point was driven home in a fourth comment,

[4] Interestingly, in the light of his position when First Deputy Managing Director of the IMF, he wrote: 'I fear rather that much of Washington does believe strongly that financial capital flows should not be constrained, but that it has simply not yet focused on the problem.'

by Patricio Meller of CIEPLAN in Santiago de Chile. They were, of course, correct, but it was too late to change the terminology.

In the months that followed, I participated in several meetings where I not only argued that the policies included in my ten points were in fact being adopted fairly widely in Latin America, as our conference had confirmed, but also that this was a good thing and that lagging countries should catch up. I know that I never regarded those ten points as constituting the whole of what should be on the policy agenda, but perhaps I was not always as careful in spelling that out as I should have been.

The two points in my original list that seem to me in retrospect the least adequate as a summary of conventional thinking are the two identified by Allan Meltzer—namely, financial liberalization and exchange rate policy. The agenda for financial liberalization went broader than interest rates, to include most importantly the liberalization of credit flows, and (as Joseph Stiglitz has often pointed out) it needed to be supplemented by prudential supervision if it were not to lead almost inexorably to financial crisis. We already had the experience of the Southern Cone liberalization of the late 1970s to emphasize that point, so I clearly should not have overlooked it. On exchange rate policy, I fear I was guilty of wishful thinking in suggesting that opinion had coalesced on something close to my own view, which implies an intermediate regime, whereas in fact I suspect that even then a majority of Washington opinion would have plumped (like Meltzer) for one of the poles.

In arguing that lagging countries should catch up with the policy reforms on my list, I argued on occasion that the East Asian Newly Industrialized Economics (NIEs) had broadly followed those policies. A Korean discussant (whose name I regret to say escapes me) at a conference in Madison challenged this contention; he argued that their macro policies had indeed been prudent, but also asserted (like Alice Amsden and Robert Wade) that their microeconomic policies had involved an active role for the state quite at variance with the thrust of points 4 and 6 through 9 of my list. I think one must concede that some of the East Asian countries, notably Korea and Taiwan, were far from pursuing laissez-faire during their years of catch-up growth, but this does not prove that their rapid growth was attributable to their departure from liberal policies, as critics of the Washington Consensus seem to assume axiomatically. There were, after all, two other East Asian economies that grew with comparable rapidity, in which the state played a much smaller role. Indeed, one of those—namely, Hong Kong—was the closest to a model of laissez-faire that the world has ever seen. It would seem to me more natural to attribute the fast growth of the East Asian NIEs to what they had in common, such as fiscal prudence, high savings rates, work ethic, competitive exchange rates, and a focus on education, rather than to what they did differently, such as industrial policy, directed credit, and import protection. Incidentally, one should compare the policy stance of Korea and Taiwan with that of other developing countries, not with a textbook model of perfect competition. Most of the countries that failed to grow comparably quickly were even less liberal. So even if it was wrong to treat the East Asian NIEs as pin-up examples of the Washington Consensus in action, it is even more misleading to treat them as evidence for rejecting microeconomic liberalization. That controversy cannot be resolved by any simple appeal to what happened in East Asia.

But arguments about the content of the Washington Consensus have always been secondary to the wave of indignation unleashed by the name that I pinned on this list of policy reforms. Some of the reformers obviously believed that I had undercut their local standing by calling it a 'Washington' agenda, and thus suggesting that these were reforms that were being imposed on them rather than being adopted at their own volition because they recognized that those were the reforms their country needed. When I invented the term I was not thinking of making propaganda for economic reform (insofar as I was contemplating making propaganda, it was propaganda for debt relief in Washington, not propaganda for policy reform in Latin America). From the standpoint of making propaganda for policy reform in Latin America, Moisés Naím (2000) has argued that in fact it was a good term in 1989, the year the coalition led by the United States emerged victorious in the Cold War, when people were searching for a new ideology and the ideology of the victors looked rather appealing. But it was a questionable choice in more normal times, and a terrible one in the world that George W. Bush has created, where mention of Washington is hardly the way to curry support from non-Americans. It was, I fear, a propaganda gift to the old left.

Varying Interpretations

To judge by the sales of *Latin American Adjustment: How Much Has Happened?*, the vast majority of those who have launched venomous attacks on the Washington Consensus have not read my account of what I meant by the term. When I read what others mean by it, I have discovered that it has been interpreted to mean bashing the state, a new imperialism, the creation of a laissez-faire global economy, that the only thing that matters is the growth of GDP, and doubtless much else besides. I submit that it is difficult to find any of these implied by the list of ten policy reforms that I presented earlier.

One event that I found extraordinary was to learn that many people in Latin America blamed the adoption of Washington Consensus policies for the collapse of the Argentine economy in 2001. I found this extraordinary because I had for some years been hoping against hope that Argentina would not suffer a collapse like the one that occurred, but was nonetheless driven to the conclusion that it was highly likely because of the fundamental ways in which the country had strayed from two of the most basic precepts of what I had laid out. Specifically, it had adopted a fixed exchange rate that became chronically overvalued (for reasons that were mainly not its fault), and—while its fiscal deficits were smaller than in the 1980s—it had not used its boom years to work down the debt/GDP ratio. Its fiscal policy as the crisis approached was not nearly restrictive enough to sustain the currency board system. None of the good reforms along Washington Consensus lines that Argentina had indeed made during the 1990s—trade liberalization, financial liberalization, privatization, and so on—seemed to me to have the slightest bearing on the crisis. Yet Latin American populists and journalists, and even a few reputable economists, were asserting that the Washington Consensus was somehow to blame for the Argentinean implosion. I am still hoping to learn the causal channel they have in mind.

One must conclude that the term has been used to mean very different things by different people. In fact, it seems to me that there are at least two interpretations of the term beside mine that are in widespread circulation.

One interpretation refers to the policies the Bretton Woods institutions applied towards their client countries, or perhaps the attitude of the US government plus the Bretton Woods institutions.[5] This seems to me a reasonable, well defined usage. In the early days after 1989, there was not much difference between my concept and this one, but over time some substantive differences emerged. The Bretton Woods institutions increasingly came to espouse the so-called bipolar doctrine (at least until the implosion of the Argentine economy in 2001, as a direct result of applying one of the supposedly crisis-free regimes), according to which countries should either float their exchange rate 'cleanly' or else fix it firmly by adopting some institutional device like a currency board. As pointed out above, that is directly counter to my version of the Washington Consensus, which called for a competitive exchange rate, which necessarily implies an intermediate regime since either fixed or floating rates can easily become overvalued. Again, the Bretton Woods institutions, or at least the IMF, came in the mid-1990s to urge countries to liberalize their capital accounts, whereas my version had deliberately limited the call for liberalization of capital flows to FDI. Both of those deviations from the original version were in my opinion terrible, with the second one bearing the major responsibility for causing the Asian crisis of 1997. But there were also some highly positive differences, as the Bank and Fund came to take up some of the issues that I had not judged sufficiently major in Latin America in 1989 to justify inclusion—in particular, governance and corruption, in the case of

[5] For years I was oblivious to this obvious interpretation; I owe my enlightenment to Yaw Ansu of the World Bank. The fact that this usage is widespread was brought home to me vividly at a conference in Havana earlier in 2004. In my presentation to the conference I thought I had gone to pains to distinguish three concepts: my original one and the two variants described in the text. When my presentation was summarized by Fidel Castro, he told the assembled throng that Williamson had said he disagreed with the Washington Consensus in two ways, naming the ways (exchange rate policy and capital account liberalization) in which I had said that this version was inferior to mine!

the Bank, and financial sector reform as reflected in standards and codes, in the case of the Fund. And by the late 1990s, both institutions had replaced their earlier indifference to issues of income distribution with a recognition that it matters profoundly who gains or loses income.

The third interpretation of the term 'Washington Consensus' uses it as a synonym for neoliberalism or market fundamentalism.[6] This I regard as a far more dramatic deviation from the original intent and a thoroughly objectionable perversion of the original meaning. Whatever else the term 'Washington Consensus' may mean, it should surely refer to a set of policies that command or commanded a consensus in some significant part of Washington, either the US government or the IFIs or both, or perhaps both plus some other group. Even in the early years of the Reagan administration, or during Bush 43, it would be difficult to contend that any of the distinctively neoliberal policies, such as supply-side economics, monetarism, or minimal government, commanded much of a consensus, certainly not in the IFIs. And it would be preposterous to associate any of those policies with the Clinton administration. Yet most of the diatribes against the Washington Consensus have been directed against this third concept, with those using the term this way apparently unconcerned with the need to establish that there actually was a consensus in favor of the policies they love to hate.[7]

Why should the term have come to be used in such different ways? I find it easy enough to see why the second usage emerged. The term initially provided a reasonable description of the policies of the Bretton Woods institutions (indeed, the list was constructed as an attempt to portray the essence of what the institutions were preaching), and as these evolved, the term continued to refer to what these currently were.

What puzzles me is how the third usage became so popular. One possible hypothesis is that this was an attempt to discredit economic reform by bundling a raft of ideas that deserve to be consigned to oblivion along with the list of common sense, pro-reform proposals that constituted my original list. This was doubtless facilitated by the name that I had bestowed on my list, which gave an incentive to anyone who disliked the policies or attitudes of

[6] For example, Stiglitz (2002: 74) writes 'The Washington Consensus policies . . . were based on a simplistic model of the market economy, the competitive equilibrium model, in which Adam Smith's invisible hand works, and works perfectly. Because in this model there is no need for government—that is, free, unfettered, "liberal" markets work perfectly—the Washington Consensus policies are sometimes referred to as "neo-liberal", based on "market fundamentalism" . . . '

[7] I find it ironic that one of the chairmen of President Clinton's Council of Economic Advisers should have adopted this usage, since my understanding of the definition of the word consensus would preclude a Washington Consensus including anything to which he took serious objection while in office as either chairman of the US Council of Economic Advisers or Chief Economist at the World Bank.

the US government or the IFIs to join in a misrepresentation of the policies they were promoting. But an alternative hypothesis is that some people really do believe that the IFIs, or at least the IMF (and perhaps the US Treasury too), promote market fundamentalism and minimal government. Stiglitz (2002) certainly writes as though he believes this, and therefore treats the second and third senses as synonymous. I must say I find this rather preposterous: I have often found the IMF's positions to be more conservative than my own views, but never that its policy positions depended upon the far-fetched contention that markets work perfectly. Stiglitz's view that the IMF has a theological belief in market fundamentalism is pure assertion, unsupported by a single citation.

In any event, surely intellectual integrity demands a conscientious attempt in the future to distinguish alternative concepts of the Washington Consensus. Semantic issues may not be the most exciting ones, but being clear about the way in which terms are being used is a necessary condition for serious professional discussion. The practice of dismissing requests for clarification as tedious pedantry should be unacceptable. Perhaps then more critics would follow the example of the Korean discussant to whom I referred earlier, who laid out precisely to which elements of my original agenda he objected. Or if a critic chooses to use the third concept, then surely he should say that he is talking about a concept of the Washington Consensus that has never commanded a consensus in Washington.

The Future

However much exception I may take to some of the assaults that have been made on the Washington Consensus, I have to admit that I too am uncomfortable if it is interpreted as a comprehensive agenda for economic reform. Even in 1989, there was one objective of economic policy that I regard as of major importance but that found only very tenuous reflection in the Consensus.[8] Since then 15 years have passed, and it would be remarkable (and depressing) if no new ideas worthy of inclusion in the policy agenda had emerged. Hence there are two reasons why my policy agenda of today can differ from the Washington Consensus as I laid it out in 1989: because I am not limiting myself to doctrines able to command a consensus but am presenting what I believe deserves to be done, and because time has passed and ideas have developed.

[8] I am referring to equity, which did not play a larger role because I regret to say that I could not convince myself that the Washington of 1989 (or 2004, for that matter) agreed that equity was of any consequence. The one respect in which it did appear was in the second point, which said that public expenditure should be redirected from non-merit subsidies, defense, and administration towards things like primary education, health, and infrastructure that would be both pro-growth and pro-equity. This doctrine had by then become well-established in the World Bank.

A book that I co-edited last year (Kuczynski and Williamson 2003) addressed the issue of delineating a policy agenda appropriate for Latin America in the current decade. Note that this new agenda, like the original Washington Consensus, was aimed specifically at Latin America at a particular moment of history, rather than claiming to be a text for all countries at all times as many critics have interpreted it to be. We identified four major topics that ought to be included.

The first of these is stabilization policy. The need for more proactive policies to keep the economy on an even keel has been driven home with great force in recent years by the horrifying price that many emerging markets have paid for the crises to which so many have been exposed. When I drew up the Washington Consensus the overwhelming need—at least in Latin America—was to conquer inflation, so that was the macroeconomic objective that I emphasized. Had it occurred to me that my list would be regarded in some quarters as a comprehensive blueprint for policy practitioners, I hope that I would have added the need for policies designed to crisis-proof economies and stabilize them against the business cycle (the sort of measures that Ricardo Ffrench-Davis has advocated under the heading of 'reforming the reforms').

A first implication is to use fiscal policy as a countercyclical tool, insofar as possible. The most effective way to do this seems to be to strengthen the automatic stabilizers and let them operate. (It seems unlikely that emerging markets would have more success with discretionary fiscal policy than the developed countries have had.) Most developing countries have been precluded from doing even this by a need to keep the markets happy, which has required deflationary fiscal policy during difficult times. The way to end this is to use booms to work down debt levels to a point at which the market will consider them creditworthy, which means that countercyclical fiscal policy can be initiated only during the boom phase of the cycle. Chile in the 1990s is an example of what other developing countries should try to do.

Obviously there are other tools besides fiscal policy that may help minimize the probability of encountering a crisis and its cost, if it nevertheless occurs. Exchange rate policy may be the most crucial, since many of the emerging market crises of recent years have originated in the attempt to defend a more or less fixed exchange rate. For this reason most countries have abandoned the use of fixed or predetermined exchange rates in favor of some version of floating. However, there is still an important difference of view between those who think of floating as implying a commitment on the part of the government not to think about what exchange rate is appropriate, versus those who take the view that floating is simply avoidance of a commitment to defend a particular margin.

In the latter view, which I share, it is still perfectly appropriate for a government to have a view on what range of rates would be appropriate, and to slant policy with a view to pushing the rate towards that range, even if it avoids guaranteeing that the rate will stay within some defined margins. In particular, I would argue that while a government should freely allow depreciation in order to avoid or limit the damage of a crisis, it should, if necessary, be proactive in seeking to limit appreciation in good times, when investors are pushing in money. If a country has a sufficiently efficient and uncorrupt civil service to be able to make capital controls work (like the Chilean uncompensated reserve requirement of the 1990s), then it should be prepared if necessary to use capital controls to limit the inflow of foreign funds and hence help to maintain a competitive exchange rate.

Monetary policy is also highly pertinent to countercyclical policy. Many countries, especially those that have abandoned a fixed exchange rate and were therefore seeking a new nominal anchor, have told their central banks to use an inflation targeting framework to guide monetary policy. This appears a sensible choice, provided at least that it is not interpreted so rigidly as to preclude some regard for the state of the real economy when setting monetary policy.

Recent experience has demonstrated conclusively that the severity of a crisis is magnified when a country has a large volume of debt denominated in foreign exchange (see, e.g., Goldstein and Turner 2004). This is because currency depreciation, which does—and should—occur when a crisis develops, increases the real value of the debts of those who have their obligations denominated in foreign currency. If the banks took the exchange risk by borrowing in foreign currency and on-lending in local currency, then their solvency will be threatened directly. If they sought to avoid that risk by on-lending in foreign currency, then their debtors' financial position will be undermined (especially if they are in the non-tradable sector) and the banks are likely to end up with a large volume of bad loans, which may also threaten their solvency. If the government contracted foreign currency debt (or allowed the private sector to shield itself by unloading its foreign currency debt when conditions turned threatening), then the effect of a currency depreciation will be to increase public sector debt and thereby undermine confidence at a critical time. Whatever the form of such borrowing, it can intensify any difficulties that may emerge. The solution is to curb borrowing in foreign currency. The government can perfectly well just say no when deciding the currency composition of its own borrowing, and issue bonds in local currency (as more and more emerging markets are now starting to do). Bank supervision can be used to discourage bank borrowing and lending in foreign exchange. The more difficult issue is foreign currency borrowing by corporations. To prevent that would require the imposition of controls on the form of foreign borrowing. Perhaps it makes more sense to be content with discouraging, rather than completely preventing, foreign currency denominated borrowing. That could be achieved by taxation policy, which could give less tax relief for interest payments on foreign currency loans, and/or charge higher taxes on interest receipts on such loans.

Obviously crisis-proofing an economy may require attention to other issues. For example, in many countries, sub-national government units face a soft budget constraint, which for well-known reasons is not good for stabilization policy. But the purpose of this section is to give an idea of the issues that are important in designing a policy agenda, not to write a comprehensive account of every issue that may face a policy practitioner, so I will leave this first issue.

The second general heading of our policy agenda consisted of pushing on with the liberalizing reforms that were embodied in the original Washington Consensus, and extending them to areas like the labor market where economic performance is being held back by excessive rigidity. One does not have to be some sort of market fundamentalist who believes that less government is better government and that externalities can safely be disregarded in order to recognize the benefits of using market forces to coordinate activity and motivate effort. This is a proposition that is such a basic part of economic thinking that it is actually rather difficult to think of a work that conclusively establishes its truth. But there are a variety of indirect confirmations, from the universal acclaim that meets the abandonment of rationing to the success of emissions trading in reducing pollution at far lower cost than was anticipated.

It is certainly true that the move to adopt a more liberal policy stance in many developing countries over the past two decades has as yet had the hoped-for effect of stimulating growth in only a few countries, like India. The results have not been comparably encouraging in, say, Latin America (Kuczynski and Williamson 2003; Ocampo 2004). But the blame for this seems to me to lie in the misguided macroeconomic policies—like allowing exchange rates to become overvalued and making no attempt to stabilize the cycle—that accompanied the microeconomic reforms, rather than in the latter themselves. The same was true in the UK under Mrs Thatcher and in New Zealand when Roger Douglas was Finance Minister; both undertook far-reaching microeconomic liberalizations that can now be seen to have arrested and even reversed the relative decline of those countries, but their peoples saw no benefits for the best part of a decade because of the primitive macro policies that accompanied the micro reforms.

When we asked what is most in need of liberalization in Latin America today, we concluded that it is the labor market. Around 50 percent of the labor force in many Latin American countries is in the informal sector. This means that they do not enjoy even the most basic social benefits, like health insurance, some form of safeguard against unemployment, and the right to a pension in old age. What people do get is the right to maintain, through thick and thin, a formal sector job if they are lucky enough to have one, and a wide range of social benefits that go along with all formal sector jobs. Not all these benefits appear to be highly valued, to judge by the stories of workers taking second jobs to supplement what they can earn in their guaranteed maximum of 40 hours, or taking another job during their guaranteed summer vacations. So we proposed to flexibilize firing for good reason and curtail the obligation to pay those elements of the social wage that appear less appreciated, in the belief that this will reduce the cost of employing labor in the formal sector and so lead to more hiring and greater efficiency. There is an abundant economic literature that concludes that the net effect of making it easier to fire workers is to increase employment net.

The third element of our proposed policy agenda consists of building or strengthening institutions. This is hardly novel; the importance of institution building has in fact become the main new thrust of development economics in the 15 years since the Washington Consensus was first promulgated. Which particular institutions are most in need of strengthening tends to vary from one country to another, so the possibility of generalizing is limited, but archaic judiciaries, rigid civil service bureaucracies, old-fashioned political systems, teachers' unions focused exclusively on producer interests, and weak financial infrastructures are all common.

One institutional reform that we certainly did not advocate was the introduction of industrial policy, meaning by this a program that requires some government agency to 'pick winners' (to help companies that are judged likely to be able to contribute something special to the national economy). As argued before, there is little reason to think that industrial policies were the key ingredient of success in East Asia (see also Noland and Pack 2003). But we did have a lot more sympathy for a cousin of industrial policy usually referred to as a national innovation system. This does not require government to start making business judgments; instead, government seeks to create an institutional environment in which those firms that want to innovate find the necessary supporting infrastructure. A national innovation system is about government creating institutions to provide technical education, to promote the diffusion of technological information, to fund precompetitive research, to provide tax incentives for R&D, to encourage venture capital, to stimulate the growth of industrial clusters, and so on. While there is still ample scope for productivity to increase in Latin America by copying best practices developed in the rest of the world, it may need an act of Schumpeterian innovation—and therefore the sort of technologically supportive infrastructure that comprises a national innovation system—to bring world best practice to Latin America (ECLAC 1995: part 2).

The final element of the policy agenda is intended to combat the neglect of equity that was as true of the Washington Consensus as it has long been of economics in general. We suggested that it is important for governments to target an improved distribution of income in the same way that they target a higher rate of growth. Where there are opportunities for win–win solutions that will both increase growth and improve income distribution (such as, maybe, redirecting public education subsidies from universities to primary schools), they should be exploited. But the more fundamental point is that there is no intellectual justification for arguing that only win–win solutions deserve to be considered. One always needs to be aware of the potential cost in terms of efficiency (or growth) of actions to improve income distribution, but in a highly unequal region like Latin America, opportunities for making large distributive gains for modest efficiency costs deserve to be seized.

Progressive taxes are the classic instrument for redistributing income. One of the more questionable aspects of the reforms of the past decade in Latin America has been the form that tax reform has tended to take, with a shift in the burden of taxation from income taxes (which are typically at least mildly progressive) to consumption taxes (which are usually at least mildly regressive). While the tax reforms that have occurred have been useful in developing a broader tax base, it is time to reverse the process of shifting from direct to indirect taxation; effort should now focus on increasing direct tax collections. For incentive reasons one may want to avoid increasing the marginal tax rate on earned income, but that still leaves at least three possibilities:

1. The development of property taxation as a major revenue source (it is the most natural revenue source for the sub-national government units that are being spawned by the process of decentralization that has rightly become so popular).
2. The elimination of tax loopholes, not only so as to increase revenue but also to simplify tax obligations and thus aid enforcement.
3. Better tax collection, particularly of the income earned on flight capital parked abroad, which will require the signing of tax information sharing arrangements with at least the principal havens for capital flight.

Increased tax revenue needs to be spent on basic social services, including a social safety net as well as education and health, so that the net effect will be a significant impact in terms of reducing inequality, particularly by expanding opportunities for the poor.

With the best will in the world, however, what is achievable through the tax system is limited, in part by the fact that one of the things that money is good at buying is advice on how to minimize a tax bill. Significant improvements in distribution will come only by remedying the fundamental weakness that causes poverty, which is that too many people lack the assets that enable them to work their way out of poverty. The basic principle of a market economy is that people exchange like value for like value. Hence, in order to earn a decent living, the poor must have the opportunity to offer something that others want and will pay to buy: those who have nothing worthwhile to offer because they have no assets are unable to earn a decent living. The solution is not to abolish the market economy, which was tried in the communist countries for 70 years and proved a disastrous dead end, but to give the poor access to assets that will enable them to make and sell things that others will pay to buy. That means:

1. *Education*. There is no hope unless the poor get more human capital than they have had in the past.
2. *Titling programs* to provide property rights to the informal sector and allow Hernando de Soto's 'mystery of capital' to be unlocked (de Soto 2000).
3. *Land reform*. The Brazilian program of recent years to help peasants buy land from latifundia landlords provides a model. Landlords do not feel their vital interests to be threatened and therefore they do not resort to extreme measures to thwart the program. Property rights are respected. The peasants get opportunities but not handouts, which seems to be what they want.
4. *Micro credit*. Organizations to supply micro credit are spreading, but in most parts of the world, they still serve only a small minority of the poor. One big obstacle to an expanded program often consists of high real interest rates, which mean either that micro credit programs have a substantial fiscal cost and create an incentive to divert funds to the less poor (if interest rates are subsidized), or otherwise that they do not convey much benefit to the borrowers. Macro policy in a number of countries needs to aim to reduce market interest rates over time, which will inter alia facilitate the spread of micro credit.

In the best of worlds, such policies will take time to produce a social revolution, for the very basic reason that they rely on the creation of new assets, and it takes time to produce new assets. But, unlike populist programs, they do have the potential to produce a real social revolution if they are pursued steadfastly. And they could do so without undermining the well-being of the rich, thus holding out the hope that traditionally fragmented societies might finally begin to develop real social cohesion.

Concluding Remarks

Some may ask whether it matters whether people declare themselves for or against the Washington Consensus. If the battles are essentially semantic, why don't we all jump on its grave and get on with the serious work of developing an updated policy agenda? Good question, but there is an answer. When a serious economist attacks the Washington Consensus, the world at large may interpret that as saying that they believe there is a serious intellectual case against disciplined macroeconomic policies, the use of markets, and trade liberalization—three core ideas that were embodied in the original list and that are identified with the IFIs. Perhaps there is such a case, but I have not found it argued in Stiglitz (2002) or anywhere else. On the contrary, Stiglitz supports those causes much like any other economist (see his remarks about fiscal and monetary prudence (e.g., on p.87), his ready assumption that markets promote efficiency (e.g., on p.224), and his critique of protectionism (e.g., on p.251)). Alternatively, his use of the term as a pseudonym for market fundamentalism may lead the public to believe that the IFIs are committed to market fundamentalism, which is a caricature. We have no business to be propagating caricatures.

Everyone agrees that the Washington Consensus did not contain all the answers to the questions of 1989, let alone that it addresses all the new issues that have arisen since then. So of course we need to go beyond it. That is the purpose to which I hope the penultimate section of this chapter will contribute.

References

Balassa, B., Bueno G., Kuczynski, P. P., and Simonsen, M. H. (1986). *Towards Renewed Economic Growth in Latin America*. Washington: Institute for International Economics.

de Soto, H. (2002). *The Mystery of Capital: Why Capitalism Triumphs in the West and Fails Everywhere Else*. London: Black Swan.

ECLAC (Economic Commission for Latin America and the Caribbean) (1995). *Latin America and the Caribbean: Policies to Improve Linkages with the Global Economy*. Santiago: ECLAC.

Goldstein, M. and Turner, P. (2004). *Controlling Currency Mismatches in Emerging Markets*. Washington: Institute for International Economics.

Kuczynski, P. P. and Williamson, J. (eds.) (2003). *After the Washington Consensus: Restarting Growth and Reform in Latin America*. Washington: Institute for International Economics.

Naím, M. (2000). 'Washington Consensus or Washington Confusion?' *Foreign Policy*, Spring.

Noland, M. and Pack, H. (2003). *Industrial Policy in an Era of Globalization: Lessons from Asia*. Washington: Institute for International Economics.

Ocampo, J. A. (2004). 'Latin America's Growth and Equity Frustrations During Structural Reforms'. *Journal of Economic Perspectives*, 18/2: 67–88.

Stiglitz, J. E. (2002). *Globalization and Its Discontents*. New York and London: Norton.

Williamson, J. (1990). *Latin American Adjustment: How Much Has Happened?* Washington: Institute for International Economics.

3

Inequality and Redistribution

Paul Krugman

Introduction

At the time John Williamson introduced the famous concept of the 'Washington Consensus,' discussions of economic inequality did not play a large role in economic debate, either in developed or in developing countries. Instead, the focus was on macroeconomic stability and growth, with the assumption that progress on these fronts would benefit everyone.

Today, given the evidence of widening inequality in many countries, coupled with disappointments on the growth front, inequality has become a more obviously crucial subject. In this chapter, I will try to summarize briefly the reasons for a renewed focus on inequality, our (limited) understanding of why it has increased in some developing countries, and what the implications for a 'post-Washington Consensus' policy consensus might be.

Inequality: The US Case

Even though the focus of this book is on policy in developing countries, the renewed interest in inequality is partly driven by experience in the United States, which offers an object lesson—based on much better data than those which we have for most developing countries—on how important changes in inequality can be in affecting income growth. So let me begin this chapter with a brief review of the US experience.

Figure 3.1 shows the most commonly cited data on income growth in the United States; it shows census estimates of the rate of growth of average family income by income quintiles and for the top 5 percent. The data are divided into two periods: 1967–79, an era of generally stable

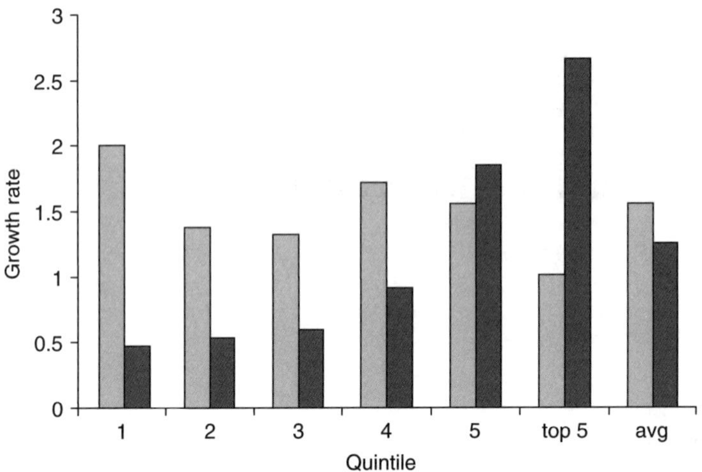

Figure 3.1. Most Commonly Cited Data on Income Growth, US
Source: US Census.

income distribution, and 1979–2003, an era of widening inequality. Average income growth was somewhat slower in the latter period—1.2 percent versus 1.6 percent. But growth for families in the middle quintile and below was *much* slower, while income gains for the top 5 percent were much higher; the bulk of gains in the last quarter-century have gone to high-income families.

And by high income, we mean *really* high income. Census data do not break down the top 5 percent, largely because it's well-known that the data fail to track really high incomes. The Congressional Budget Office has helped fill that gap with estimates that combine census and IRS data; these estimates also adjust for family size. Unfortunately, the CBO estimates only go as far back as 1979—that is, they cover only the recent era of rising inequality. Still, what they show, as illustrated in Figure 3.2, which shows percentage increases from 1979 to 2001, is the huge disparity between slow income growth for the middle and lower quintiles, and very rapid growth further up the scale. For reference, in 2001, average income in the top 1 percent of families was US$1.05 million.

Finally, the work of Piketty and Saez (2000), using income tax data, gives us a look within the top 1 percent: Piketty and Saez show that since 1970, income growth has been faster the higher one goes up the distribution, with the share of the top 0.01 percent in income rising at least six-fold since 1970. On their estimates, almost all income growth in the United States over the past 30 years has gone to the top 1 percent.

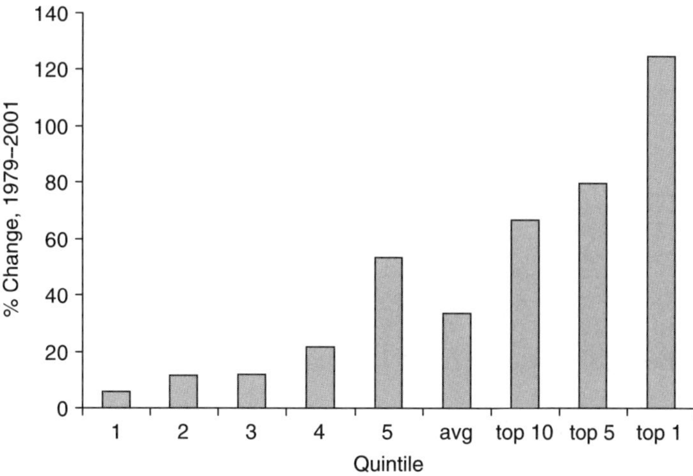

Figure 3.2. Percentage Increases in Income from 1979 to 2001, US
Source: Congressional Budget Office.

There are two important points that we can learn from the US case. The first is that income distribution is not a second order issue. Rising inequality can create a gap between average income growth and the income growth of middle- and lower-income families of, say, 1 percentage point per year over a period of several decades. Since even optimistic estimates of the effects of improved economic policies on overall growth are rarely that large (but see my discussion of outward looking policies, below), distribution deserves to be treated as an issue as important as growth.

The second important point is that analyzing the causes of increasing inequality is difficult under the best of circumstances. Economists became aware of a major upward trend in US inequality by around 1987 or 1988, and that trend quickly became a focus of intense discussion and analysis. The data on income distribution in the United States are as good as we can find anywhere: we have consistent surveys over time, very long-term time series from income tax data, and detailed breakdowns from the Congressional Budget Office. Yet the history of inequality in the United States remains somewhat mysterious. We do not know why the 'great compression' of income that took place during World War II (Goldin and Margo 1992) persisted for three decades. We do not know why inequality began surging circa 1980, or why there has been a sharp increase in wage inequality among people with similar levels of education. So we should not expect too much from attempts to understand inequality trends in developing countries, where the data are much less helpful.

Table 3.1. International Comparisons of Inequality

	Date	Gini	Bottom quintile	Top quintile
Sweden	2000	25	9	37
Korea	1998	32	8	37
France	1995	33	7	40
United States	2000	41	5	46
Argentina	2001	52	3	56
Mexico	2000	55	3	59
Brazil	2001	59	2	63

Source: World Bank WDI database.

International Comparisons of Inequality

The difference between US inequality today and inequality a quarter-century ago, though large, is still small compared with cross-country differences in inequality. Table 3.1 shows World Bank data on income distribution for a selection of advanced and developing countries, ranked from most equal to most unequal. The table shows the year to which the World Bank data apply, the Gini for each country, the income share of the bottom quintile, and the income of the top quintile.

The table offers several insights. First, the United States is a radical outlier among developed countries, with much higher inequality than European nations. (The fact that the US accepts a level of inequality that would be unthinkable in other advanced countries may have some relevance to the way inequality was downplayed in the original version of the Washington Consensus, as discussed below.) Second, there is a drastic difference between the newly industrialized economies of Asia, which have European levels of inequality, and the experience of Latin America. (Taiwan isn't included in the World Bank data, but its numbers look similar to those of Korea.) Third, Latin American inequality is very, very high. In particular, the income share of the bottom quintile is so low that even a modest degree of redistribution could produce large percentage income gains at the bottom.

So here is the question: Given the apparent importance of international differences in inequality, why was the issue of inequality almost absent from policy discussion when the Washington Consensus reigned?

What was the Washington Consensus on Inequality?

As John Williamson likes to emphasize, many policy recommendations that have been attributed to the Washington Consensus cannot be found in his original formulation. And it is often tricky and inherently unfair to give a modern version, with 20/20 hindsight, of what people thought a considerable time ago. This is particularly true when the issue is one, like inequality, that was not even considered a crucial topic of discussion.

But let me offer a caricature—as much a description of what I believed circa 1990 as of what dreaded neoliberals in general believed.

Circa 1990, I would suggest, the general view was that concerns about inequality were not a major reason to worry about a shift by developing countries to outward-looking economic policies, or to pro-market policies in general. There were two reasons for this. First, people expected the positive effects of liberalization on growth to be large. In the 1985 World Development Report, which in some ways represents the high water mark of intellectual faith in trade liberalization as an engine of development, the World Bank estimated that countries with 'outward-looking' policies grew about 2 percentage points faster than those with 'inward-looking' policies. That is enough to make up for a lot of increased inequality (although the US example, described above, shows that increasing inequality can cause the income growth of large segments of the population to diverge from average growth by amounts nearly that large).

Second, there was a general view that free trade policies would tend to be equalizing rather than unequalizing. This view came partly from theoretical considerations: a simple Heckscher-Ohlin trade model suggests that opening labor abundant economies to trade should raise wages while depressing rents of capital or land. It was also based on the experience of the original newly industrializing economies, which were both highly open and surprisingly egalitarian. I at least was guilty of the belief that the low levels of inequality in South Korea and Taiwan were, at least in part, the result of their outward-looking policies. And I was not alone in the belief that a shift to outward-looking policies would have an equalizing effect.

Unfortunately, in Latin America, where the Washington Consensus had the greatest impact on policy, both of these expectations proved unfounded. Growth didn't take off, and inequality rose instead of falling.

Growth and Inequality After Liberalization: What Do We Know?

Some at the Barcelona Conference described the long, confusing history of econometric estimates of the effects of reform and liberalization on growth. Suffice it to say that the case for a reliably strong positive growth effect from reform and liberalization has at least become questionable as researchers have taken increasing care to adopt measures of openness that are not in some sense measures of economic success as well. Perhaps more crucial in the policy debate has been the failure of post-Washington Consensus Latin America to experience an East Asian-type takeoff. The point is that few people at this point would be willing to promise, as the 1985 World Development Report seemed to, that liberalization will produce increased growth of a couple of points per year, enough to brush aside concerns over increasing inequality.

Meanwhile, expectations that trade liberalization would reduce inequality were contradicted by experience.

It is not possible to create figures like Figures 3.1 and 3.2 for Latin America: countries do not conduct household surveys annually, or even at predictable intervals. Moreover, as Goldberg and Pavncik (2004) point out, surveys that are not part of a regularized, periodic plan are not necessarily comparable over time: apparent changes in inequality may reflect differences in survey construction or coverage, not real changes in the economy. Such problems are why I used US data, despite their limited relevance to developing countries, which are a good place to demonstrate how important changes in inequality can be.

Still, the survey evidence seems to suggest rising inequality during the 1990s. (But see Milanovic (2005) for a different take.) Szekely (2001), weeding out surveys highly likely to have problems, estimated annual trends in the Gini index for Latin American countries during the 1990s, finding a positive trend for every country except Colombia, the Dominican Republic, and Costa Rica. Moreover, he finds a clear correlation between changes in inequality and progress or the lack thereof in reducing poverty. Figure 3.3 shows this

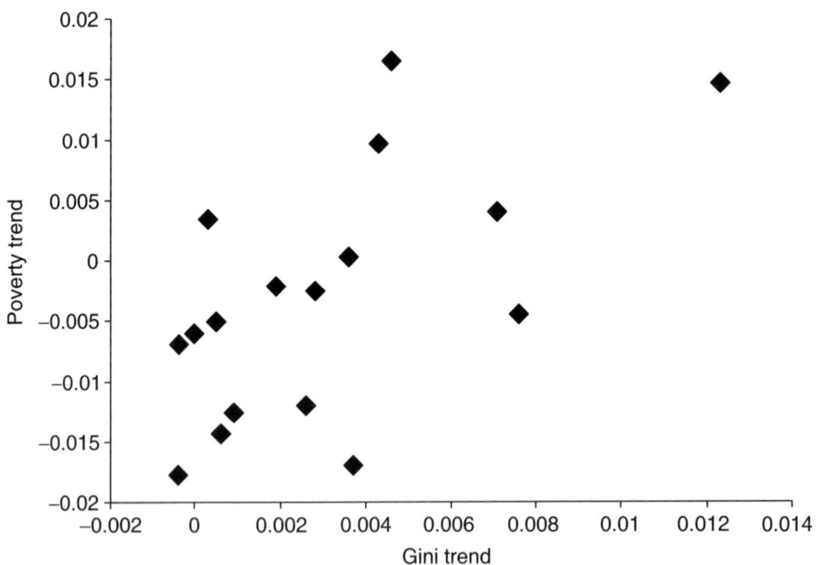

Figure 3.3. Correlation between Changes in Inequality and Progress/Lack of Progress in Reducing Poverty
Source: Szekely 2001.

correlation: the 'Gini trend' is the estimated annual rate of change in the Gini index by country, the 'poverty trend' is the estimated annual trend in the poverty rate. The association between rising inequality and rising poverty remains even when differences in economic growth are taken into account.

The point is that survey data do suggest an increase in inequality during the era of liberalization and reform—the reign of the Washington Consensus. Given the problems with these data, the specific numbers from survey data should not be taken too seriously. But the numbers do agree with casual observation.

More solid evidence comes from data on the structure of wages. A number of papers, such as Cragg and Epelbaum (1996), have documented a sharp rise in the skill premium in Mexico following trade reform. Behrman et al. (2003) clean up survey data to focus on prime age male wage earners classified by education level. They show that the premium for higher education over primary education rose a logarithmic 60 percent in Latin America as a whole during the 1990s. Taken together with the broader survey data and general observation, it seems clear that inequality has increased in Latin America during the era of 'neoliberal' or Washington Consensus policies, and in some cases that rise in inequality is very sharp.

What Happened to Heckscher-Ohlin?

In my caricature of early Washington Consensus views, I argued that people—certainly, me—expected trade liberalization to be equalizing in the developing world, because labor abundant countries would export labor intensive goods and import capital intensive goods, raising wages while depressing returns on other factors. Clearly, that has not happened in Latin America. Why?

There are two obvious possibilities: our trade and income distribution model is wrong, or other factors besides trade policy are responsible. These possibilities are not, of course, mutually exclusive.

Hanson and Harrison (1999), who carefully examine the Mexican data, partly resolve the puzzle, by showing that highly protected sectors under the preliberalization regime tended to be labor intensive, not capital intensive. In other words, Heckscher-Ohlin—or, more properly, Stolper-Samuelson—may still apply; we were just wrong about what was being protected.

But how is it possible that labor abundant countries were protecting labor intensive products from import competition? What's the general equilibrium story? The underlying logic of the Hanson and Harrison argument is that in the case of Mexico, at least, a two-factor, two-good model is deeply misleading. On the eve of the big liberalization of the late 1980s, Mexico was for the most part an exporter of resource intensive products. In 1985, exports of fuels and mineral products, overwhelmingly oil, were 30 percent larger than exports of manufactures. (This figure plunged the next year, along with the price of oil, but the figures from 1985 and earlier are relevant if we're trying to get a picture of the preliberalization situation.) One can also argue that the size of manufactures exports preliberalization seriously overstates their importance to the economy, because of the low domestic content of maquiladora production. Finally, one can argue that Mexico's tourism imports, which are largely driven by climate and beachfront, should be considered a resource-based export.

Given this resource base, import substituting industrialization did not have the effect of shifting factors from labor intensive exports to capital intensive import competing industries. Instead, it shifted factors from resource intensive export industries and nontraded goods to labor intensive import competing industries, with at least some equalizing effect on income distribution. And, according to Hanson and Harrison, unwinding that protection has been an unequalizing policy.

It is not hard to see how a similar argument could be made in other Latin American countries, such as Argentina. There may also be other parts to the story, including reduction in rents, some of which accrued to labor, and perhaps some effects involving induced technical change.

The alternative approach is to ask whether other policy changes were responsible for the increase in inequality. The Washington Consensus was, after all, a package that included much more than trade liberalization. Behrman et al. (2003) study five indices: trade policy, financial policy, tax policy, external capital transactions policy, privatization policy, and labor policy. All of these indices moved together: there was a general movement towards liberalization, greater reliance on markets, in Latin America.

Behrman et al. do a yeoman job of statistical analysis, teasing out correlations between an overall index of liberalization and its components, on one side, and inequality as measured by skill differentials, on the other. Without criticizing this approach, let me point out that few would argue for adopting this approach to analyzing trends in inequality in developed countries. We know, or think we know, that a reduced form estimate of the effects of policies on inequality in advanced countries, whether in time series, cross-section, or both, is simply too crude to work: it's a good bet that the estimated effects of Reagan's and Thatcher's policies would be far larger than we could derive from any structural economic model, and economists would be quick to invoke omitted variables—including variables that are hard to measure, such as union power and social norms.

Why, then, should we expect such an approach to work for Latin America? To be fair, there is one possible reason: the policy changes, especially trade policy changes, were more dramatic and rapid than anything we see in developed countries, which may reduce the omitted variables problem. Still, I think we should be cautious about reading too much into the results of cross-country regressions, no matter how carefully done.

For what it's worth, however, Behrman et al. (2003) find that an index that combines all five indicators of liberalization is clearly associated with rising inequality, accounting for about a third of the rise in the skill differential. Their efforts to tease out the effects of the different components suggest, however, that trade policy has little effect: financial policy and tax policy, not trade policy, are the factors driving the impact of liberalization on inequality. There is also evidence in the data that the effects of liberalization fade out over time, that the initial impact on inequality is larger than the final impact. Nonetheless, the authors write: 'Do our results suggest that policy liberalization has been bad for equality concerns in Latin America—a "class act" favoring the relatively highly schooled upper classes because their net effect has been to exacerbate earnings differentials? Our answer is a qualified yes.'

One further note: regional inequality is an important story for developing countries, especially China. One way to reconcile widening income disparities with a conventional Heckscher-Ohlin picture of trade is to combine that picture with internal transport costs and agglomeration economies, leading to a sharp rise in incomes in some parts of a country while other regions lag behind.

Policy Implications?

Clearly, in Latin America liberalization and reform have not yielded the growth results everyone hoped for, while they have been associated with—and, to some degree, caused—a sharp increase in inequality. What are the policy implications?

Despite the disappointments, it's hard to make a case for a return to inward-looking, import substituting policies. One doesn't have to be a true believer in the magic of the market to conclude that import substituting industrialization had reached a dead end by 1980 or so. And the upside possibilities of outward-looking policies still seem much greater, even if we now have a much more realistic sense of how hard it is for many countries to take advantage of these possibilities.

But what can be done about rising inequality and, probably, declining real incomes at the bottom of the distribution?

At the risk of sounding trite, the answer is that if you want to help the poor, help the poor. Because income distribution is so unequal in Latin American countries, modest programs of aid to the poor, measured as a share of GDP, can have large impacts on the quality of life for the poor. So although we may be chastened and somewhat dismayed at the failure of liberalizing policies to deliver broad-based gains, the answer is deliberate policies to help the poor, not a reversal of liberalization.

References

Behrman, J., Birdsall, N., and Szekely, M. (2003). 'Economic Policy and Wage Differentials in Latin America', Center for Global Development Working Paper, No. 29.

Cragg, M. I. and Epelbaum, M. (1996). 'Why has Wage Dispersion Grown in Mexico? Is it the Incidence of Reforms or the Growing Demand for Skills?' *Journal of Development Economics,* 51: 99–116.

Goldberg, P. K. and Pavcnik, N. (2004). 'Trade, Inequality, and Poverty: What Do We Know?' NBER Working Paper, No. 10593.

Goldin, C. and Margo, R. (1992). 'The Great Compression: The U.S. Wage Structure at Mid-Century'. *Quarterly Journal of Economics,* 107: 1–34

Hanson, G. and Harrison, A. (1999). 'Trade and Wage Inequality in Mexico'. *Industrial and Labor Relations Review,* 52/2: 271–88.

Harrison, A. and Hanson G. (1999). 'Who Gains from Trade Reform? Some Remaining Puzzles'. *Journal of Development Economics,* 59: 125–54.

Milanovic, B. (2005). 'Global Income Inequality: What it is and Why it Matters'. HEW OSI2001, EconWPA. Available at: http://ideas.repec.org/p/wbk/wbrwps/3865.html

Piketty, T. and Saez, E. (2003). 'Income Inequality in the United States, 1913–1998'. *The Quarterly Journal of Economics,* 115/1 (February).

Szekely, M. (2001). 'The 1990s in Latin America: Another Decade of Persistent Inequality, but with Somewhat Lower Poverty', Inter-American Development Bank Working Paper, No. 443.

4

Is there a Post-Washington Consensus Consensus?

Joseph E. Stiglitz[1]

If there is a consensus today about what strategies are most likely to promote the development of the poorest countries in the world, it is this: there is no consensus except that the Washington Consensus did not provide the answer. Its recipes were neither necessary nor sufficient for successful growth, though each of its policies made sense for particular countries at particular times.

By the Washington Consensus I mean, of course, the oversimplified rendition of policies recommended by international financial institutions and the US Treasury, especially during the period of the 1980s and early 1990s, before they became such a subject of vilification in both the north and the south—not the more subtle work of John Williamson, who actually coined the term (Williamson 1990, 1999). Whatever its original content and intent, the term 'Washington Consensus,' in the minds of most people around the world, has come to refer to development strategies that focus on privatization, liberalization, and macro stability (meaning, mostly, price stability). (The policies are often referred to as 'neoliberal' policies, because of the emphasis on liberalization, and because like nineteenth century liberalism, they emphasized the importance of a minimal role for the state.) To most people, the Washington Consensus represents a set of policies predicated upon a strong faith—stronger than warranted either by economic theory or historical experience—in unfettered markets and aimed at reducing, or even minimizing, the role of government.[2] This development strategy stands in

[1] The author would like to thank the Ford Foundation, the MacArthur Foundation, and the Mott Foundation for financial support. Research assistance from Megan Torau is also gratefully acknowledged. This is a slight revision of a paper presented at a conference sponsored by Foundation CIDOB and the Initiative for Policy Dialogue held in Barcelona in September 2004, 'From the Washington Consensus Towards a New Global Governance.'

[2] How the term 'Washington Consensus' is widely understood is then an important difference between this chapter/paper and John Williamson's paper presented at the same

marked contrast to the successful strategies pursued in East Asia, where the *development state* took an active role.

The Consensus on the Failures of the Washington Consensus

The post-Washington Consensus consensus goes further in detailing the nature of the failures of the Washington Consensus.[3] There was a failure in understanding economic structures within developing countries, in focusing on too narrow a set of objectives, and on too limited a set of instruments.

The Limits of Market Fundamentalism: Theory

For instance, markets by themselves do not produce efficient outcomes when information is imperfect and markets are incomplete (true in all countries, but especially in developing countries) or when technology is changing as a result of R&D expenditures or learning, or more generally, when there is learning, for instance, about markets.

The intellectual foundations of the Washington Consensus had been badly eroded even before its doctrines became widely accepted. The fundamental theorems of welfare economics provided the rigorous interpretation of Adam Smith's invisible hand, the conditions under which and the sense in which markets lead to efficient outcomes. Under these theorems, it turned out, markets were efficient only if capital markets were impossibly perfect—at least in the sense that there be no missing risk or intertemporal markets. There could be no externalities (no problems of air or water pollution), no public goods, no issues of learning, and no advances in technology that were the result either of learning or expenditures on R&D. Greenwald and Stiglitz (1986) went further and showed that there also could not be any imperfections of information, changes in the information structure, or asymmetries of information. These problems are serious in any economy, but are at the heart of development. There are important externalities in these dynamic processes, which give rise

conference—'A Short History of the Washington Consensus'—in which Williamson, referring to me, asserts that 'when a serious economist attacks the Washington Consensus, the world at large interprets that as saying that he believes there is a serious intellectual case against disciplined macroeconomic policies, the use of markets, and trade liberalization...' At any rate, that is not my case against the Washington Consensus polices, as I use the term; this should be evident from what follows in this chapter. On the particular points raised by Williamson, my view is that the Washington Consensus has come to mean both more and less than Williamson suggested. For instance, Williamson does not include in his list capital market liberalization, which has come to be one of the pillars of the Washington Consensus, as it has come to be applied. Williamson talks about reducing public deficits, one of the keys to macro stability. But macro stability itself under the Washington Consensus *as applied* has focused too narrowly on price stability. See, for instance, Williamson (2004).

[3] See, for instance, Stiglitz (1998). This chapter extends and updates the arguments I made in that paper.

to an important role for government. The successful East Asian countries recognized this role; the Washington Consensus policies did not. In short, *there is no theoretical underpinning to believe that in early stages of development, markets by themselves will lead to efficient outcomes.*

The Limits of Market Fundamentalism: History

Historical experience also provided little support to the belief that markets, by themselves, would lead to rapid development. While there is an active debate about the particular role of each of the industrial policies undertaken by each of the East Asian countries, there is a clear link between the policies and the successes.[4] The township and village enterprises in China (publicly owned at the local level) were central to China's success in the 1980s and early 1990s. The individual responsibility system, which was far short of full privatization of land (which market fundamentalists claimed was necessary), was responsible for the enormous increase in agriculture productivity. And it is hard to conceive that Korea or Taiwan would have become the industrial players of today without having undertaken active industrial policies. All of the countries in East Asia had high savings rates, and it is at least plausible that the government policies designed to stimulate savings actually did what they were intended to do. While firms in the rest of the world complain about a shortage of capital, the governments of East Asia provided capital to those firms that were proving their mettle by exporting, especially in technology sectors where there were likely spillovers to the rest of the economy.[5] To be sure, all of this could have been an accident; it is even possible that, as some critics of these policies claim, the East Asian countries might have grown even faster in the absence of industrial policies. Anything is *possible*, but there is no reason to believe that this is the case, and the weight of the evidence points in the other direction.

If the success of East Asia suggests the desirability of a larger role for government in successful development than was traditionally emphasized in the Washington Consensus policies, the failures in sub-Saharan Africa and Latin America have reinforced the doubts about the Washington Consensus strategies (Stiglitz 2002a). Growth in Latin America during the 1990s—the decade of reform—was just half of what it was in the 1960s and 1970s, the decades marked by the 'failed' policies of import substitution. Surely, there were problems with the import substitution strategy and it would have had to evolve, as it did in East Asia, into a strategy based more on exports. It was the debt crisis, however, and not the shortcomings of the development strategy that brought an end to the period of high growth. Success under reform

[4] See, for instance, World Bank 1993; Wade 2003.

[5] The general theory for why such policies may be desirable is set forth in Greenwald and Stiglitz (2006).

was even more short lived (less than a decade), and the end of that success (beginning in 1997) was directly related to the failures of the reform strategy. The openness of capital markets exposed the countries to the volatility of international capital markets, which had adverse consequences in the global financial crisis of 1997–98.

In Africa, the costs of a simple-minded belief in the magic of the market were palpable and huge. For example, policy conditionalities imposed on the region's countries too often focused much too narrowly on liberalization of agricultural prices without adequate attention to the prerequisites to make such liberalization effective, for example, functioning markets for inputs and outputs, credit availability, and infrastructure (especially roads). The insistence on static comparative advantage foreclosed the kind of dynamic changes that underlay the successes in East Asia—had Korea stuck with its static comparative advantage, it would still be growing rice. But there were a further set of problems, illustrating the fallacy of composition, whereby increasing exports of commodities by many countries with similar comparative advantages led to a collapse in their prices. Financial sector reforms focused excessively on making interest rates market-determined in very thin and rudimentary markets, which often led to prolonged periods of very high interest rates without improving the availability of credit.

If there were fruits of the Washington Consensus, they are yet to be enjoyed, at least by the average citizens of many developing countries. Early followers of the Consensus, such as Bolivia, still ask: 'We have felt the pain, when do we get the gain?' If Consensus reforms exposed countries to greater risk, the policies did not provide the citizens of their countries with adequate protections, with the kinds of safety nets that could even partially insulate them from the consequences; nor did they provide these countries with the strength for a rapid recovery; in Latin America as a whole, there followed almost a half decade of declining per capita income.

The fact that countries that followed the Washington Consensus policies grew more slowly than those that did not should, by itself, have been enough to lead countries to abandon these strategies. But the International Monetary Fund (IMF) urged patience developing countries were told that growth was just around the corner. They were told that if they abandoned the Washington Consensus policies, all the pain and suffering that they had experienced would be for naught.[6]

It was the crises, especially in countries like Argentina that had received an A+ grade from the IMF, that finally resulted in global disillusion with the Washington Consensus, as marked by the Barcelona conference.

But even before this, there was growing awareness that several of the policies that they had pushed seemed flawed: privatizations marred by corruption,

[6] The reluctance to abandon failed strategies is a well-documented phenomenon in all bureaucratic institutions (sometimes referred to as the principle of escalating commitment).

for instance, and which resulted in monopolies that led to higher prices for consumers. Of course, when such problems occurred, the IMF would say, the problem was not with privatization, itself, but with the way that it was implemented. But that response was disingenuous: they had urged countries to privatize rapidly, as if to say that even a flawed privatization—and the more rushed the privatization, the more likely was it that it would be flawed—was better than a postponed privatization. Moreover, policies have to be designed to be implemented by ordinary mortals, and when country after country faced similar problems in 'implementation,' it became clear that the roots of the problem were deeper.

Several distinct problems were identified: we have already seen how the Washington Consensus policies relied on market fundamentalism, a view of the market economy that was neither in accord with modern economic theory or historical experiences. The IMF/Washington Consensus sometimes confused means with ends; but the set of ends—objectives—that they pursued was also too narrow; they used too narrow a set of instruments to achieve even the ends they sought. In part, the problem was that underlying the Washington Consensus was more than just an economic agenda.

More than an Economic Agenda

This is illustrated by the discussions during the East Asia crisis, focusing on corporate governance and transparency. While the points were well-taken—improvements in corporate governance and transparency would be beneficial—in succeeding years, it has become increasingly evident that politics, rather than economic analysis, lay behind the framing of the agenda. For instance:

- The IMF and the US Treasury, while pushing the transparency agenda, remained among the least transparent of public institutions.
- The US Treasury had even resisted reforms in the United States that would have improved transparency of America's accounting frameworks, e.g., related to stock options.
- Scandinavia, the last set of countries to be afflicted by financial crises, was among the most transparent.
- When the debate about transparency turned to Western institutions, hedge funds, and secret bank accounts, the US Treasury even began to argue against excessive transparency, and eventually vetoed (before 9/11) the OECD initiative on bank secrecy.
- While continuing, rightly, to inveigh against corruption, the developed countries have refused to take easy steps that would make such corruption more difficult, e.g., allowing tax deductions only for those payments

to governments that are 'published' (and adopting other measures of the extractive industries transparency initiative).

- IMF accounting practices continue to put a roadblock in the way of market-based land redistribution.

While the IMF talked about the need for greater safety nets, it did not focus squarely on the factors that contributed to economic volatility, including capital market liberalization. Instead, it continued to advocate capital market liberalization, long after the adverse effects on stability became clear and evidence mounted that it did not contribute to economic growth.[7] The IMF continued to focus on the inadequacies in the developing countries and not those in the Washington Consensus policies; blame was squarely placed on the developing countries for their problems, especially those related to lack of transparency and poor governance.

A Balanced Role for Markets and Government

The political agenda was most evident in the Washington Consensus' reliance on *market fundamentalism*—the belief that markets by themselves lead to economic efficiency, that economic policies should focus on efficiency, and that distributional concerns could and should be taken care of elsewhere in the political process. The policies pursued by the international financial institutions that came to be called 'Washington Consensus policies' or 'neoliberalism' entailed a much more circumscribed role for the state than was embraced by most of the East Asian countries, a set of policies that (in another simplification) came to be called the 'development state.'

To be sure, governments can make matters worse. No doubt, the Washington Consensus represented, in part, a reaction to failures of the state in attempting to correct failures of the market. But the pendulum swung too far in the other direction and for too long. The Washington Consensus policies often assumed the worst about the nature and capability of *all* governments, and, in its quest to find a 'one-size-fits-all' policy, gave up on trying to improve governments, arguing that it was better simply to rely on markets *by themselves*. This resulted in a strong bias against basing policy advice on an analysis of what interventions are appropriate in what contexts, or building the institutions or capacity of states to intervene effectively.

What is at issue then is not just the size of government, but its role—what activities should it undertake—and the balance between government

[7] Finally, in March of 2003, even the IMF recognized these problems—almost six years after it had tried to change its charter to force developing countries to liberalize their capital markets. It remains uncertain, however, the extent to which these findings have altered the policy prescriptions that it gives at the country level. See, for instance, Prasad et al. (2003).

and the market. The post-Washington Consensus consensus recognizes that there is a role for markets; the question is to what extent do the neoliberals recognize that there is a role for the state, beyond the minimal role of enforcing contracts and property rights? The post-Washington Consensus consensus recognizes too that there are government failures, just as there are market failures. But it believes that there are systematic ways to improve the performance of the government, just as there are systematic ways to improve markets. Governments and markets are seen as complementary, with government actually often playing an important role in addressing market failures, helping markets to work better.

Defining Objectives

The Washington Consensus failed so systematically largely because of its failure to understand development and developing countries; but its failure is also attributable to the fact that the objectives of development reflected in the Washington Consensus were too narrowly defined: the objective of policy should not have been limited to an increase in GDP—putting aside for the moment the measurement problems associated with that measure—but should have included sustainable increases in standards of living, as well as the promotion of democratic and equitable development.

The issue of equity, in particular, often received short shrift. Is a society in which the vast majority of its citizens are becoming worse off, while a few at the top are doing so well that average incomes are rising, better off than a society in which the vast majority are doing better, even if total GDP is growing more slowly? While there may be disagreements—and those at the very top may well stress that average income is the appropriate measure—the possibility that increases in GDP may not benefit most individuals means that we cannot simply ignore issues of distribution. Some economists argued that distribution concerns could be ignored because they believed in trickle-down economics, that somehow everybody would benefit in the way that a rising tide would lift all boats. But the evidence against trickle-down economics is now overwhelming, at least in the sense that an increase in average incomes is not sufficient to raise the incomes of the poor for prolonged periods. Some economists argued that distribution concerns could and *should* be ignored, because such concerns were outside the province of economics. Economists should focus on efficiency and growth alone; distribution was a matter for politics. The fundamental theorems of welfare economics gave economists some comfort, for those results suggested that one could separate out equity and efficiency concerns, and any desired distribution of income could be achieved simply by a redistribution of initial endowments. But advances in economic theory (especially those related to the economics of information) showed that that was simply not true; lump sum redistributions were not generally feasible, and efficiency and equity were inextricably interlinked.[8] Interestingly, several sources of these interlinkages (e.g., associated with agency problems) had been analyzed *in the context of developing countries* 15 years *before* the formulation of the Washington Consensus (see, e.g., Stiglitz 1974).[9]

Ignoring distributional concerns meant that sometimes even improvements in efficiency were compromised. For instance, land reform, which would have reduced the scope for (and inefficiencies associated with) agency problems in tenancy, would have simultaneously improved equity and efficiency. Sharecropping, a prevalent form of land tenancy in developing countries, has resulted in an effective tax rate of 50 percent, and in some cases 66 percent, on some of the poorest people. It is ironic that while the IMF and the advocates of the Washington Consensus often railed against the distortions arising from high tax rates, land reform, which should have been even more important, was seemingly not high on the agenda. While the international financial institutions talked a great deal about 'getting incentives right,' they never addressed this incentive problem.

Confusing Ends with Means

Even worse than the formulation of too narrow a set of objectives was the fact that, too often, the IMF confused means with objectives—privatization and liberalization, for instance, became not means to an end, but ends in themselves. *Sometimes* privatization makes sense. But it matters how privatization is done; if done in the wrong way, growth can be reduced and societal welfare lowered. The pursuit of rapid privatization in the former Soviet Union contributed to the enormous increase in inequality, compromising the legitimacy of private rights, at least those acquired in the privatization process, and perhaps even of the market system. Low inflation was seen as an objective in itself; excessively tight monetary policy led to the growth of barter, which undermined market efficiency as equally as inflation. Capital market liberalization did not lead to faster economic growth, but did lead to more instability.

The Evolving Washington Consensus

As the failures of the Washington Consensus became increasingly evident—especially after the crises, beginning with the Mexican crisis and followed

[8] See in particular the discussion in Stiglitz (1994).

[9] There are other connections. Capital constraints may limit access to education, implying that many individuals' full potential is never realized. See, e.g., Birdsall (1999). Large inequalities may give rise to social tensions, and are even systematically associated with civil strife, which itself has a very negative effect on growth. See, e.g., Deininger (2003).

by the East Asian crises, the Russian crisis, and the Argentine crisis—it has evolved, to what is sometimes called the 'Washington Consensus Plus.' The advocates of the Washington Consensus successively tried to modify the prescription. But even as it changed, the underlying problems, based on a flawed understanding of market economics and a too narrow set of objectives (even if those objectives did expand slightly), persisted.

From Resources to Policies

The Washington Consensus represented an advance in one respect over earlier approaches to development, which saw developed and less developed countries differing largely in their *resources*. Thus to make more resources available, a 'bank' was put at the center of the world's efforts to promote development. Interestingly, the creation of the World Bank (as well as the IMF) reflected recognition of the importance of market failures. If the neoclassical model *were* correct, the shortage of capital would be reflected in higher returns to capital, and private markets would ensure the flow of capital from the capital-rich advanced industrial countries to the capital-poor developing world. But particularly at the time of the founding of the World Bank, such flows were limited; and even in the temporary heyday of capital flows, the mid-1990s, before the global financial crisis, the funds went mostly to a limited number of countries, and for limited types of investment. Many countries seemingly faced credit constraints (see, e.g., Eaton and Gerzovitz 1981). (It was in this sense ironic that international institutions founded in recognition of a market failure should premise so much of their analysis on models that paid insufficient attention to these failures.)

By the early 1980s, however, it was recognized that projects were not enough. The Washington Consensus thus focused on *policies*—policies of privatization, liberalization, and stability (which meant, in practice price stability).

From the Washington Consensus to the Washington Consensus Plus

When these policies failed to produce the hoped-for results, the diagnosis changed, and it was argued that these policies needed to be supplemented with additional policies: the Washington Consensus Plus. What was added depended on the criticism that was being leveled and on the nature of the failure that was being recognized.

When growth failed to materialize, 'second generation reforms,' including competition policies to accompany privatizations of natural monopolies, were added. When problems of equity were noted, the 'Plus' included female education or improved safety nets.

Mexico showed that even if a country got its own fiscal house in order and kept inflation in check, it could have a crisis. The problem, supposedly, was a lack of domestic savings. But when East Asian countries faced crisis—countries with the highest rates of savings in the world—a new explanation was sought. Now, it was lack of transparency (they seemingly forgot that the last set of crises were in the Nordic countries, which were among the most transparent in the world). Weak financial institutions were to blame, but if such weak institutions were found in the United States and other advanced industrial countries (which had banking crises in the late 1980s and early 1990s), what hope did the developing countries have? By this point, the IMF/US Treasury/Washington Consensus[10] advice rang hollow: ex post, they could always find something that was wrong, and add something to the increasingly long laundry list of what countries should do.[11]

From the Washington Consensus Plus to the Washington Consensus Plus Plus

When all of these versions of the Washington Consensus Plus also failed to do the trick, a new layer of reforms was added: one had to go beyond projects and policies to the reform of institutions, including *public institutions*, and their governance.

In some ways, this represented a more fundamental change in perspectives, but in other ways it was a continuation of the same mindset. Government had long been viewed as the problem and markets as the solution. The questions should have been: what can we do to improve the efficiency of *both* markets and the government? What is the right balance between the market and government and how should that balance change over time, as markets improve and the competencies of governments change? Rather than asking these questions, the Washington Consensus had ignored market failures, viewed government as the problem, assumed that governments could not be reformed, and proposed massive scalebacks in government. Belatedly, it recognized the need to improve government, and that many of the countries where development was not proceeding suffered not from too much government but from too little. But there remained a lack of balance. For instance, rather than asking if public pension systems could be strengthened, the Washington Consensus continued to focus its attention on privatization.

[10] I deliberately drop the World Bank from the trilogy, because by this point, it had joined the critics on many of the elements of the Washington Consensus.

[11] Jason Furman and I tried to do a somewhat serious job of ascertaining what might be meant by a country having policies or institutions that made it 'vulnerable' to a crisis, by looking across countries to see what, if any, characteristics were systematically associated with an increased likelihood of having a crisis. Not surprisingly, the East Asian countries that the IMF had suggested were particularly vulnerable do not appear to be so in our analysis. See Stiglitz and Furman (1998).

When deficiencies in private pension schemes were noted (e.g., their higher administrative costs, problems of adverse selection, the failure to insulate old age pensioners against risks of market volatility or inflation, and the difficulty of preventing fraud), the problems were ignored or attempts were made to address the *market failures*, but it was simply assumed that it would be easier to make markets work than to make public institutions work.

Nor was the link between policies and institutions, or between institutions and society, adequately recognized. The IMF told countries to have good institutions, and examples of good institutions were exhibited, but there was little to say about how to create such institutions. It was easy to instruct countries on good economic policies: simply cut the budget deficit. But an injunction to have honest institutions was much more complicated.

Just as there was controversy about what constituted good policies, so too was there controversy about what was meant by good institutions. Countries were told to be democratic, but there is no subject of greater concern to the citizens of most developing countries than economic performance. To make matters more confusing, developing countries were told that one central ingredient, monetary policy, was too important to be trusted to democratic processes. As part of the conditionality imposed to obtain loans, countries were given short deadlines to reform social security programs or to privatize or to change the charter of their central banks, to engage in reforms that the democracies of many advanced industrial countries had rejected. There was a failure to recognize that the issuance of such demands put public institutions into an impossible bind: if governments failed to comply, they lost credibility, as they were accused of not doing what was right for their country. If governments acceded to the demands, they also lost credibility, as they appeared to be simply following the orders of the new colonial masters. When the reforms failed to deliver on the promises, which happened in country after country, the governments again lost credibility. The weaknesses in public institutions were thus caused in part by the Washington institutions.

There were other important instances of policies interacting with institutions in ways that were adverse to economic performance. High interest rate policies in Russia (and the failure to create viable financial institutions to supply credit to new and expanding enterprises) made asset stripping more attractive than wealth creation; and weakened support for the creation of the kind of rule of law that would have facilitated wealth creation (see, e.g., Hoff and Stiglitz 2004).

Thus, even as the Washington Consensus began to expand the list of what was to be done, its perspectives remained too narrow. Broader goals and still more instruments were required. A more fundamental change in mindset was needed.

But the criticism now went further. One of the longstanding criticisms of the Washington Consensus and the IMF was not just the failure to understand economics; it was argued that they failed to take into account adequately politics and political processes, and how they are intertwined with economics. But governance entails political processes, and while the attention newly focused on governance was welcome, these limitations—and the imperfections in the international institutions' own governance itself[12] meant that the IMF and the Washington Consensus had less to contribute on the subject than one might have hoped. Even when what they said may have had more than a grain of truth, the international economic institutions lacked the credibility required for their messages to have the desired impact.

Institutional Failures at the International Level

The focus on institutions had one salutary effect: it shifted attention to the problems in the international economic institutions themselves. One of the problems, the 'democratic deficit,' and the lack of political legitimacy, is discussed at greater length in Chapter 14, on 'The Future of Global Governance' (as well as elsewhere, e.g., Stiglitz 2002a). Close links with financial markets (not just its governance structure, which is directly accountable to finance ministers and governors of central banks, both typically from financial markets, but also through a 'revolving door', through which staff go from and return to financial markets) contribute to its seeing the world through a lens similar to those that predominate there (accounting for greater faith in markets than either theory or evidence warrants)—and taking actions that reflect their interests (the interests of foreign creditors) more than the interests of the developing countries, which was so evident during the East Asian crisis. But institutional imperatives even account for one of the aspects for which the IMF has been so roundly criticized, its one-size-fits-all prescriptions, also evident during the East Asia crisis, when it tried prescriptions that might have been appropriate during the Latin American crisis, on the countries in the region. There was no subtlety of diagnosis—an attempt to recognize the defining characteristics of East Asian economies, that had contributed to their success over a period of more than three decades—that one might have hoped for. But in defense of the institution, countries that call upon the IMF have to receive the same treatment, the same advice, *no matter who the institution sends to the country*; it is far easier to accomplish this if there is a strong doctrine, a simple recipe, which can mechanically be followed in the analysis of each country's problem. Moreover, IMF staffers have to be 'replaceable parts,' and this in turn makes it a place less attractive to those with the capacities and drive to understand the subtle but often important ways in which countries differ.

[12] A subject I have written about extensively, e.g., in Stiglitz (2002a).

Some Elements of an Emerging Consensus

So far, I have described several elements of an emerging consensus—or, at least, a broadly shared view—about the inadequacies of the Washington Consensus and its excessive belief in market fundamentalism. There is also a broad consensus that the international economic institutions have created unfair rules of the game (most evident in the case of trade, see, e.g., Stiglitz and Charlton 2005) and have foisted failed policies on developing countries that are dependent on these institutions and on donors for assistance. While many of the policies of the developing countries have themselves contributed to their own failure, the difficulties of development need to be recognized: tilting the playing board against developing countries makes their task all the more difficult, even for an honest and committed government.

I have written extensively elsewhere on what accounted for these failures: the role of historical experiences and honest differences in economic analysis and in the interpretation of statistical evidence, versus the role of ideology and special interests. In recent years, the economics profession has paid more attention to institutions, the incentives confronting the institutions and those within the institutions, and the relationships between governance, organization design, and organization behavior. Such analyses have provided insights into the behavior of the IMF and the WTO (see, e.g., Stiglitz 2001). Of concern is not only what has been done, but what has not been done—for instance, the failure to address the problems posed by the international reserve system, sovereign defaults, and the inadequacy of the system of sharing the risks of interest rate and exchange rate fluctuations between developed and less developed countries.

There are several more elements of a post-Washington Consensus. The first is that a post-Washington Consensus consensus cannot be arrived at simply within the confines of Washington. The development of a successful development strategy will have to involve those in the developing world in an important and meaningful way.

The second is that one-size-fits-all policies are doomed to fail. Policies that work in one country may not work in others. The contrast between the success of the East Asian economies, which did *not* follow the Washington Consensus, and those that did has become increasingly clear. However, the question remains, to what extent can the policies that worked so well in East Asia be *transferred* to other countries?

A third is that there are some areas in which economic science has not yet provided sufficient evidence, sufficiently strong theory, or empirical evidence, to result in a broad consensus about what countries should do. There may be a broad consensus against 'excessive protectionism' that only serves the interests of special interests, but there is no consensus that rapid liberalization, especially in a country with high unemployment, will lead to faster economic growth. It may only lead to more unemployment. The usual argument that liberalization frees resources to move from unproductive, protected sectors into more productive export sectors is unconvincing when there are ample unutilized resources already available. In these cases, there is an emerging consensus: *countries should be given room to experiment, to use their own judgment, and to explore what might work best for them.*

A fourth is that successful development requires not the minimal role assigned to the state by the Washington Consensus, but a *balanced role*. The exact role may differ from country to country, depending on the stage of development of market and public institutions. In *every* successful country, government plays a critical complementary role with markets, for example in regulating financial institutions. In the most successful countries, government has taken on the broader set of roles associated with the *developmental state.*

A fifth point of consensus is that development requires strengthening of both market and state institutions.

And a final point of consensus is that success is to be measured not just by an increase in GDP, but by a broader set of measures—including those that assess environmental and social sustainability. Greater attention must be paid too to issues of distribution; a development strategy that leads to increases in GDP with most citizens not sharing in the fruits of that growth is not a success; and such a development strategy will almost surely not be sustainable over the long run.

Though it may not be possible to formulate simple prescriptions applicable to all countries, there may still be some principles and a range of instruments to be adapted to the circumstances of each country. The Barcelona Conference provided us an opportunity to explore some of the possible principles and some of the possible reforms, both in the policies pursued by individual countries and by the global community.

We addressed two broad sets of issues: first, what can each country, on its own, do to enhance sustainable, stable, equitable, and democratic development? As the developing countries approach this problem, they must take the world as it is, with the inequities in the global trading system and the instabilities in the global financial system. But that brings us to the second question: How should the global economic architecture be changed, to make the global economy more stable, to promote equity among countries, and to enhance the ability of developing countries to pursue their objectives—especially the goals of sustainable, stable, equitable, and democratic development? While it is difficult to touch upon all the facets of this question, we can discuss, or at least touch upon, a few of the central reforms, including, or especially, reforms in global governance.

References

Birdsall, N. (1999). 'Education: The People's Asset'. CSED Working Paper, No. 5 (September).

Deininger, K. (2003). 'Causes and Consequences of Civil Strife: Micro-Level Evidence from Uganda'. World Bank Working Paper, No. 3045 (May).

Eaton, J. and Gerzovitz, M. (1981). 'Debt with Potential Repudiation: Theoretical and Empirical Analysis'. *Review of Economic Studies*, 48: 289–309.

Greenwald, B. and Stiglitz, J. E. (1986). 'Externalities in Economics with Imperfect Information and Incomplete Markets'. *The Quarterly Journal of Economics*. May 1986: 229–64.

—— —— (2006). 'Helping Infant Economies Grow: Foundations of Trade Policies for Developing Countries'. *American Economic Review: AEA Papers and Proceedings*, 96/2: 141–6 (May).

Hoff, K. and Stiglitz, J. E. (2004). 'After the Big Bang? Obstacles to the Emergence of the Rule of Law in Post-Communist Societies'. *American Economic Review*, 94/3: 753–63 (June).

Prasad, E., Rogoff, K., Wei, S., and Kose, A. M. (2003). 'Effects of Financial Globalization on Developing Countries: Some Empirical Evidence'. IMF Occasional Paper, No. 220 (September).

Stiglitz, J. E. (1974). 'Alternative Theories of Wage Determination and Unemployment in L.D.C.'s: The Labor Turnover Model'. *Quarterly Journal of Economics*, 88/2: 194–227 (May). (Subsequently published in D. Lal (ed.) (1992). *Development Economics*, 1. London: Elgar, 288–321.)

—— (1994). *Whither Socialism?* Cambridge, MA: MIT Press.

—— (1998). 'More Instruments and Broader Goals: Moving Towards the Post-Washington Consensus'. The 1998 WIDER Annual Lecture, Helsinki (January), reprinted in H.-J. Chang (ed.) (2001). *The Rebel Within*. London: Wimbledon Publishing Company, 17–56.

—— (2001). 'The Role of International Financial Institutions in the Current Global Economy', in H.-J. Chang (ed.), *The Rebel Within*. London: Wimbledon Publishing Company, 172–93. Originally Address to the Chicago Council on Foreign Relations, Chicago, February 27.

—— (2002a). *Globalization and its Discontents*. New York: W.W. Norton & Company.

—— (2002b) 'Reforming Reform: Towards a New Agenda for Latin America'. Prebisch Lecture, ECLAC, Santiago, Chile.

—— and Charlton, A. (2005). *Fair Trade for All*. New York: Oxford University Press.

—— and Furman, J. (1998). 'Economic Crises: Evidence and Insights from East Asia'. *Brookings Papers on Economic Activity*, 2: 1–114. (Presented at Brookings Panel on Economic Activity, Washington, September 3.)

—— Greenwald, B. (2003). *Towards a New Paradigm for Monetary Policy*. London: Cambridge University Press.

Wade, R. (2003). *Governing the Market: Economic Theory and the Role of Government in East Asian Industrialization*. Princeton, NJ: Princeton University Press.

Williamson, J. (1990). 'What Washington Means by Policy Reform', in J. Williamson (ed.), *Latin American Adjustment: How Much Has Happened?* Washington, DC: Institute for International Economics.

Williamson, J. (1999). 'What Should the Bank Think About the Washington Consensus'. Background Paper to the World Bank's World Development Report 2000 (July).

—— (2004). 'A Short History of the Washington Consensus'. Paper presented at Foundation CIDOB Conference, 'From the Washington Consensus Towards a New Global Governance', Barcelona, September.

World Bank (1993). *The East Asian Miracle: Economic Growth and Public Policy (World Bank Policy Research Reports)*. Washington, DC: World Bank Publications.

5

The Barcelona Development Agenda

We*, a group of economists from developing and developed countries, met in Barcelona on September 24 and 25, 2004 to consider the prospects for growth and development around the world. We discussed the effects of economic reforms adopted by many developing nations over the last two decades, the lessons for economic policymaking that emerge from this experience, and the performance of the international economic system into which poor and middle-income countries are increasingly integrated.

We noted three encouraging trends:

- The gains made in human rights, democracy, and the rule of law in many—but regrettably not all—developing nations.

* Alice Amsden, Barton L. Weller Professor of Political Economy, Massachusetts Institute of Technology; Olivier Blanchard, Professor of Economics, Massachusetts Institute of Technology; Ramón Caminal, Professor of Economics, CSIC; Guillermo Calvo, Professor of Economics, Public and International Affairs, Columbia University; Daniel Cohen, Professor of Economics, Paris School of Economics, Paris; Antón Costas, Professor of Economics, CSIC; Guillermo de la Dehesa, Chairman of the Centre for Economic Policy Research (CEPR); Jeffrey Frankel, James W. Harpel Professor of Capital Formation and Growth, Kennedy School of Government, Harvard University; Jordi Galí, Director of CREI, University Pompeu Fabra; Ricardo Hausmann, Professor of Economic Development, Harvard University; Louka Katseli, Director, Development Center, OECD; Martin Khor, Director, Third World Network; Paul Krugman, Professor of Economics, Princeton University; Deepak Nayyar, Professor of Economics, Jawaharlal Nehru University; José Antonio Ocampo, Co-President of IPD and Professor, Columbia University; Dani Rodrik, Professor of International Political Economy, Kennedy School of Government, Harvard University; Jeffrey D. Sachs, Director, Earth Institute, Columbia University; Miguel Sebastián, Lecturer of Economics, Complutense University of Madrid; Narcís Serra, President of CIDOB Foundation; Shari Spiegel, Senior Portfolio Manager, New Holland Capital; Joseph E. Stiglitz, Co-President of IPD and University Professor, Columbia University; Ernesto Talvi, Executive Director, CERES; Joan Tugores, Professor of Economics, University of Barcelona; Andrés Velasco, Sumitomo-FASID Professor of International Finance and Development, Kennedy School, Harvard University; Jaume Ventura, Professor of Economics, CREI, University Pompeu Fabra; Xavier Vives, Professor of Economics and Finance, INSEAD; John Williamson, Senior Fellow, Peterson Institute for International Economics.

- The growth takeoff in several countries—including India and China—which has the potential to pull tens of millions more people out of poverty.
- The increasing recognition of the importance of macroeconomic stability, which, for instance, has led to a dramatic reduction in inflation in historically inflation-prone Latin America.

But we also noted at least three reasons for concern:

- The recurrence and severity of systemic financial crises affecting developing nations, including some that have undertaken adjustment and stabilization policies following international guidance.
- The mediocre record of reforms in igniting sustained economic growth in many regions of the world.
- The persistence—and often the worsening—of highly unequal distributions of wealth and income in many developing countries.

Our discussion was primarily focused on policy lessons and the need for changes in both rich and poor nations. There was broad agreement on seven sets of lessons, which in turn serve as priorities for reform.

First, both basic economic reasoning and international experience suggest that institutional quality, such as respect for the rule of law and property rights, plus a market orientation with an appropriate balance between market and state, and attention to the distribution of income, are at the root of successful development strategies. Moreover, the institutions that put these abstract principles into reality matter, and developing countries should work hard to improve their institutional environments. But effective institutional innovations are highly dependent on a country's history, culture and other specific circumstances. Encouraging developing nations to copy mechanically the institutions of rich countries—as international financial institutions tend to do—is not guaranteed to yield results, and can do more harm than good.

Second, experience has shown again and again that large debts, both public and private, poorly regulated banks and loose monetary policies are serious hindrances to development. Not only do these practices fail to stimulate growth in the medium term, but they can also expose nations to financial and debt crises that carry tremendous costs, especially for the poor. Developing nations that hope to prosper should therefore pursue prudent financial, monetary, fiscal, and debt policies. But a prudent fiscal stance, for instance, is not the same as a balanced budget every year, regardless of circumstances. Macroeconomic policies that are countercyclical are both more efficient and also ultimately more sustainable politically. Developing countries ought to build the institutions to make countercyclical policies feasible. International financial institutions should encourage such policies whenever possible. The macroeconomic accounting frameworks used by these institutions should also have the necessary built-in flexibility—for instance by treating productive infrastructures and R&D investment as asset purchases and not as current expenditures, for a given fiscal target.

Third, there is no single set of policies that can be guaranteed to ignite sustained growth. Nations that have succeeded at this tremendously important task have faced different sets of obstacles and have adopted varying policies regarding regulation, export, and industrial promotion, and technological innovation and knowledge acquisition. Countries should be free to experiment with policies suited to their specific circumstances, and international lending organizations and aid agencies should encourage such experimentation. But freedom to experiment is not the same as an 'anything goes' approach to development. Neither should this freedom be used to disguise policies that merely transfer income to politically powerful groups. The priority is to identify the most binding constraints to growth and to address them through microeconomic and macroeconomic policies. Micro interventions should be aimed at redressing specific market failures, and incentives should be contingent on improved performance by recipients.

Fourth, multilateral trade negotiations should proceed in a manner that promotes development. Agricultural and textile protectionism in developed countries represent an important obstacle to the participation of developing countries in the global economy. But some of the developing countries may limit their potential growth through inappropriate trade policies. We encourage a successful conclusion of the Doha Round that will provide more opportunities for world growth, thereby creating more room for developing countries to pursue their own growth strategies.

Fifth, international financial arrangements are not working well. Poor countries remain largely cut off from private financial flows and official aid levels are insufficient. Private capital flows to middle-income countries are highly volatile, and this volatility is largely unrelated to economic fundamentals in the recipient countries. Systemic capital account shocks continue to be common, and contagion increasingly hits countries widely regarded as having sound policies. At the core of the problem is the absence of markets and instruments that would permit a more efficient risk sharing among countries. Multilateral lending institutions do not do enough to overcome these failings of private financial markets. A focus on 'moral hazard' as the driving force behind crises has diverted attention from other causes of financial instability. Talk of reforming the international financial architecture has produced few tangible results. One reason may be that developing nations' views are under-represented in the decision making of the multilateral lenders. The allocation of votes in the boards of these institutions still reflects power relations of the past, and has little to do with the present day weight of countries in the world economy. In short: reforming international financial arrangements should be a priority for rich and poor countries.

Sixth, current international arrangements deal with movements of capital and labor asymmetrically. International financial institutions and G8 governments generally treat capital mobility as something to be encouraged. The same is not true of international labor mobility. But reasons of both equity and efficiency argue for allowing for greater international migration. We need a set of international rules and institutions to guide cross-border movements of people, including guest workers and service providers, and to promote the use of remittances from migrants as an additional source of financing. Improving the rights of migrants will facilitate their integration into the job market and limit exploitation.

Seventh, the worsening of the environment, including problems of global warming, need to be tackled with sustainable development policies at both national and global levels. This is an area in which both rich and poor countries have work to do.

There is much not to like about the state of the world today. The fact that over a billion human beings live in abject poverty should be a cause for unrelenting concern. AIDS and other epidemic diseases represent a tragedy for the least developed countries, mainly in Africa. In the Millennium Development Goals donor nations committed to increase aid to address these and other problems, but that commitment remains largely unfulfilled. It also is easy to be discouraged by the failure of all kinds of magical recipes for development. But concern is not the same as despair. Nor should concern for the poor serve to justify unthoughtful anti-growth attitudes. Over the last half-century a number of countries have pulled themselves out of poverty, and others are doing the same today. There are hopeful lessons to be learned from these experiences, some of which we have tried to summarize in this agenda. Equitable and progressive development paths are conceivable. No set of policies can guarantee success, but we know more today about where to look for the keys to that success.

Citizens of developing countries know full well that development is a long and arduous path. If their leaders embark upon it, and if rich countries help reform international arrangements that hinder rather than ease this path, there is still reason for hope.

Part II

Analyses of Central Issues in Development

6

A Broad View of Macroeconomic Stability

José Antonio Ocampo[1]

Introduction

The concept of macroeconomic stability has undergone considerable changes in the economic discourse over the past decades. During the post-war years dominated by Keynesian thinking, macroeconomic stability basically meant a mix of external and internal balance, which in turn implied, in the second case, full employment and stable economic growth, accompanied by low inflation. Over time, fiscal balance and price stability moved to center stage, supplanting the Keynesian emphasis on *real* economic activity. This policy shift led to the downplaying and even, in the most radical views, the complete suppression of the countercyclical role of macroeconomic policy. Although this shift recognized that high inflation and unsustainable fiscal deficits have costs, and that 'fine tuning' of macroeconomic policies to smooth out the business cycle has limits, it also led to an underestimation of both the costs of real macroeconomic instability and the effectiveness of Keynesian aggregate demand management.

This shift was particularly sharp in the developing world, where capital account and domestic financial liberalization exposed developing countries to the highly pro-cyclical financial swings characteristic of assets that are perceived by financial markets as risky, and thus subject to sharp changes in the 'appetite for risk.' In the words of Stiglitz (2003), such exposure replaced Keynesian automatic stabilizers with automatic *de*stabilizers. Thus, contrary to the view that financial markets would play a disciplinary

[1] This is a revised version of a paper previously presented at the seminar 'From the Washington Consensus Towards a New Global Governance' at the Universal Forum for Cultures, Barcelona, September 24–5, 2004. I thank participants in the Forum and Stephany Griffith-Jones, Maria Angela Parra, Lance Taylor, and Camilo Tovar for their comments on the prior version of this chapter.

role, dependence on financial swings actually encouraged the adoption of pro-cyclical monetary and fiscal policies that increased both *real* macroeconomic instability and the accumulation of risky balance sheets during periods of financial euphoria which led, in several cases, to financial meltdowns.

There is now overwhelming evidence that pro-cyclical financial markets and pro-cyclical macroeconomic policies have not encouraged growth; they have in fact increased growth volatility in developing countries that have integrated to a larger extent in international financial markets (Prasad et al. 2003). This has generated a renewed but still incomplete interest in the role that countercyclical macroeconomic policies can play in smoothing out—that is, in reducing the intensity of—business cycles in the developing world. At the same time, since the Asian crisis, it has been increasingly recognized that liberalized capital accounts and financial markets tend to generate excessively risky private sector balance sheets, and that an excessive reliance on short term external financing enhances the risks of currency crises. Preventive (prudential) macroeconomic and financial policies, which aim to avoid the accumulation of unsustainable public and private sector debts and balance sheets during periods of financial euphoria, have thus become part of the standard recipe since the Asian crisis. This represents, however, only a partial return to a countercyclical macroeconomic framework, for no equally strong consensus has yet emerged on the role of expansionary policies in facilitating recovery from crises.

Thus, the menu of macroeconomic policies has broadened in recent years. We have only come part of the way, however, to the full recognition that macroeconomic stability involves multiple dimensions, including not only price stability and sound fiscal policies, but also a well-functioning real economy, sustainable debt ratios, and healthy domestic financial and nonfinancial private sector balance sheets. A well-functioning real economy requires, in turn, smoother business cycles, moderate long-term interest rates, and competitive exchange rates, all of which may be considered intermediate goals of the ultimate Keynesian objective: full employment. Such a broad view of macroeconomic stability should recognize, in any case, that there is no simple correlation between its various dimensions and, thus, that multiple objectives and significant trade-offs are intrinsic to the design of 'sound' macroeconomic frameworks.

This view should lead to the recognition of the role played by two sets of policy packages, whose relative importance will vary depending on the structural characteristics, the macroeconomic policy tradition, and the institutional capacity of each country. The first involves a mix of countercyclical fiscal and monetary policies with appropriate (and, as we will argue, generally intermediate) exchange rate regimes. The second includes a set of capital management techniques designed to reduce the unsustainable accumulation of public and private sector risks in the face of pro-cyclical access to international capital markets.

To encourage economic growth, such interventions through the business cycle should lead to sound fiscal systems that provide the necessary resources for the public sector to do its job, as well as a competitive exchange rate and moderate long-term real interest rates. These conditions, together with deep financial markets that provide suitably priced investment finance in the *domestic* currency with sufficiently long maturities, are the best contribution that macroeconomics can make to growth.

This chapter calls for a broad view of macroeconomic stability and for active countercyclical macroeconomic policies supported by the equally active use of capital management techniques. It is divided into four sections. The first section identifies some 'stylized facts' about financial and real macroeconomic instability in developing countries. The subsequent two sections each analyze one of the aforementioned policy packages. The last takes a brief look at the implications of this framework for international cooperation.

Some Stylized Facts

The Characteristics and Costs of Capital Account Volatility

Trade—including terms of trade—fluctuations continue to play a major role in the determination of business cycles in developing countries, particularly in commodity dependent economies. Domestic factors, including political and climatic variables, also continue to play a role. Nonetheless, the distinguishing feature of developing country business cycles since the 1970s has been the leading role played by *capital* account fluctuations, particularly in those economies with access to international private capital markets (the 'emerging' economies).

These new sources of vulnerability are associated with the flow and balance sheet effects of *capital* account fluctuations on the behavior of domestic financial and nonfinancial agents. Rather than the price and wage rigidities emphasized by traditional macroeconomic models, financial variables—such as capital account cycles, their domestic financial multipliers, and their reflection in asset prices—have thus become the major determinant of growth volatility (Easterly et al., 2001). Furthermore, whereas some of the effects of financial instability are transmitted through public sector accounts (as the first generation of crisis models tended to emphasize), the dominant feature of the 'new generation' of business cycles in developing countries is the sharp fluctuation in *private* spending and balance sheets. The resulting implication is that 'twin' external and domestic financial crises have become more frequent since the breakdown of Bretton Woods exchange rate arrangements in the early 1970s (IMF 1998; Bordo et al. 2001).

Boom–bust capital account cycles in developing countries are characterized by the twin phenomena of volatility and contagion. The first is associated with significant changes in risk evaluation of what international market agents consider to be risky assets, which involve the alternation of periods of 'appetite for risk' (or, more properly, underestimation of risks) with periods in which there is a 'flight to quality' (risk aversion). The second implies that, due to the costs of and asymmetries in information, developing countries (or groups of them) are pooled together in risk categories viewed by market agents as being strongly correlated. Beyond any objective criteria that may underlie such views, this practice turns such correlations into self-fulfilling prophecies. Countries are then pulled in the same direction by the herding behavior of investors, generating both a contagion of optimism and a contagion of pessimism. Furthermore, market sensitive risk management practices, as well as other features of financial market operations (such as benchmarking and evaluation of managers against competitors), tend to increase this herding behavior (Persaud 2000).

As a result of these factors, developing countries were pulled together into the financial boom that started in the early 1990s (Calvo et al. 1993), but they have also been subject to a clustering of 'sudden stops' in external financing since the Asian crisis (Calvo and Talvi 2008), in both cases with some independence from the 'fundamental' macroeconomic factors. In turn, financial market evaluations are subject to pro-cyclical patterns—as reflected, for example, in the highly pro-cyclical variations of credit ratings (Reisen 2003). They are also subject to the inconsistent judgment of individual economies over time, which may lead to some 'success' stories being reclassified as financial pariahs (e.g., Argentina) and pariahs reclassified as 'investment grade' (e.g., Russia). Interestingly, due to herding behavior, countries viewed by markets as 'success' stories are almost inevitably drawn into the boom, inducing sizeable private sector deficits (Ffrench-Davis 2001; Marfán 2005) that may subject them to the endogenous unstable dynamics, which have been analyzed by Minsky (1982) and Taylor (1998), among others.

Volatility is reflected in the pro-cyclical pattern of spreads (narrowing during booms, widening during crises), but also in variations in the *availability* of financing (the presence or absence of credit rationing) and in maturities (reduced availability of long-term financing during crises, or the use of options that have a similar effect). The feedback between increases in spreads (country risk premia), debt accumulation, and short-term macroeconomic expectations during crises can be highly destabilizing, particularly in the presence of high debt/export ratios (Frenkel 2005). Different types of capital flows are subject to different volatility patterns. In particular, the greater volatility of short-term capital indicates that reliance on such financing is highly risky (Rodrik and Velasco 2000), whereas the smaller volatility of FDI vis-à-vis all forms of financial flows is considered a source of strength.

Capital account cycles involve short-term movements, such as the intense movements of spreads and the frequency of interruption (rationing) of financing. These phenomena were observed during the Asian and, particularly, the Russian crises. Perhaps more importantly, however, they also involve *medium-term* fluctuations, as the experience of the past three decades indicates. Indeed, during these decades, the developing world has experienced two such medium-term cycles that left strong imprints in the growth rates of many countries: a boom of external financing (mostly in the form of syndicated bank loans) in the 1970s, followed by a debt crisis in a large part of the developing world in the 1980s; and a new boom in the 1990s (then mostly portfolio flows), followed by a sharp reduction in net flows since the Asian crisis.

There is widespread evidence that ample private sector financing encourages, and certainly rewards, pro-cyclical macroeconomic policies during booms. On the other hand, authorities are expected to behave in ways that generate 'credibility' for financial markets during crises, which means that they are judged according to their capacity to adopt pro-cyclical austerity policies. This generates, in turn, economic *and* political economy pressures to also adopt pro-cyclical policies during booms. Financial and non-financial agents resist then the restrictions that authorities may impose on their ability to spend or lend, whereas authorities are only too happy to have some breathing space after a period of austerity. Thus, contrary to the notion that financial markets would have a disciplinary effect, unstable external financing has, in a strong sense, distorted the incentives that *economic agents* and *authorities* face throughout the business cycle, inducing pro-cyclical behavior from both economic agents and macroeconomic policies.

The costs of financial volatility in terms of economic growth are high. Volatility leads to a high average rate of under-utilization of production capacity, which reduces the productivity of capital. In turn, the uncertainty associated with variability in growth rates has adverse effects on capital accumulation (Loayza et al. 2003). More importantly, in the presence of increasing returns, strong recessions generate significant losses of resources that may have cumulative effects (Easterly 2001: ch. 10). In the most favorable case, this will be reflected in a once and for all loss in GDP (as in the experience of Korea during the Asian crisis); in the most adverse case, it will lead to a displacement in the long-term growth *trajectory* (as in most Latin American countries in the 1980s, or in Indonesia during the Asian crisis).

The Underlying Financial and Macroeconomic Asymmetries

The dynamics of boom–bust cycles are deeply rooted in the operation of financial markets, but also in some basic asymmetries of the world economy, which are largely (though not exclusively) of a center–periphery character (Ocampo 2003b; Ocampo and Martin 2003). In the financial area, these asymmetries are reflected in three basic facts: (a) the incapacity of most countries to issue liabilities in their own currencies, a phenomenon that has become known as 'original sin' (Eichengreen et al. 2003; Hausman and Panizza 2003); (b) differences in the degree of domestic financial and capital market development, which lead to an under-supply of long-term financial instruments; and (c) the small size of developing countries' domestic financial markets vis-à-vis the magnitude of the speculative pressures they may face (Council on Foreign Relations 2000). Taking the first two of these phenomena together, this implies that domestic financial markets in the developing world are significantly more 'incomplete' than those in the industrial world, and thus that some financial intermediation must necessarily be conducted through international markets. As a result, developing countries are plagued by variable mixes of currency and maturity mismatches in the balance sheets of their economic agents. This also implies that integration into international financial markets is an integration between unequal partners (ECLAC 2000: ch. 8).

Financial asymmetries are reflected, in turn, in macroeconomic asymmetries, particularly in the capacity to undertake countercyclical macroeconomic policies. Industrialized countries, whose currencies are the international currencies, have larger degrees of freedom to undertake countercyclical macroeconomic policies and to induce a stabilizing response from markets. In contrast, as we have seen, developing countries have more limited degrees of freedom to do so, and face pro-cyclical pressures from financial markets (Kamisky et al. 2004). In this sense, developing countries are both *'business cycle takers'* and *'policy takers'* (Ocampo 2002).

The risks associated with financial instability can be partly corrected by domestic policy actions. Indeed, this chapter addresses ways of dealing with such vulnerabilities. Such actions, however, are not costless because 'self-insurance' is costly. Furthermore, some of the policy actions that emerging economies can adopt to manage risks merely shift those risks, rather than correct them. For example, larger short-term capital flows can be counterbalanced by a simultaneous accumulation of international reserves, but this route implies a loss equivalent to the spread between lending and borrowing interest rates on the accumulated reserves. Also, the risks faced by the domestic financial sector can be counterbalanced by more strict prudential regulations of domestic financial activities than international (Basle) standards, but this raises the cost of financial intermediation and may restrict the development of new financial services. The move to a currency board regime or dollar/euroization can reduce or eliminate currency risks, but it may also make economic activity more volatile, given the restrictions placed on the adoption of countercyclical policies. There is, therefore, a very profound sense in which the financial and macroeconomic asymmetries that affect developing countries are inescapable. In this context, the search for shortcuts and 'silver bullets' does not eliminate the difficult trade-offs that such asymmetries generate, and it may actually increase the costs incurred in the absence of a broad framework for macroeconomic stability.

Countercyclical Macroeconomic Policy

The Exchange Rate Regime and the Scope for Monetary Autonomy

The traditional instruments of trade and balance of payments management used by developing countries throughout most of the post-war period became severely criticized as a source of inefficiency and rent seeking; in recent years, therefore, they have been weakened or dismantled altogether. Interestingly, the countercyclical role that they played in economies where the business cycles are largely of an external origin has been generally overlooked. Thus, protection and export subsidies were used to encourage trade restructuring during periods of adverse external shocks, while trade liberalization and reduction of export subsidies were used to reduce the expansionary effects of export booms. Capital controls and dual exchange rates were also used to manage pro-cyclical swings in capital flows. In practice, trade and capital account liberalization thus eliminated instruments that could be used to manage externally generated business cycles.

This left the exchange rate as the major and, in many cases, the only instrument of balance of payments management. The exchange rate can play a countercyclical role by encouraging trade restructuring through the business cycle—in promoting exports and efficient import substitution during periods of foreign exchange scarcity, and the opposite during periods of abundance. As the literature on the contractionary effects of devaluation (expansionary effects of appreciation) indicates, however, the aggregate demand effects of exchange rate fluctuations may be pro-cyclical, at least in the short run (Krugman and Taylor 1978; Díaz Alejandro 1988: ch. 1).

Furthermore, real exchange rate fluctuations are not without costs if tradable sectors face learning and other dynamic economies of scale. In particular, appreciation pressures during periods of foreign exchange abundance (an increase in commodity prices or capital flows) may have long-term de-industrialization effects, as indicated in the literature on the 'Dutch disease' (van Wijnbergen 1984; Krugman 1990: ch. 7). Real exchange rate instability is also costly if entry into tradable sectors has fixed costs (fixed capital investments or fixed costs of building a clientele in foreign markets). In broader terms, in open developing economies, the real exchange rate is one of the crucial determinants of investment, growth and employment (Frenkel 2004).

In any case, in a world of capital account volatility, trade effects are overshadowed by the *wealth* effects that exchange rate fluctuations have in economies with currency mismatches in their balance sheets (net external liabilities denominated in foreign currencies). The capital gains generated by appreciation during upswings help to fuel the private spending boom, whereas the capital losses generated by depreciation have the opposite effect during downturns. Furthermore, such gains induce additional net inflows (including net variations of flight capital) when there are expectations of exchange rate appreciation, and the opposite effect if depreciation is expected, thus providing endogenous reinforcement to the capital account cycle.

Countercyclical monetary and fiscal policies could, in principle, counteract the pro-cyclical effects that real exchange rate fluctuations are likely to have in developing countries. A crucial factor is the degree of monetary autonomy allowed by different exchange rate regimes. In this regard, it has long been accepted that fixed exchange rate regimes eliminate monetary autonomy whereas flexible exchange rates provide room for autonomous monetary policies. As we will see, this traditional view of flexible exchange rates is not entirely valid. Indeed, recent evidence indicates that the degree of exchange rate flexibility may not be as crucial a determinant of the ability to undertake countercyclical macroeconomic policies as traditionally thought (Kamisky et al. 2004).

These considerations imply that, in today's open developing economies, the exchange rate regime is subject to conflicting and not easily reconcilable demands. These conflicts are exacerbated by capital account volatility, by the strong aggregate demand and *supply* effects of exchange rates on developing economies, and by the reduced degrees of freedom enjoyed by authorities in a world of limited policy instruments.

Although these contradictory demands can be expressed in different ways, they can usefully be defined as the tensions faced by exchange regimes between the demand for stability and the demand for flexibility (Ocampo 2002). The demand for stability comes from trade, but also from domestic price stability and the need to avoid the pro-cyclical wealth effects of exchange rate fluctuations. The demand for flexibility comes from the need to have some degrees of freedom to manage trade and capital account shocks. Authorities will thus tend to choose the exchange rate regime based on their preferences, but also on the relative benefits ('price') of flexibility versus stability, which are determined by both the external environment and objective factors. Increased international instability (such as the breakdown of the dollar standard, a period of turmoil in world finance for 'emerging' markets or a world recession) will increase the relative benefits of flexibility, whereas a period of tranquillity (as in the heyday of the Bretton Woods system or a period of stable world economic growth) will increase the relative advantages of stability. In turn, while the benefits of flexibility will be higher for larger, less specialized economies, the benefits of nominal stability will be greater for smaller, more specialized economies.

Another way to characterize these conflicting demands begins, as does this chapter, with the understanding that a broad framework for stability implies that economic authorities have, in fact, multiple objectives: low inflation, smoother business cycles, competitive real exchange rates, stable long-term interest rates, and sound balance sheets. Achieving these multiple objectives requires some additional instruments, particularly countercyclical fiscal policies and prudential regulation and supervision of domestic financial systems (see below). Even if helped by these instruments, however, monetary authorities must not disregard their multiple objectives. Particularly, in addition to inflation targeting, they should not disregard the countercyclical role of monetary policy (output and employment targeting). Furthermore, to the extent that a stable, real exchange rate is a crucial determinant of growth and employment in open economies, an element of real exchange rate targeting is also an essential component of adequate macroeconomic management in developing countries (Frenkel 2004). As indicated at the start of this section, this is particularly important when, as the result of liberalization, countries have given up their traditional trade policy instruments.

The call to choose polar exchange rate regimes does not capture the relevance of these conflicting demands. Rather, the defense of polar regimes is based on the argument that any attempt to manage the conflicting demands on exchange rate policy is futile and should thus be abandoned.

Hard pegs certainly introduce built-in institutional arrangements that provide for fiscal and monetary discipline and help to avoid currency mismatches and their pro-cyclical effects (Calvo 2001), but this choice is made at the cost of eliminating the output and real exchange rate objectives of monetary policy. Thus, under this type of regime, adjustment to overvaluation (if the economy gets 'locked' into an overvalued exchange rate during the transition, or as a result of devaluations by major trade partners, or of appreciation of the currency to which the exchange rate is pegged) is painful, and it may lead to low structural rates of growth mixed with strong business cycles. Nor is this regime speculation proof, as evidenced by the experiences of Argentina in 1994–95 and 1998–2001, of Hong Kong in 1997 and, for that matter, of the gold standard in the periphery. More price flexibility could help, but it may nonetheless generate adjustment problems that are generally disregarded today.[2] In particular, during the gold standard era, price flexibility tended to generate additional domestic financial risks during crises, due to the rapid increase in real debt burdens generated by deflation (which may be thought of as equivalent to very high *real* short-term interest rates). The gold

[2] See, however, Easterly et al. (2001) for a similar view to that exposed here.

standard also generated a strong short-term bias in bank lending, which was necessary to rapidly reduce nominal portfolios during periods of monetary contraction.

On the other hand, the volatility characteristic of freely floating exchange rate regimes increases the costs of trade transactions, thus reducing the benefits of international specialization. As developing countries are largely net importers of capital goods, exchange rate uncertainty also affects investment decisions. Its major benefit is thus the degree of monetary autonomy that it provides—that is, the ability to determine monetary policies on the basis of domestic factors, thus generating some room for countercyclical macroeconomic policies. But this benefit is unlikely to materialize fully, for two different reasons.

The first reason relates to the links between the exchange rate and the domestic price level in open economies. If monetary authorities follow strict inflation targeting rules, these effects are pro-cyclical. This is most visible in two widely used pro-cyclical policies: anchoring the price level to a fixed exchange rate during periods of foreign exchange abundance, and counterbalancing the inflationary effects of devaluation through contractionary monetary policies during periods of foreign exchange scarcity. Expressed in terms of the literature on open economy inflation targeting, strict inflation targeting will generate more output volatility than flexible inflation targeting, which takes into account other objectives of monetary policy, particularly reducing the output gap (Svensson 2000).

The second reason why inflation targeting in a floating exchange rate regime is unlikely to result in countercyclical macroeconomic management relates to the effects of capital mobility. The key problem faced by the authorities during booms is that capital surges exert expansionary aggregate demand effects that are enhanced by the downward pressure on interest rates and/or exchange rate appreciation. Any attempt by policymakers to counteract these aggregate demand effects through contractionary monetary policies will be partly self-defeating, as the higher interest rates will induce additional capital inflows, and thus additional appreciation pressures. During crises, the reduction of capital inflows will have a direct effect on aggregate demand, which will be combined with a mix of devaluation and interest rate hikes. Any attempt to avoid the latter by using expansionary monetary policy will encourage a stronger devaluation. Thus, if authorities consider that the exchange rate fluctuations generated by boom–bust cycles are too strong to start with, they may be encouraged to use pro-cyclical monetary policy to smooth out those fluctuations. In other words, contrary to the traditional argument about the additional degrees of freedom for monetary policy provided by floating exchange rates, such a regime may in fact lead, in the presence of open capital accounts and inflation targeting, to pro-cyclical monetary policies. The only way to guarantee adequate degrees of freedom for countercyclical monetary policies may thus be to give up free floating, free capital mobility, or both.

The frequency of regimes with limited exchange rate flexibility (Reinhart and Rogoff 2004) may be seen as a reflection of the revealed preference of authorities in the developing world for striking a balance between the conflicting demands they face by choosing intermediate exchange rate regimes. These regimes can take several forms: (a) quasi-fixed exchange rate regimes with large central bank interventions in foreign exchange markets; (b) managed exchange rates, such as crawling pegs and bands; and (c) dirty floats.[3] All these regimes can be understood to include an element of 'real exchange rate targeting' in the design of macroeconomic policy, and many or most of them are also mixed with different capital account regulations. According to the arguments presented above, this type of mix may be a rational choice when authorities face multiple objectives. Furthermore, to the extent that smoothing out real exchange rate fluctuations has a countercyclical effect, 'real exchange rate targeting' can serve the objective of smoothing output volatility.

Thus, intermediate regimes may provide a better framework for effective 'monetary autonomy' than floating exchange rates. This approach implies, of course, that monetary authorities will *not* have a single objective and that they will coordinate their actions with the fiscal authorities. Nonetheless, the scope for monetary autonomy is limited. First of all, that autonomy will depend on the effectiveness of capital account regulations as a macroeconomic policy tool, an issue we will deal with below. Second, all intermediate options are subject to speculative pressures if they do not generate credibility in markets, and the costs of defending the exchange rate are high in this context. This is particularly true of any pre-announcement (of the rate of the crawl of a band or of a specific exchange rate target), which should thus be avoided. Third, intermediate regimes will generally require sterilized intervention in foreign exchange markets. Although the additional reserves accumulated during booms will provide additional 'self-insurance' during the ensuing crises, the simultaneous accumulation of assets and liabilities in external currency generates quasi-fiscal losses.

In any case, one of the advantages of intermediate regimes is that they allow for a *graduated flexibility*, with the appropriate level of flexibility being determined by the relative benefits of stability versus flexibility that we have analyzed. This implies that any specific intermediate regime has an embedded 'exit option.' Also, if some degree of exchange rate flexibility is available before an external crisis hits, this would provide scope to avoid the real interest rate

[3] For defenses of intermediate regimes, see ECLAC (2000: ch. 8), Williamson (2000), Ocampo (2002), and Ffrench-Davis and Larraín (2003). For interesting reviews of controversies on exchange rate regimes, see Frankel (1999), Velasco (2000), and Braga de Macedo et al. (2001).

overshooting that characterizes the transition towards freer exchange rates in developing countries.[4]

Countercyclical Fiscal Policies

Regardless of which exchange rate and capital account regime a country chooses, fiscal policy can always provide a useful countercyclical device. Indeed, it is frequently argued that fiscal policy is a more powerful countercyclical instrument than monetary policy in an open economy. But this argument runs against two strong facts.

The first is that there are objective restrictions on the capacity of fiscal policy to play a strong countercyclical role. Some of them are inherent to fiscal policy: spending inertia plays a very strong role in fiscal affairs, and there exist time lags between the point when a change in the course of policy becomes desirable and when either the government or parliament decides on the new course of action. Others are of a political economy character. In particular, there are objective limits to the capacity of fiscal authorities to convince the public that they should generate large fiscal surpluses during upswings in order to compensate rising private deficits (Marfán 2005). The public may actually reject such a policy choice, given that it would generate substantial distributive effects, as the recipients of goods and services provided by the public sector are not the same agents that benefit from private spending. Furthermore, to the extent that social spending would be affected, the distributive effects of a spending cut would be regressive.

The second fact is that the pro-cyclical swings in external and domestic financing generate strong incentives for fiscal policies to behave in a pro-cyclical way. This is enhanced by the pro-cyclical performance of public sector revenues in the context of high GDP volatility, which implies that spending will be partly financed by temporary revenues during booms, and that temporary reductions in revenue will lead to pro-cyclical cuts in spending. Also, the explosion of the debt service as a result of the variations of interest and exchange rates generated by adverse external shocks implies that primary fiscal spending must adjust pro-cyclically to meet short-term fiscal targets during crises. The orthodox expectation that cuts in the fiscal deficit will then 'crowd in' private spending, thereby avoiding the contractionary effects of fiscal adjustment, is not generally met (see, for example, in relation to IMF programs, IMF 2003).

At the same time, other pro-cyclical patterns have become more important than in the past, particularly those associated with the granting of explicit or implicit guarantees to the private sector. A first case in point is the explicit and

[4] Indeed, the atypical phenomenon identified by Hausmann (2000)—when rising interest rates accompany the adoption of a more flexible exchange rate—is only a feature of transition periods.

implicit guarantees issued to financial agents and depositors in the financial system. These also include public sector guarantees for private sector investments in infrastructure (such as minimum revenue or profit guarantees, or explicit coverage of interest or exchange rate risks). Both types of guarantees have three elements in common: (a) they are not always transparent; (b) they encourage *private* spending during booms (it is during periods of euphoria that implicit public sector spending, in the form of an equivalent 'insurance premium,' is actually incurred, indicating an underestimation of accrued public sector spending during these periods); and (c) disbursements (cash spending) are incurred during crises, increasing borrowing requirements and crowding out other public sector spending.

There is indeed widespread evidence that fiscal accounts are highly pro-cyclical in the developing world (Kaminsky et al. 2004). In Latin America, for example, the evidence provided by Martner and Tromben (2003) indicate that out of 45 episodes of cyclical swings in 1990–2001, 12 were neutral (in the sense that the structural fiscal deficit remained unchanged through the improvement or deterioration of fiscal accounts), 25 were pro-cyclical and only eight countercyclical.

The costs of pro-cyclical fiscal policies are high. Given the higher flexibility of public sector investment, they are likely to be reflected in large swings in this variable, a pattern that will tend to reduce its efficiency. During upswings, abundant financing may lead authorities to initiate some projects that have low social returns. During downswings, cuts in spending may mean that investment projects are left unfinished or take much longer to execute than planned, thereby raising their effective cost. In turn, extended cuts in public sector investment may have long-term effects on growth (Easterly and Servén 2003; IMF 2004a). To the extent that current spending is reduced during downswings, some valuable social programs may be cut, the existing structure for the provision of public and social services may become disjointed, and reductions in real wages may lead to the loss of valuable staff. Thus, in general, 'stop–go' cycles significantly reduce the efficiency of public sector spending.

This means that fiscal reforms must both firmly establish the principle of fiscal sustainability and adopt targets that avoid pro-cyclical biases in fiscal policy. Fiscal policies, however, cannot be expected to serve by themselves as the major instrument of countercyclical management, compensating not only the pro-cyclical effects of financial markets, but also those of pro-cyclical monetary and exchange rate policies.

The major reflection of the principle of fiscal responsibility should be the adoption of targets for the public sector deficit and/or maximum debt to GDP ratios. The definition of such rules is not an easy task, as indicated by the recent debates over the European Growth and Stability Pact (GSP). In any case (and contrary even to the practice of the GSP), deficit targets should be designed on the basis of the *structural* stance of fiscal policy. Indeed, setting fiscal deficit targets independently of the business cycle transforms fiscal policy into a pro-cyclical instrument, leading both to spending on the basis of transitory revenues during the boom and to cuts in spending during crises due to equally transitory reductions in revenue. The surplus or deficit target should then be determined on the basis of a structural stance and current deviations from potential GDP and other relevant variables. In this regard, an interesting experience in the developing world is that of Chile, which in recent years has set a structural public sector surplus equivalent to 1 percent of GDP.

Defining a structural stance is also a difficult task. In general, the trend of GDP growth will *not* be independent of cyclical swings, particularly in countries experiencing substantial shocks (Heyman 2000). Furthermore, in developing countries, it would be important to determine also the cyclical stance of commodity prices that have a strong impact on public sector finances, but this is not easily done when these price deviations result from a random walk or from temporary deviations from a long run-trend, which may itself be subject to change.

A first major instrument of countercyclical policy is fiscal stabilization funds to sterilize temporary public sector revenues (Davis et al. 2003). The experience gained from the management of stabilization funds for commodities that have a significant fiscal impact (the National Coffee Fund of Colombia and the copper and petroleum funds in Chile, for example) must be extended to develop broader fiscal stabilization funds (ECLAC 1998). The counterpart of the resources accumulated in these funds would be sterilized foreign exchange reserves, which would then provide 'self-insurance' against sudden stops of external financing, as well as reduced currency appreciation.

To the extent, however, that these funds sterilize the additional revenues generated by a commodity or capital boom, this would make fiscal policy at most cycle-*neutral*. A complementary instrument, of a clearly *counter*cyclical character, would be to design flexible tax rates, particularly to manage sharp private sector spending cycles. The best candidate is a tax on the source of the spending booms. This is the traditional argument for taxing exports subject to temporary price surges, which has served as the basis for the design of commodity stabilization funds. A similar argument can be used to justify a tax on capital inflows, as this is the major source of private sector spending booms today (Marfán 2005).[5] It is interesting to note that this argument is additional to those associated with the greater monetary autonomy that such a tax on capital flows may provide. A second-best argument can also be made for temporary hikes of Value-Added Tax (VAT) rates during private spending booms (Budnevich and Le Fort 1997).

[5] It should be emphasized that the tax collection could be done by the central bank (the equivalent tax for unremunerated reserve requirements on capital inflows), and the revenues could be sterilized in the form of a quasi-fiscal surplus not transferred to the government.

To the extent that, as argued above, cyclical swings may reduce the efficiency of public sector spending and that time lags inevitably occur in the decision-making process, the alternative of using discretionary changes in public spending as a countercyclical device is sub-optimal. Indeed, a strong claim can be made that the growth of public sector spending should be determined on the basis of an essentially long-term criterion: the balanced supply of public and private goods. In any case, a well-designed social safety net to protect vulnerable groups during crises (preferably as part of permanent social protection systems) is an automatic, countercyclical instrument that can play a useful macroeconomic (as well as social) role.

These tax and spending policies must be complemented by adequate mechanisms to manage public sector guarantees. With respect to financial sector risks, regulatory policies are the proper answer. In the case of public sector guarantees of private infrastructure projects, it is necessary that the 'insurance premium equivalent' of such guarantees be regularly estimated and budgeted, with the corresponding resources transferred to special funds created to serve as a backup in the event that the corresponding contingencies materialize. The estimated contingent liabilities should be added to the public sector debt.[6]

A major problem with these guarantees is that they generate significant distortions in public sector accounting. As argued earlier, they have pro-cyclical effects. If deficit targets are in place, the guarantees also clearly discriminate against public sector investment, for they create a strong incentive for governments to promote private investment in infrastructure to circumvent the targets. Dealing with all these issues simultaneously can only be achieved by combining a target for the *current* fiscal balance of the general public sector administration (such as a structural 'golden rule'[7] or a structural primary surplus) with a public sector debt target that includes all contingent liabilities. Also, to avoid discriminating against investment by public sector firms versus private investment in infrastructure, the same criteria must be used in both cases: the fiscal risk incurred by the public sector administration in either case.[8] Indeed, the only other option is a full accounting of guaranteed private sector investments within fiscal targets.

[6] The IMF (2004a) has argued that contingent liabilities should be included alongside public sector debt, but it does not propose similar treatment of the current account of the public sector. The treatment we propose here is more complete and symmetrical.

[7] This rule would determine that the current account of the general administration, including costs equivalent to the depreciation of the public sector capital stock, should be balanced—once cyclical factors are netted out.

[8] This rule would be simpler and much better than the stringent criteria suggested by the IMF (2004a) to determine whether an investment by a public sector firm will be excluded from the public sector accounts. The latter includes criteria that may be contrary to the legal principles that define a public sector firm in some countries, and that have nothing to do with the fiscal risks incurred (such as total managerial independence, stock listing, and rights of minority shareholders).

Capital Management Techniques

The Case for Capital Account Regulations

The accumulation of macroeconomic risks during booms depends not only on the magnitude of private and public sector debts, but also on the maturity and currency mismatches on their balance sheets. Therefore, capital account regulations potentially have a dual role: as a macroeconomic policy tool, which provides some room for countercyclical monetary policies that smooth out spending and avoid excessive debt ratios, and as a 'liability policy', which encourages improvements in private sector external debt profiles. The emphasis on *liability structures*, rather than on national balance sheets, recognizes the fact that, together with liquid assets (particularly international reserves), the liability structures play the crucial role when countries face liquidity constraints; other assets play a secondary role in this regard.

Viewed as a macroeconomic policy tool, capital account regulations target the direct source of boom–bust cycles: unstable capital flows. If successful, they will provide some room to 'lean against the wind' during periods of financial euphoria, through the adoption of a contractionary monetary policy and/or reduced appreciation pressures. If effective, they will also reduce or eliminate the quasi-fiscal costs of foreign exchange reserve accumulation. During crises, they provide 'breathing space' for expansionary monetary policies. In both cases, capital account regulations improve the authorities' ability to mix a countercyclical monetary policy with a more active exchange rate policy.

Viewed as a liability policy, capital account regulations recognize that the market rewards sound external debt profiles (Rodrik and Velasco 2000). This reflects the fact that, during times of uncertainty, the market responds to *gross* (rather than merely net) financing requirements, which means that the rollover of short-term liabilities is not financially neutral. Under these circumstances, a maturity profile that leans towards longer-term obligations will reduce domestic liquidity risks. This indicates that an essential component of economic policy management during booms should be instruments that improve the maturity structures of the external and domestic liabilities of both the private and public sectors. On the equity side, foreign direct investment (FDI) should be preferred to portfolio flows, as the former has proved to be less volatile than the latter. Both types of equity flows have the additional advantage of allowing all risks associated with the business cycle to be shared with foreign investors, and FDI may bring other benefits (access to technology and external markets). These benefits should be balanced against the generally higher costs of equity financing.

In macroeconomic terms, capital market regulations work by *segmenting* the domestic capital market from international markets. As such, it can be seen as a 'second-best' policy that aims to correct the fundamental market failures identified above: the inability of most countries to issue liabilities in international markets denominated in their domestic currencies ('original sin'), and the undersupply of long-term financing in these currencies (the greater 'incompleteness' of domestic capital markets). A 'first-best' solution would require at least three conditions: (a) the creation of a long-term demand for domestic currency denominated assets abroad, a measure that may be impossible according to the 'original sin' literature; (b) coverage of the risks incurred by domestic agents with either international reserves (a costly 'self-insurance' device) or with debt issued in the domestic currency by multinationals (an option that has been available to some countries according to the same literature—see Hausman and Panizza 2003); and (c) the development of deep markets for long-term debt and securities in *domestic* currencies. But some of these solutions are either unavailable or take a long time to develop. Capital account regulations thus recognize that, given the *existing* segmentation, it may be optimal to respond to this market imperfection by further segmenting the market through regulations, rather than designing economic policy as if such segmentation did not exist.

Traditional controls—which many developing countries, including large ones such as China and India, continue to use in diverse ways—basically work by segmenting the domestic and foreign capital markets through rules that openly differentiate between residents and non-residents and, among the former, between corporate and non-corporate residents. This includes forbidding domestic firms and residents from borrowing in foreign currency, except for some specific transactions (trade financing and long-term investment) by some agents (corporations), subject perhaps to ceilings. The rules also forbid foreign residents from holding assets or debt denominated in the domestic currency, except for the domestic operations of foreign investors (and even in this case debts may be restricted or forbidden). Finally, they prohibit domestic banks from holding deposits by residents in foreign currencies or from lending in foreign currencies (except when intermediating the allowed external credit lines).

For countries that choose to be more fully integrated into international capital markets, the possibilities are varied and can be combined in different forms. A first option is to introduce rules not unlike traditional quantitative (administrative) controls that temporarily segment the market between residents and non-residents; this was Malaysia's choice in 1994 (in relation to inflows) and 1998 (to outflows). Another option is to introduce price-based regulations that effectively tax inflows or outflows. Taxing inflows was the choice pioneered by Chile in 1991 and Colombia in 1993 (where it was applied more aggressively), using the mechanism of an unremunerated reserve requirement (URR) on capital inflows; in both cases, URRs were reduced and eventually dismantled during the Asian crisis. Taxing outflows was introduced by Malaysia in February 1999 as a substitute for its 1998 regulations; the exit tax was then gradually reduced until it was dismantled in May 2001. The basic advantage of price-based regulations is their non-discretionary character.

Other rules, which can be combined with any of the previous two systems or can stand by themselves, include more permanent prohibitions or strong discouragement of domestic financial dollar/euroization, and of offshore markets and the international use of the domestic currency (strongly discouraged by the Singaporean authorities and part of the 1998 Malaysian controls). Also, portfolio flows can be subject to direct regulation, in terms of the amounts that can be brought into the country and the domestic securities in which they can invest (as in Colombia). Direct borrowing abroad or issuance of American Depositary Receipt (ADRs) and similar instruments may be subject to prudential regulations that apply to the issuer. And minimum stay requirements can be established (as in Chile, where the requirement was lifted in May 2000).

A comparative evaluation of these experiences leads to four major conclusions.[9] First of all, controls on both inflows and outflows can work, but it is essential to build the capacity to administer the regulations, while avoiding loopholes and, particularly, corruption. As the experience of Malaysia indicates, however, no direct previous experience of capital account regulations is necessary for success. In this regard, according to IMF evaluations, simple traditional quantitative restrictions that rule out certain forms of indebtedness may be easier to administer than price-based controls (Ariyoshi et al. 2000) and may thus be preferable for countries with weaker administrative capacity. Also, in countries characterized by deeper domestic financial development, it may be easier to circumvent controls, but some tools may work even under those conditions, as the experiences of Chile and Malaysia indicate. A good administration requires, however, dynamic adjustment to close loopholes and, generally, to respond to changing market conditions. For this reason, maintaining *permanent* regulatory regimes that are tightened or loosened through the business cycle or in response to other market conditions may be better than alternating different capital account regimes.

Second, in terms of macroeconomic effectiveness, traditional exchange controls and capital account regulations may be the best option if the policy objective is to reduce significantly the domestic sensitivity to international capital flows. This is reflected, in particular, in the lower sensitivity to such flows during the Asian crisis by countries that maintained more traditional regulations vis-à-vis Latin American countries that used price-based regulations. Also, a comparative analysis of the price-based controls of Chile and Colombia versus the quantity-based controls of Malaysia indicates that the

[9] See, in this regard, the comparative evaluations of some of these experiences by Ariyoshi et al. (2000); Rajaraman (2001); Palma (2002); Epstein et al. (2003 and 2008); Ocampo (2003a); Ocampo and Palma (2008). See also the evaluation of the Indian experience by Reddy (2001) and Nayyar (2002) and that of the Malaysian experience by Kaplan and Rodrik (2001).

Malaysian controls had stronger effects on the magnitude of capital flows (inflows or outflows, depending on the target variable) and, more generally, on compensating the expansionary or contractionary macroeconomic pressures generated by the capital account (Ocampo 2003a; Ocampo and Palma 2008). Despite the fact, however, that URRs may have only temporary effects on capital inflows (if they are not dynamically reinforced in the face of a continuous capital surge), they are not ineffective in macroeconomic terms. In particular, there is strong evidence that they influence interest rate spreads.[10] Thus, in broader terms, the usefulness of URR as a macroeconomic policy tool is reflected in the capacity to affect capital flows, domestic interest rates, or both, with the particular combination subject to other macroeconomic conditions and to policy choice.

Third, contrary to the heated controversies regarding the macroeconomic effectiveness of reserve requirements, particularly of URRs, broad agreement exists on their effectiveness in reducing short-term debt flows and thus in improving or maintaining good external debt profiles. As such, they have proven to be a useful preventive macroeconomic policy tool.

Finally, it is important to emphasize that capital account regulations should be seen—and, in fact, have been seen by countries adopting them—not as a substitute for, but as a complement to other 'sound' macroeconomic policies. Moreover, they improve fundamentals. In particular, they provide additional degrees of freedom to adopt countercyclical macroeconomic policies.

It should probably be emphasized that, in order to guarantee the effectiveness of capital account regulations, some regulations on *current* account transactions (export surrender requirements or the obligation to channel trade transactions through certain approved intermediaries) may be necessary. As already pointed out, it is also essential to avoid the internationalization of the domestic currency and domestic financial dollar/euroization (Reddy 2001).

Prudential regulation and supervision can complement but also partly substitute for the role played by capital account regulations. Indeed, the distinction between capital controls and prudential regulations affecting cross-border flows is not so clear cut. In particular, higher liquidity (or reserve) requirements for the financial system's foreign currency liabilities can be established, and domestic lending to firms operating in non-tradable sectors can be forbidden or those firms can be discouraged from borrowing in foreign currencies, through more stringent regulatory provisions on the financial intermediaries involved in the transaction.

The main problem with these options is that they only indirectly affect the foreign currency liabilities of *non*-financial agents and, indeed, may encourage

[10] See De Gregorio et al. (2000) in relation to Chile, and Villar and Rincón (2003) in relation to Colombia. This is also the interpretation of the Chilean experience provided by Williamson (2000: ch. 4). Indeed, according to this interpretation, the conflicting evidence on the Chilean system largely disappears.

them to borrow directly abroad. Accordingly, they need to be supplemented with other regulations, including rules on the types of firms that can borrow abroad and prudential ratios with which they must comply; restrictions on the terms of corporate debts that can be contracted abroad (minimum maturities and maximum spreads); public disclosure of the short-term external liabilities of firms; regulations requiring rating agencies to give special weight to foreign exchange exposure; and tax provisions applying to foreign currency liabilities (see on the latter, Stiglitz and Bhattacharya 2000). Some of the most important regulations of this type concern external borrowing by firms operating in non-tradable sectors. A simple rule that should be considered is the strict prohibition against borrowing in a foreign currency by non-financial firms with no foreign currency revenues. Alternatively, restrictions could be placed on the maturities (only long-term) or end use (only investment) of such borrowing. Price-based capital account regulations may thus be simpler to administer than an equivalent system based on prudential regulations and additional policies aimed at non-financial firms.

Capital controls obviously have costs. First, they increase the costs of financing during capital surges.[11] This is precisely the desired effect, however, as the increase in those costs has the expected countercyclical effect. A second, longer-term effect may be the impact of controls on domestic financial development. Derivatives markets will have more limited room to develop, and the operations of foreign institutional investors that may act as 'market makers' in domestic capital markets will be restricted. The trade-offs that authorities face in the short run are not simple in this regard, but authorities should clearly aim to avoid the adverse effects that controls can have on the development of deeper, liquid domestic capital markets.

The Macroeconomic Dimensions of Prudential Regulations

The origins of problems that erupt during financial crises are associated with both excessive risk taking during booms, as reflected in a rapid increase in lending, and with the inevitable mix of maturity and currency mismatches that characterize balance sheets in developing countries. Inadequate risk analysis by financial agents and weak prudential regulation and supervision of domestic financial systems exacerbate this problem. This issue became evident during the first wave of financial crises that hit Latin America in the early 1980s (Díaz-Alejandro 1988: ch. 17), but it was broadly ignored in later episodes of financial liberalization in the developing world. Since the Asian crisis, the principle that financial liberalization should take place within a suitable institutional setting has been firmly adopted. Indeed, it is now

[11] Given asymmetries in direct access to external markets, this effect may disproportionately affect SMEs.

widely recognized that properly regulated and supervised financial systems are structurally superior in terms of risk management.

Prudential practices have traditionally focused on microeconomic risks. In recent years, however, increasing attention has been placed on risks that have a clear *macroeconomic* origin. The basic problem in this regard is the inability of individual financial intermediaries to internalize the collective risks assumed during boom periods, giving rise to coordination problems beyond the control of any single agent. In terms of the terminology used in portfolio risk management, whereas microeconomic risk management can reduce non-systematic risks (those that depend on individual characteristics of each borrower) through diversification, they cannot reduce systematic risks (those associated with common factors that market agents face, such as economic policy and the business cycle).

Moreover, traditional regulatory tools, including both Basle I and Basle II standards, have a pro-cyclical bias.[12] The basic problem in this regard is the highly pro-cyclical nature of a system in which loan loss provisions are tied to loan delinquency or to short-term expectations of future loan losses. Under this system, the precautionary signals may be ineffective in hampering excessive risk taking during booms, when expectations of loan losses are low. On the other hand, the sharp increase in loan delinquency during crises reduces financial institutions' capital and, hence, their lending capacity, possibly triggering a 'credit squeeze.' This reinforces the downswing in economic activity and asset prices and, thus, the quality of the portfolios of financial intermediaries.[13] These problems may be particularly severe in developing countries, where due attention should thus be given to the links between domestic and external financing; the links among these two factors, asset prices and economic activity; and the links between domestic financial risks and variations in interest and exchange rates.

Given the central role that all of these processes play in the business cycles of developing countries, the crucial issue is to introduce a countercyclical element into prudential regulation and supervision. In this regard, the major innovation is the Spanish system of forward-looking provisions introduced in December 1999. According to this system, provisions are made when loans are *disbursed* based on the *expected* ('latent') losses; such 'latent' risks are estimated for homogenous categories of credit, estimated on the basis of a full business cycle (Poveda 2000; Fernández de Lis et al. 2001). This system implies, in

[12] For analyses of these issues and policy options for managing them see, BIS (2001: ch. VII); Borio et al. (2001); and Clerc et al. (2001). In relation to Basle II, see Griffith-Jones et al. (2003) and United Nations (2003: 54–7). Since credit ratings are also pro-cyclical, basing risk on such ratings, as proposed by Basle II, is also a pro-cyclical practice.

[13] For this reason, the sudden introduction of strong regulatory standards during crises may worsen a credit squeeze. Thus, although authorities must adopt clearly defined rules to restore confidence, the application of stronger standards should be gradual. In any case, to avoid moral hazard problems, authorities must never bail out the owners of financial institutions.

fact, that provisioning follows the criteria traditionally used by the insurance industry (where provisions are made when the insurance policy is issued), rather than by the banking industry (where they are made when loans become due).

Under this system, provisions[14] build up during economic expansions and are drawn upon during downturns. They are accumulated in a fund, together with special provisions (traditional provisions for non-performing assets or for borrowers under stress) and recoveries of non-performing assets. The fund can be used to cover loan losses, thus in effect entirely substituting for special provisions if resources are available in adequate amounts. Although the accumulation and drawing down of the fund has a countercyclical dynamic, this only reflects the cyclical pattern of bank lending. Thus, the system is, strictly speaking, 'cycle neutral,' rather than countercyclical, but it is certainly superior to the traditional pro-cyclical provisioning for loan losses or forward-looking provisioning based on shorter time horizons.

Therefore, such a system should be complemented by strictly countercyclical prudential provisions, which can be decreed by the regulatory authority for the financial system as a whole or for some sectors or economic agents, or by the supervisory authority for special financial institutions on the basis of objective criteria. These criteria could include the excessive growth of credit (relative to some benchmark), the bias in lending to sectors characterized by systematic risks and the growth of foreign currency denominated loans to non-tradable sectors.

A system of provisions such as this is certainly better than the possible use of capital adequacy ratios to manage the effects of business cycles. Capital adequacy requirements should focus instead on long-term solvency criteria, rather than on cyclical performance. Insofar as developing countries are likely to face more macroeconomic volatility, a case could be made for requiring higher capital/asset ratios (see additional arguments below), but no convincing case exists for capital adequacy requirements, as such, to be countercyclical. Focusing on provisions rather than capital requirements has an additional advantage, in that the quality of the capital may be difficult to guarantee in developing countries (Rojas-Suarez 2008).

These provisions should be supplemented by more specific regulations aimed at controlling currency and maturity mismatches (including those associated with derivative operations), and at avoiding the overvaluation of collateral generated by asset price bubbles. The strict prohibition of currency mismatches in the portfolios of financial intermediaries is the best rule. As we have seen, authorities should also closely monitor the currency risk of

[14] Under this system, provisions are estimated using either the internal risk management model of the financial institution or the standard model proposed by Banco de España. The latter establishes six categories, with annual provisioning ratios that range from 0 percent to 1.5 percent.

non-financial firms operating in non-tradable sectors, which may eventually become credit risks for banks. Regulations can be used to establish more stringent provisions and/or risk weighting for these operations, or a strict prohibition on lending in foreign currencies to non-financial firms without revenues in those currencies.

In addition, prudential regulation needs to ensure adequate levels of liquidity for financial intermediaries so that they can handle the mismatch between the average maturities of assets and liabilities, which is inherent in the financial system's essential function of transforming maturities, and which generates risks associated with volatility in deposits and/or interest rates. This underscores the fact that liquidity and solvency problems are far more closely interrelated than traditionally assumed, particularly in the face of macroeconomic shocks. Reserve requirements, which are strictly an instrument of monetary policy, provide liquidity in many countries, but their declining importance makes it necessary to find new tools. Moreover, their traditional structure is not geared to the specific objective of ensuring financial intermediaries' liquidity in the face of the inherent maturity mismatches in their portfolios. The best system could be one in which liquidity or reserve requirements are estimated on the basis of the residual maturity of financial institutions' liabilities, thus generating a direct incentive for the financial system to maintain an appropriate liability structure.

The valuation of assets used as collateral for loans also presents problems when these assets exhibit price volatility because, in many cases, prices used to value collateral may be significantly higher than ex post prices. Limits on loan to value ratios and/or rules to adjust the values of collateral for cyclical price variations should be adopted.

It must be emphasized, in any case, that any regulatory approach has clear limits and costs that cannot be overlooked. Prudential regulation involves some non-price signals, and prudential supervision is full of information problems and is a discretionary activity susceptible to abuse. Experience also suggests that even well-regulated systems in industrial countries are subject to periodic episodes of euphoria, when risks are underestimated. The crisis of the early 2000s in Argentina is a specific case in which a system of prudential regulations considered to be one of the best in the developing world—and working within the framework of a financial sector characterized by the large scale presence of multinational banks—clearly failed to avert the effects of major macroeconomic shocks on the domestic financial system.

Moreover, many regulatory practices aimed at correcting risky practices on the part of financial intermediaries *shift* the underlying risks to non-financial agents, rather than eliminate them. This may generate indirect credit risks. Thus, for example, lower risk ratings for short-term credit and strong liquidity requirements reduce direct banking risks, but they also reinforce the short-term bias in lending. Maturity mismatches are thus displaced to non-financial agents and may result in reduced fixed capital investment. Also, prudential regulations forbidding banks from holding currency mismatches in their portfolios may encourage non-financial agents to borrow directly from abroad. The higher spreads that stricter prudential regulation entails generate a similar incentive. As we have seen, the risks assumed by corporations operating in non-tradable sectors will eventually be translated into the credit risk of domestic financial institutions that are also their creditors. In all these cases, therefore, the reduced direct vulnerability of the domestic financial sector will have, as a corollary, the maturity and currency mismatches of *non*-financial agents.

Public Sector Liability Management

In any developing country, the public sector faces some of the most severe maturity and currency mismatches. Its investments are long term in character and, except in the case of a few public sector firms, it produces non-tradable goods and services. Beyond that, moral hazard issues are paramount. Thus, specific legal limits and regulations are required, although, as argued here, strong fiscal responsibility laws can help maintain healthy debt ratios and structures by establishing clear rules on public sector indebtedness, direct mechanisms for controlling foreign borrowing, and rules establishing minimum maturities and maximum spreads at which public sector entities can borrow. The Ministry of Finance or the central bank can play a leading role in either of these areas, establishing rules that should apply not only to the central administration, but also to autonomous public sector agencies and sub-national governments.

Several financial crises have underscored the importance of the maturity structure of the *domestic* liabilities of the public sector. The basic reason for this is the highly liquid nature of public sector securities, which facilitates asset substitution and, thus, capital flight. Thus, when gross borrowing requirements are high, the interest rate will have to increase to make debt rollovers attractive. Higher interest rates will then feed into the budget deficit, contributing to the rapid increase of debt service and the acceleration of indebtedness. In addition, rollovers may be viable only if risks of devaluation or future interest rate hikes can be transferred to the government, thus generating additional sources of destabilization. This was the case prior to the Mexican crisis of 1994 and the Brazilian crisis of 1999, when fixed interest bonds were swiftly replaced by variable rate and dollar denominated securities. On the contrary, given Colombia's tradition of issuing public sector securities with a minimum one-year maturity, no substitution of a similar magnitude was observed in this country during its 1998–99 crisis (Ocampo 2003a).

Although the currency mismatches that characterize the public sector would recommend borrowing exclusively in the domestic currency, there are two reasons why this rule should not be strictly followed. The first reason is macroeconomic in character: the public sector can play an essential role in compensating the highly pro-cyclical pattern of external private capital flows. This means that, during capital account surges, the public sector should adopt a liability policy aimed at substituting external for domestic liabilities. In contrast, during phases of reduced private capital inflows, the public sector may be one of the best net suppliers of foreign exchange, thanks to its preferential access to external credit, including that from multilateral financial institutions. Such borrowing may also be helpful in maintaining a better external debt profile and avoiding private borrowing abroad at excessively high spreads during crises.

The second reason relates to the depth of domestic bond markets, which determines the ability to issue longer-term domestic debt securities. This attribute includes the existence of secondary markets and market makers that provide liquidity for these securities. In the absence of these pre-conditions, the government faces a serious trade-off between maturity and currency mismatches. It may thus make sense to opt for a debt mix that includes an important component of external liabilities, despite the associated currency mismatch. In the long run, the objective of the authorities should be, in any case, to deepen the domestic capital markets. Indeed, due to the lower risk levels and the greater homogeneity of the securities it issues, the central government has a vital function to perform in the development of longer-term primary and secondary markets for domestic securities, including the creation of benchmarks for private-sector debt instruments.

In Lieu of Conclusions

A major conclusion of this chapter is that a broad view of macroeconomic stability is essential to the design of 'sound' macroeconomic frameworks. Such a framework necessarily involves multiple objectives and significant trade-offs. This implies that, although a broad focus on sustainability, including external, fiscal, and financial sector sustainability, is correct (IMF 2004b), equally important emphasis should be given to the *countercyclical* dimensions of macroeconomic and financial policies.

Managing such countercyclical frameworks policies is no easy task. Given existing asymmetries in the international economic order, financial markets generate strong pro-cyclical effects and strong incentives to follow pro-cyclical policy rules in the developing world. Moreover, globalization places objective limits on national macroeconomic policy autonomy. In this context, as we have seen, self-insurance is costly and may merely shift the underlying macroeconomic and financial risks, rather than correct them. For this reason, international cooperation in the macroeconomic policy area should be designed with the clear objective of overcoming these incentives and constraints.

This means that the first role of international financial institutions, from the point of view of developing countries, is to counteract the pro-cyclical effects of financial markets. This can be achieved by smoothing out boom–bust cycles at their source through regulation, and by increasing the incentives and degrees of freedom that developing countries have to adopt countercyclical policies. This should be done through adequate surveillance and incentives to avoid the build up of risky macroeconomic and financial conditions during periods of financial euphoria, together with sufficient financing and appropriate debt management and restructuring mechanisms that avoid the explosive debt dynamics that characterize periods of sudden stops of external financing. As is well-known, major issues in these areas are the weak signals that surveillance may give in a period of financial euphoria; the absence of some essential lending facilities (such as the failed contingency credit line or an invigorated contingency financing facility) and limits on the use of others, matters that have been the subject of recurrent debate in the IMF Board; and the absence of an agreed international framework for debt standstills, write-offs, and rescheduling. A second and equally essential role of international financial cooperation is to counter the concentration of lending by providing access to those countries and agents that tend to be subject to rationing in private international capital markets. This is, of course, a persistent problem for some developing countries (the poorest among them), but a cyclical one for others (the 'emerging market' economies). Lending should therefore follow a countercyclical pattern, not only in the case of the IMF (a fact that is widely recognized), but also of multilateral development banks.[15]

Development banks can also help to create new financial instruments with a clear countercyclical focus. Particularly, government counterpart funds can be temporarily detached from bank disbursements to generate these effects. Thus, governments can actually 'save' counterpart funds in multilateral banks during booms for disbursement, together with bank financing, during crises. This would be a particularly effective instrument for the design of social safety net financing. Also, greater use could be made of contingency repayment clauses, according to which loan amortization would be accelerated or slowed down on the basis of some indicators of GDP growth, terms of trade, or the availability of private external financing. Development banks could also play a role as 'market makers' for new private sector lending instruments that reduce developing country risks, such as GDP linked and commodity linked bonds.

[15] For an analysis of some of these issues see Griffith-Jones and Ocampo (2003).

This leads to two interesting implications of the analysis of the asymmetries in financial markets that underlie the pro-cyclical risks that developing countries face. The first is related to the 'original sin.' In recent years, there has been a boom in domestic bond markets in developing countries. Foreign investors have been active in those markets, but largely to benefit from the appreciation trends of several emerging market currencies. So, it is unclear whether this trend can be viewed as 'redemption.' A more ambitious idea would involve the creation of private funds that, by spreading risk among a large number of currencies, can lend in the currencies of the developing countries (Dodd and Spiegel 2004). Multilateral development banks should also start lending in those currencies, covering the risks of such currency exposure by becoming, at the same time, important players in the long-term bond markets of developing countries. The second implication is closely related. The analysis presented in this chapter indicates that there is no substitute for *long*-term lending in the *domestic* currencies of developing countries. The development of deep domestic financial markets in the currencies of developing countries should thus be strongly supported by the international financial institutions. An essential corollary of this statement is that *reversing* (and, obviously, avoiding new cases of) dollar/euroization should be an element of that support.

The macroeconomic toolkit of developing countries must be preserved and even enhanced. This means that developing countries should maintain the autonomy to impose capital account regulations, and thus, the freedom to re-impose controls if they deem them useful. It also means that the tools for financial sector management should be improved. Since the Asian crisis, this has been, of course, a centerpiece of the IMF/World Bank's Financial Sector Assessment Program, as well as of their technical assistance activities. Nonetheless, this chapter shows that much more emphasis should be given to forward-looking provisioning and other countercyclical tools of prudential regulation, which have not received adequate attention. Indeed, experience and analysis (including recent debates on Basle II) indicate that traditional regulatory instruments may increase, rather than reduce pro-cyclicality.

Finally, this chapter also suggests that, given the multiple objectives and trade-offs faced by macroeconomic authorities, solutions are likely to differ according to the conditions that characterize each country. This means not only that 'one size fits all' solutions are entirely inadequate, but also, and very importantly, that the principle of 'ownership' by developing countries of their macroeconomic policies should be strictly respected.

References

Ariyoshi, A., Habermeier, K., Laurens, B. et al. (2000). 'Capital Controls: Country Experiences with Their Use and Liberalization'. Occasional Paper, No. 190, International Monetary Fund, Washington, DC.

BIS (2001). 71st *Annual Report*. June, Bank for International Settlements, Basle.

Bordo, M., Eichengreen, B., Klingebiel, D., and Martínez-Peria, M. S. (2001). 'Is the Crisis Problem Growing More Severe?' *Economic Policy*, 32: 51–82 (April).

Borio, C., Furfine, C., and Lowe, P. (2001). 'Pro-cyclicality of the Financial System and Financial Stability: Issues and Policy Options'. *Marrying the Macro- and Micro-Prudential Dimensions of Financial Stability*. BIS Paper, No. 1 (March), Bank for International Settlements, Basel, 1–57.

Braga de Macedo, J., Cohen, D., and Reisen, H. (eds.) (2001). 'Monetary Integration for Sustained Convergence: Earning Rather than Importing Credibility', in J. Braga de Macedo et al. (eds.), *Don't Fix, Don't Float*. Paris: OECD Development Centre Studies, 11–53.

Budnevich, C. and Le Fort, G. (1997). 'Fiscal Policy and the Economic Cycle in Chile'. *CEPAL Review*, 61 (April).

Calvo, G. (2001). 'The Case for Hard Pegs in the Brave New World of Global Finance', in J. Braga de Macedo et al. (eds.), *Don't Fix, Don't Float*. Paris: OECD Development Centre Studies, 77–84.

—— Talvi, E. (2008). 'Sudden Stop, Financial Factors and Economic Collapse: A View from the Latin American Frontlines', in J. E. Stiglitz and N. Serra (eds.), *The Washington Consensus Reconsidered: Towards a New Global Governance*. New York: Oxford University Press.

—— Leiderman, L., and Reinhart, C. (1993). 'Capital Inflows and Real Exchange Rate Appreciation in Latin America: The Role of External Factors'. *IMF Staff Papers*, 40 (March): 108–51.

Clerc, L., Drumetz, F., and Jaudoin, O. (2001). 'To What Extent are Prudential and Accounting Arrangements Pro- or Countercyclical with Respect to Overall Financial Conditions?' *Marrying the Macro- and Micro-Prudential Dimensions of Financial Stability*. BIS Papers, No. 1 (March), Bank for International Settlements, Basel: 197–210.

Davis, J., Ossowski, R., Daniel, J. A., and Barnett, S. (2003). 'Stabilization and Savings Funds for Nonrenewable Resources: Experience and Fiscal Policy Implications', in J. Davis, R. Ossowski, and A. Fedelino (eds.), *Fiscal Policy Formulation and Implementation in Oil-Producing Countries*. Washington, DC: International Monetary Fund, ch. 11.

De Gregorio, J., Edwards, S., and Valdés, R. (2000). 'Controls on Capital Inflows: Do They Work?' *Journal of Development Economics*, 63/1: 59–83 (October).

Díaz-Alejandro, C. F. (1988). *Trade, Development and the World Economy: Selected Essays*, ed. Andrés Velasco. Oxford: Basil Blackwell.

Dodd, R. and Spiegel, S. (2004). 'Up From Sin: A Portfolio Approach to Salvation'. Paper prepared for the XVIII Technical Group Meeting of the Group of 24, Geneva, March.

Easterly, W. (2001). *The Elusive Quest for Growth*. Cambridge: MIT Press.

—— Servén, L. (eds.) (2003). *The Limits of Stabilization: Infrastructure, Public Deficits, and Growth in Latin America*. Palo Alto and Washington, DC: Stanford University Press and World Bank.

—— Islam, R., and Stiglitz, J. E. (2001). 'Shaken and Stirred: Explaining Growth Volatility', in B. Pleskovic and N. Stern (eds.), *Annual Bank Conference on Development Economics 2000*. Washington, DC: World Bank, 191–211.

ECLAC (1998). *The Fiscal Covenant: Strengths, Weaknesses, Challenges*. Santiago: Economic Commission for Latin America and the Caribbean.

—— (2000). *Equity, Development and Citizenship*. Santiago: Economic Commission for Latin America.

Eichengreen, B., Hausman, R., and Panizza, U. (2003). 'Currency Mismatches, Debt Intolerance and Original Sin: Why They are Not the Same and Why They Matter'. NBER Working Paper, No. 10036 (October), National Bureau for Economic Research, Cambridge, MA.

Epstein, G., Grabel, I., and Jomo, K. S. (2003). 'Capital Management Techniques in Developing Countries', in A. Buira (ed.), *Challenges to the World Bank and the IMF: Developing Country Perspectives*. London: Anthem Press.

—— —— —— (2008). 'Capital Management Techniques in Developing Countries: Managing Outflows in Malaysia, India and China', in J. A. Ocampo and J. E. Stiglitz (eds.), *Capital Market Liberalization and Development*. New York: Oxford University Press.

Fernández de Lis, S., Martínez, J., and Saurina, J. (2001). 'Credit Growth, Problem Loans and Credit Risk Provisioning in Spain'. *Marrying the Macro- and Micro-Prudential Dimensions of Financial Stability*, BIS Paper, No. 1 (March). Basel: Bank for International Settlements, 310–30.

Ffrench-Davis, R. (2001). *Financial Crises in 'Successful' Emerging Economies*. Washington, DC, and Santiago: Brookings Institution Press and ECLAC.

—— Larraín, G. (2003). 'How Optimal are the Extremes? Latin American Exchange Rate Policies during the Asian Crisis', in R. Ffrench-Davis and S. Griffith-Jones (eds.), *From Capital Surges to Drought: Seeking Stability for Emerging Markets*. London: Palgrave Macmillan, 245–68.

Frankel, J. (1999). *No Single Currency Regime Is Right for All Countries or at All Times*. Essays in International Finance, No. 215, International Finance Section, Department of Economics, Princeton University, Princeton, NJ.

Frenkel, R. (2004). 'Real Exchange Rate and Employment in Argentina, Brazil, Chile and Mexico'. Paper prepared for the Group of 24, Washington, DC, September.

—— (2005). 'External Debt, Growth and Sustainability', in J. A. Ocampo (ed.), *Beyond Reforms: Structural Dynamics and Macroeconomic Vulnerability*. Palo Alto and Santiago: Stanford University Press and ECLAC, 189–209.

Griffith-Jones, S. and Ocampo, J. A. (2003). *What Progress on International Financial Reform? Why So Limited?* Stockholm: Almqvist & Wiksell International for Expert Group on Development Issues (EGDI).

—— Persaud, A., with Spratt, S. and Segoviano, M. (2003). 'The Pro-cyclical Impact of Basel II on Emerging Markets and its Political Economy'. Paper prepared for the Economic Commission for Latin America and the Caribbean, Santiago.

Hausmann, R. (2000). 'Exchange Rate Arrangements for the New Architecture'. *Global Finance from a Latin American Viewpoint*. Paris: Inter-American Development Bank (IDB) and Organization for Economic Co-operation and Development (OECD), 81–94.

Hausmann, R. and Panizza, U. (2003). 'On the Determinants of Original Sin: An Empirical Investigation'. *Journal of International Money and Finance*, 22: 957–90.

Heyman, D. (2000). 'Major Macroeconomic Upsets, Expectations and Policy Responses'. *CEPAL Review*, 70: 13–29.

IMF (1998). *World Economic Outlook, 1998—Financial Crises: Characteristics and Indicators of Vulnerability*, International Monetary Fund, Washington, DC, May.

IMF (2003). *Fiscal Adjustment in IMF-Supported Programs*. Washington, DC: Independent Evaluation Office, International Monetary Fund.

____ (2004a). 'Public Investment and Fiscal Policy'. Document presented to the Board, International Monetary Fund, Washington, DC, March 12.

____ (2004b). 'Assessing Sustainability'. Document presented to the Board, International Monetary Fund, Washington, DC, May 28.

Kaminsky, G L., Reinhart, C. M., and Végh, C. A. (2004). 'When It Rains, It Tours: Procyclical Capital Flows and Macroeconomic Policies'. NBER Working Paper, No. 10780 (September), National Bureau for Economic Research, Cambridge, MA.

Kaplan, E. and Rodrik, D. (2001). 'Did the Malaysian Capital Controls Work?' NBER Working Paper, No. 8142 (February), National Bureau for Economic Research, Cambridge, MA.

Krugman, P. (1990). *Rethinking International Trade*. Cambridge: MIT Press.

____ Taylor, L. (1978). 'Contractionary Effects of Devaluations'. *Journal of International Economics*, 8: 445–56.

Larraín, F., Labán, R., and Chumacero, R. (2000). 'What Determines Capital Inflows? An Empirical Analysis for Chile', in F. Larraín (ed.), *Capital Flows, Capital Controls, and Currency Crises: Latin America in the 1990s*. Ann Arbor: University of Michigan Press, 61–82.

Marfán, M. (2005). 'Fiscal Policy, Efficacy and Private Deficits: A Macroeconomic Approach', in J. A. Ocampo (ed.), *Beyond Reforms: Structural Dynamics and Macroeconomic Vulnerability*. Palo Alto and Santiago: Stanford University Press Economic Commission for Latin America and the Caribbean, 161–88.

Martner, R. and Tromben, V. (2003). 'Tax Reforms and Fiscal Stabilization in Latin America'. *Tax Policy*, Public Finance Workshop Proceedings, Banca d'Italia Research Department, Rome, 140–71.

Minsky, H. P. (1982). *Can 'It' Happen Again? Essays on Instability and Finance*. Armonk, NY: M. E. Sharpe.

Nayyar, D. (2002). 'Capital Controls and the World Financial Authority—What Can We Learn from the Indian Experience?' in J. Eatwell and L. Taylor (eds.), *International Capital Markets—Systems in Transition*. New York: Oxford University Press, 99–126.

Ocampo, J. A. (2002). 'Developing Countries' Anti-Cyclical Policies in a Globalized World', in A. Dutt and J. Ros (eds.), *Development Economics and Structuralist Macroeconomics: Essays in Honour of Lance Taylor*. Aldershot: Edward Elgar, 374–405.

____ (2003a). 'Capital Account and Counter-Cyclical Prudential Regulation in Developing Countries', in R. Ffrench-Davis and S. Griffith-Jones (eds.), *From Capital Surges to Drought: Seeking Stability for Emerging Markets*. London: Palgrave Macmillan, 217–44.

____ (2003b). 'International Asymmetries and the Design of the International Financial System', in A. Berry (ed.), *Critical Issues in Financial Reform: A View from the South*. New Brunswick, NJ: Transaction Publishers, 45–74.

____ Martin, J. (2003). *Globalization and Development*. Palo Alto and Santiago: Stanford University Press and Economic Commission for Latin America and the Caribbean.

—— Palma, G. (2004). 'Dealing with Volatile External Finances at Source: The Role of Preventive Capital Account Regulations'. Processed, Initiative for Policy Dialogue Columbia University, New York.

Palma, G. (2002). 'The Three Routes to Financial Crises: The Need for Capital Controls', in J. Eatwell and L. Taylor (eds.), *International Capital Markets—Systems in Transition*. New York: Oxford University Press, 297–338.

Persaud, A. (2000). *Sending the Herd off the Cliff Edge: The Disturbing Interaction between Herding and Market-sensitive Risk Management Practices*. State London: Street Bank.

Poveda, R. (2000). *La Reforma del sistema de provisiones de insolvencia*. Madrid: Banco de España.

Prasad, E. S., Rogoff, K., Wei, S., and Kose, M. A. (2003). 'Effects of Financial Globalization on Developing Countries: Some Empirical Evidence'. IMF Occasional Paper, No. 220, International Monetary Fund, Washington, DC.

Rajaraman, I. (2001). 'Management of the Capital Account: A Study of India and Malaysia'. Processed, National Institute of Public Finance and Policy, New Delhi, March.

Reddy, Y. V. (2001). 'Operationalising Capital Account Liberalisation: The Indian Experience'. *Development Policy Review*, 19/1: 83–99 (March).

Reinhart, C. M. and Rogoff, K. (2004). 'The Modern History of Exchange Rate Arrangements: A Reinterpretation'. *Quarterly Journal of Economics*, 119/1: 1–48 (February).

Reisen, H. (2003). 'Ratings Since the Asian Crisis', in R. Ffrench-Davis and S. Griffith-Jones (eds.), *From Capital Surges to Drought: Seeking Stability for Emerging Markets*. London: Palgrave Macmillan, 119–38.

Rodrik, D. and Velasco, A. (2000). 'Short-Term Capital Flows'. *Proceedings of the Annual World Bank Conference on Development Economics 1999*. Washington, DC: World Bank, 59–90.

Rojas-Suárez, L. (2008). 'Domestic Financial Regulations in Developing Countries: Can They Effectively Limit the Impact of Capital Account Volatility', in J. A. Ocampo and J. E. Stiglitz (eds.), *Capital Market Liberalization and Development*. New York: Oxford University Press.

Stiglitz, J. E. (2003). 'Whither Reform? Towards a New Agenda for Latin America'. *CEPAL Review*, 80: 7–38.

—— Bhattacharya, A. (2000). 'The Underpinnings of a Stable and Equitable Global Financial System: From Old Debates to a New Paradigm'. *Proceedings of the Annual World Bank Conference on Development Economics 1999*. Washington, DC: World Bank, 91–130.

Svensson, L. E. O. (2000). 'Open-economy Inflation Targeting'. *Journal of International Economics*, 50: 155–83.

Taylor, L. (1998). 'Capital Market Crises: Liberalisation, Fixed Exchange Rates and Market-Driven Destabilisation'. *Cambridge Journal of Economics*, 22/6: 663–76 (November).

United Nations (2003). *World Economic and Social Survey 2003*. New York: United Nations.

Van Wijnbergen, S. (1984). 'The Dutch Disease: A Disease After All?' *Economic Journal*, 94: 41–55.

Velasco, A. (2000). *Exchange-Rate Policies for Developing Countries: What Have We Learned? What Do We Still Not Know?* Geneva and Cambridge, MA: United Nations Conference on Trade and Development (UNCTAD) and Center for International Development, Harvard University.

Villar, L. and Rincón, H. (2003). 'The Colombian Economy in the Nineties: Capital Flows and Foreign Exchange Regimes', in A. Berry (ed.), *Critical Issues in Financial Reform: A View from the South*. New Brunswick, NJ: Transaction Publishers, 353–82.

Williamson, J. (2000). 'Exchange Rate Regimes for Emerging Markets: Reviving the Intermediate Option'. *Policy Analyses in International Economics*, 60. Washington, DC: Institute for International Economics.

7

The Wild Ones: Industrial Policies in the Developing World

Alice H. Amsden

Introduction

With the dawn of decolonization in Africa, Asia, and the Middle East, rates of growth and employment soared throughout the developing world. The period from 1950 through 1980 has become known as a 'Golden Age,' because fast growth coincided with the freedom of former colonies to use their own brainpower and innovate new development approaches, most controversially import substitution. Whereas the North knew little about the South's economies, the South's educated elite knew a lot about its own economies as well as those of the North, where it lived, studied, and worked. The more freedom developing countries have to brainstorm their own economic policies, the faster they will grow.

The first American empire (1945–79) that overlooked the Golden Age had a mixed record. The Cold War destroyed many opportunities for sensible policies, not least of all in Cuba and Vietnam. Apart from the Green Revolution, American private foreign investors patronized only the richest developing countries, and even these received only a trickle. Nevertheless, unlike in the period after 1980, the United States did the developing world a great favor. It left it relatively alone—a new form of 'laissez-faire.' To create modern factories and skilled employment, the developing world could use unorthodox economic policies rather than laissez-faire. Some Third World countries—those with prewar manufacturing experience, mostly in Japan's 'East Asian Co-Prosperity Sphere'—succeeded spectacularly in barging into world markets in higher and higher end goods. Others lost their way, leaving millions of people disappointed and destitute.

Where import substitution did not work well because manufacturing experience was small, corruption and political unrest intensified. Corruption in many countries came before manufacturing, killing it and making corruption even worse.

Present at the Creation

The huge task of economic development fell on the shoulders of Third World nationals. The initiative to move from underdevelopment to development was not taken by multinational firms, international banks, US technical assistants, or the US Treasury, no matter how much each portrayed itself retrospectively as a catalyst. Whatever role these foreign agents ultimately played, whatever influence the Bretton Woods institutions eventually had, they were not the first risk takers (lending to the Third World by the World Bank was anemic until at least 15 years after the end of World War II). Nor were the bush whackers that collaborated with colonial rulers—traditional tribal chiefs or clerics, plantation managers, or import–export merchants. Traders, called 'indentors' or 'compradores' in Chinese, preferred earning profits from importing rather than from investing locally in risky new ventures; they were opponents of industrialization, although some changed and gave manufacturing a boost. Instead, the movers and shakers, the new, foreign educated cadre of risk takers, public and private, were the military men and business managers, teachers, distributors, engineers, technocrats, and other professionals who despised colonialism but who were often Western in outlook or conversant with Western ways.

Leaving the Free Market Model Behind

The Third World rejected the development model of rich countries because it did not have their stupendous assets to compete. How could it be expected to play on a level field? Without big domestic markets, Ghana's cocoa was processed in the UK. Without knowledge to produce efficiently, to expand at low cost, and to invent new products, the law of comparative advantage was violated. The low wages of the Third World couldn't hold their own against the technology and marketing finesse of the First World.

Europe and the US enjoyed a tight marriage between new technology and free markets: a happy relationship for over two centuries. Market forces provided incentives for the development of new products and processes, sometimes epochal. In turn, innovations led to market power, earning the finance for further innovation. In sharp contrast, no matter how free their markets, the Third World originally had no state of the art innovations, minor or major, labor intensive or capital intensive. Free markets simply meant deadly competition from experienced foreign firms, before local enterprises had enough oxygen to compete at international prices. The 13 American colonies prospered partly because their gap with England in technological capabilities and organizational skills was small. As Adam Smith stated: 'The Colony of a civilized nation which takes possession either of a waste country, or of one so thinly inhabited, that the natives easily give place to the new settlers, advances more rapidly to wealth and greatness than any other human society.'[1]

The presence or absence of commercial and technological knowledge determined the difference in policy between early and late industrializers. One relished the free market, the other was ravaged by it. Smith didn't say what happened to a country like Brazil, who took possession of a wasteland (using slaves, like the US), but which was far behind Sheffield or Lancashire in skills.

Even in the most labor intensive manufacturing industries, low wages were no match for the know-how of advanced countries, limiting the applicability of Ricardo's famous 'comparative advantage' thesis. As the prestigious Pearson Commission observed in its study of the Third World in the 1960s: 'the American (and European) market is one in which *the less-developed countries' price advantage alone is usually not sufficient without detailed knowledge.*' Ricardo himself did not assume that all firms in an industry have equal knowledge, but later interpretations of his work did. This false assumption turned out to be dogmatic and dangerous for actual policymaking. At market prices, many poor countries had no comparative advantage at all.

Korea and Taiwan, now among the world's top ten exporters, could at first only export manufactures of plywood and wigs of human hair. Despite the pittance earned by their female workers, despite martial law and repression of trade unions, despite US aid for new equipment, despite two of the Third World's best education systems and physical infrastructures, Korea and Taiwan could *still* not compete in the 1960s against the mighty Japanese textile industry at market prices and production costs. Thus began their adventures with industrial policy and government economic intervention in order to help private firms build the assets they needed to complement their rock-bottom labor costs. Textile companies required better machinery, more experience in mixing raw cotton and setting the speeds and feeds of equipment, maintaining old equipment, and switching rapidly to manufacture the types of yarns and fabrics that came into vogue in different parts of the world. Without these skills and market information, which took more time and money to acquire than most private entrepreneurs could sustain, Korea's and Taiwan's low wages could not match Japan's high productivity. Without an industrial policy to overwrite free trade theory, these countries were doomed to export products with the lowest skills.

[1] Smith, A. (1976). *An Inquiry Into The Nature and Causes of The Wealth of Nations*, Canaan (1904 edition, PT II), University of Chicago, 75.

Table 7.1. Who Exports Labor Intensive Textiles, 2001–02

	Developed countries	Developing countries
Textile yarn	45%	53%
Cotton fabrics	45%	54%
Woven manmade fibers	43%	56%
Knitted fabrics	35%	64%
Textile articles	35%	64%
Pharmaceutical products	93%	6%

Source: United Nations Conference on Trade and Development, Trade and Development Report, 2004.

Developed countries often remained number one even in labor-intensive industries, long after their comparative advantage in low wages had disappeared. Their skills, their protective tariffs, their high-end consumer tastes, and their migrant labor kept them in business. Table 7.1 shows the export market shares in the 1990s of developed and developing countries in garments and textiles, two of the most labor intensive industries since the first Industrial Revolution. These industries are naturals for developing countries, but the market share of developed countries is still high.

Thus, the life-and-death challenge of late industrializers was to exploit their wage advantage and *learn marketable skills*, moving up the ladder of comparative advantage from low-tech, mid-tech (industries like steel, cement, chemicals, rubber, glass, shipbuilding, machinery, and automobiles), to 'mature high-tech,' where high-tech products, already familiar in world markets, are out-sourced to developing countries as profit margins fall. Despite the diversity of developing countries, they shared a common compulsion to learn, especially those with prewar manufacturing experience, which led to similar policies and organizations. Starting with Japan, the same seed grew in different flowerpots. Depending on the country, however, the flowers were more or less hardy. Some blooms perished at birth. Some were stronger and sweeter than others.

What, then, was the nature of the Third World's unorthodox system that enabled it to create skilled industries? Why were some countries far better at exploiting this system than others? How did the system work at all, given what critics later obsessed as the inevitable corruption and inefficiencies of government economic intervention?

The Wild East

With their nationalist rhetoric and visions of wealth, the great leaders of colonial independence inspired hundreds of millions of poor people to sacrifice and save in the name of development. But late development was arguably less a product of charismatic leaders than of capable civil servants, managers and efficient bureaucracies, public and private, all entangled in the 'developmental state.'

Third World countries created their developmental institutions at roughly the same time. The 'winds of change' that blew away imperialism (in the words of Britain's last colonial Prime Minister, Harold Macmillan), were buffeting the whole developing world. Independence, nationalism, socialism, Keynesianism, and economic development were all in the air, in the newspapers, and in people's minds.

Alongside this euphoria, something sinister was shaking the Third World's economic scaffolding, and the response mechanisms of the free market were not doing enough to fix it. Countries everywhere began to suffer from a hard currency shortage. The motive behind government intervention became 'necessitarian'—governments intervened out of necessity, to solve money or other problems, and to take advantage of an opportunity that private domestic firms were too weak to exploit. To be sure, governments also intervened to enrich themselves and their friends. But if corruption were the main motive for government intervention in the 1950s and 1960s, then the timing of such intervention would have been different. Instead of appearing everywhere at the same time, which the developmental state did, it would have appeared at different times in different places, because corruption itself wouldn't arise everywhere simultaneously.

Like clockwork, systems to promote skill intensive industries were constructed in the late 1950s or early 1960s. In Thailand, for instance, a coup brought a general to power with pro-private business sympathies. A Promotion of Industrial Investment Act in 1960 created a board of investment that quickly began strengthening manufacturing activity. In Malaysia, a pioneer industry ordinance of 1958 sparked industrial promotion that then intensified after race riots in 1969. In Indonesia, a new military government that came to power in 1966 under General Soeharto started the long road to industrialization using many institutions established by the deposed leftist president Sukarno. In Mexico, the new presidency of Miguel Alemán made industrialization his *only* economic goal and along with a 'new group' of progressive industrialists, launched a vigorous plan to bolster manufacturing activity. Even China, with the least tolerance for market forces and an entirely different political economy, intensified its attempts at industrialization in 1958 with a 'great leap forward.'

Argentina was the sad exception—nothing much progressed there organizationally in the late 1950s or early 1960s, creating a mystery for development economists. Juan Peron's corrupt banks and nepotistic public agencies, dating from the 1940s or earlier, 'crowded out' the professionally managed developmental machinery that arose in other countries. In the 1950s, the government of Arturo Frondizi adopted the American-backed policy of welcoming foreign investment, but foreign investors never provided strong leadership for diversification. As the bureaucratic machinery in other countries began to grind away, Argentina's once rich economy atrophied.

Although not nearly as industrialized as Argentina, the Philippines' story is similar. De-colonization in these countries didn't witness the expulsion of foreign-owned firms that occurred in most of Asia, from China to Taiwan. No developmental machinery was created, and the state's role was among the smallest in the Third World (the US ruled from 1898 to 1946, and defeated a communist insurgency in the early 1950s). The economics Nobel Laureate, Gunnar Myrdal, referred to the Philippines as a 'soft state.' Its bureaucracies were corrupt due to patronage, the wealthy evaded tax collection, and growth was feeble. The Philippines, like many other former colonies, was burdened with foreign companies controlling its rich natural resources, with little to show for it in the form of diversification into manufacturing (Amsden 2007).

Budget Busters

After a short spending spree financed by the war-related windfalls, the Third World's foreign exchange became extremely scarce. Solving this problem involved the government's traditional macroeconomic ministries, especially the ministry of finance, as well as a new generation of bureaucracies related to industrial policy. In 1950, the Third World's dollar value of exports and imports was about equal. By 1960, imports exceeded exports by over 10 percent, with no obvious way to pay for the shortfall (Victorian Britain covered its own shortfall with invisible exports like financial services and insurance). The traditional market remedy to balance of payments deficits is to let wages fall and thereby increase labor intensive exports. But developmental states were in no position to cut wages that were typically close to subsistence. They did something new, and some succeeded stupendously.

In the absence of tariffs, a typical balance of payments' buster was the family of air conditioners, TVs, and sewing machines. In the family of transportation equipment, payments deficits were worse. To grow, countries needed trucks to move materials and buses to transport people. Demand for cars was lively among the elite. As imports of internal combustion engines climbed, the balance of payments was imperiled (especially if gas had to be imported as well). In desperation, governments tried to assemble locally imported 'kits' of automobile parts and components, but sometimes assembling the kits of a car or bus cost more than importing the finished product.

As local demand sky rocketed for the new, exciting consumer durables of the 1950s, deficits in the Third World's balance of payments worsened.

There are two ways to reduce the foreign exchange gap: export more, or substitute domestic production for imports. The latter, 'import substitution industrialization (ISI),' provided a roadmap to entrepreneurs of what products

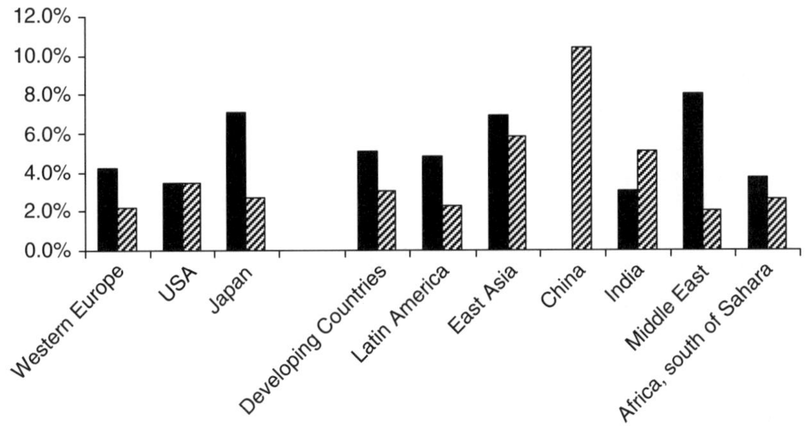

Figure 7.1. Growth in Income: 1950–80 and 1980–2000

Notes: ■ 1950–80, ▨ 1980–2000.

were in local demand. Governments provided state-owned enterprises and private-owned enterprises (SOEs and POEs) with tariffs and cheap finance to make IS investments feasible. Then they offered them other incentives to improve efficiency and improve product design. Import substitution increased output, saved foreign exchange, and came to represent a prosperous era of industrial transformation in a newly politically independent Third World. It was during this golden age of import substitution that developing countries enjoyed the fastest growth rate in their history (see Figure 7.1).

The virtues of exporting over import substituting for the balance of payments were calculated by the great 'enlightenment' economists: exporting respects the law of comparative advantage. By manufacturing at free market prices those products that require inputs widely available locally, efficiency and exporting are maximized. Efficiency is *not* maximized and exporting is not possible with import substitution, because *any* import can be produced and sold locally if its tariff protection is high enough and, due to human nature, most tariffs never tend to fall.

Agriculture and raw material processing were still considered the developing world's comparative advantage at the end of the 1960s. Almost 90 percent of Third World exports derived from primary products. In 75 percent of countries, these exports were concentrated in three crops. If their price fell, a farmer's livelihood plummeted. Certainly agriculture in the early post-war years deserved more public spending than it got—farming, after all, is what most people did to survive. But the developmental state rejected agriculture as the engine of export-led growth. Chile was the most successful country to target agriculture, exporting counterseasonally subsidized tropical fruits and vegetables to the US. But Chile had a highly unequal income distribution due to the concentration of raw materials. It also started the post-war period with a per capita income roughly twice that of Taiwan's, an emerging manufacturer, but ended the century with a per capita income barely half that of Taiwan's. Manufacturing was at the heart of modern economic growth because it had the power to create new skills and pay higher wages.

Raul Prebisch, the Argentine who headed the United Nation's regional office in Chile, was one of the fathers of import substitution theory. He argued in the 1950s that there was a systematic tendency for the prices of many primary products to fall relative to those of manufactures, which benefited from intellectual property rights and new technologies that replaced natural resources with synthetics. As incomes in developed countries rose, the demand for raw materials rose, but by less. The deterioration in the 'terms of trade' was impoverishing. More raw material exports had to be given just to get the same amount of manufactured imports in exchange. For his heterodoxy of attacking comparative advantage, Prebisch was 'Satanized' by the American development establishment, as described by a former head of Peru's central bank, Richard Webb. But Prebisch was right, both in terms of the Third World's long run deterioration in the terms of trade and its disruptive short run commodity price fluctuations. Even at the end of the century developing countries were acutely suffering from terms of trade losses. The loss was about US$5 billion a year from 1981–85, almost US$55 billion a year from 1989–91, to US$350 billion for the period 1980–92. The terms of trade loss was a major factor in the rise of these commodity exporters' foreign debt, as they strove to maintain a minimum of essential imports.[2] The burden of commodity price recession fell disproportionately on Sub-Saharan Africa, the least able region to make structural adjustments.

Upward mobility inspired millions of youths to migrate from the countryside to the towns and drove the struggle for colonial independence. The imperial idea that natural resources would forever be the engine of growth—especially when they already accounted for nearly 90 percent of total exports—was politically and economically disdained and discarded, especially since life as an agricultural worker was so difficult. Right or wrong, hostility towards agro-led growth, and resentment towards comparative advantage, cleared the way for Third World industrialization.

Much hotter as an engine of growth than exporting natural resources was the export of *manufactures*. In the 1960s at the lowest end of the skill spectrum (hand assembly of, say, integrated circuits). By the 1970s some developing countries began exporting automobiles, chemicals, and shipbuilding. Industrialization was really getting underway.

[2] Maizels, A. (2003). 'Economic Independence in Commodities', ed. Y. Toye. *Trade and Development: Directions for the 21st Century*. Cheltenham: Edward Elgar.

But labor-intensive manufacturing had its own intellectual critics. Whether in industrial estates or urban neighborhoods, labor intensive exporting went hand in hand with low wages, unsafe working conditions, and dead-end jobs, as foreign investors moved on to yet lower wage locales. Nevertheless, exporting labor intensive manufactures gave a developing country an enormous boost. Employment expanded and everyone wanted a job. Young women workers found new freedom away from their families and, to reduce labor turnover, companies producing labor intensive products like textiles sometimes provided high school educations for their employees. Savings rose and foreign exchange became slightly more abundant. Local managers in foreign plants got state-of-the-art experience. In Taiwan, foreign-owned firms were a rarity by the 1990s, especially in electronics, but most top managers in the 2000s apprenticed with RCA, a foreign TV company in the 1960s.

The leader of exporting labor intensive manufactures to high wage countries was Japan, which also was a leader in import substitution. When Japanese wages rose rapidly in the 1960s under Japan's 'growth doubling' plan, foreign firms fled, seeking cheaper labor in Japan's backyard—Korea, Taiwan, Hong Kong, Singapore, and—later—Thailand, Malaysia, and Indonesia. To attract these escapees, East Asian countries created 'export processing zones'—companies locating in these zones could import all their inputs duty free so long as they exported all their output. Washington played along, listening to the voices of America's big foreign investors. No tariffs were paid in the US on the share of an import accounted for by an American-made component or part. Only the labor costs of foreign assembly got taxed. By the 1960s, the sonic boom in out-sourcing from the US and importing from the Third World had begun.

The problem with export was not exploitation, but not enough exploitation. Because of intense competition for foreign investments, only a handful of Third World countries benefited from export led growth. Asia surpassed all others, owing to contacts with Japan and relatively reliable trans-Pacific transportation. Asia also had good infrastructure and *extremely* low wages, given its high population density. Low wages made all the difference. The manufacture of televisions, for example, was one of the first American industries to relocate overseas. Producers like RCA assembled in Mexico, but wages were too high there and they headed for Taiwan.

Over time, more and more American, European, and Japanese enterprises chased cheap labor, and moved their labor intensive operations overseas. But export led growth lacked the punch it had when it was concentrated in only a few countries. By the mid-1990s, production was spread over as many as 225 export processing zones in Asia and 41 in Latin America. Owing to an excess of suppliers, exporting low end manufactures ceased being an engine of growth

Exporting more skill intensive products was a better bet, of course, but infinitely harder. Korea, for example, built a chemical plant in the 1960s to serve both the domestic and export markets. During construction, the minimum efficient plant scale rose worldwide. At great cost, Korea enlarged its capacity. When it finally began exporting on the international market, foreign firms in the chemical industry began dumping, driving down the price. Korea's shipbuilding giant, part of the Hyundai group, was late delivering the first three ships it ever built. This gave buyers the chance to cancel their contracts in a soft market. Hyundai was thus stuck with a huge inventory. So it diversified further, created a merchant marine company, which then bought its own three ships. What saved the day was the Korean government's decree that all crude oil exported to Korea had to be carried in Korean owned vessels.

These are not the stories of export markets inciting private entrepreneurs along free trade lines. These are more complicated stories of the developmental state at work, from building export processing zones to keeping an infant shipbuilder afloat. Only one simple story tends to repeat itself: behind the rise of every export was an earlier import substitution investment.

Import Substitution

Developing countries with small domestic markets, many in Sub-Saharan Africa, achieved a light dusting of manufacturing industry in the 1960s and 1970s. They produced beer, flour, and other foodstuffs, construction materials like bricks, steel tubes, and cement, and miscellaneous manufactures like matches, metal boxes, and the assembly of consumer durables including cars. But virtually all small countries failed to enter the orbit of modern world industry because they were so far behind the world technological frontier, in contrast to their European colonists 100 years earlier, when small could be beautiful and markets could be free (Switzerland, one of history's few real free traders, could avoid being devoured by its protectionist neighbors by virtue of its innovative watch industry, superb machinery building industry, gnomes of Zurich, tourist business, and multinational firms in pharmaceuticals and food processing).

Some of the North Atlantic's biggest firms in the nineteenth century emerged in the smallest countries. They did so by innovating in industries with a high content of skilled labor, which were becoming a big part of world trade. From these specializations came great manufacturers in small countries. No small Third World countries had skill endowments comparable to those of their forebears a century earlier, however, so most failed at both import substitution and export led growth. Many large countries succeeded at both (Brazil, Mexico, Turkey, India, Iran, China, Indonesia, and Korea), but some failed (Argentina, Bangladesh, and Pakistan). Country size is thus a poor predictor of success. But it is noteworthy that import substitution operated in the developing world at *all* stages of industrialization—early, middle, and late—and some small countries succeeded along the way.

An example of a low-tech transformation was Korea, which then moved up the ladder to the top. To modernize its textile industry in the 1950s, Korea turned to import substitution behind the back of the American security empire, which was helping it buy textile machinery. Korea closed its markets to foreign exporters, including the most ferocious competitor of all, Japan. It also prohibited Japanese textile companies from acquiring Korean textile companies. Then Korean firms set out to learn. A major source of know-how was Korea's textile machinery suppliers (British and Japanese). Independent Japanese textile engineers—either moon-lighters or retirees—were hired as consultants. The Korean government created a graduate engineering major in textiles at Seoul National University, which was modeled along the lines of Tokyo National University. The government also pushed companies to export (tariff protection was made contingent on exporting), and with larger scale, textile companies diversified into the manufacture of garments. With integrated production, textiles and apparel became a huge employer. It was a cradle for small and medium size Korean enterprises and earner of foreign exchange.

Automobiles, the big balance of payments buster, emerged early almost everywhere in the Third World by dint of import substitution. One of the most frequently cited horror stories concerned Chile, a country with less than ten million people in the 1960s. Thanks to government incentives, Chile attracted around 20 automobile assemblers, each operating on an *infinitesimally* small scale. The government considered restricting entry to only one or two firms, but did not know what criterion to use. There was no weeding out process by the market, leaving one or two players to compete, and soon Chile's entire automobile industry collapsed. Brazil was the first latecomer to impose 'local content' requirements on automobile assemblers, an import substitution policy designed to ease balance of payments constraints, create small and medium size national companies, and strengthen technological skills.

> Assemblers had to meet an extremely ambitious domestic-content schedule to be eligible for the full range of financial subsidies. Each year their vehicles had to contain an increased percentage of domestically purchased components. By July 1, 1960, trucks and utility vehicles were to contain 90 percent domestic content and jeeps and cars, 95 percent... By offering the financial incentives for only a limited period, the plan would put laggardly entrants at a competitive disadvantage.[3]

Generally, by forcing final assemblers to buy parts locally, assemblers were given a strong incentive to make their local suppliers more efficient. The whole local content process became an intense learning experience for small

[3] Shapiro, H. (1994). *Engines of Growth: The State and Transnational Auto Companies in Brazil*. Cambridge: Cambridge University Press.

parts suppliers, which also became an important political ally of many governments.

From Import Substitutes to Exports

Whatever the stage of development, import substitution has tended to occur *before exporting*, according to country reports.[4] Economists separated import substitution and export led growth analytically, as though they were bi-polar opposites: one bad, one good; but the two were tightly intertwined insofar as one preceded the other. In Japan, 'unit costs were reduced by increased domestic demand and mass production before the export-production ratio in growing industries began to be boosted.' Similarly in Brazil, in the period 1960–80 'exports resulted not only from further processing of natural resources . . . which . . . enjoyed a comparative advantage, but also from manufactures that firms learned to produce during the import-substitution phase.' In fact, 'export performance after the 1960s would not have been possible without the industrialization effort which preceded it as export growth was largely based on sectors established through ISI in the 1950s.' Later, 'import substitution policies created the capacity to export; the dominant export sectors of the 1980s and 1990s were the auto industry and those intermediate and heavy industries targeted for import substitution in the wake of the 1973 oil shock.' In Mexico, the chemical, automobile, and metalworking industries were targeted for import substitution in the 1970s and began exporting 10–15 percent of their output in the 1980s. 'Much of the rise in non-oil exports during 1983–88 came from some of the most protected industries.' Regarding the Chilean economy and its ability to adjust to an abrupt change in policy in 1973, 'a portion of this response capacity, especially in the export sector, was based on the industrial development which had been achieved earlier through import-substitution policies.'

In Korea, 'the shift to an export-oriented policy in the mid-1960s did not mean the discarding of import-substitution. Indeed, the latter went on along with the export-led strategy. Export expansion and import substitution were not contradictory activities but complemented each other.' In electronics, 'the initial ISI phase of the 1960s was critical to the development of the manufacturing skills that enabled (the chaebol) to become the efficient consumer electronics and components assemblers of the 1970s. Indeed, ISI in consumer electronics parts and components continued in the 1970s after domestic demand from export production justified it.' By 1984, heavy industry had become Korea's new leading export sector, exceeding light industry in value,

[4] The sources of the quotations in this section may be found in Amsden, A. H. (2001). *The Rise of 'the Rest': Challenges to the West from Late-Industrializing Economies.* New York: Oxford University Press.

and virtually all of Korea's heavy industries had come out of import substitution, just as textiles had done in the 1950s and 1960s.

In Taiwan 'in the first half of the 1960s, most of the exports came from the import substitution industries. Protection from foreign competition was NOT lifted. Getting subsidies to export was extra.' In Taiwan's electronics industry,

> there is no clear-cut distinction between an import substitution phase and an export promotion phase. Even though the export of electronics products speeded up since the early 1970s, the domestic market for electronics products was still heavily protected through high import tariffs. Whether protection was necessary for the development of local electronics firms is controversial. However, we do observe that the protection of consumer electronics products forced Japanese electronics firms to set up joint ventures with local entrepreneurs and to transfer technologies to local people which helped to expand their exporting capabilities. (Amsden and Chu 2003)

In Thailand, approximately 50 percent of exports (excluding processed foods) in 1985 emerged out of import substitution. In the case of Turkey in the 1980s,

> it is important to recognize that the growth in manufactured exports did not stem from the establishment of new export industries, but from existing capacity in industries that before had been producing mostly for the domestic market (that is, industries which had originally been established from import substitution). (Amsden 2001)

Decades later, China's leading firms were also first building their capabilities through import substitution, and only then venturing into export markets. TCL was formed in 1981 with a US$5,000 loan from a local government in Guangdong province, and became a leading Chinese brand name in TVs, personal computers, air conditioners, and cell phones. TCL 'aims to become a global household name, but first it has to succeed at home' where it faces local competitors battling for turf on the basis of low wages, and multinationals leveraging their reputations and know-how. 'What TCL lacks, as with most Chinese consumer electronics companies, is proprietary technology, something it aims to rectify with the establishment of five research and development centres, including one in Guangdong with 700 researchers.'[5]

Some exports did not come out of the import substitution process directly, but were produced by *firms* that emerged out of it. The managerial and technological expertise of import substituting firms in Asia gained them a business reputation and contracts with American firms searching for a lower wage locale than Japan to produce their parts and components. This sequence was also true of most of the Third World's diversified business groups, which was the model of big business after World War II in Asia, Latin America, and the Middle East, given their absence of proprietary technology. These groups typically first began serving the domestic market and then diversified into exporting.

[5] McGregor, R. (2001). 'The World Begins at Home for TCL'. *Financial Times*, 23.

Simply exporting proved to be too tough a first step for firms lacking original know-how or connections to advanced country markets, no matter what the enlightenment fathers and market theorists said. Subsidization of domestic capacity was the only practical policy to stem the hemorrhaging in the balance of payments, and to industrialize without world class technological skills.

Unfortunately, government economic intervention is typically vulnerable to corruption, abuse, and inefficiency. 'Government failure' may be as detrimental to development as 'market failure.' But the presumption that governments simply throw subsidies around without any controls on them turns out to have been misguided. What lay behind successful post-war industrialization was a monitored system of controls on subsidies. Neither import substitution nor export led growth was a free for all.

Performance Standards

To minimize the inefficiencies of import substitution, countries built a complex set of institutions that amounted to a control system. These systems attached performance standards to subsidies, including the tariffs, entry restrictions, and cheap credit that governments gave away to pioneering enterprises. Just as developed countries gave innovators patents by way of an incentive and reward, developing countries gave learners protection and other financial aids, but not for nearly as long as the duration of a patent, and not for nearly the same amount of imperial support. The guiding principle of the best bureaucracies—politics permitting—was to give nothing away for free. Reciprocity was the ideal. If the government gave a firm a financial incentive, the firm would have to give something back to the government in exchange, like reaching a certain export target, output level, investment rate, or management practice.

The development bank, flag star of the developmental state, subjected its clients to monitorable performance standards.[6]

In the case of Brazil's preeminent development bank, BNDES,[7] its contracts with borrowers stipulated clear and comprehensive performance obligations. A contract with a leading pulp and paper manufacturer in the 1970s, for example, stated that the company had to prove that it had hired a Brazilian engineering company to do the detailed design for an expansion; BNDES had to approve the company's general plans to establish an R&D department; the company had to have its technology contracts registered with the appropriate government organization to insure that they were not overpaying for foreign technology. Another company had to hire two consultants (one Swedish, one

[6] See Amsden, A. H. (2001). *The Rise of 'the Rest': Challenges to the West from Late-Industrializing Economies*. New York: Oxford University Press.

[7] 'The Politicized Bureaucracy: Regimes, Presidents and Economic Policy'. Banco Nacional des Economie et Social, Working Paper.

Finnish) and these consultants had to approve the company's choice of technology. BNDES had to approve the company's contracts with the consultants.

A contract for financial strengthening between BNDES and a leading capital goods manufacturer, 1983–86, specified that in 60 days, the company had to present an administrative program for the reduction of operating costs. In 120 days it had to present a plan for divesting itself of one operating unit. Another capital goods supplier had to show BNDES a plan for relocation of certain production capacity, improvement of productivity, and strengthening of financial variables. As part of the reorganization program, the company had to hire a controller and implement an information system that was modern and that widened the company's scope of data processing. The company also had to modernize its cost system and improve its planning and control of production (within so many days). In a steel contract for expansion, the steel maker was required by BNDES to modernize its management system, including a revision of its marketing and distribution function for domestic and foreign sales. Its cost system had to be upgraded with a view towards reducing its number of personnel as well as inventory, according to prespecified benchmarks.

With respect to finance, BNDES made clients reach a certain debt/equity ratio and liquidity ratio to insure financial soundness. The debt/equity ratio (amount of debt a company carried in relationship to the equity it held) was based on American banking standards, possibly because the US had been an early lender to BNDES. Brazil's debt/equity ratio was low by East Asian standards—typically debt could not exceed 60 percent of total assets. Hence, 'large' Brazilian companies tended to be small by East Asian standards, whose debt equity ratios were around 3.1 or even 4.1. Through its performance standards, BNDES could thus influence firm size. Bank clients were also prohibited from distributing their profits to stockholders of a controlling company. Companies were not allowed to make new investments of their own or change their fixed capital without BNDES approval. In the case of a company that required financial restructuring, it was forced by BNDES to divest itself of non-production related assets.

In all countries, performance standards with respect to policy goals, as distinct from technical goals, were specified at the highest political level; bureaucrats only implemented them, but this gave them a lot of power. Export expansion was a major policy goal and performance standard.

South Korea, with the world's highest post-war growth rate of exports, induced firms to become export oriented by making their subsidies—especially tariff protection of the domestic market—contingent on achieving export targets. In exchange for tariff protection, firms had to reach a certain export goal. This reciprocity was negotiated jointly by business and government and aired at high level monthly meetings, as in Japan. These meetings were attended regularly by Korea's president, Park Chung Hee, and were designed to enable bureaucrats to learn and lessen the problems that prevented business from exporting more. Reciprocity also involved long term policy lending by the Korea Development Bank. Starting in 1971, at the commencement of Korea's heavy industrialization drive, the KDB began to offer credit 'to export enterprises recommended by the Ministry of Commerce and Industry.' The more a company exported, the more likely it was to receive cheap long-term loans. After 1975 the government made a lucrative license to form a 'general trading company' contingent on big businesses reaching a certain level and diversity of exports. These qualifications unleashed fierce competition among Korea's big business groups at a time when the emergence of heavy industries was dampening competition at the industry level. If a targeted firm in Korea proved itself to be a poor performer, it ceased being subsidized—as evidenced by the high turnover among Korea's top ten companies from 1965–85.

Taiwan, with the world's second highest growth rate of exports, also tied subsidies to exporting. In the case of the cotton textile, steel products, pulp and paper, rubber products, cement, and woolen textile industries, all formed industry associations and agreements to restrict domestic competition and subsidize exports. Permission to sell in Taiwan's highly protected domestic market was made conditional on a certain share of production being sold overseas. In the 'strategic promotion period' of Taiwan's automobile industry, 1977–84, the Ministry of Economic Affairs required new entrants into the industry to export at least 50 percent of their output (only parts producers succeeded).

Other countries also connected subsidies with exporting, only in different ways and with different degrees of success. Thailand's Board of Investment changed its policy towards the textile industry after the first energy crisis in 1973. Overnight it required textile firms (whether foreign, local, or joint venture) to export at least half their output to qualify for continued BOI support. In terms of labor 'exports' of high-tech managers from Japan to Thailand, to run Japan's Thai subsidiaries, the government allowed only short-term import contracts so that Japanese companies had to train Thai replacements.

In Indonesia, 'counterpurchase regulations' stipulated that foreign companies that were awarded government contracts, and that imported their intermediate inputs and capital goods, had to export Indonesian products to non-traditional markets of equal value to the imports they brought into Indonesia. In the case of timber, concessionaires were required to export processed wood rather than raw timber; in the mid-1980s plywood accounted for about one-half of Indonesia's manufactured exports. Moreover, joint venture banks and branches of foreign banks were required to allocate at least 50 percent of their total loans, and 80 percent of their offshore funds, to export activity (a policy that the East Asian financial crisis of 1997 destroyed).

Turkey tried to promote exports starting in the 1960s, making them a condition for capacity expansion by foreign firms. In the case of a joint venture between a Turkish development bank, Sümerbank, and a German multinational, Mannesmann, both the Turkish and German managing directors believed that the Turkish government was constantly willing to help the company in its operations. Nevertheless, one point irritated foreign investors: any capital increase required the consent of the Turkish government. It also became government policy to agree only to a capital increase by forcing companies to take on export commitments. The government held that, in general, any profit transfers abroad had to be covered by exchanges through exports. Since Turkish industry (steel pipes in the case of the Sümerbank–Mannesmann joint venture) could not yet compete at world market prices, export sales did not cover costs, and export quotas were regarded as an incentive to increase efficiency.

In the case of Mexico's oil company, Pemex, in the late 1970s it guaranteed private petrochemical producers a ten year price discount of 30 percent on their feedstock in exchange for their willingness to export at least 25 percent of their installed capacity and maintain permanent employment (the debt crisis of 1981–82, however, led to the cancellation of this plan). Then, the North American Free Trade Agreement and American investment stimulated a surge in exports to the US, to the exclusion of almost any other country.

India made exporting a condition for subsidies and privileges of various sorts but usually the terms of the agreement were unworkable. In the textile industry, for example, in the 1960s the government agreed to waive restrictions on firm's restructuring if they agreed to export 50 percent of their output—but few did because they lacked the capital to restructure. In 1970, export obligations were introduced for various industries; industries or firms were required to export up to 10 percent of their output. But the government could not enforce many export requirements except possibly in industries that were already export oriented, like garments and software. In the case of software, for example, the right to import computers was dependent on software exports within a certain number of years after purchase.

Performance standards were thus an antidote to abuse and inefficiency in government intervention. They hardly worked perfectly. But because the technological capabilities of developing countries were weak, governments conceived a new and unique system of controlled intervention to promote industrialization. The rapid skill formation and industrialization in a few countries that consequently occurred in the 30 years after World War II are a tribute to a generation of managers and bureaucrats who worked diligently, and with little disabling dishonesty.

Monitoring

As development banks imposed operating standards on their clients, they themselves tightened their own monitoring skills and procedures. Monitoring was increasingly built into lending arrangements such that compliance at one stage was made contingent on further loan disbursement. Development banks undertook careful appraisals of prospective clients, examining their managerial and financial status, past performance, and the merits of their proposed project.

Regarding the Korea Development Bank, in 1970 it 'strengthened review of loan proposals and thoroughly checked up on overdue loans to prevent capital from being tied up. Business analyses and managerial assistance to clients were conducted on a broader scale.' In 1979 the KDB introduced a new procedure to tighten control over lending.

> In order to ensure that loan funds are utilized according to their prescribed purpose, disbursements of loan proceeds are not made immediately upon commitment. Instead, loan funds are transferred into a Credit Control Account in the name of the borrower and the money may be withdrawn only for actual expenditures. The Bank is therefore able to monitor closely the progress of each project. (Amsden 2001)

In India, 'appraisal notes' included conditionalities. For every loan, the Industrial Development Bank of India (IDBI) insisted on the right to nominate a director to a company's board. This practice was comparable to that of the big German banks, but the purpose of the IDBI was not to gain control of its clients' strategic decisions. Rather, it was to gain information about them with a view towards exerting discipline over their operations. Other conditionalities in 'appraisal notes' varied by loan. For example, in a loan to a large steel pipe manufacturer that represented 10 percent of IDBI's net worth, a condition of lending was that the firm form a project management committee to the satisfaction of IDBI for the purpose of supervising and monitoring the progress of the project's implementation.

Thailand's Board of Investment appraised and monitored clients thoroughly, and if a company failed to meet BOI terms (stipulated in a promotion certificate), its certificate was withdrawn. Between January and December 1988, 748 firms received certificates for new projects, of which 37 certificates were withdrawn. In the case of Thai firms, 24 out of 312 certificates, or 8 percent, were withdrawn.

Where the capabilities of borrowers—*and lenders*—were poor, the quality of development banking also suffered. In the case of Malaysia's development banks, which were designed to lend to local Malays in order to raise their relatively backward economic position vis-à-vis Malaysian Chinese entrepreneurs, operations were hampered by 'the poor performance of many debtors.' A failure rate on loans of about 30 percent was reported because of a shortage of viable projects. But even the best projects did not properly prepare their business proposals. Hence, Bank Industri

> has a thorough research team on which it relies heavily. It has adopted a target market approach, and the research staff plays the key role in identifying and evaluating new

areas of the economy for the bank to penetrate. The researchers undertake very detailed industry studies, looking at all aspects of a potential project in order to gain familiarity with its strengths and weaknesses... (Amsden 2001)

Once a project has been approved, the Bank Industri 'insists on being an active partner. It stays jointly involved in the financial management with its partner, often operating joint bank accounts with its clients, which requires the bank to countersign all checks for payment of expenses.'

Generally, development banks were successful in creating a managerial culture in their clients because they themselves were managerial, often representing the most elite bureaucracy of the early post-war period.

In the case of Mexico's development bank, NAFINSA (data on NAFINSA were destroyed in an earthquake), its

técnicos became a respected voice in government affairs... Its influence has been diffused throughout the Mexican economy. Since its founding in 1934, the institution has been the training ground for numbers of bright and active men (sic) whose technical and political expertise has moved them into important government positions.

(Amsden 2001)

Concerning Brazil's BNDES, it had 'a strong sense of institutional mission, a respected "administrative ideology" and a cohesive *esprit de corps*.' According to two executives of Dow Chemicals Latin America, interviewed three years before the Pinochet military coup, the National Development Corporation in Chile (CORFO), excelled for its

organization and thoroughness of planning... which sets Chile apart from some of the other countries that have engaged in similar activities... The management of key Chilean Government agencies... are outstanding professionals who do not automatically change with each succeeding political regime.[8]

The Best and the Brightest

We are now in a position to offer a reason why some developing countries performed better than others and what, if anything, that implies for the world economy.

The top ten latecomers that joined the orbit of modern world industry all had *prewar manufacturing experience*, as measured by the share and diversity of manufacturing activity in their gross national products. However scarce their engineers, they knew something about production and project execution. Their managers had a working knowledge of accounting and finance. The

[8] Willis, E. J. (1990). Manuscript, Boston College, 17; and Blair, C. P. (1964). 'Nacional Financiera: Entrepreneurship in a Mixed Economy', ed. R. Vernon, *Public Policy and Private Enterprise in Mexico*. Cambridge, MA: Harvard University Press, 191–240.

countries with the most prewar manufacturing experience included Brazil, Chile, China, India, Indonesia, Malaysia, Mexico, Taiwan, Thailand, and Turkey. Many of these had a relatively large domestic market (the markets of two, China and India, were tremendous, measured by population), but all had production and project execution capabilities. All understood the socially complex institution of the firm. This enabled them to take the first big steps towards import substitution and export led growth ahead of other low wage competitors.

The definition of 'manufacturing experience' emerges out of the development experience itself. Writing about Indonesia's millions of peddlers, Muslims who were energetic and enterprising but failed to expand, Clifford Geertz, a renowned anthropologist, writes that

> what they lack is the power to mobilize their capital and channel their drive in such a way as to exploit the existing market possibilities. They lack the capacity to form efficient economic institutions; they are entrepreneurs without enterprises.[9]

Manufacturing experience should thus be defined as the ability to *establish* and *operate* efficient enterprises (in the manufacturing sector).

Without prewar manufacturing experience, investments from private sources failed to materialize; no one wanted to lend money to an entrepreneur without a good reputation and know-how, as was the case for entrepreneurs in many parts of Africa. Loans from development banks were squandered and wasted because the chances of financial success were perceived by the borrower to be small—it was hard to come up with any sensible business plan, so plans failed or entrepreneurs took the money and ran. What was borrowed was not repaid, and the development bank itself went broke. As poverty destroyed the dreams and expectations that national independence had inspired, poverty itself made economic growth more difficult. Many African and Latin American countries were trapped when they tried producing anything other than their traditional cash crop. By contrast, in countries that had accumulated manufacturing experience before the war, capital came out of the woodwork. Managerial capabilities convinced investors that their money was in good hands.

The source of prewar manufacturing experience differed among the top ten. No one pattern held for all. India, China, and Turkey were former empires (Mughal, Chinese, and Ottoman), so manufacturing experience went far back in time. Later, under imperial rule, India and China developed modern textile mills owned by Indian and Chinese nationals, with foreign technology transfer. Turkey's know-how came partly from Europeans who had lived in the Middle East for centuries, as was the case in the silk industry of Bursa.

[9] Geertz, C. (1963). *Peddlers and Princes: Social Development and Economic Change in Two Indonesian Towns*. Chicago: University of Chicago Press.

Argentina, Brazil, Chile, and Mexico had acquired know-how from *émigrés* and later foreign firms—Pirelli, as early as 1917, became the first Italian multinational to invest in Argentina.

A very popular teacher in Asia of manufacturing know-how was Japan, although Japan's militarism had an ambivalent effect. During the war, when Japan had taken control of Vietnam, the Japanese army needed the transportation lines Vietnam had in order to move food and war materials for its own troops. Rice did make it to the north, and of ten million north Vietnamese people, one million died of starvation. Japan invaded China's Manchurian province in 1938 and established some heavy industries there, such as coal mining and steel making. Today, many Japanese plants still operate in China, as do Japanese trolley cars from the 1930s. New heavy industries in Manchuria have also grown, such as the First Auto Works and automobile joint ventures. Because Korea and Taiwan were Japanese colonies, they were used as beachheads for foreign invasion—Korea into Manchuria and Taiwan into Southeast Asia. When Japan conquered Manchuria, Korean businessmen cheered. Japanese investment in the late 1920s provided Korean entrepreneurs with diverse know-how. Koreans sat on the boards of directors of Japanese regional companies. They rose almost to the top in some banks. Many worked in cement plants and textile mills. Taiwan experienced a big jump in manufacturing activity when Chinese entrepreneurs, mostly from Shanghai, fled communist China after 1948 and resettled in Taiwan, Hong Kong, and Singapore.

Japan also influenced the industrialization of other Asian neighbors. The Japanese and Thai militaries worked together in the 1930s, gaining experience in building a few ordnance factories. A crown company held a monopoly in manufacturing cement. Thailand's agriculture had a high level of market activity, which was conducive to the growth of trade. In turn, a financial services industry arose out of trade, from which came new businesses, including textiles.

As Japan's war drums beat harder in the 1930s, European empires industrialized their Asian colonies in order to fortify them against Japanese attack. The Dutch began to arm Indonesia, and when Dutch property was finally nationalized starting in 1957, the Indonesians inherited a rich laboratory for learning: 489 Dutch corporations, including: 216 plantations, 161 mines and industrial establishments (GM had opened an automobile assembly plant in Indonesia in 1927), 40 trading firms, and 16 insurance companies.

Malaysian companies first emerged out of mining (tin and rubber) and agro-industry (copra oil, palm oil, and pineapples). From these industries emerged British conglomerates, and the top five owned as many as 220 manufacturing enterprises until they were taken over on the London Stock Exchange by the independent Malay government. A heavy engineering company had arrived in Malaya as early as 1881, making Malaysia's manufacturing experience over 100 years old.

Some countries had prewar manufacturing experience but it was narrowly focused on a single industry, such as Venezuela (petrochemicals), the Philippines (agro-industry), and Egypt and Pakistan (textiles). Even the smallest, poorest countries got a powdering of import substitution industrialization after the war, in foodstuffs (beer and flour), building materials (rolled steel and cement), and consumer non-durables (matches and ceramics). But these investments went nowhere, along the same sorry trail as the import substitution of some big countries (Pakistan and Bangladesh). The ten latecomers with the most manufacturing experience not only included many with large markets, but also 'extra-large' markets (Brazil and Indonesia) and 'super-large' markets (China and India), but also some small countries (Malaysia and Taiwan). However diverse, every single country that industrialized after World War II had accumulated prewar manufacturing experience. Whatever the popularity in the past of explaining success by culture, macroeconomic policy, ethnic homogeneity, education, or political stability, it is now clear that manufacturing experience mattered.

Between 1950 and 1980, a whole new set of developing countries acquired manufacturing experience, including countries such as Algeria, Egypt, the Philippines, Ecuador, and Peru. But these countries failed to industrialize after 1980. The reason is not a lack of capabilities but, rather, misguided policy constraints placed on their growth from the second American empire and related institutions such as the IMF and World Bank.

Conclusion

Under the first American empire, developing countries determined their own economic fate, which ultimately depended on learning. Leadership emerged from a new elite of educated private and public technocrats, managers, and engineers. All recognized that exporting anything but natural resources or shiny trinkets meant acquiring more knowledge to compete against multinational corporations from developed countries, typically enjoying monopolistic powers due to their inventions and brand names. No matter how experienced from prewar years, latecomers could not compete until they had accumulated modern know-how through import substitution. Jumping into export markets for anything other than raw materials and shiny trinkets was infeasible without gaining confidence at home. Latecomers thus took upon themselves the challenge of import substitution, manufacturing domestically what they had formerly imported. Instead of confining themselves to manufacturing low-end products according to their 'comparative advantage' and cheap labor costs, they produced according to their demand, as revealed by what their economy was importing. Imports were a source of information on demand and included high end products that forced new investors to move quickly down their learning curve, before more domestic competitors appeared or imperial powers forced the lifting of tariffs. Only imperial powers themselves had the luxury of keeping tariffs in perpetuity, as in the US textile and steel industries. In producing according to demand instead of supply, David Ricardo stepped aside for John Maynard Keynes.

Import substitution gave rise to industries such as textiles, cement, steel, heavy electrical equipment, and automobiles. These industries demanded mid-level managerial know-how, and created high wage jobs and salaried professionals. To induce entrepreneurs to invest in these industries, the developmental state gave them a battery of incentives, including low cost credit and tariff protection. The government in countries that had acquired a threshold of manufacturing experience, also recognized that if these subsidies were to be used efficiently, a system was necessary to impose performance standards in exchange for subsidies. The goal—not always attained—was to give away nothing for free. The principle was reciprocity.

With intense government promotion and performance standards, import substitution was efficient enough to generate diverse manufactured exports. Import substitution was the mother of all but the most labor intensive exports. Export targets became a performance standard in and of itself (in exchange for protection of the domestic market, firms had to meet export quotas). In the leading economies, import substitution and export led growth became one, instead of opposites—good and evil—the way they are disparaged in academic and policy circles. The incentives each receives cannot be separated, because long-term capital can be used for both.

The Third World's climb up the ladder of comparative advantage after World War II turned out to be highly innovative and original. The linkage of performance standards to subsidies changed the way government intervention worked. Instead of handouts, subsidies became incentives for greater productiveness. Instead of 'government failures,' the economic interventions of government, under conditions of reciprocity and technocratic elitism, led to learning, and the accumulation of manufacturing experience for the next generation. The Third World countries that now make a difference in the world economy—by no means all of them—came out of this process.

Since the rise of the second American empire in response to Japan's competitive challenge, the history of the golden age (as just told) is being rewritten by a new generation of economists, whose anti-statist theories are beautiful in their simplicity but whose assumptions make their theories irreconcilable with reality. By the year 2000, the argument against the *visible* hand had stumbled on three assumptions. One is that states are paralyzed by corruption, and no one can deny that there is corruption. But in developing countries, corruption tends overwhelmingly to be confined to two industries (infrastructure and raw materials) and to the poorest countries, with little chance of making money honestly. The rest of the world has corrupt governments, but different institutions are used to make government perform well enough to keep society going. A second cast-in-concrete given is that 'picking winners' is impossible. In fact, it is no big deal for latecomers that have a live model in the form of a developed economy to follow. Picking winners is also like corruption—it is everywhere. Successful state 'pickers' range from the US Department of Defense to the Egyptian Planning Board. Finally, the biggest truism for opposing the visible hand is that import substitution has slowed down, so there is no turning back. Import substitution has always been tied to exporting, so it is not slowing down. ISI products may be determined by demand rather than factor proportions, but many products that are demanded have appropriate factor proportions, which ISI changes. The question is whether market theory can accept the close connection between the two. The visible hand is needed to coordinate their connection, so the mother–child relationship between them was never explored in market theory. Yet it tells the story of post-war economic development.

As the leading developing countries enter into 'mature high-tech' industries (Amsden and Chu 2003), a whole new set of institutions arise-the developmental state is overtaken by the science park, that performs many of the same functions. Import substitution is alive and well, without tariff protection but with a whole new set of institutions to sustain it. Continuity rather than discontinuity characterizes the transition from the Golden Age to the Dark Ages (1980–2010), because market rules can never supercede innovative and adaptive learning in the process of catching up.

References

Amsden, A. H. (2001). *The Rise of 'the Rest': Challenges to the West from Late-Industrializing Economies*. New York: Oxford University Press.

—— (2007). *Escape from Empire: The Developing World's Journey from Heaven to Hell*. Cambridge, MA: MIT Press.

—— and Wan-wen Chu (2003). Beyond Late Development: Toiman's Upgrading Policies. Cambridge, mass: MIT Press.

Blair, C. P. (1964). 'Nacional Financiera: Entrepreneurship in a Mixed Economy', in R. Vernon (ed.), *Public Policy and Private Enterprise in Mexico*. Cambridge, MA: Harvard University Press, 191–240.

Geertz, C. (1963). *Peddlers and Princes: Social Development and Economic Change in Two Indonesian Towns*. Chicago: University of Chicago Press.

Maizels, A. (2003). 'Economic Dependence on Commodities', in Y. Toye (ed.), *Trade and Development: Directions for the 21st Century*. Cheltenham: Edward Elgar.

McGregor, R. (2001). 'The World Begins at Home for TCL'. *Financial Times*, 23.

Shapiro, H. (1994). *Engines of Growth: The State and Transnational Auto Companies in Brazil*. Cambridge: Cambridge University Press.

8

Sudden Stop, Financial Factors, and Economic Collapse in Latin America: Learning from Argentina and Chile[1]

Guillermo A. Calvo and Ernesto Talvi[2]

Introduction

Latin America does not grow. It occasionally hits an ice patch where output speeds up, only to fall on its face when the ice patch ends. Moreover, in the glorious 1960s when the region was hurtling along at high speed, it was outpaced by other regions, including the OECD. Thus, in contrast to advanced economies (in the north), in which the business cycle has given way to growth as the main subject of professional attention, in Latin America business fluctuations remain the name of the game. Reducing volatility and avoiding the exhilaration of the ice patch have become primary policy commandments.

Unfortunately, false starts and painful crashes have not given rise to a solid academic literature comparable to the one dealing with problems in the north. Rather, the failure of a false start is quickly attributed to the skates used on the ice patch. Thus, after the crash policymakers go quickly to the store to buy a new pair of skates instead of learning how to skate on an ice patch that is less than totally smooth. Instead of analysis and ideas, new slogans are

[1] This chapter is based on a paper prepared for the debate 'From the Washington Consensus Towards a New Global Governance' held at the Forum Barcelona, in Barcelona, Spain, September 24–6, 2004. We would like to thank very specially Diego Pereira and the rest of CERES's research assistants, Ignacio Munyo, Virginia Olivella, and Inés Levin, for their excellent work and John Dunn Smith for superb editorial support.

[2] Guillermo Calvo is Professor of Economics, Public and International Affairs at Columbia University and former Chief Economist of the Inter-American Development Bank. Ernesto Talvi is currently the Executive Director of CERES, a public policy research institution in Montevideo, Uruguay, specializing in the economic analysis of Latin American economies and the design of public policies.

printed on political banners declaring 'the model has failed,' 'the model is exhausted,' or other empty statements of that nature. When the debt crisis erupted in the early 1980s, politicians, cheered by international multilateral institutions, declared the failure of import substitution and bought a brand new pair of Washington Consensus skates. Few stopped to think that the 1982 crisis in Latin America had systemic elements and followed a sharp increase in US interest rates that precipitated a collapse of capital flows to the region.[3] After the 1998 Russian crisis, which set off a string of emerging market (EM) financial crises, politicians started to sneak out of their Washington Consensus skates and again went shopping for a new pair. It is still too early to know what will be the new fashion, but some very prestigious ice skate producers are forcefully vying for attention!

Intellectual fickleness, however, militates against credibility, and without credibility policy is likely to be ineffective, if not counterproductive.[4] Thus, we strongly believe that a deeper understanding of financial crises in the region constitutes one of the most productive projects. We said 'productive,' not 'easy,' because typically the observer is limited by a very small number of observations relative to the shocks and regime changes during the observation period.

This chapter will focus on the last gasps of the Washington Consensus, which began to be heard in the aftermath of the 1998 Russian crisis. In contrast to much current thinking, we do not fault the Washington Consensus for what it says. Rather, we fault it for what it does *not* say, particularly for ignoring several key financial factors. Thus, for example, the Washington Consensus ignored the key role of high volatility of international capital markets. The Washington Consensus also ignored central characteristics of domestic capital markets in Latin America and other EMs such as the high incidence of foreign currency debt (liability dollarization).

We will argue that poor growth performance and the new crop of crises in Latin America in the late 1990s and the early years of the new millennium were largely the result of the Russian crisis, which brought about an unprecedented, across-the-board increase in interest rates for EMs, and a systemic collapse of capital flows to the region. This is vividly suggested by Figure 8.1. Nevertheless, the implications of the Russian crisis for Latin America are still badly understood, and they have given rise to the erroneous notion that reforms do not work.

Furthermore, we will argue that the systemic collapse in capital flows, when combined with *domestic* financial vulnerabilities that acted as amplifiers of the external shock, also goes a long way towards explaining how individual countries in Latin America fared during the late 1990s: who was badly hit (Argentina), experiencing a major financial crisis and economic collapse with

[3] However, see Calvo and Borensztein (1989). [4] See, for example, Calvo (1989).

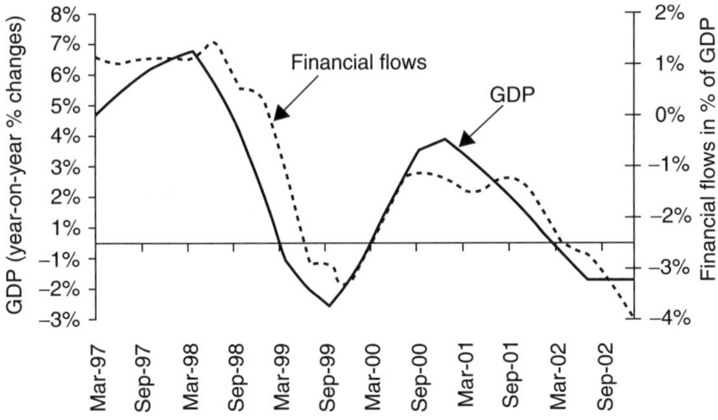

Figure 8.1. LAC-7 External Financial Flows and Economic Growth*

Notes: *LAC-7 is the simple average of the seven major Latin American countries: Argentina, Brazil, Chile, Colombia, Mexico, Peru, and Venezuela. These countries represent 93% of Latin America's GDP.

Sources: Corresponding central banks.

severe social consequences, and who suffered painful macroeconomic adjustments (Chile) but emerged largely unscathed.

This alternative interpretation of the disappointing performance and recent crop of crises in Latin America in the late 1990s has very important policy implications. Once one takes into account financial factors, most of the pieces of the puzzle fall into place. Thus, these crises imply no momentous break from the conventional wisdom prevailing in the 1990s, as doomsayers would have us believe. Rather than throwing overboard the reform efforts of the 1990s, EMs should focus on identifying and fixing key 'points of financial vulnerability' and reinforcing policy credibility. In turn, the focus of attention of the international community should be redirected to fixing the international financial architecture in ways that resources, financial and otherwise, can be mobilized in a more efficient and stable manner from central to peripheral countries. This topic is highly relevant because there are incipient signs of resumption in capital flows to emerging market economies. Thus, it is extremely important to contain the seeds of future crises before they have time to germinate.

The next section documents the boom and bust, in other words, the systemic, large, and largely unexpected interruption in external capital flows to Latin America (i.e., a sudden stop) following the Russian crisis. As this 'sudden stop' affected a very large number of heterogeneous countries in very different regions of the world at about the same time, it is very difficult to construe this sudden stop as the result of a coordinated re-assessment of the economic fundamentals of individual countries or regions. Rather, we argue that the root cause of the sudden stop lies in developments in the central financial markets. The next section in this chapter describes the anatomy of Latin America's painful macroeconomic adjustment and sharp reduction in growth rates following the sudden stop in capital flows. Special attention is paid to the case of Chile, as Chile suffered a severe sudden stop in capital flows and a painful macroeconomic adjustment in the aftermath of the Russian crisis, in spite of its very solid economic fundamentals and tight controls on capital inflows. However hard the landing and painful the adjustment, the Chilean economy experienced no financial crisis and did not collapse as did Argentina's economy. In the third section of this chapter we use the comparative experiences of Chile and Argentina after the sudden stop in capital flows in the aftermath of the Russian crisis, to address the key domestic financial vulnerabilities that acted as amplifiers of the initial external financial shock, transforming an otherwise painful macroeconomic adjustment into a full blown financial crisis and economic collapse. The last section of the chapter concludes with some reflections on policy.

Life after Russia, or the Chronicle of a 'Sudden Stop'

The 1990s was a decade of formidable economic expansion of the US economy. The revolution in information and communications technology produced an investment boom, and investment in the US rose at an average rate of 6.7 percent between 1991 and 2000, compared to 3.7 percent in the previous decade. This investment was stimulated by both the emergence of new firms and the incorporation of new technologies into existing firms. As a result, the US economy saw formidable advances in productivity that led to a boom in stock market values: the Dow Jones multiplied by 4.5 and the NASDAQ by 14 between October 1990 and early 2000. This huge increment in financial wealth also precipitated an equally large increment in the financial resources available for firms and households.

Emerging economies were direct beneficiaries of this enormous increase in investment and financial resources. Starting in 1989–90 there was a huge increase in capital flows to emerging economies, in the form of both direct investment and financing. According to IMF figures, net capital flows went from US$29 billion in 1989 to US$227 billion in 1996, when they reached their peak, an eight-fold increase in a very short period of time. This huge wave of capital inflows to EMs in the first half of the 1990s makes the previous wave of inflows that occurred between the mid-1970s and the early 1980s pale by comparison. We believe that the year 1989 could justifiably be considered the beginning of financial globalization in the modern era.

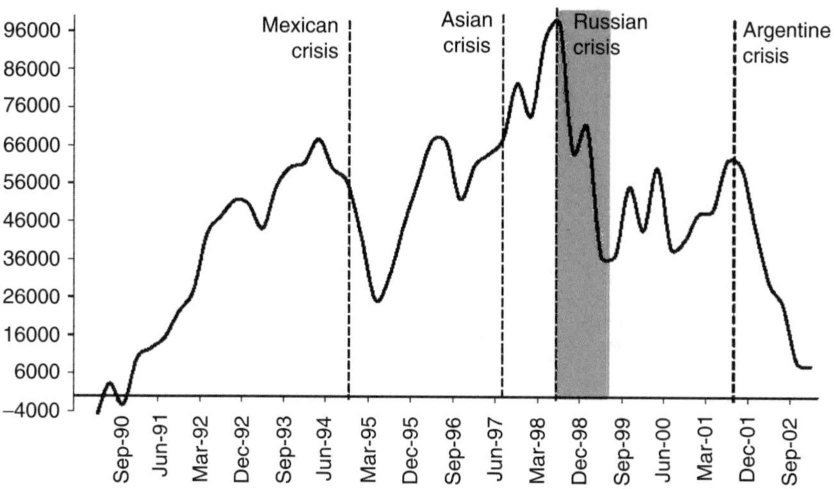

Figure 8.2. Boom and Bust in Capital Flows to LAC-7, 1990–2002* (in millions of US dollars, last four quarters)

Notes: * LAC-7 includes the seven major Latin American countries, namely, Argentina, Brazil, Chile, Colombia, Mexico, Peru, and Venezuela. These countries represent 93% of Latin America's GDP.
Sources: Corresponding central banks.

By the end of the 1980s, with the implementation of the Brady Plan, Latin American countries were on the verge of finally resolving the 1980s debt crisis and hence renewing their access to international capital markets. As a result, Latin America also benefited from the huge wave of capital inflows that started in the early 1990s. As illustrated in Figure 8.2, external capital flows to the major Latin American countries (henceforth LAC-7), which all but vanished after the debt crisis of the early 1980s, jumped from minus US$13 billion (or minus 1.1 percent of GDP) by the year ending in IV-1989 to US$100 billion (or 5.5 percent of GDP) in the year ending in II-1998 (see Figure 8.2).[5] At their peak, external capital flows to LAC-7 were financing 24 percent of total investment in the region.

This new wave of capital inflows was not only large, but also widespread, as illustrated in Table 8.1. Cheap and abundant capital and financing were pouring into every country in the region. At their peak in mid-1998, net capital flows to LAC-7 had increased by close to seven percentage points of GDP relative to 1989, and the swing was positive and significant in every country. This highly synchronized and widespread increase in capital inflows to a variety of very diverse countries suggests that the root cause of this bonanza

[5] LAC-7 includes the seven major Latin American economies, namely, Argentina, Brazil, Chile, Colombia, Mexico, Peru, and Venezuela. These countries represent 93 percent of Latin America's GDP.

Table 8.1. Boom and Bust in Capital Flows per Country (in % of GDP, last four quarters)

Country	Boom	Bust	
	Avg 1985–1990 vs peak 1998	peak 1998 vs trough 1999	peak 1998 vs 2002
Chile	9.3	−7.9	−5.2
Peru	16.0	−7.2	−4.7
Colombia	2.1	−6.6	−3.5
Brazil	8.5	−5.8	−3.8
Venezuela	5.4	−3.5	−17.4
Argentina	8.5	−2.2	−19.5
Mexico	3.8	−1.9	−1.7
Average	7.7	−5.0	−8.0

Sources: Corresponding central banks.

must lie in common external factors, in other words, developments in central rather than in peripheral countries.[6] However, external does not necessarily mean that capital inflows are independent of domestic fundamentals. This important and subtle difference is precisely the topic of our third section.

A key feature of the 1990s was that non-FDI financial flows to Latin America were in the form of portfolio flows, while other emerging markets, such as the emerging Asian countries, were mainly recipients of bank loans. Calvo (2002) suggests that a relevant factor could have been the creation of a secondary market for sovereign bonds in Latin America as a result of the Brady Plan, which transformed bank loans into bonds. The Brady debt reduction plan, which mostly focused on Latin America, created for the first time a critical mass of long-term bonds that needed to be managed and traded by specialists. The creation of this market allowed fund managers of risky portfolios to include Latin American risk and made it worthwhile to invest in information on Latin American economies, expanding investors' interest in the region as their knowledge of the region grew.

Mexico's Tequila Crisis in 1994–95 produced only a temporary reversal in capital flows to Latin America, and its effects were limited in scope, mainly affecting Argentina (see Figure 8.2). However, a key lesson learned from the Mexican experience was that countries were financially more fragile than previously thought: even if their long term capacity to pay was sufficient to cover obligations, they could be rendered insolvent if a critical mass of investors refused to roll over short-term bonds (Mexico) or bank deposits (Argentina). In such a situation, investors could rationally refuse to lend, and a crisis would ensue.[7]

[6] The role of external factors in explaining inflows and outflows of capital and economic performance in emerging economies has been emphasized in Calvo et al. (1993).

[7] See Calvo (1998).

The second crisis episode was the Asian crisis of 1997. This crisis hit countries with very high saving rates and an impeccable record of high growth.[8] It became apparent that liquidity crises were also a possibility not only in the case of bonded debt, but also in the case of bank lending, whether intermediated through the domestic banking system or directly allocated to local firms. However, not even the Asian crisis interrupted the exponential increase in capital flows to Latin America. Rather, the Asian crisis hit Latin America through trade channels by depressing commodity prices: non-fuel commodity prices fell by nearly 30 percent from their peak in II-1997 to their trough in early 2002. This decline in commodity prices contributed in some specific cases, notably Chile and Peru, to a deceleration in growth rates.

It was Russia's default in August 1998, however, that represented a fatal blow for Latin America. This default precipitated a sudden, synchronized, large, and persistent increase in interest rates for EMs. In tandem with the rest of emerging markets, interest rate spreads for LAC-7 rose from 450 basis points prior to the Russian crisis to 1,600 basis points in September 1998, more than tripling the cost of external financing in a period of weeks. As a result, capital inflows to LAC-7 countries came to a sudden stop, falling from US$100 billion (or 5.5 percent of GDP) in the year ending in II-1998 prior to the Russian crisis, to US$37 billion (or 1.9 percent of GDP) one year later (see Figure 8.2). The sudden reversal is explained by the collapse in non-FDI flows, which fell by US$80 billion during that period.

After the initial blow, capital flows to LAC-7 suffered an additional blow after the Argentine crisis in 2001 (which, as we will argue, was triggered by Russia's crisis) and, later, the ENRON scandal that had a major—albeit temporary—effect on both US junk bonds and emerging markets.[9] By the year ending in IV-2002 capital flows to LAC-7 were less than US$10 billion, back to the very low levels of the late 1980s.

The Russian virus affected every major country in Latin America, with the exception of Mexico (see Table 8.1). Even Chile, a country with very solid economic fundamentals—a track record of sound macroeconomic management, a highly praised and sustained process of structural and institutional reforms that completely transformed and modernized Chile's economy, and an average rate of growth of 7.4 percent per year between 1985 and 1997, the highest growth rate in LAC-7—and tight controls on the inflows of foreign capital, experienced a sudden and severe interruption in capital inflows. In

[8] In the aftermath of the devaluation of the Thai currency in July 1997 capital flows to emerging Asian countries, i.e., Indonesia, Korea, Malaysia, Philippines, and Thailand, fell from US$47 billion (or 4.3 percent of GDP) in the year ending II-97, to minus US$58 billion (or –5.5 percent of GDP) one year later.

[9] For a brief analysis of the relationship between the ENRON scandal and emerging market bond spreads see Calvo and Talvi (2002).

fact, the sudden stop in Chile in the year following the Russian crisis was 7.9 percent of GDP, the largest in LAC-7.

That a partial debt default in Russia, a country that represented less than 1 percent of world GDP and had no meaningful financial or trading ties with Latin America, could precipitate a financial contagion shock wave of such proportions posed a puzzle for the profession. In our view, the kind of explanation that is consistent with the evidence—in other words, a sudden, synchronized, and widespread increase in interest rates for EMs—is that financial contagion was caused by the impact of Russia's crisis on the balance sheet of financial intermediaries investing in emerging markets. These intermediaries were highly leveraged, and the accumulation of losses after Russia's default led to a liquidity crunch, forcing a sell-off of EM bonds across the board at fire sale prices to meet margin calls.[10] In fact, during the Russian crisis big players in the central capital markets were subject to a liquidity crunch, prompting the Fed and the ECB to lower interest rates as a result. Unfortunately, however, liquidity relief came only when the crisis threatened the stability of US and European markets—too late to restore confidence in EMs.

An alternative systemic explanation for the widespread effect of the Russian crisis is 'reverse moral hazard.' According to this explanation, the IMF refusal to bail out Russia sent a strong signal to the market that the IMF would no longer support blanket bailouts. This, in turn, increased the perceived risk of investing in EMs and orchestrated a run on EM securities. Reverse moral hazard is complementary to the one relying on liquidity crunch in the central capital market and, furthermore, reinforces the view that EMs were badly hit by the Russian crisis. Although this is not the place to engage in a debate about the relevance of the reverse moral hazard view, we believe that this view is highly debatable, given that the IMF has since arranged generous packages for Brazil and Turkey.[11]

To be fair, there is another possible interpretation for the reversal in capital flows in the 1990s, and this view lays the blame on domestic reform. Some critics of the reforms of the early 1990s, such as Stiglitz (2003), argue that the global financial crisis was itself the product of capital market liberalization, which was an integral part of the reform agenda of the 1990s. Although one could argue that the opening of the capital account could have facilitated destabilizing capital flows (i.e., 'hot money'), this does not explain the *synchronized* nature of the reversal in capital flows that occurred in Latin America in 1998. Moreover, those who find fault with an open capital account will be hard-pressed to explain why capital flow reversal also took place in countries that had imposed controls on capital inflows, like Chile.

[10] For a theoretical explanation of this kind of contagion see Calvo (1999a) and Calvo and Mendoza (2000). For empirical evidence supporting this class of explanations see Kaminsky and Reinhart (2001, 2003).

[11] See Calvo (2002).

In summary, the deterioration in international financial conditions for emerging economies and the consequent interruption in capital flows to a variety of very heterogeneous countries—in terms of exchange rate regimes, capital controls, fiscal stance, track record of structural and institutional reforms, and growth performance—was so sudden, synchronized, and widespread that it appears implausible to argue it was caused by a sudden and coordinated reassessment of the economic fundamentals of individual countries in the region.[12] Rather, a more straightforward explanation is that the dramatic increase in interest rates for Latin American economies and the ensuing interruption in capital flows was the result of a disruption in international financial markets in the aftermath of Russia's default.

'Sudden Stops' and Macroeconomic Adjustment in Latin America

The sudden stop in capital flows precipitated a very severe and painful macroeconomic adjustment and a sharp reduction in economic growth in Latin America.[13] The anatomy of this adjustment in LAC-7 is illustrated in Figure 8.3. The following are its main characteristics.

1. *A very large and persistent increase in the cost of external financing and a collapse in asset prices.* The increase in interest rate spreads and the cost of external financing for LAC-7 was not only large—spreads tripled in a matter of weeks—but also persistent: it took nearly five years for spreads to return to the levels prevailing prior to the Russian crisis (see Figure 8.3a).

   Such a severe tightening in monetary and credit conditions in such a short period of time has no parallel in developed countries. It should come as no surprise that it resulted in a severe drop in asset prices. LAC-7 stock markets, which had already started to decline after the Asian crisis, collapsed by an additional 48 percent from their relative peak in II-1998 to their trough in IV-2002, after experiencing a ten-fold increase between 1991 and 1997 (see Figure 8.3b).
2. *A sudden stop in external financial flows and domestic bank credit and sharp financial deleveraging.* The dramatic tightening in monetary and credit conditions, both external and internal, and the reduction in the value of collateral signaled that current debt levels were unsustainable. The result was a sudden stop in external financial flows and domestic bank

[12] The diversity in the degree of advancement of structural reforms has been extensively documented in Lora (2001).

[13] This represents a 'hard landing,' to use the term that, paradoxically, currently is associated with concerns regarding the size of the external current account deficit of the US economy (5 percent of GDP) and fears that a change in market sentiment (a sudden stop?) might force a major macroeconomic adjustment in the US.

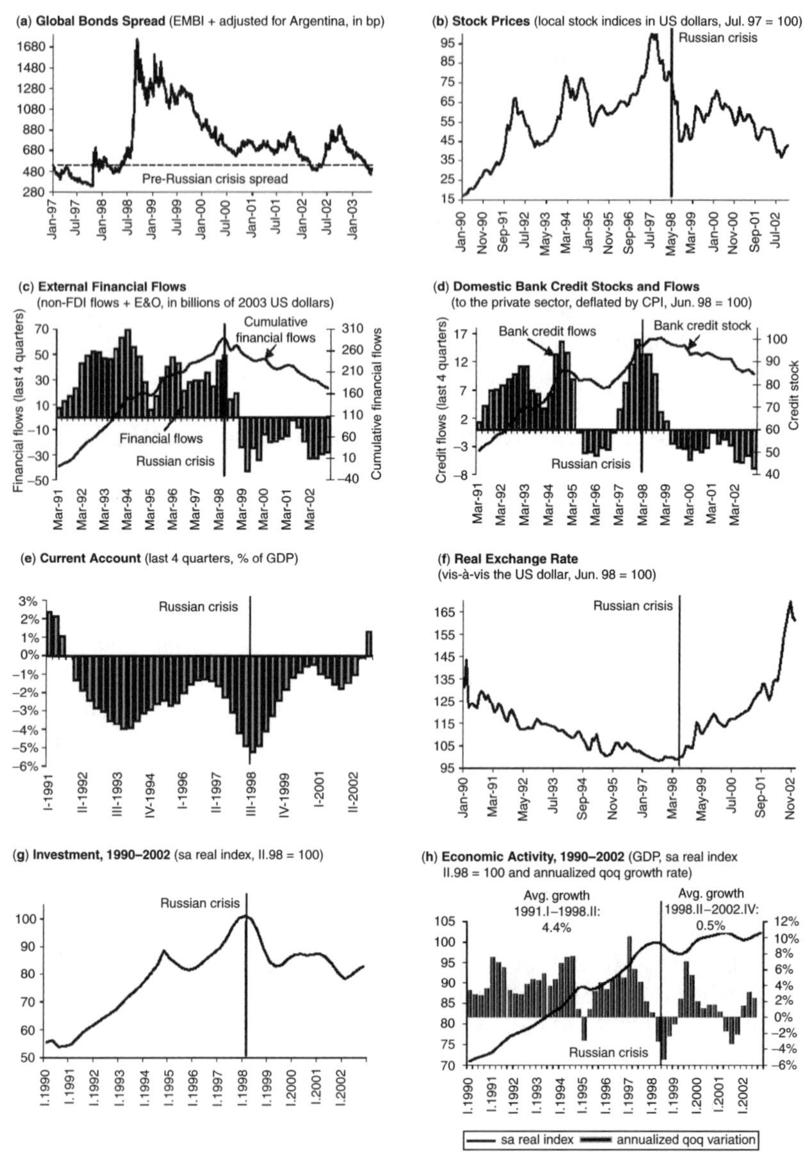

Figure 8.3. Sudden Stop and Macroeconomic Adjustment in LAC-7, 1990–2002*

Notes: * LAC-7 is the simple average of the seven major Latin American countries, namely, Argentina, Brazil, Chile, Colombia, Mexico, Peru, and Venezuela. These countries represent 93% of Latin America's GDP.

Sources: Corresponding central banks.

credit flows which did not merely decline but in fact turned negative. As a result, the sudden stop was accompanied by a very sharp and persistent financial deleveraging on the part of LAC-7 households and firms.

External financial flows (i.e., non-FDI financial inflows) experienced a dramatic turnaround in the immediate aftermath of the Russian crisis, falling from US$40 billion in the year to II-1998 to minus US$40 billion one year later, and they have remained persistently negative since then. This means LAC-7 countries have been transferring net financial resources abroad, in sharp contrast with the period preceding the Russian crisis. As a result, external financial flows fell from a cumulative total of (real) US$200 billion between I-1990 and II-1998 and to a cumulative total of (real) US$120 billion dollars by the IV-2002, a reduction of 40 percent (see Figure 8.3c).[14]

Domestic bank credit flows to the private sector also came to a sudden stop and actually turned persistently negative (see Figure 8.3d). As a result, financial deleveraging also took place at the domestic level in LAC-7: domestic bank credit to the private sector declined by 20 percent in real terms (see Figure 8.3d). It took a very protracted period of financial deleveraging and a substantial improvement in international financial conditions (i.e., a large reduction in US interest rates) for interest rate spreads of emerging economies and the cost of external financing to return to pre-Russian levels in early 2003. However, capital flows to LAC-7 recovered only slightly in 2003 and 2004 and still remain substantially below their previous heights.

To understand this apparent puzzle it is important to stress the nature of the shock and the corresponding adjustment. Borrowing in international markets can smooth an adverse shock to current income, such as a fall in the terms of trade. Such a shock would be associated with a deteriorating current account and an increase in inflows of foreign capital. However, the type of shock experienced by the Latin American economies in the aftermath of the Russian crisis is not an adverse income shock but an adverse *shock to the capital account*, in other words, a shock to the cost and availability of capital and credit. This type of shock is by definition undesirable if not impossible to smooth. On the contrary, it induces a major adjustment in the *stocks of debt*, which under the new and tighter conditions are too 'expensive' to sustain. It is precisely this adjustment in debt stocks or deleveraging on the part of firms and households that allows for an *endogenous* reduction in the cost of external financing. However, the endogenous reduction in the cost of external financing can only be sustained by lower stocks of debt and, in turn, lower capital inflows.

[14] 'Real' dollars are 2003 dollars, using the US CPI as a deflator.

Table 8.2. Current Account Reversals and the Real Exchange Rate (RER) per Country

Country	Current account in % of GDP, 1998–2002. Year to II-1998	IV-2002	Reversal	RER depreciation Jun. 98 vs. Dec. 02
Argentina	−4.7	8.9	13.6	185.3
Venezuela	−2.5	9.2	11.7	20.3
Chile	−6.5	−1.3	5.2	47.5
Peru	−7.0	−2.0	5.0	22.4
Colombia	−6.5	−1.8	4.7	61.2
Brazil*	−3.9	−1.7	4.2	151.0
Mexico	−3.0	−2.2	0.8	−13.9
Average	−4.9	1.3	6.5	67.7

Note: * Year to II-2003.
Sources: Corresponding central banks.

The sudden stop in capital flows and external financial deleveraging (or the transfer of net financial resources abroad) had its counterpart in a sharp current account adjustment and real currency depreciation. The current account of LAC-7 went from a deficit of 5 percent of GDP in the year ending in II-1998 to a surplus of 1.3 percent of GDP in the year ending in IV-2002, an adjustment equivalent to 6.3 percentage points of GDP (see Figure 8.3e). During the same period, the real value of domestic currencies in LAC-7 vis-à-vis the US dollar depreciated by 70 percent (see Figure 8.3f). As illustrated in Table 8.2 the adjustment in the current account and currency values was highly synchronized: every country in LAC-7—with the notable exception of Mexico—experienced large current account adjustments and currency depreciation during this period.

3. *Severe and sustained contraction of investment and a sharp reduction in economic growth.* The other side of the coin of financial deleveraging and the large current account adjustment was a severe and sustained reduction in investment levels. To see this, let us consider how the stocks of debt in the balance sheets of households and firms can be reduced. There are essentially three ways. First, for any given level of investment, households and firms must forego consumption in order to increase savings and, hence, increase the resources available to reduce debt levels. Alternatively, for any given level of savings, households and firms must reduce investment in order to use part of their savings to reduce debt levels. Finally, debt levels can be reduced through negotiated debt restructuring with creditors.

Although in practice the three modes of balance sheet adjustment are typically observed, the reduction in investment in LAC-7 has played a major role in the adjustment to tighter international financial

Table 8.3. Growth and Investment Reversals

	GDP (avg. annual % change)			Investment (avg. annual % change)			Investment ratio (% GDP)			
Country	1991–97	1999–2002	Reversal	1991–97	1999–2002	Reversal	1991	1997	2002	Reversal
Argentina	6.1	−4.9	−10.9	14.8	−17.9	−32.7	14.6	19.4	13.9	−5.5
Chile	8.3	2.2	−6.2	13.7	−5.0	−18.8	22.6	27.2	21.1	−6.1
Venezuela	3.4	−2.2	−5.6	18.5	−4.8	−23.4	18.7	21.0	14.3	−6.7
Colombia	4.0	0.4	−3.5	9.3	−2.2	−11.5	15.9	22.0	15.1	−6.9
Peru	5.3	2.5	−2.8	11.5	−6.5	−18.0	17.3	24.0	18.4	−5.6
Brazil	3.1	2.0	−1.1	4.3	0.1	−4.2	19.8	21.5	18.1	−3.4
Mexico	2.8	2.7	−0.1	6.9	1.6	−5.3	23.3	25.9	24.1	−1.8
Average	4.7	0.4	−4.3	11.3	−5.0	−16.3	18.9	23.0	17.9	−5.1

Sources: Corresponding central banks.

conditions. Investment declined by 18 percent in the immediate aftermath of the Russian crisis, and by the fourth quarter of 2002 still showed no signs of recovery (see Figure 8.3g). Investment growth rates collapsed from an average of 9 percent per year between 1991 and 1997 to minus 5 percent per year between 1999 and 2002, and investment ratios fell from 23 percent of GDP in 1997, prior to the Russian crisis, to 18 percent of GDP in 2002, a reduction of five percentage points. In fact, it was the reduction in investment ratios, rather than an increase in saving rates, that made the largest contribution to the current account adjustment.

As was the case with the slowdown of capital flows, the collapse in the growth rates of investment and investment ratios was also synchronized and widespread and affected every single country in the region (see Table 8.3). In fact, with the sole exception of Mexico, average investment growth was negative between 1999 and 2002 in every LAC-7 country.

Not surprisingly, growth in LAC-7 also experienced sharp reduction. GDP growth fell from an average of 4.4 percent per year between 1991 and the year ending in II-1998, when international financial resources were abundant and cheap, to 0.5 percent between 1999 and 2002 after the sudden stop (see Figure 8.3h). Again, the reduction in growth rates was both synchronized and widespread. As Table 8.3 illustrates, growth reversals occurred in every country of the region, ranging from 11 percentage points in Argentina and 6 percentage points in Chile and Venezuela, to 1.5 and 0.1 percentage points in Brazil and Mexico, respectively.

The Chilean Experience

As noted, Chile was also affected by a severe sudden stop in the aftermath of the Russian crisis and experienced a hard landing as a result. The anatomy of Chile's macroeconomic adjustment following the sudden stop was qualitatively and quantitatively a carbon copy of the average Latin American country described above. Figure 8.4 illustrates its main characteristics.

In the aftermath of the Russian crisis, Chile also suffered a large and persistent increase in the cost of external financing and a collapse in asset prices and currency values. Interest rate spreads more than tripled, albeit from lower levels than those of the average LAC-7 country, from 120 basis points prior to the Russian crisis to 390 basis points in October 1998 (see Figure 8.4a).

The tightening in monetary and credit conditions further resulted in a severe drop in asset prices: the stock market in Chile collapsed by 37 percent between II-1998 and IV-2002 compared to 48 percent in LAC-7, after having already experienced a substantial decline since the Asian crisis (see Figure 8.4b).

The severe tightening in monetary and credit conditions and the reduction in the value of collateral also precipitated in Chile a sudden stop in external financial flows that actually turned negative. As a result, the sudden stop was accompanied by a sharp and persistent external financial deleveraging on the part of households and firms. After the Russian crisis, external financial flows fell from a cumulative total of (real) US$20 billion to a cumulative total of US$10 billion—a 47 percent reduction (see Figure 8.4c). Likewise, domestic bank credit flows to the private sector came to a sudden stop but turned negative for only a brief period of time (see Figure 8.4d). Although the stock of bank credit continued to grow, it did so at substantially lower rates. Bank credit growth declined from an average of 13.5 percent in the period I-1991 to II-1998 to 2.9 percent in the aftermath of the Russian crisis.

Chile, like the average LAC-7 country, also required a very protracted period of external financial deleveraging and a substantial improvement in international financial conditions (i.e., a large reduction in US interest rates) in order for its interest rate spreads and the cost of external financing to return to pre-Russian crisis levels.

The sudden stop in capital flows and external financial deleveraging in Chile also had its counterpart in a sharp current account adjustment and real currency depreciation. The current account went from a deficit of 6.5 percent of GDP in the year ending in II-1998 to virtual balance one year later, a similar adjustment to LAC-7 overall but in a shorter time span (see Figure 8.4e). From June 1998 to December 2002, Chile's currency depreciated by close to 50 percent vis-à-vis the US dollar, compared to 70 percent in LAC-7 (see Figure 8.4f).

Finally, as in the average LAC-7 country, Chile's financial deleveraging and large current account adjustment were obtained through a severe and sustained reduction in investment. Investment declined by 23 percent in the immediate aftermath of the Russian crisis, and by the fourth quarter of 2002 it was still 12 percent below its pre-Russian levels (see Figure 8.4g). Between 1999 and 2002 average growth in investment was negative, and the

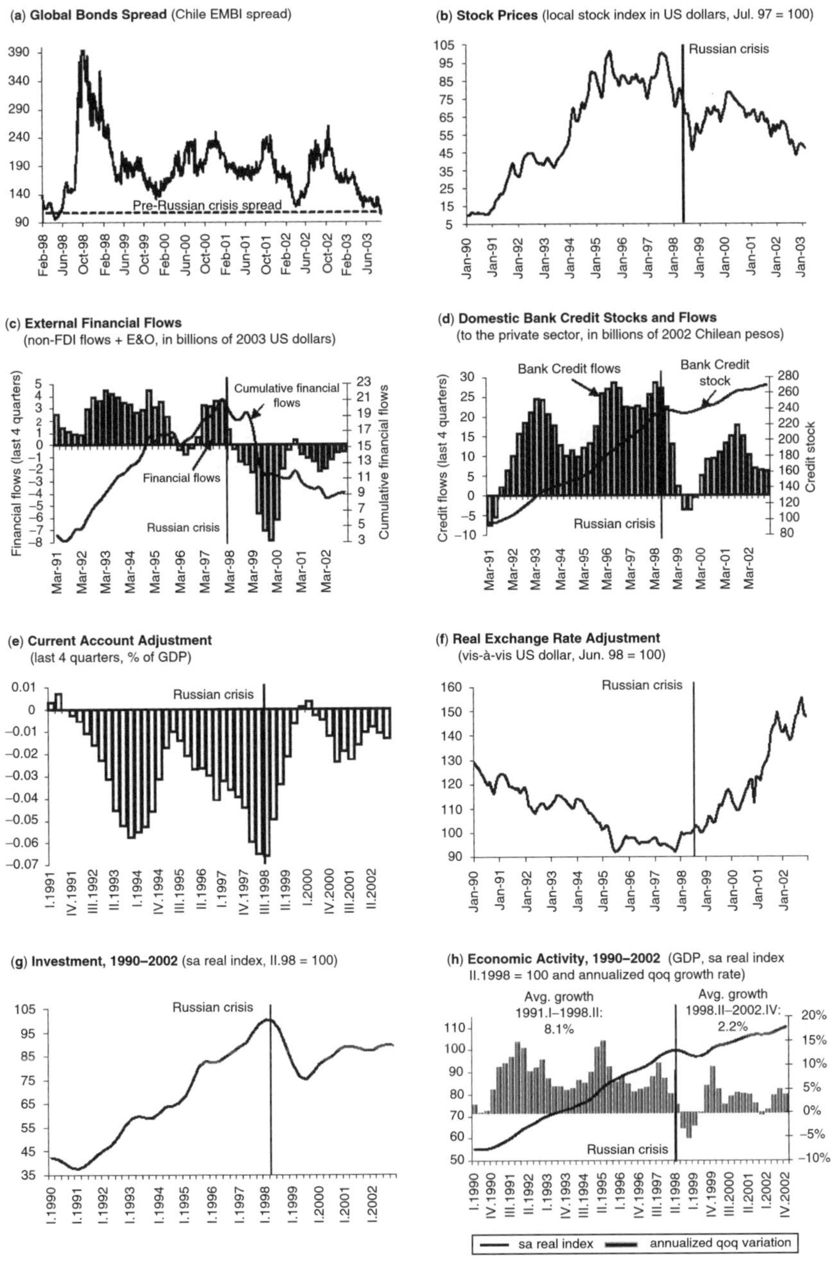

Figure 8.4. Sudden Stop and Macroeconomic Adjustment in Chile, 1990–2002

Sources: Central bank of Chile.

investment ratio fell from 27 percent of GDP in 1997, prior to the Russian crisis, to 21 percent of GDP in 2002; this reduction of six percentage points explains the bulk of the current account adjustment (see Table 8.2). The drop in investment ratios was associated with a correspondingly sharp reduction in growth rates (Figure 8.4h). Growth in Chile fell from an average of 8 percent per year between 1991 and 1997 to 2 percent per year between 1999 and 2002—after the sudden stop.

In summary, the evidence strongly suggests that the poor growth performance of the region in the late 1990s and early 2000s is the result of the macroeconomic adjustment set in motion by the sudden stop in capital flows following Russia's crisis. As credit dried up and existing degrees of leverage could not be sustained, LAC-7 economies went through a protracted period of relatively low investment as households and firms adjusted their balance sheets to the new situation. Every major country in LAC-7 was affected to a greater or lesser degree (with the notable exception of Mexico, which is tightly linked to the US business cycle), including Chile, by far the best performer in the region.

From Macro Adjustment to Financial Crisis and Economic Collapse: The Polar Cases of Chile and Argentina

However hard the landing and painful the adjustment, the Chilean economy did not experience the financial crisis and economic collapse that Argentina's did. This is puzzling in light of the fact that the sudden stop in capital flows in Chile and Argentina from II-1998 to II-2001—the period prior to the beginning of the bank run in Argentina—displayed a similar time pattern and, if anything, was larger in Chile than in Argentina (see Figure 8.5).

A cold spell affects different people in different ways: some catch a mild cold, while others end up at the hospital. Clearly, the outcome will depend on the physical strength or fragility of the person affected. Similarly, a sudden stop in capital flows originating in external factors can have a very different impact depending on the strength or the vulnerability of each economy.

In this section we identify two key *domestic* factors that contribute to attenuate or intensify the effects of a sudden stop. These are: trade openness and 'liability dollarization.'[15] In what follows we discuss the mechanisms through which these factors operate, focusing on the case of Argentina.

[15] Calvo et al. (2004) perform formal econometric tests on the role of openness and financial dollarization as determinants of sudden stops.

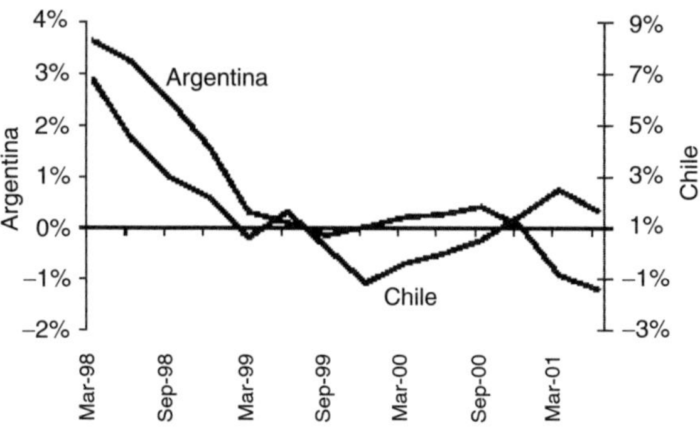

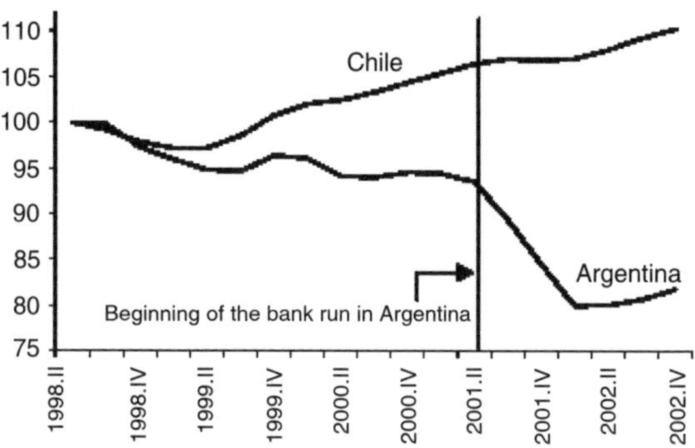

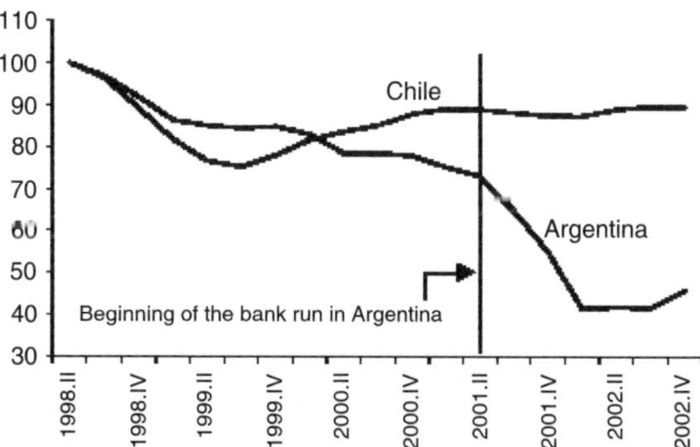

Figure 8.5. Sudden Stop and Economic Performance in Argentina and Chile
Sources: Corresponding central banks.

Table 8.4. Sudden Stop, Openness, and Real Exchange Rate (RER) Adjustment in Argentina and Chile

Country	Openness (share of tradables in GDP, avg. 1991–97*)	Current account deficit Year to II.1998		Required change in the equilibrium RER** (scaled to Chile's observed depreciation)
		% of GDP	% of imports	
Chile	35%	6.5%	22%	48%
Argentina	24%	4.7%	36%	75%

Notes: * The share of tradables in total production is proxied by the participation of the primary and manufacturing sectors In GDP; **see Calvo, Izquierdo, Talvi (2003).

Openness

As we showed in the previous sections, a sudden stop in capital flows was typically accompanied in the average LAC-7 country (Chile included) by a rapid and large adjustment in the current account, and by a large real depreciation of the domestic currency.

Openness is an essential link in the chain mapping an external liquidity shock to a financial crisis and an economic collapse. The reason is that the change in the real exchange rate to accommodate a sudden stop in capital flows is larger in a closed economy than in an open economy.[16]

As illustrated in Table 8.4, Chile's economy prior to the Russian crisis and the sudden stop was approximately 50 percent more open than that of Argentina if we use the share of tradables in GDP as our measure of openness: Chile's tradable sector averaged 35 percent of GDP compared to 24 percent in Argentina for the period 1991–97 prior to the Russian crisis.[17] Although Argentina's current account deficit prior to the sudden stop was smaller than Chile's (4.7 percent as opposed to 6.5 percent), due to its relatively closed economy Argentina would have required a larger *real* depreciation than Chile in order to eliminate the current account deficit. This is so because Argentina's current account deficit, when measured in percentage of imports prior to the sudden stop, was 60 percent larger than Chile's. Hence, Argentina

[16] For a formal proof in the context of a simple model see Calvo et al. (2003). The intuition is that in the short run, in other words, when the supply of tradables is relatively fixed, an adjustment to the current account of any given size requires a larger *proportional* reduction in domestic absorption of tradables, the smaller the supply of tradables relative to domestic expenditure of tradables. Under standard assumptions of preferences (homotheticity), the absorption of non-tradables must fall by the same proportion as tradables. In the short run, in other words when the supply of non-tradables is relatively fixed, the required change in the equilibrium real exchange rate will be larger, the smaller the supply of tradables relative to domestic expenditure on tradables.

[17] The share of tradables in GDP is proxied by the participation of the primary and manufacturing sectors in GDP. Traditional measures of openness—the share of imports plus exports as a share of GDP—averaged 56 percent in Chile and 19 percent in Argentina for the period 1991–97, prior to the Russian crisis.

may have required a real depreciation of 75 percent after the sudden stop if we scale Argentina's required depreciation to Chile's observed depreciation (and assume that the elasticity of substitution in consumption between tradables and non-tradables is about the same in both countries). Let us recall that Chile eliminated its current account deficit and its currency depreciated by 48 percent after the sudden stop.[18]

Under normal circumstances, a real devaluation would be part of the solution for an economy that requires substantial external adjustment. However, under extensive liability dollarization a large devaluation was bound to be part of the problem, not part of the solution.

'Liability Dollarization'

Figure 8.6a illustrates that private debt in Argentina was highly dollarized.[19] Prior to the sudden stop, 80 percent of private debt, whether domestic or foreign, was denominated in US dollars, compared to 38 percent in Chile. The high dollarization of private debt implied large financial mismatches in the balance sheets of Argentinean households and firms, since only 25 percent of productive activities are in the tradable sector, and therefore, potentially capable of generating earnings in hard currency. In contrast, Chile's tradable sector is much larger (the share of tradable goods in GDP prior to the sudden stop was 35 percent) and similar in size to the share of dollar debts in total private debt. Hence, the aggregate balance sheet of Chile's private sector was likely to be much less sensitive to movements in the real exchange rate.[20]

In the presence of these very large financial mismatches, a real devaluation of 75 percent in Argentina implied a huge revaluation in the value of private debts. For the typical debtor, with 80 percent of its liabilities denominated in US dollars and one-quarter of its income generated in US dollars, the ratio of the stock of debt relative to income would be expected to increase by 35 percent. For a debtor whose income was 100 percent in local currency the situation would be even worse: the ratio of debt to income would be expected to rise by 61 percent (see Figure 8.6b).

Let us pause for one second to stress why a large expected real devaluation and the implied revaluation of private debt stocks was bound to create severe financial stress. After the sudden stop, interest rate spreads for emerging economies skyrocketed and the value of collateral plummeted, signaling the unsustainability of outstanding debt stock. This situation was bound to be

[18] See Calvo et al. (2003) for a formal derivation of the relative size of the required real depreciation by Argentina and Chile to eliminate the current account deficit.

[19] Private debt is defined as domestic bank credit to the private sector plus foreign lending to the non-financial domestic private sector.

[20] For micro evidence on the absence of any significant balance sheet mismatches in Chile see Cowan et al. (2004).

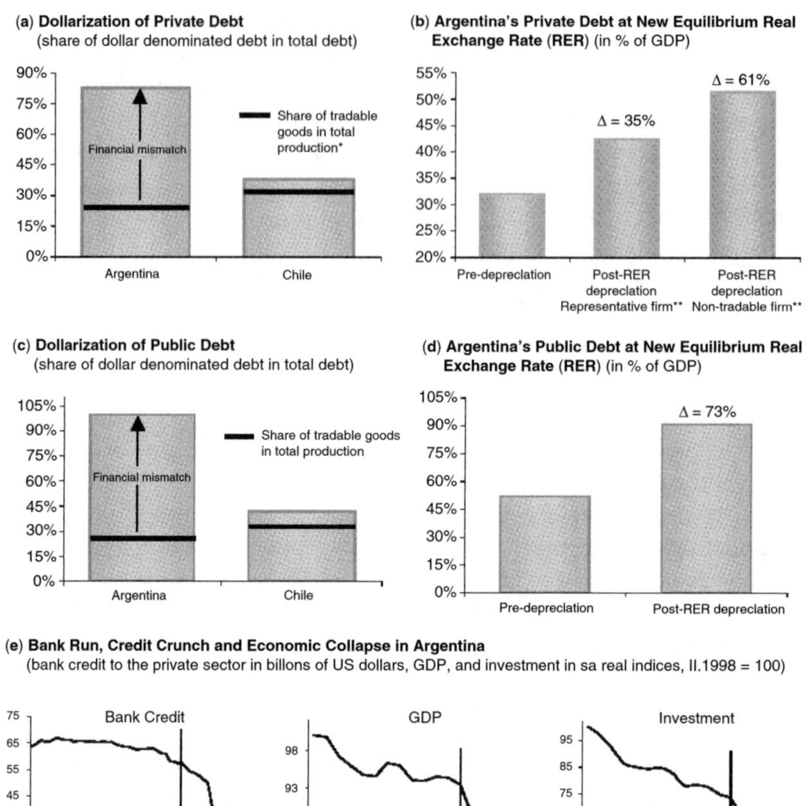

Figure 8.6. Sudden Stop, Dollarization, Financial Crisis, and Economic Collapse: Argentina in the Light of Chile

Notes: * The share of tradable goods in total production is proxied by the share of the primary and manufacturing sectors in GDP; ** the representative firm and the non-tradable firm are assumed to generate 75 percent and 100 percent, respectively, of their income in domestic currency.

Sources: Corresponding central banks and own estimations.

exacerbated by currency devaluation (another consequence of sudden stop), by increasing private debt ratios even further. This 'double whammy,' namely, the sharp rise in external financing costs and the revaluation in the stock of private debt, forces a much larger adjustment in debt stocks and sets in motion a potentially disruptive credit crunch (i.e., the inability to roll over existing stocks of debt) that could strangle investment and production.

Even if only the group of firms with balance sheet mismatches runs into financial trouble (i.e., is hit by the inability to rollover its stock of debt), much of the rest of the economy becomes suspect. This is the case because in most market economies inter-enterprise credit plays a prominent role in business transactions. In such an environment, credit to firms whose debts would have automatically been rolled over is conditioned on passing more in-depth viability tests. The latter, in turn, is a costly information-gathering exercise, and more so during a crisis, because it requires information about the inter-enterprise credit network to which the firm in question is connected. Like highway congestion caused by an accident, which can stop the flow of traffic, this may represent a major negative supply shock.[21]

Under these circumstances of severe financial stress, the public sector could have been part of the solution by, for example, 'collateralizing' private debts (as Korea did in 1997), by implicitly offering future tax revenues as collateral to prevent or mitigate the credit crunch of the private sector. But Argentina's public sector was bound to be part of the problem, not part of the solution. Close to 100 percent of Argentina's public debt, domestic and foreign, was denominated in US dollars, compared to 44 percent in Chile (see Figure 8.6c). Thus, a real devaluation of 75 percent—which, as argued above could have been called for by the sudden stop—would be expected to result in an increase of the public debt/GDP ratio from 54 to 93 percent (see Figure 8.6d).

In order to sustain those higher levels of public debt under tighter external financial conditions, Argentina's public sector would have been required to significantly increase its primary surplus in a sustained and credible manner to the tune of three percentage points of GDP (or 15 percent of government expenditures).[22] Since government expenditures largely consist of wages and pensions, it is close to impossible for a democratically elected government to explicitly engineer such a reduction through the normal budget process.[23] The alternative—to increase taxes on the private sector at the time when the private sector was also experiencing a severe credit crunch—simply meant plugging one hole by opening another. Clearly, the expected revaluation of debts, both private and public, was a national problem, and the private sector could not be counted on to bail out the public sector through higher taxes, and the public sector could not be counted on to bail out the private sector by socializing private debts. Under these circumstances, the credit crunch would be felt *simultaneously* by both the private and the public sector. Given the sheer magnitude of the problem caused by the 'double whammy' and the

[21] See Calvo (2000) for a discussion. [22] See Calvo et al. (2003).

[23] Adjustments of this size, and even larger, in public sector wages and pensions have been regularly observed in Latin America. However, they are typically engineered through an 'inflationary shock' that dilutes the real value of nominal wages and pensions rather than through an explicit decision of the government through the budgetary process.

inability to continue rolling over existing stocks of debt, it was unlikely that the adjustment in debt stocks would *not* have been expected to include some kind of debt restructuring, both public and private.

Let us now turn to the banking sector, a major factor in spreading the crisis across the economy. In the case of Argentina, bank assets consisted primarily of loans to the private and public sectors. Thus, financial trouble of the sort described above implied a severe deterioration of the quality of banks' loan portfolios. As it became increasingly clear that the sudden stop was systemic and persistent, and that a realignment of the exchange rate in Argentina was bound to be large and close to inevitable, the seeds of a bank run were sown. From the perspective of depositors, there was nobody around to bail them out in the event of a large devaluation, and therefore they ran for the exits. From February to December 2001, when the '*corralito*' was implemented, Argentina's banks lost close to 50 percent of their deposit base.[24] The bank run exhausted the central bank's international reserves, and the worst nightmare finally came true: the 'convertibility' regime—the fixed one-to-one peg to the US dollar—was abandoned and the peso experienced a very large depreciation. Not surprisingly, bank credit to the private sector also collapsed, along with the deposit base, and there was a huge collapse of investment and economic activity. GDP and investment fell by 25 percent and 70 percent, respectively, from (the year to) III-1998 to (the year to) III-2002, when they reached a minimum (see Figure 8.6e).

Before concluding this section, a note on the convertibility regime is in order. Many economists believe that had Argentina decided to abandon convertibility and devalue its currency early on, the protracted recession and ultimate financial crisis and economic collapse could have been avoided or largely attenuated. Chile's case is often cited as an example of a country that recognized early on that the currency needed to be adjusted in the aftermath of the sudden stop and successfully did so.

Although we acknowledge these Keynesian elements might have played a role in the early stages of Argentina's recession, they are not at center stage in explaining the ensuing collapse. Contrary to popular opinion, we believe that whatever the flaws of the convertibility regime (and there may be many),[25] the exchange-rate regime was a side show in this crisis. Had the Argentinean authorities decided to abandon it by engineering an early devaluation of the currency in the immediate aftermath of the sudden stop, the financial crisis would have occurred earlier. This is the case because the key problem was the real devaluation per se (and the revaluation of private and pubic debts it implied). In our view, the delay in abandoning the convertibility regime

[24] The '*corralito*' was the popular name given to the prohibition dictated by the government to withdraw money from bank accounts, except for very small and predetermined weekly amounts.

[25] See Calvo (1999b).

and in recognizing (what turned out to be) an inevitable realignment of the Argentinean currency was not the main cause of the crisis. Rather, the crisis was the consequence of Argentina's very high liability dollarization and the large real devaluation required by the sudden stop. This explains why devaluation of the Argentinean currency was delayed until it became patently obvious that there was no other choice.

Reflections on Policy

The recent crop of crises in emerging economies has revealed the importance of *external* financial factors, confirming once again the findings in Calvo et al. (1993). Therefore, this section will discuss policy responses to *systemic* shocks originating in international financial markets. We first offer some remarks on a variety of *crisis prevention policies* that have taken center stage in current policy debates, namely self-insurance, capital controls, the exchange rate regime, and de-dollarization. In addition we discuss the role of trade policy in crisis prevention, which emerges naturally from our previous analysis. We will then discuss the role of fiscal and interest rate policy in dealing with the crisis *after* it has occurred. Finally, we conclude this section with some brief remarks on what can be done at the global level to prevent or reduce the likelihood of systemic financial shocks affecting EMs.

Crisis Prevention Policies

The relevance of systemic shocks—shocks that apply to more than one EM economy at a time—became apparent after the 1998 Russian crisis, which brought about a sudden stop (of capital inflows) in several countries, despite Russia's small role in trade and financial markets. What can a single country do to offset such a negative shock? Typically, policymakers come forward asserting that their country is different—and, typically, this does not work. Multilateral financial institutions also join the chorus in a typically vain attempt to stave off a crisis, only to be quickly and rudely dismissed by the market (unless they are prepared to put enough money on the table). As we will discuss below, standard policies are not very effective either. Credit dries up, so expansive fiscal policy is infeasible (unless, once again, multilateral financial institutions or generous donors come forward with the necessary finance). Low central bank interest rates do not generate more credit (unless the central bank is prepared to spend its international reserves). In sum, standard policy is not effective unless some form of new credit is made available.

What can an individual country do to attenuate the effects of systemic crisis prior to crisis? Here the options are more varied, although by no means easy or costless.

SELF-INSURANCE

Let us focus on a sudden stop, in other words a credit crunch suffered by the country as a whole. If the government is over-indebted, the public sector is part of the problem. However, if public debt is small, then the public sector could help to ameliorate the credit squeeze by tapping multilateral financial institutions and putting up future tax revenue as collateral (as Korea did in 1997); or, equivalently, by employing its international reserves (as Hong Kong and Brazil did in 1998 and 2002, respectively). These observations suggest the following policy alternatives prior to crisis: (1) contingent credit lines from private/public international institutions and (2) a 'war chest' of international reserves. We will now say a few words about them.

1. *Contingent credit lines.* They are effective complements to international reserves, and were implemented by Argentina and Mexico. However, these lines tend to dry up as crisis looms. Moreover, the amounts are typically insufficient to prevent a sharp current account adjustment.
2. *'War chest.'* This is becoming a popular idea. The example that is usually mentioned is the Chilean Copper Stabilization Fund, which is supposed to grow during the expansion phase of the business cycle, and fall during downswings. The Chilean system does not fully address systemic shocks, since in principle the latter are not necessarily correlated with domestic business cycles. However, the basic idea is the same: minimize adjustment costs during downturns, and, especially, avoid having to implement tight fiscal policy during recessions. One problem with war chests is that the ruling party may have strong incentives to violate its operating rules and sacrifice the war chest for the sake of popularity at the polls. This observation is particularly relevant for a case in which the war chest is created to bail out the banking system. In that case the sums involved could amount to 20–30 percent of GDP. Thus, we feel that a war chest is unlikely to stand on its own. It will likely have to be complemented with contingent credit lines, because the latter involve third parties that could better ensure compliance with operating rules.

A problem faced by the types of policies described above is *moral hazard.* Anticipating a bailout, the private sector will likely change its behavior, possibly offsetting the effects of the bailout. Thus, bailouts must be made costly, especially for those agents who will be their direct beneficiaries.[26]

CAPITAL CONTROLS

There are few other topics that are as badly understood as the effect of capital controls on the probability of financial crises, more specifically, sudden stops.

[26] See IADB (2005).

A common, and misleading, intuition is that if one prevents short-term ('hot') capital from flowing in, then capital will not gush out, and a sudden stop will thus be prevented. Plausible as it may sound, this intuition is wrong for more than one reason. In the first place, capital outflow can take place even in the absence of capital inflow. For example, exporters could keep export proceeds in a foreign bank instead of bringing them home, and multinational firms could increase the rate of profit repatriation or use financial transactions that imply capital outflows to hedge the risks of immobile assets in their balance sheets. Second, a sudden stop entails *lower* capital inflows, not necessarily capital *outflows*. Thus, a sudden stop would take place if foreign direct investment (FDI) slows down (as happened in Peru in 1998), even though FDI is the polar opposite of hot capital. This shows, incidentally, that not even effective controls on capital outflows (as in Malaysia in 1997) could prevent sudden stop. Third, as shown in previous sections, empirical evidence cast serious doubts on the effectiveness of controls on capital inflows. After 1998, Chile suffered the largest sudden stop in Latin America, despite having consistently, and for an extended period of time, imposed controls on capital inflows. Furthermore, it is possible to conceive of circumstances in which the imposition of controls may exacerbate the extent of a sudden stop, because the government would have revealed its predisposition to meddle with the market.

EXCHANGE RATE REGIME

This is another topic where confusion is king. Some seem to think that crises could be entirely wiped out if the exchange rate was free to float. This is an extreme view, and an easy one to dismiss. However, it is perhaps fair to say that most observers believe that pegged exchange rates are dangerous for EMs. Interestingly, while the debate leans against fixed exchange rates, accession countries in Europe are eagerly queuing up to join the euro, and China—with a splendid sustained growth record—has pegged its currency to the US dollar since 1995. Moreover, not even the pro-floaters appear to be disturbed by the fact that economies so geographically diverse as the regions of the US have only one currency, and are proud and happy to do so. Although California has gone through a deep recession in recent years, we have never heard a respectable pro-floater say that what California needs is to issue a new currency and devalue!

Exchange rates have recently been discussed in Calvo and Mishkin (2003), and we have little to add here. The bottom line is that exchange rates are a sideshow. Issues like institutions and credibility take the center stage. Sudden stop episodes involve a sharp drying up of credit, bringing about severe domestic repercussions, especially if the economy is highly 'liability dollarized' (i.e., foreign exchange denominated debts). Under those circumstances, a floating exchange rate is of little help and may even aggravate the crisis.

Calvo et al. (2004) show that the probability of a sudden stop increases with liability dollarization (more precisely, *domestic* liability dollarization, in other words, foreign exchange debts to the domestic banking system), while the exchange rate regime does not appear to be a contributing factor.

DE-DOLLARIZATION

As noted, liability dollarization appears to increase the chances of a sudden stop. Thus, the question arises, is there a way to remove the dollarization scourge? We probably reflect conventional wisdom on this matter in saying that liability dollarization is likely a consequence of many years of monetary mismanagement. Thus, it is unlikely that it will go away as a result of actions taken by present policymakers, unless there is an assurance that future policymakers will not revert to business as usual. Forceful de-dollarization on the other hand, is likely to result in a drastic shrinkage of the financial system and a reduction in the maturity of deposits.

A possibility that has received some attention is to try to steer the domestic financial system away from indexing to a foreign currency and towards some domestic price level. A successful example in Latin America is the Chilean UF (*Unidad de Fomento*). In Chile most financial and formal sector wage contracts are UF-indexed. This allowed Chile to carry out a large real devaluation after 1998 without disrupting the domestic capital market. Can this be replicated in other countries, and is this always a desirable policy? The first part of the question does not have a promising answer. In the first place, Chile was never heavily dollarized, even so it took about 30 years to make the UF operational.[27,28] As to the second part of the question, 'Is it desirable?', we do not have a good answer yet. Financial problems arise when there is a mismatch between the denomination of assets and liabilities at financial institutions and/or firms in general, and liability dollarization is a clear case of mismatch in the non-tradables sector. But any index is likely to be imperfect when the economy is faced with a large change in relative prices. Thus, for example, as a result of a sudden stop housing prices are likely to show a precipitous fall. Since the index will only partially reflect housing prices, mortgage obligations are bound to surge relative to housing values—causing financial difficulties, as households will have much lower incentives for honoring their housing financial obligations.

TRADE POLICY

As noted above, given the current account deficit, the change in relative prices brought about by a sudden stop is in inverse relation to the degree

[27] See Landerretche and Valdes (1997).

[28] Bolivia recently attempted to adopt an UF-type system to de-dollarize its banking system to no avail.

of openness. Thus, the larger the tradables sector, the less likely that a sudden stop will generate serious financial problems. Actually, for the purposes of this discussion 'tradables' are goods that could be quickly transformed into exports when there is a collapse in domestic demand. Thus, a better term for 'tradables' in this context is 'exportables.' Evidence of exportability is offered by Chile after the 1998 Russian crisis: exports in Chile contributed to 50 percent of the current account adjustment. In sharp contrast, in Argentina 98 percent of the current account adjustment after 1998 (and prior to the bank run in II-2001) was triggered by a reduction in imports.

These observations provide new support for trade opening. Here the argument is not the standard one in trade theory, in which issues like comparative advantage or product variety are at center stage. Rather, the argument is that economies with a large exportables sector will exhibit stable real exchange rates—thus lowering the deleterious incidence of liability dollarization. What is important in this context is that tradable goods can quickly be transformed into exports—and for this, availability of *trade credit* is essential. Recent episodes, however, show that trade credit can dry up as quickly as other types of credit. This is very disconcerting because one would expect exports to be good collateral for international creditors. Recent conversations with bankers and policymakers in Brazil and Uruguay, however, indicate that exports' value as collateral is jeopardized by the expectation of disarray after a sudden stop. For example: (a) strikes and social upheaval may prevent exports from reaching the port, making them non-exportable; and (b) the government may impose foreign exchange controls that either impede the repayment of external debt or make it extraordinarily onerous. Therefore, under those circumstances, to make tradable goods exportable the government will have to be prepared to dip into its war chest or contingent credit lines to support the export sector.[29]

Post-crisis Policies

The debate on how fiscal and interest rate policy should be conducted after crisis has been heated. Should fiscal and monetary policy be tight, as usually recommended by the IMF? Or should these policies be loose, as recommended by authors like Joseph Stiglitz, a harsh critic of IMF policies during the Asian crisis?[30] Although we do not intend to resolve the striking differences of opinion on this issue here, some comments are in order.

[29] The central bank of Brazil extended credit to the export sector in 2002, in the midst of a sudden stop that was partly provoked by uncertainty regarding the political transition about to take place in December.

[30] See Stiglitz (2002).

FISCAL POLICY

If the government does not have the resources or cannot access the capital market, there is little the public sector can do to alleviate the situation. Thus, under these conditions, it would be impossible to implement expansive fiscal policy. This, incidentally, does not imply that tight fiscal policy—beyond what is strictly required by capital market conditions—is desirable either. The only exception would be if tight fiscal policy improves the economy's credibility and facilitates capital market access by the private sector.[31] This is hard to determine in practice, but we believe that the success of super-tight fiscal policy depends on whether the crisis is systemic or localized. If the crisis is systemic, then super-tight fiscal policy is likely to be unnecessarily contractionary, undermining policy credibility and aggravating the crisis.[32] On the other hand, if the crisis is localized, then fiscal super-adjustment might help, particularly if it is accompanied by generous funding from multilateral financial institutions or it takes place during a favorable phase in the capital market for EMs.

INTEREST RATE POLICY

Low interest rates are likely not to be implementable unless the country has a war chest, contingent credit lines, or a generous transfer from the international community. However, as with fiscal policy, there is the question of how tight monetary policy should be. Furman and Stiglitz (1998), for example, are skeptical of super-tight monetary policy; and we agree, especially after sudden stops. A sudden stop breaks the link between domestic and international credit markets, at least momentarily, thus making it possible for super-tight monetary policy to be contractionary.[33] Therefore, policymakers have to sail the narrow stretch between the Scylla of contraction and the Charybdis of inflation and monetary disarray—by no means an easy task!

[31] This was the strategy followed by Argentina in August 1996, when Minister Cavallo was fired by President Menem, and the new Minister (Roque Fernandez) had to show he was a fiscal conservative vis-à-vis the capital market. The strategy seems to have been successful, but partly because external financial conditions were favorable, as will be discussed below.

[32] We conjecture that the failure of Argentina's 2000 fiscal adjustment program had a great deal to do with the fact that it was carried out in the midst of the sudden stop that affected many EMs after the 1998 Russian crisis.

[33] Calvo and Coricelli (1992) discussed this issue in regard to the IMF 1990 Poland stabilization plan, where monetary policy was extraordinarily tight. For example, on January 1, 1990, the start of the stabilization program, the National Bank of Poland increased interest rates in zlotys from 7 to 36 percent per month! Calvo and Coricelli (1992) argue that this policy was responsible for the sharp output decline in 1990, because Poland had no access to international capital markets (hence, it was operating under conditions similar to those that prevail under a sudden stop).

Global Policies

Our previous discussion suggests that even under the best of circumstances, systemic shocks cannot be entirely palliated by domestic policy. Is there something further that can be done at a global level to prevent a systemic shock?

The answer to the question depends, of course, on the causes of systemic shocks. Take, for example, the case in which credit to EMs dries up as a result of a liquidity crunch at the center of the capital market, a leading explanation for the spread of the 1998 Russian crisis.[34] In such a case the obvious solution is to relieve the global liquidity crunch by, for example, lowering US and EU interest rates (as eventually happened after the Russian crisis). The problem is that US/EU central banks are not supposed to react to liquidity problems that affect other economies. Thus, liquidity relief may arrive when the systemic shock is already in full swing and has already caused irreversible damage in EMs. This demonstrates the need to create a global central bank to manage global liquidity problems. Unfortunately, however, a moment's reflection shows that such a project is fraught with forbidding regulatory problems, stemming from national sovereignty constraints. A more modest proposal is the creation of an emerging market fund (EMF) which would attempt to stabilize the price of EM bonds in case of a global liquidity crunch.[35]

The main difference between these proposals and current international arrangements is that IMF liquidity assistance in the event of a credit crunch to EMs is targeted at individual countries, rather than at financial intermediaries suffering from a liquidity crunch. A global central bank or EMF, in contrast, would mitigate the liquidity crunch of financial intermediaries in EM bonds. This is akin to the actions undertaken by a central bank when confronted by a bank run that would result in a credit crunch as banks recall their outstanding loans to repay depositors: liquidity is directly provided to the banks and not to the bank's individual debtors.

Other proposals to mitigate the impact of systemic shocks emphasize the role of multilateral institutions in fostering the development of financial instruments to allow for a more efficient international risk sharing. One such proposal, advanced by Eichengreen and Hausmann (2003), intended to attenuate the incidence of liability dollarization claims that multilateral institutions should lend a portion of their funds to EMs in inflation indexed instruments denominated in their own currency. Multilateral institutions in turn would issue debt instruments denominated in an inflation-indexed basket that would be placed with institutional investors. The implied basket would suffer less from idiosyncratic risk and, therefore, may enjoy higher liquidity than the country-specific bonds.

[34] See Calvo (1999a).

[35] See Calvo (2000) for a discussion.

Proposals such as the SDRM (a sort of international bankruptcy proceeding sponsored by the IMF) or the inclusion of collective action clauses in sovereign bond issues are intended to be an efficient resolution of a sovereign debt crisis once it has occurred. Such mechanisms for orderly restructurings of sovereign defaults have several limitations that have been extensively discussed by the international financial community. For our purposes it is sufficient to say that proposals along these lines could have positive features but would not necessarily result in crisis prevention.

References

Calvo, G. A. (1989). 'Incredible Reform', in G. A. Calvo, R. Findlay, P. Kouri, and J. B. de Macedo (eds.), *Debt, Stabilization and Development*. New York: Basil Blackwell. (Reprinted in Calvo, G. A. (ed.) (1996). *Money, Exchange Rates, and Output*. Cambridge, MA: MIT Press.)

—— (1998). 'Varieties of Capital-Market Crises', in G. Calvo and M. King (eds.), *The Debt Burden and its Consequences for Monetary Policy*. London: Macmillan.

—— (1999a). 'Contagion in Emerging Markets: When Wall Street is a Carrier'. Online paper available at: www.bsos.umd.edu/econ/ciencrp8.pdf (shorter version, *Publisher in the Proceedings from the International Economic Association Congress*, vol. 3, Buenos Aires, Argentina, 2002).

—— (1999b). 'On Dollarization'. Online paper available at: www.bsos.umd.edu/econ/ciecpn5.pdf (also in *Economics of Transition Journal*, 2002).

—— (2000). 'Balance of Payments Crises in Emerging Markets: Large Capital Inflows and Sovereign Governments', in P. Krugman (ed.), *Currency Crises*. Chicago: University of Chicago Press.

—— (2002). 'Globalization Hazard and Delayed Reform in Emerging Markets'. *Economia*, 2/2.

—— and Borensztein, E. (1989). 'Perspectivas sobre el Problema de la Deuda'. *Trimestre Económico* (special issue on *Crecimiento, Equidad y Financiamiento Externo*), 67: 39–72.

—— and Coricelli, F. (1992). 'Stabilizing a Previously Centrally Planned Economy: Poland 1990'. *Economic Policy* (April): 176–208. (Reprinted in G. A. Calvo (ed.) (1996). *Money, Exchange Rates, and Output*. Cambridge, MA: MIT Press.)

—— and Mendoza, E. (2000). 'Rational Contagion and the Globalization of Securities Markets'. *Journal of International Economics*, 51/1: 79–113.

—— and Mishkin, F. (2003). 'The Mirage of Exchange Rate Regimes for Emerging Markets Countries'. *Journal of Economic Perspectives*, 17/4.

—— and Talvi, E. (2002). 'Lula Effect? Look Again!' Policy Note, No. 12, CERES, Montevideo, Uruguay.

—— Reinhart, C., and Leiderman, L. (1993) 'Capital Inflows and Real Exchange Rate Appreciation in Latin America: The Role of External Factors'. *IMF Staff Papers*, 40/1: 108–51.

—— Izquierdo, A., and Talvi, E. (2003). 'Sudden Stops, the Real Exchange Rate, and Fiscal Sustainability: Argentina's Lessons'. NBER Working Paper, No. 9828, National Bureau of Economic Research, Cambridge, MA.

—— —— and Mejia, L. F. (2004). 'On the Empirics of Sudden Stops: The Relevance of Balance-Sheet Effects'. NBER Working Paper, No. 10520, National Bureau of Economic Research, Cambridge, MA.

Cowan, K., Hansen, E., and Herrera, L. O. (2004). 'Currency Mismatches, Balance Sheet Effects and Hedging in Chilean Non-Financial Corporations'. Prepared for the conference Vulnerabilidad Externa y Políticas de Prevención, Central Bank of Chile (forthcoming in conference volume).

Eichengreen, B. and Hausmann, R. (2003). 'The Road To Redemption', in B. Eichengreen and R. Hausmann (eds.), *Debt Denomination and Financial Instability in Emerging Market Economics*. Chicago: University of Chicago Press.

Furman, J. and Stiglitz, J. E. (1998). 'Economic Crises: Evidence and Insights from East Asia', Brookings Papers on Economic Activity, No. 2, Brookings Institution Press, Washington, DC, 1–114.

IADB. (2005). *Unlocking Credit, Economic and Social Progress Report*. Washington, DC: Inter-American Development Bank.

Kaminsky, G. and Reinhart, C. (2001). 'Bank Lending and Contagion: Evidence From the Asian Crisis', in T. Ito and A. Krueger (eds.), *Regional and Global Capital Flows: Macroeconomic Causes and Consequences*. Chicago: University of Chicago Press for the NBER, 73–99.

—— —— (2003). 'The Center and the Periphery: The Globalization of Financial Shocks'. NBER Working Paper, No. 947, Cambridge, MA.

Landerretche, O. and Valdés, R. (1997). 'Indización: Historia Chilena y Experiencia Internacional'. Central Bank of Chile Working Paper, No. 21, Santiago, Chile.

Lora, E. (2001). 'Structural Reforms in Latin America: What Has Been Reformed and How to Measure It'. RES Working Paper, No. 466, Inter-American Development Bank, Washington, DC.

Stiglitz, J. E. (2002). *Globalization and its Discontents*. New York: Norton & Co.

—— (2003). 'El Rumbo de las reformas: hacia una nueva agenda para América Latina'. *Revista de la CEPAL*, 80.

9

Towards a New Modus Operandi of the International Financial System

Daniel Cohen[1]

Introduction

The Bretton Woods system was conceived as a fixed exchange rate regime, allowing for a few devaluations, with the IMF supplying a line of credit to countries in 'transitory' difficulties. It was far less ambitious than the idea put forward by Keynes, who wanted to switch directly to a truly international monetary system based upon a world currency, the *bancor* as he meant to call it.[2] Sixty years later, the advent of the euro in Europe has shown that the idea of a supranational currency was not infeasible after all. One clearly sees, however, the set of political and economic difficulties at hand. The stability pact, to give one example, which was geared toward imposing fiscal discipline on the member states, has proved extremely difficult to implement. As Argentina or Brazil have demonstrated in a different context, it is indeed very difficult to hold the 'provinces' accountable to financial discipline when there is a 'free lunch,' namely a common currency. After the war, the US was willing to lend or grant money to the rest of the world (as the Marshall plan later demonstrated), but not as a matter of principle.

On the other hand, a supranational currency is at least consistent with greater financial integration. Given the 'Mundell triangle,' something has to give with free capital mobility: either an independent monetary policy (and, one would add, a fiscal stance as well) or a fixed exchange rate. The collapse of the Bretton Woods (BW) system—formally in the 1970s, in practice as early as

[1] This chapter draws on joint work with Richard Portes (Cohen and Portes 2003), Charles Vellutini (Cohen and Vellutini 2003), and Thibault Fally and Sebastien Villemot (Cohen et al. 2004). I thank them all for inspiration. The usual disclaimer applies.

[2] An intriguing question is whether Harry Dexter White, the US counterpart to Keynes, was, as ascertained in a recent book (Craig 2004), a Soviet 'correspondent.' If proven, this could somehow weaken the thesis that the IMF was only designed to enhance US interests.

in the early 1960s—can be interpreted as driven by the Mundell logic, when monetary policy would not surrender despite financial integration. As capital mobility expands, the system becomes rapidly untenable. As devaluations are anticipated, exchange rate crises often get out of control. As financial integration deepens, the need for credit lines is of a different nature. The role of the IMF is no longer to finance 'transitory' balance of payments disequilibria, which almost by definition can be dealt with by financial integration. If financial markets refuse to assist a country, this must arise from some kind of crises. Some of them have to do with the intrinsic instability of financial markets, others with the lack of self-imposed discipline from the debtor countries themselves. Overall, for most emerging countries, the post-BW world has been as much a risk, say, as an opportunity. As shown by Eichengreen and Bordo, crisis frequency has risen, being now about twice as frequent than in the period 1880–1913. Three quarters of financial crises after 1973 took place in developing countries. The widespread debt crisis of the 1980s became 'the lost decade' for Latin America, and the banks ultimately had to accept substantial write-offs. The Asian crisis of 1997–98 was devastating at the time. The Russian default of August 1998 was settled relatively quickly, but even quicker were the shock waves it sent out to the financial markets—with some role in the failure of LTCM, a sharp rise of all emerging market bond spreads, and the subsequent Brazilian exchange rate crisis. Dealing with country debt crises is always very messy, often protracted, and very costly to both debtor and creditors.

Orderly resolution of sovereign debt crises has in fact become more difficult in the past decade. The shift from the syndicated bank loans of the 1970s to a mix of short-term bank finance and bonds has created a much wider group of creditors and instruments. This exacerbates the 'rush to exits' by creditors in a crisis and the collective action problems involved in debt restructuring. What seems rational for an individual creditor trying to get their money out becomes counterproductive when all try to do so simultaneously, or when they cannot agree to accept some loss if some think they can do better acting alone.

The debtor knows that restructuring will be difficult in these circumstances and therefore may do everything possible to delay the inevitable, as a result often making it worse when it does come. Then, once a restructuring is finally agreed by most creditors, holdout ('rogue') creditors can seek to extract full payment—so all creditors are concerned *ex ante* about such free-rider behavior, and that itself impedes agreement. During a protracted restructuring, the debtor faces severe financing problems—it may be impossible to get 'new money,' often including trade credit. The abrupt compression of imports and shift into exports can be a very painful adjustment, often accompanied by deep falls in output. The absence of a framework for orderly workouts increases the pressure on the IMF and G8 to step in with bailout packages, because a disorderly workout appears too unpalatable.

There are alternatives. After the Mexican crisis of 1994–95, Jeffrey Sachs[3] proposed an international bankruptcy regime modeled on chapter 11 of the US bankruptcy code. Eichengreen and Portes (1995) argued instead for a combination of contractual and institutional changes that would not require an international bankruptcy court.[4] The G10 deputies issued a report in May 1996 that advocated the latter route.[5] Nothing was done, because the G10 left any action to the initiative of market participants. But the lenders had already expressed their opposition to any measures that would, as they put it, 'make default easier.' It should instead be as 'bad and ugly' as possible, they said, in order to deter any violation of the sanctity of contracts.

The discussions on the international financial architecture that followed the Asian crisis of 1997–98 revived the debate, but both the conclusions and the results were the same as before: no change. The crises in Turkey and Argentina were handled in much the same way as the Asian crises—a pre-crisis period of exchange rate rigidity endorsed by the IMF, followed by big bailout packages when trouble came. Only the debacle and default of Argentina broke the pattern, and the consequences are disastrous for that country, if not for the international financial system. One proposal came from Stanley Fischer, declaring to be in favor of IMF action as lender of last resort (LLR). Another one was by Anne Krueger (Fischer's successor as the Fund's number two), advocating a sovereign debt restructuring mechanism (SDRM), a mechanism facilitating declaration of insolvency for overindebted countries along the lines of chapter 11. One of the institutional manifestations of the Fischer proposal is the use of the CCL facility, which enables countries affected by a contagion crisis to draw on additional lines of credit. No country, however, made use of this facility which was eventually shelved in 2004. The Krueger proposal was also eventually shelved although, four months after her first declaration, she responded to criticism by significantly reducing the implementing role of the IMF; but her plan would still have required an international treaty or amendment of the IMF Articles of Agreement. John Taylor, US Undersecretary of the Treasury for International Affairs, responded immediately with a version of the proposals for contractual changes that had appeared in 1995–96. The then-G7 endorsed the US position, and at the end the whole exercise was abandoned.

Both these proposals (LLR and SDRM) have proved, with the benefit of hindsight, too ambitious. The LLR reform, to take this one first, must have

[3] Sachs, J. (1995). 'Do We Need an International Lender of Last Resort?' Graham Lecture, Princeton University.

[4] Eichengreen, B. and Portes, R. (1995). *Crisis? What Crisis? Orderly Workouts for Sovereign Debtors*. London: Centre for Economic Policy Research.

[5] BIS (1996). *The Resolution of Sovereign Liquidity Crises*. London: BIS.

at its disposal either the resources to inject an indeterminate quantity of fresh liquidity or perfect information regarding solvent and insolvent financial intermediaries. As the latter assumption is virtually ruled out by the very nature of financial crises, the former is tantamount to giving the IMF the means to create liquidity *ex nihilo*. Such a transfer of monetary sovereignty—and we have seen how difficult it was to implement in the European case—seems unrealistic on a world scale. If there is to be a world LLR, it is rather for the large central banks (Fed, ECB, and BoJ) to play this role, but it is hard to imagine that this could be formalized in a systematic way, although some commentators have offered to reactivate the SDR as a means for creating world liquidity (e.g., Soros). The proposal of a bankruptcy court, for its part, has also been the subject of intense discussions (see Rogoff and Zeltmeyer, 2003, for a review). Here too, the political difficulty of setting up an international court with authority over the handling of sovereign debt, an excellent idea in itself, has appeared to be unattainable for essentially the same reason; in other words, the substantial transfer of sovereignty that would be needed in order to give an international court the statutory possibility of suspending legal procedures against a country. This is why a realistic agenda of reforms needs to be one step below this ambitious proposal. At the risk of appearing to be too cautious, I will suggest in this report a new modus operandi rather than a big bang approach to the reform of the system.

Content of the Chapter

The rest of the chapter comes as follows. We first offer a brief history of financial crises after 1973, highlighting the differences between the 1980s and the 1990s. We then discuss a platform of reforms for the middle-income countries. In the last section we address the poorest countries' needs.

A Brief History of Financial Crises after 1973

From the 1970s into the 1980s

A popular view in the 1970s was that world excess savings (brought about by the oil shocks) were efficiently recycled to the developing countries through the euro/dollar market. According to this view, current account deficits of the developing countries were an 'equilibrium' phenomenon which enabled these countries to absorb aggregate shocks smoothly. For all practical matters, the balance of payments was portrayed as following a pattern mimicking the cash flow of an infinitely lived individual subject to an

Table 9.1. Debt Reschedulings in the 1980s

D/X	Probability of rescheduling
200%	60%
250%	69%
300%	93%

Source: Cohen (2001).

intertemporal budget constraint. Thanks to financial integration, nobody should worry about the current account disequilibria.[6]

The 1980s, however, became the decade when the debt accumulated in the 1970s became a bitter component of the developing countries' lives. World interest rates shot up and the time horizon of the lenders consequently got shorter. Against the view that balance of payments disequilibria were equilibrium phenomena rose the opposite view that debt could well be unsustainable. Table 9.1 relates the probability of a debt crisis to the level of debt accumulated in the early 1980s by a developing country.

The new question was: given the shock to the interest rate and given the new impatience of creditors to reduce their exposure on the poor countries, would the country be willing to service its debt in full?[7] A number of approaches have been tried which converge on a narrow range of answers. Whatever the methodology, there was no question that the debt had (eventually) to be written down. An early proponent of debt write-off in the 1980s was Kenen (1983). (In defense of voluntary debt write-off, see also Williamson, 1988.) Why it took almost a decade to reach such a conclusion is one of the most troublesome questions of the period.

One aspect that made the need for a debt write-down obvious was the fact that the debt of most middle-income debtors was quoted on a secondary market that would simply reveal what the lenders themselves were thinking. In cases such as Bolivia, the discount on the debt came down as low

[6] The analysis of a country's balance of payments in an intertemporal framework was renewed by the work of Bazdarich (1978); Dornbusch and Fischer (1980); Sachs (1981); and Razin and Svensson (1983). The guiding line of these papers was to apply the permanent income theory to the case of a nation portrayed as an infinitely lived agent and to interpret the so-called 'disequilibria' of the balance of payments as an equilibrium phenomenon. Further models paid specific attention to the problem of aggregating the intertemporal budget constraints of an infinite number of finitely lived agents. The key papers include Buiter (1981); Dornbusch and Fischer (1985); and the work by Frenkel and Razin (1989).

[7] The theory of debt repudiation has then been brought to life by the work of Eaton and Gersovitz (1981). Early work on the topic also includes Kharas (1984); Kletzer (1984); Cohen and Sachs (1986); Ozler (1986); and Krugman (1988). The early survey by Sachs (1984) and Eaton et al. (1986) as well as the other papers in the special issue of the *European Economic Review* (June 1986) give an overview of the state of the art in 1985.

Table 9.2. Market Value of Debt Circa 1990

D/X	Market value	Marginal price
150%	78.5%	30%
200%	87.9%	9.5%
250%	90%	2.1%
300%	89%	−3%

Source: Cohen 2001.

as 95 percent, which meant that the creditors were willing to sell a claim nominally priced at US$1 for 5 cents. The Brady initiative itself offered to cut the nominal value of the debt by a significant amount. In the (extreme) case of Bolivia, for instance, the Brady deal carried an 84 percent discount. In the less severe cases of Brazil and Mexico, one of the key options offered to the commercial banks involved a 35 percent discount. For Ecuador, the write-off discount agreed upon after the Brady deal amounted to 45 percent. Yet, even in the immediate aftermath of the Brady deal, the debt was still quoted at a significant discount. In the case of Argentina, the discounted bond was traded at 61 cents on the dollar in July 1992. In the case of Nigeria, which is closer to the HIPC problem to be examined below, the debt was quoted at 25 cents on the dollar (i.e., a 75 percent discount). These numbers, which were an integral part of the debate at the time of the Brady deal, were strong evidence of the discrepancy between the market and the face values of the debt at the time when the Brady deals were signed.

In order to analyze the potential of debt write-off as a solution to the debt crisis, Bulow and Rogoff (1989a) have offered a critical distinction between average and marginal value of debt (see also Cohen and Verdier 1995). When a country owes a debt that already extends its ability to service it, at the margin, accumulating an extra US$1 of credit will bring nothing to the investors as a whole, although one individual investor would clearly be richer. Conversely, when a creditor reduces its claim on a debtor by US$1, by how much does it really reduce the burden of the debtor? Obviously by less than the face value of the write-off but also by less than the average (market) value of the debt. In the extreme example where, no matter what, the country will always pay a fixed number, the marginal price of the debt is zero so long as the debt is larger than that number. Building upon these insights, I have calibrated the difference between the average and the marginal price of the debt such as it was quoted prior to the Brady deal for emerging countries. The results are shown in Table 9.2.

One sees from Table 9.2 that countries whose debt-to-export ratio is above 250 percent have reached the stage where the marginal value of the debt is estimated to be nil by secondary market participants. In those cases, one could speak of a 'Debt Laffer Curve' problem, as Paul Krugman once put it: more debt reduces its market value, something labeled as a 'debt overhang' in the literature. A debt-to-export ratio of 250 percent then appears, in this context, as the absolute maximum for debt accumulation. We return below to this critical dimension to analyze the lessons of the HIPC initiative.

Are the Financial Crises of the 1990s Different from Those of the 1980s?[8]

In the period leading up to 1982, when Mexico suspended payment on its debt, spreads were very low, rarely exceeding 200–250 basis points, as most bankers at the time thought that countries did not default. Spreads on both Mexican and Brazilian debt did rise in the few months before the debt moratoria, but the syndicated bank lending of the 1970s and early 1980s showed no signs of recollection of the 1930s. Although spreads did vary somewhat with the characteristics of the borrower, there was no perceptible market analysis of the risk involved. The bulk of the financial crises involved syndicated loans with very low spreads, and the average real rate of interest on sovereign borrowing in the 1970s was negative. The debt crisis of the 1980s was simply not anticipated by the lenders. This changed, to a large extent, in the 1990s. The agents became different. Corporate borrowers joined sovereign debtors. Lenders were different too: bondholders replaced bank loan syndicates. The 1980s story according to which high public deficits created high debt was not the only one at hand. Confidence crises created new scenarios. Crises were more complex: the Asian crises, the Mexican crisis, and the Russian crisis give a range of cases that are difficult to subsume under one story. Some crises were expected, some were unexpected, and quite often, in each case, for good reasons. During the 1990s, the critical questions became to investigate the extent to which 'confidence' crises could disrupt a country without any references to its fundamentals, and whether a new global monitoring of the financial system was needed.

In order to create a typology of new debt crises in the nineties, let us distinguish cases where the spread before the crisis was large enough that one could speak of 'foretold' crises from cases where they were telling nothing about the likelihood of a forthcoming crisis. Take, for instances of the first category, the cases of Argentina and Ecuador (Table 9.3); and, at the other extreme, take Korea or Mexico (Table 9.4).

From the comparison of these two cases, it is fairly clear that Argentina and Ecuador were fundamentally insolvent, at least with respect to one of the two criteria which are commonly used: debt-to-export ratio above 200 percent and/or debt-to-GDP ratio above 50 percent (note, however, that it takes both indicators to anticipate a crisis, on which more later). Huge spreads

[8] This section is based on Cohen and Portes (2003).

Table 9.3. Case 1: Foretold Crises in Argentina and Ecuador (data two years before the crisis)

	Argentina	Ecuador
D/X	380%	250%
D/GDP	36%	85%
Spreads (basis points)	1,000	1,000
Current account (% of GDP)	−5%	−11%

were paid, and at the time when the crisis erupted, no lender could claim that it was taken by surprise. Yet despite this apparent market discipline, many lenders were taken by surprise; and the discipline of higher spreads had little perceptible effect on the policies of Argentina or its creditors. Argentina was able to borrow at excessive spreads, which simply worsened its fiscal position and exacerbated the crisis and its consequences. This is a case where a write-down of the debt is needed, in order to return to sustainable growth as soon as possible.

Case 2 (Table 9.4) is exactly the opposite. No major macroeconomic disequilibria were observable, insofar as the outstanding stocks were concerned; spreads were correspondingly low. In the case of Mexico, however, it is clear that the large current account deficit was creating liquidity pressures. On the other hand, Korea failed by none of these criteria. Indeed, its weakness came from elsewhere—the short-term nature of its debt. As the current account demonstrates, however, there was no particular need for a major exchange rate adjustment.

In Case 3 (see Table 9.5), the sovereign risk pertains to the nature of the debtor. Despite good macroeconomic performance, creditors could examine the macroeconomics and perceive the risk of defaults that the shaky government or the shaky banking system could create. The spreads were correspondingly high.

Let us summarize the discussion so far with Table 9.6.

Table 9.4. Case 2: Unexpected Crises in Mexico and Korea (data two years before the crisis)

	Mexico	Korea
D/X	180%	76%
D/GDP	35%	25%
Spreads (basis points)	200	150
Current account (% of GDP)	−7.2%	−1.9%

Table 9.5. Case 3: Foretold Crises Without Apparent Macroeconomic Disequilibria (data two years before the crisis)

	Turkey	Russia
D/X	194%	121%
D/GDP	54%	26%
Spreads (basis points)	500	800
Current account (% of GDP)	−0.7%	+0.7%

Compared to the 1980s, then, it does not appear to be the case that large disequilibria went unnoticed by the markets. The high debt/low spread cell is empty.

The Dynamics of High Debt/High Spreads

Case 1 is a case where high debt comes with high spreads. Clearly high debt is bound to cause high spreads, but the reverse is also true: high spreads cause high debt through the snowball effect of the interest bill on debt accumulation. In order to shed some light on this debate, we have decomposed the debt dynamics into the following identity:

Increase of the Debt-to-GDP ratio =

real interest rate * Debt-to-GDP ratio

– Growth rate of the economy* Debt-to-GDP ratio

– Primary Surplus/GDP

The real interest rate is the nominal rate (risk-free rate + spread) adjusted for the deviation of the exchange rate from PPP. The dynamics are computed up to the year of the debt crisis itself. We present this decomposition below by dividing each of the three terms of the right-hand side by the sum of their absolute values (the sum of absolute value then adds to one). We reach the results set out in Table 9.7.

The first term is roughly interpreted as a *confidence premium*, the second term as a measure of the underlying fundamentals and the third term as a measure of the policy choices. We see that, on average, the growth component (second

Table 9.6. Summary Table

	High debt	Low debt
Low spread	None	Case 2
High spread	Case 1	Case 3

Table 9.7. Debt Dynamics

	Int+Change	Growth	Deficit
Argentina	0.16	−0.51	0.33
Brazil	0.47	−0.51	0.02
Colombia	0.01	−0.98	−0.01
Korea	0.22	−0.26	0.52
Ecuador	0.42	−0.54	−0.04
India	0.35	−0.49	0.16
Indonesia	0.10	−0.73	0.17
Malaysia	−0.07	−0.49	0.44
Mexico	−0.45	−0.51	0.04
Pakistan	−0.25	−0.45	0.30
Panama	0.07	−0.40	−0.54
Papoua	0.51	−0.37	0.12
Peru	0.25	−0.73	−0.02
Philippines	−0.46	−0.07	−0.47
Russia	+0.50	−0.50	0
Thailand	−0.06	−0.33	0.61
Turkey	0.52	−0.10	−0.39
Uruguay	−0.85	0.00	0.14
Venezuela	−0.41	−0.08	−0.51
Zimbabwe	0.29	−0.50	−0.20

Note: Each item expressed as a fraction of the sum of absolute value.

column) is the critical factor behind the dynamics of debt. The confidence premium factor (first column) is the second important item, while the deficit itself appears to play the least important role. Some countries are heavily burdened by the confidence crisis term: Brazil, Ecuador, Turkey, and Russia are all instances where it almost entirely cancels the (beneficial) growth factor. This decomposition suggests two policy implications. Given the fact that bad 'fundamentals' are also a major part of the story, we conclude that debt write-off may also be needed. Finally, the role of the confidence term suggests that efficient measures (taken ex ante and ex post) could alleviate the importance of that term.

A Brief Investigation into the Lucas Paradox[9]

While default in the 1980s came as a surprise to many lenders (whose maxim at the time was that countries do not default), it was certainly not news to economic historians. A collection of papers in Eichengreen and Lindert (1989) reminded the profession, in retrospect, of the history of past defaults in the nineteenth century and in the 1930s. In a recent paper, Reinhart and Rogoff (2003) call the phenomenon 'serial default' and make the link between the pattern of default of many emerging countries (especially Latin American)

[9] This section is based on Cohen and Soto (2002).

Table 9.8. Capital/Output Ratio (volume, Summers-Heston data)

	Physical output to physical capital
Rich countries	1
Middle- and low-income countries excluding SSA	1.86
Sub-Saharan Africa (SSA)	3.77

Sources: See Cohen and Soto (2002) for sources and sample used.

and what is called the Lucas Paradox. The paradox is that capital does not flow into the poor countries where capital is scarce, against the neoclassical view that the return to capital accumulation should be higher where capital is rare. Lucas concludes that the neoclassical paradigm should be abandoned, while Reinhart and Rogoff conclude that the risk premium due to bad behavior is the main culprit. Following my work with Marcelo Soto, I want to sketch here why there is in fact no paradox at all, once account is taken of the lack of integration of the goods and services markets.

In Cohen and Soto (2002), we present capital stock data that first confirm that capital accumulation is indeed significantly lower in poor countries. The data come as follows (see Table 9.8).

The capital output ratio is about three times lower in Africa and about 50 percent lower in Latin America than in the rich countries. These data, however, are used in volume terms, using Summers and Heston data after PPP corrections (as they should be from the perspective of a producer). But these results clearly do not hold when using current values. When investments and output are evaluated in current dollars (at current exchange rates), there is no paradox at all: the capital output ratios are fairly identical across countries (see Table 9.9).

This sheds a new perspective on the cause of capital shortage. No foreign investors would invest in a local grocery store. Its market value, in current prices, is too low, due to the fact that its customers are essentially too poor. This is precisely what the Summers and Heston data intend to correct. From a Wall Street perspective, however, this is not good enough. The reason why capital markets do not deliver an equalization of capital ratios has therefore more to do with the fact that goods markets remain poorly integrated (the

Table 9.9. Capital/Output Ratio (value, current dollars)

	Physical output to physical capital
Rich countries	1
Middle- and low-income countries excluding SSA	1.02
Sub-Saharan Africa (SSA)	0.90

Table 9.10. Capital/Output Ratio (manufacturing)

	Physical output to physical capital
Rich countries	1
Middle- and low-income countries excluding SSA	1.33
Sub-Saharan Africa (SSA)	1.76

Source: See Causa and Cohen (2004) for sources and sample used.

share of non-traded goods remaining a critical dimension of most economies) than because of capital imperfections themselves.

As proof that this is indeed the case, one can simply measure the capital/output ratio in manufacturing (the traded good sector) (see Table 9.10). In this case, one finds that the capital/output ratio is in fact higher in the poor countries than in the rich, and even much higher in Africa than in other poor countries.

Table 9.10 shows that in poor countries there is no shortage of capital. In fact, Africa—which was among the least endowed countries in infrastructure—appears to be among the best capitalized countries in terms of physical capital. More generally, in Causa and Cohen (2004), we find that the capital/output ratio is, in general, the highest among the poor countries. This can be coined as an *anti-Lucas Paradox*. The intuition that we offer is that poor countries, lacking other inputs such as infrastructure, use physical capital as a substitute for the scarcity of those missing inputs. If we take this line of interpretation, this means that poor countries do not borrow too little. The problem seems rather that they borrow too much, borrowed capital being one way to supplement other missing inputs. It should then come as no surprise, from a neoclassical perspective, that the returns to foreign capital are low. This sheds a different light on what one should expect the financial markets to perform. Rather than focusing on raising the transfer of capital from rich to poor countries, financial markets are more needed to diversify risk or to accommodate shocks. This is unfortunately the function that they do worse. This is why the resolution of crises, which are the worst way to deal with unforeseen events, comes first on the list of any agenda of reform of the financial architecture.

An Agenda of Reforms

The debate over debt sustainability has gained a number of critical insights over the course of the last three decades. We know more about the willingness of countries to sustain external debt in the face of an adverse shock; we know more about the market value of external debt and its determinants. We also learned much about the role of confidence crisis in undermining the solvency of a country. Where we have learned little, however, is on how to avoid debt crises being endlessly repeated, how to address them when they start, how to close them when they erupt. This is the topic that we now address.

Bankruptcy Court

In November 2001, Anne Krueger, First Deputy Managing Director of the IMF, advocated a sovereign debt restructuring mechanism (SDRM) to facilitate a declaration of insolvency for an overindebted country along the lines of chapter 11 of the US Bankruptcy Code (Krueger 2001). Despite subsequent revisions that reduced the role of the IMF (Krueger 2002), the SDRM was shelved at the April 2003 meetings, specifically because it would have required an amendment to the articles (IMF 2003). Setting up an international court with authority over the handling of sovereign debt would entail a substantial transfer of sovereignty in order to give the court the statutory basis for suspending legal procedures against a country. This was felt to go too far, especially by the US government.

Beyond these political constraints, a number of authors have argued that one should be careful before making a comparison between sovereign and corporate debts. For one thing, a firm that goes bankrupt keeps an intrinsic value, which can be sold by creditors. This is not the case for a country. Aggregate GDP is not something that can be shipped home by the creditors. Some kind of willingness to pay on the part of the country is always needed. Second, because creditors have no collateral, the value of their claim is proportionate to the harm that they can inflict on defaulting countries. Defaults need to be 'bad and ugly' if one wants to deter debtors from reneging on their debt. This is bad ex post for the country but may be good ex ante, insofar as it may raise the supply of credit. This is one reason why many big debtors such as Brazil are reluctant to participate in an SDRM: they fear that the mechanism would frighten their creditors and precipitate the crisis.

Neither of these arguments is fully convincing, however. For one thing, although it is true that payment always depends on the 'willingness to pay' of indebted countries, it is also clearly the case that this willingness, being conditioned by the threat of sanctions, is proportional to GDP or exports, although clearly by a factor lower than one (see above). But this brings us to a second argument. There are two ways of interpreting 'bad and ugly' renegotiations. Take a country that has the choice between paying its debt in full or default. Payment in full will be preferred over default whenever the debt is lower than a given threshold. Past this threshold, however, the optimum strategy is not to let the country default but to get it to pay an amount below the face value of the debt. This is obviously superior to outright default both ex post (the country is perhaps indifferent but the creditors get something) and ex ante (since this results in higher lending initially). This is why, just like any usual bankruptcy court, a mechanism that enhances collective rationality of decision-making in case of default should be welcome.

There is, however, an additional critical difference between a country and a firm that relates to the risk of a confidence crisis. If a country finds it difficult to borrow for whatever reason, then it may be endogenously obliged to default, in effect fulfilling the initial fear. Self-fulfilling debt crises are a phenomenon whose theoretical rationale has been pointed out by Calvo (1988), Cole and Kehoe (1996, 2000), and others. The intuitive rationale is quite simple: perception of high risk raises the spread, which in turn raises the debt service burden, which in turn provokes the debt crises. The reason why this may happen as a rational equilibrium is the fact that the fundamentals out of which a country can service its debt are partly endogenous to its creditworthiness. If default reduces the amount that a country can service (even reduces this ability to nothing in the case of outright default) then lenders that expect that nothing will be paid do indeed get nothing. This is less likely in the case of corporate debt if default simply amounts, say, to changing the management of the firm.

Drawing on this analogy we show analytically, in Cohen and Portes (2004), that an ex post efficient debt resolution mechanism *destroys* the risk of a self-fulfilling debt crisis. The intuition behind this proposition is straightforward. A self-fulfilling debt crisis originates from the fact that the fundamentals out of which the debt is repaid may be endogeneously lowered in case of outright default. When an efficient debt workout is implemented instead, the fundamentals are unaffected by the debt contract. The risk of a self-fulfilling debt crisis disappears. This is why focusing on efficient ex post solutions is also critical from an ex ante point of view.

CACs

In the absence of an SDRM, ex post efficient renegotiation remains a daunting issue. The broad phrase ‘collective action clauses’ has been extended to cover a wide range of proposals aimed at circumventing the absence of a bankruptcy court. As specified in Eichengreen and Portes (1995) and supplemented recently by Taylor (2002), these would bring into bond contracts (and indeed to bank lending instruments) a range of clauses that would promote orderly workouts of international debt, rather than the chaotic sequel to default that we observe now, for example, in the Argentine case. These would include initiation and engagement clauses detailing how negotiations would proceed; a clause permitting changes by a qualified majority in the terms of the debt, including amounts and dates payable; a sharing clause that would require pro rata distribution to all bondholders of any payment made to any one of them; and a non-acceleration clause to avoid having one missed payment trigger an immediate full repayment obligation.[10] An additional contractual innovation that would facilitate restructurings would be to utilize the trust deed form for bonds (common under UK law but not in New York). Here the trustee acts for all holders of a given security and centralizes enforcement of any decisions (in particular, the trustee shares among the bondholders the proceeds of any settlement).

In addition to the existing Paris Club and London Club mechanisms, which deal with debt to governments and to banks respectively, there would be a permanent (but 'light') bondholders committee—the 'New York Club,' say. It would look not unlike the previous CFB and FBPC. It would oversee bondholders' negotiations with the debtor. There might also be a new mediation agency—again, an administratively 'light' structure that would coordinate the Paris Club, London Club, and New York Club, primarily ensuring the timely exchange of information and comparison of assumptions. It would verify claims and oversee bondholder voting. It might take on other roles, for example endorsing (or not) a proposed standstill. The proposal of the Institute for International Finance to bring all creditors into a single negotiating committee seems unnecessarily to override existing structures, the Paris and London clubs, that work efficiently.

There is a relatively simple, feasible way of implementing these proposals. The mandates of the American SEC and the British FSA include duties to protect investors and to maintain orderly markets. That is sufficient justification and authority, without new legislation, for them to intervene. It is clear from the case of Argentina that those markets were and are disorderly and that investors have not been adequately protected against the eventuality of default by having adequate post-default procedures in place.

[10] It has been objected that including such clauses in international debt contracts would weaken the bonding role of debt and thereby provoke lenders to withdraw, reducing or disrupting market access for countries that now have it or aspire to it. Such objections ignore or dismiss well-supported empirical results from comparisons of 'British style' bonds, which typically do have such CACs, to otherwise equivalent 'American style' bonds, which do not. This work shows at most some tendency for terms to 'bad' borrowers to be inferior under the 'British' bonds, whereas the terms to 'good' borrowers (as measured by credit ratings) are in fact better than under the American bonds. Problems remain—for example, how to deal with old bonds that do not include such clauses? Bonds are often exchanged, and this could be facilitated with 'sweeteners' if necessary. The New York Club could deal with cross-issue coordination—there is ample historical precedent in the activities of the CFB and FBPC. It seems infeasible and perhaps undesirable to have in each instrument a 'meta-CAC' that would in effect impose qualified majority voting among all bondholders, whose result would cover all outstanding instruments of a given debtor. The 'aggregation problem' is not trivial, but the combination of new institutions and CACs can deal with it satisfactorily.

Thus we propose that the American, British, and other major financial center regulatory authorities stipulate that bonds issued or traded in their markets must include CACs and other workout friendly clauses. The IMF could organize and indeed help to fund a voluntary exchange program (with enhancements) for outstanding stocks of securities without such clauses. And the Fund should make access to the SRF (indeed, any Fund program) open only to countries that use CACs.

LLR and LFR

Drawing upon the lessons of the Asian crisis, Stanley Fischer (1999) first proposed that the IMF act as international lender of last resort (ILLR). As argued by many commentators, however (e.g., Wyplosz 2003), an ILLR must have at its disposal either the resources to inject an indeterminate quantity of fresh liquidity or perfect information regarding solvent and insolvent financial intermediaries. As the latter assumption is virtually ruled out by the very nature of financial crises, the former is tantamount to giving the IMF the means to create liquidity *ex nihilo*. As related above, such a transfer of monetary sovereignty, which was extremely difficult to implement in the European case, seems totally unrealistic on a world scale. If there is to be a world LLR, it is rather for the large central banks (Fed, ECB, and BoJ) to play this role.

The LLR role, however, is not a singled peak. Two cases can actually arise. One is in which confidence lost can only be restored by big bail outs. This is the standard LLR case such as evidenced with Mexico in 1995. Cole and Kehoe have shown, however, that another case is also possible. This is when a country which is losing the confidence of the market would want, on its own, to reduce its debt in order to restore the confidence lost. In this case, a country needs to buy time in order to willingly move out of the 'danger zone' where spreads are rising and the risk of a confidence crisis looms. This is the case of Brazil now, which attempts, despite the odds of the creditors, to escape the danger zone of high spreads/high debt. It would be a shame, for the sake of the future of the financial markets, that it would fail in this attempt. This is a case where, we argue with Richard Portes, a lender of *first* resort would be needed.

Assume that a country manages to commit itself *not* to borrow at punitive rates. Think for instance of a kind of 'usury law' that the country would apply to itself, forbidding it to borrow above a given interest threshold, say a spread over 400 basis points. In models of self-fulfilling debt crises, a debtor that is the victim of a confidence shock may want to get out of the danger zone by taking stringent actions. A country which could have gained credibility in reacting to such fears may buy time to get out of the danger zone.

Let us now investigate what it takes to make such a mechanism credible. Assume that a country initially borrows at low spreads: think of Mexico today, and assume that a new shock (fall in the price of oil...) suddenly lowers the market's assessment of its creditworthiness. If the country accepts higher spreads, it 'gambles for resurrection' by taking the chance that things will eventually settle down, or simply buys time in order to make internal adjustments. The problem with this option is that the debt may meanwhile spiral upwards, making it more difficult ex post to get the country to act decisively. For a country that is committed, say, to a 300–400 basis point spread, the IMF should work with the country on an analysis of the cause of the problem and of the remedies which could resolve it. A program would then be designed which, if agreed upon by the country, could grant access to IMF money if needed.

Nothing should be automatic in this process. Countries signal ex ante their willingness to avoid the snowball effect of rising spreads and rising debts and seek to avoid it at an early stage. But IMF support remains conditional on taking appropriate measures, so that it is not a free lunch. Furthermore, IMF money could be granted at a rate that incorporates a spread, say of 300 basis points, so that countries will not necessarily want to tap IMF resources.

One may fear that the informational content of spreads will be reduced as they become a policy variable (a version of Goodhart's law). It is true that lenders, being aware of the fact that countries will take actions against rising spreads, will change their pricing policy. If, as a result, spreads become lower, this is in itself a good thing as it reduces the snowball effect. But it is very unlikely that they could fail to detect a country that becomes insolvent. Indeed, actions to correct imbalances are voluntary, not automatic. Lenders must then keep track of a debtor's solvency. But the policy may achieve the role of making self-fulfilling spread crises if not impossible, at least less likely.

The merit of this approach, we believe, is that it allows the country to take very early corrective actions, with the support of IMF loans. By acting early the measures should not be daunting. By showing its willingness to act, the country further boosts its reputation, not too late as is often the case, but early on when the country can still see the benefit of raising its profile in the eyes of international investors. In our view this mechanism could replace the now defunct Contingent Credit Line Facility. The CCL was created to help 'first class policy' countries to face confidence shocks. The reason why no country ever decided to use the CCL was the fear of sending a wrong signal to the market, despite the quasi-pre-qualification clauses that were attached to it. Our mechanism instead is one which relies only on market signal (spreads) so that it would not run into such risk. The reason why we attach so much importance to spreads is that they both reveal a problem and contribute to creating it.

Conclusion

Building upon the previous discussion, we find it useful to distinguish three different cases pertaining to the debt accumulated by an emerging country.

- *Hair cut*: this occurs when the debt is too large, and a debt write-down is needed. This was typical of the Brady initiative, although it took too long to be acknowledged. This is the case which is usually associated to a bankruptcy court, or an SDRM.[11] The key role of the IMF should then be to act as an umpire of the debt reduction discussion between debtors and creditors. ('We provide the program, you deliver the money' as was coined by the Managing Director of the IMF in the 1980s.)
- *Big bailout*: this is the case where only a massive rescue of a country can salvage a country from a confidence crisis. This was typically the Mexican or the Asian cases. This is the branch which is usually associated with the lender of *last* resort. Many commentators argue that this is rather a role for central banks than for the IMF.
- *Lender of* first *resort*: this is a case where the country wants to take action to restore confidence, even though they still have access to the financial markets. The IMF can help, as usual with liquidity and a program, to gain time. This is the case of Brazil now.

Only when these three functions are each given an institutional recognition will it become easier to avoid the endless repetition of financial crises.

Poor Countries: A Post-HIPC Agenda[12]

The HIPC Initiative has involved 38 eligible countries. To date, debt reduction packages have been approved for 27 countries, 23 of them in Africa, providing US$31 billion (net present value terms) in debt service relief over time. Taking the 27 countries together, the NPV of total debt is projected to be reduced by 53 percent. For all HIPCs, the debt relief under the initiative accounts for a weighted average of 33 percent of their GNI. By 2005, the weighted average NPV of debt-to-exports ratio for the 27 DC countries is projected to decline from almost 300 percent before HIPC relief to 128 percent, while the weighted average NPV of the debt-to-GDP is projected to decline from 60 percent before HIPC relief to 30 percent. By 2001, the average debt service-to-exports ratio for HIPCs had already fallen below the corresponding ratio in other low-income countries.

[11] See Sachs (1981); Eichengreen and Portes (1995); Krueger (2002); Rogoff and Zettelmeyer (2003).

[12] This section relies on Cohen and Vellutini (2003).

However, although the broad picture that emerges from these facts is encouraging, a number of critical questions must be addressed, regarding the high degree of diversity in the debt situations of HIPCs. First, the dispersion among HIPCs is significant. In terms of relief to GNI, while the maximum debt relief is reaped by Sao Tomé (227 percent of GNI), at the lower end of the spectrum other HIPCs such as Senegal or Honduras are receiving debt relief for only 10 percent of their GNI. Within HIPC countries the effects of the initiative are therefore wide open. Furthermore, while debt relief is by definition well correlated to the level of debt, it has, within HIPC countries themselves, no correlation whatsoever with poverty, however defined (see Cohen and Vellutini 2003).

If one analyzes the implications of the initiative across HIPC and non-HIPC the outcomes are not better. In 1999, ODA to HIPCs accounted for 26 percent of ODA to LICs. In 2001, the proportion had risen to 32 percent. These figures are consistent with the fact that, as argued by Powell (2000), the enhanced initiative, by lowering the qualification thresholds and by setting more ambitious objectives in terms of debt reduction (namely, of ratio of debt to exports of 150 percent instead of 200 percent previously), is effectively introducing a bias in favor of HIPCs—to the detriment of other poor countries. Importantly, Powell (2000) emphasizes that this re-allocation is unrelated to poverty prevalence and policy performance. Furthermore, beyond the provision of financial resources, an important objective of the HIPC initiative is to encourage policy and institutional reforms. The integration of the HIPC process with PRSPs is in itself a positive development. There does not appear, however, to be any positive correlation between the HIPC relief and policy performance. Countries that are projected to mostly benefit from the HIPC are in fact the countries with the worst policy environments.

Finally, a central premise of the HIPC initiative is that debt relief should be additional to existing aid assistance. Ensuring additionality ex ante has been notoriously difficult, essentially because aid flows at the donors' end are affected by the very phenomenon that has proved pervasive in beneficiary countries: fungibility. Indeed, it is always an open possibility for donors to totally or partially compensate for their debt relief effort by a reduction of their other aid flows, be it at country by country level, regionally or globally. Not surprisingly, there is no formal mechanism for monitoring additionality in the initiative, let alone enforcing it. The only attempts made to assess additionality have inevitably been on an ex post basis, looking back at how debt relief has affected net aid flows. The longest experience in debt relief is by far the one of bilateral donors.[13] The evidence suggests that the additionality of the debt relief provided by bilateral donors, for which a long

[13] See for example Cohen and Vellutini (2003).

track record already exists, has been weak, to say the least (see Birdsall et al. 2002).

How to Achieve More Debt Relief

To sum up, debt relief comes up with a central problem: its impact of aid allocation across LICs. This fact thus makes it difficult to simply recommend an unqualified new round of debt relief. Despite its pitfalls in terms of resource allocation, however, debt relief has some interesting characteristics of fresh budget support—first and foremost because it is not allocated to specific projects but is rather supporting the entire governmental program. In addition, debt relief does not exhibit some of the problematic characteristics of aid flows: low stability, low predictability, and high pro-cyclicality. Several studies have found that aid flows are even more volatile than fiscal revenue or output and highly unpredictable (the difference between committed and disbursed flows, for example, is very significant).[14] They are also sometimes found to be pro-cyclical. In this context, debt reduction can be viewed as a special form of budget support that strengthens the public monitoring process. In contrast, a plethora of separate donor-funded projects makes it harder for domestic stakeholders to monitor flows of funds and implementation of government plans.

It would obviously create a perverse incentive to enhance resource transfers in the form of debt relief to countries that are debt stressed and poor while ignoring LICs that are managing their debt servicing outflows but are also subject to the same MDG financing deficits. The principles guiding ODA should be about fully funding the MDGs—whether the LICs being considered are heavily indebted or not. The risk of the debt forgiveness approach, again, is that providing additional debt relief benefits those countries that have built up large debts, at the expense of those which have not. As summed up above, one of the key problems with the HIPC initiative is the lack of correlation between poverty needs, good governance and debt reduction. The poorest nations are not receiving the most through the HIPC initiative, nor do the best governed ones. The initiative is in this respect a hybrid mix, which acknowledges that the indebted countries are too poor to sustain their debt and yet, by itself, ignores the situation of other countries which either made the effort to service their debt or were excluded in the first place from borrowing.

In response to this criticism, NGOs have proposed a common approach to financing LICs. The idea is to give an 'equivalent' amount to HIPC and

[14] See for example IMF (2003).

non-HIPC in the form of budget support. This forms the basis of the PAIR proposal which we now present.[15]

The PAIR proposal, formulated by four Belgian economists[16] and first presented by the Belgian Prime Minister at the Monterrey Conference in March 2002 and later at the OECD Ministerial Meeting in Paris in May 2002, goes a long way towards addressing this question. The proposal draws on the debt sustainability approach formulated by CAFOD and extends it in three directions: (i) the proposed eligibility criterion is defined by an HDI lower than 0.5 in 1997—this characterizes 49 countries, compared with 41 eligible HIPCs; (ii) donors should be the 23 richer countries with a financial contribution for 15 years consisting of two parts: a flat contribution equal to 0.05 percent of GDP and a variable contribution equal to the gap between their current ODA levels and the reference target of 0.7 percent of GDP; and (iii) a 15-year firm program should be established, fully funded from the start, for implementing the DAC/MDG targets and extinguishing the foreign debt of the 49 poor countries selected.

The annual contributions of the 23 countries estimated at some US$22 billion would be paid to a trust fund that would acquire all the eligible public and publicly guaranteed debt of the selected 49 countries, which in 1997 NPV terms is estimated at US$188 billion, offering a price to creditors reflecting its market value at an estimated amount of US$88 billion. Only the unsustainable part of the debt would be canceled. The sustainable part, now owed by the trust fund, would continue to be serviced with the proceeds used towards financing the Millennium Development Goals targets, in addition to the remaining budget of the fund. This approach, backed by the human development sustainability definition, corresponds to an objective of distributive fairness across poor countries, as sustainable debt service provides resources to human development in all poor countries, not only the debtor country itself.

If one were to separate the debt problem from the achievement of the Millennium Development Goals targets, the trust fund budget could be reduced from US$325 to US$88 billion. Most of the needed funding would be transferred to the fund debt instruments held by rich countries or multilateral institutions. The debt eligible for total cancellation is the long-term, public or publicly guaranteed debt (PPG), outstanding and disbursed (DOD), with respect to official (multilateral and bi-lateral) donors as well as private creditors. It also includes interest arrears on long-term debt as well as the use of IMF credit. It does not include private debt which is not publicly guaranteed nor short-term PPG debt due to private creditors.

[15] I thank, without implicating, Francis Lemoine from Eurodad for useful discussions on this topic.

[16] See Berlage et al. (2000).

As said, the debt in 1997 NPV terms of the 49 poorest countries is of US$188 billion. Its budgetary cost is estimated taking into account the fact that the debt will not realistically be fully serviced. The actual write-off of the debt from its NPV to its market or economic value is considered as a balance sheet clean-up operation. In fact, different discount rates are applied by the Belgian economists according to the nature of the creditors. For instance, the debt held by the IMF and the World Bank is valued at full NPV, given the particular seniority status of these creditors. The amount estimated to compensate multilateral creditors is thus estimated at US$55 billion, including US$21 billion for non-concessional and US$34 billion for concessional debt. For bilateral official creditors, the residual economic value is set at 30 percent of NPV for non-concessional debt and 15 percent for concessional debt; the total cost is thus estimated at US$25 billion, with US$20 billion for non-concessional and US$5 billion for concessional debt. For private creditors, assuming they agree on a *pari passu* discount, a buyback value of 30 percent to the claims yields a cost of US$8 billion.

A 'FAIR' Proposal[17]

The PAIR proposal came before the Monterrey commitments. It may be possible to present a leaner version of this project, based on the promises that have been offered, while keeping the overall approach. Britain and France, for instance, have proposed an innovative financing mechanism to double ODA quickly. According to this proposal, an international financing facility (IFF) would raise funds by issuing bonds on capital markets, and would provide predictable and guaranteed assistance flows up to 2015. After that date, with bonds falling due, aid flows would decline. The attractiveness of this scheme comes from the fact that it would provide large and predictable increases in aid in the period during which the MDGs should be met. The IFF would be supportive of best practices to reduce poverty, and be predictable enough to finance medium and long-term strategies. We would envisage our proposal within this or a similar facility.

These ODA commitments would allow the international community to proceed in a more orderly way. They offer new opportunities to further the HIPC Initiative in ways which are not detrimental to non-HIPC countries. Within the IFF framework, every poor country is entitled to a predictable amount of budget support. One idea, following the PAIR proposal, would then be to entitle HIPCs to cash in (part of) the ODA that they are entitled to, upfront, through a one-off debt reduction, while the non-HIPC countries would receive their share in due time.

[17] This section draws on useful discussions with representatives of Eurodad. The authors of the report bear obviously sole responsibility for its content.

If the one-off swap (future grants against debt cancellation) were made at face value, this would bring some benefits to the poor countries, but it is unlikely that many of them would be interested in the swap. A discount on the swap, reflecting the 'market price' of the debt could, however, be offered to those countries; by which they could turn US$100 of grant into say US$150 of debt reduction. This would have the great merit of being both consistent with the initiative's sunset clause; of giving new room for maneuver to multilateral donors and for addressing the fairness issue that has been used so often as an argument against the debt reduction process. The discount that would be offered to LICs on their external, official debt is a highly political question, but it should be grounded on the economics of debt repayment. I documented in the second section of this chapter what was the 'price' of LDC debt, based upon market valuation by the banks of middle income debt in the late 1980s. This could be a basis for action. According to the computations presented in Table 9.2, a debt that is worth 150 percent of exports, yields a 'market' value representing approximately 100 percent of exports. (By comparison, for a debt worth 250 percent of exports, the market value only represented 90 percent of exports.)

The idea of a one-off swap at a discount is supported by a number of precedents that do exist in LICs.[18] A particularly interesting example of this is a number of Paris Club agreements containing a debt swap provision, *at a discount*. It enabled creditor countries to undertake LIC debt swaps on a bi-lateral and voluntary basis. These operations may be 'debt for nature,'[19] 'debt for aid,'[20] debt for equity swaps or other local currency debt swaps. Debt to equity, for example, typically involve the sale of the debt by the creditor government—at a discount—to an investor who in turn sells the debt to the debtor government in return for shares in a local company or for local currency to be used in projects in the debtor country. The debt swap option is available for low-income countries and lower-middle-income countries. The discount rates have reportedly varied between 50 and 95 percent of face value. And the US government, which is mandated by Congress to estimate the present value of its loan portfolio in value, applies a 92 percent discount to its HIPC debt.

We can summarize this idea as follows: each country, within the Monterrey/IFF framework, is entitled in the future to a given amount of budget support. HIPCs could have the right to front load part of this budget support through a one-off swap of the grant that they expect into debt reduction. A discount on the debt would be offered. We call it a FAIR proposal.

[18] As is well known, middle-income countries have extensively used debt swaps (see for example Cohen 2000).

[19] With the objective of funding environmental projects.

[20] Essentially a similar mechanism as the one used by the HIPC Initiative, through using foregone debt service as aid—but again with a key difference: at a discount.

In Favor of a Fund to Stabilize Poor Countries' Income[21]

Debt relief is only a technical ploy. The crux of the matter for poor countries remains the fact that they are heavily dependent on a few commodities which make their income highly volatile. Because commodity prices are slow to recover from adverse shocks, any attempt to stabilize prices at a given level has failed in the past. Either there is a positive shock and the stabilization fund becomes so rich that the temptation to expropriate it becomes too strong. Or there is a bad shock and soon the fund becomes insolvent. This explains why most people have concluded that not much should be done to stabilize commodity prices.

As explained in the introduction, this should not imply that nothing should be done at all. What is needed is a less ambitious scheme which nevertheless provides some insurance to the poorest countries. In what follows, we calibrate how much it would cost to offer the poor countries an insurance scheme that would protect the price of the commodities that they sell against deviation from a moving average of past prices. By doing so, we accomplish two things. We make the income of the poor countries more predictable. We do not offer to lean against the wind. If the price of a commodity rises or falls for long, we do translate, with a lag, the change in the price levels into the income of the country. By this mechanism, we avoid the pitfalls of past stabilization schemes.

Technically, we seek to analyze how a stabilization agency could guarantee a price p_t^* to an exporting country, where p_t^* is a moving average of its previous values

$$p_{t-d-1},\ p_{t-d-2},\ \ldots,\ p_{t-d-h}$$

in which h is the time horizon over which the average is taken and d is the delay between the spot and the moving average. The stabilization is done through a fund, which is initially endowed with an amount $F_0 > 0$ in period $t > 0$. The quantity exported by the country is normalized to unity. Subsequently, for $t > 1$, the fund evolves according to the following rule:

$$F_t = (1 + r)F_{t-1} + (p_t - p_t^*)$$

The real interest rate r is assumed to be constant over time. The aim of this chapter is to determine the probability of depletion of the fund and to investigate how much resources are needed to avoid (with various degrees of probability) its bankruptcy.

In order to calibrate our results, we use monthly commodity prices reported in the International Monetary Fund's International Financial Statistics, for the period January 1957 to December 2003. The commodities used for the

[21] This section is based on Cohen et al. (2007).

Table 9.11. Selected Commodities

Commodities	Sample period	Price 7/2003	Annual value (million US$)
Bananas	1/1975–12/2003	296.3 US$/ton	3,438
Cocoa beans	1/1957–12/2003	1,556.87 US$/ton	43,287
Cotton	1/1957–12/2003	60.19 US cts/lb	4,248
Rice	1/1957–12/2003	199.48 US$/ton	3,970

study are presented in Table 9.11. For each selected commodity, it presents the sample period used for the study, the spot price in July 2003, then a figure which can be regarded as a rough estimate of the total exports of developing countries and, finally, the IFS series code of the data used. In the following analysis, all prices will be real prices, deflated by a US producer prices index, taking July 2003 as the reference.[22]

Table 9.12 reports our key results.

For example, the line of table about cocoa means that, if stabilization is done for cocoa beans: with an initial endowment of 1.8 times the annual value of trade (US$ 17.5 billion in 2003), the fund will always remain positive with probability 90 percent. With an initial endowment worth 2.6 times the volume of trade, the fund will never become negative, even at an infinite time horizon (this is in fact a general statistical property that we document in a companion working paper).

The scheme so defined could be used in a variety of fashions: either to directly help producers protect themselves against adverse shocks or to calibrate ODA to a government against the fluctuation of the economy. The scheme could also help tailor new loans to commodity-dependent countries, which could smooth their repayment pattern accordingly. The order of magnitudes that we present should allow whichever party is interested in provisioning the mechanism, and make it credible.

Still another option would be to create *new debt instruments* that explicitly account for exogenous risks. In essence, these instruments would link debt service directly to commodity prices and index the debt service profile to a commodity price index, such that commodity price declines could trigger postponement or adjustment in the debt service. This is much in the spirit of Hausmann and Rigobon (2002), who indeed have gone even further. They argue that IDA loans should be in local currencies, with only a clause pertaining to inflation. LICs have good reasons to borrow in foreign currency: domestic currency markets abroad are essentially non-existent. Even the IBRD

[22] We computed some tests to fit a statistical model for each of the price series. We have restricted ourselves to ARMA models for the price series, either stationary around a linear trend, or difference stationary. The statistical models we have fitted now enable us to simulate the behavior of the commodity prices (using Monte-Carlo simulations), and therefore the behavior of the stabilization fund.

Table 9.12. Endowment to Stabilize Prices (as a fraction of trade volumes)

Commodity	50%	90%	95%	99%	Upper bound
Bananas	0.39	1.12	1.36	1.87	2.68
Cocoa	0.78	1.8	1.97	2.19	2.68
Cotton	0.65	1.26	1.4	1.62	2.68
Rice	0.93	1.75	1.9	2.11	2.68

window of the World Bank lends in dollars because it must fund itself in the same capital markets that do not accept local currency denominations. The IDA window also lends in dollars but does not have this excuse. It is funded with fiscal resources and could lend, in principle, in any unit it wishes to. Haussman and Rigobon thus argue that it should lend in inflation indexed domestic currency. With 83 member countries, IDA should be able to achieve, they argue, a significant amount of risk diversification among its members. Such purchasing power adjusted loans would actually carry little risk given IDA's portfolio: simulating over the past 20 years the numerical implications of their recommendation they find that the IDA would have suffered no loss.

Yet such contingent loans have been rare, particularly those that would index debt service upon terms of trade fluctuations. In Cohen and Vellutini (2003) we review examples that come closest to the concept of a contingent lending facility as just defined. It can be seen that none of them in scope and in essence can be readily used for the purpose of covering exogenous shocks in LICs, except, potentially, the EC's B Envelope. Should the international community take seriously the idea that debt crisis prevention should be kept at the forefront of policy priorities, there is clearly a need for new policy instruments to act speedily upon debt signals, be it through a revived trust fund. One option would then be to prolong the trust fund, which could then keep the role that it has had in the framework of the HIPC Initiative: to enable the World Bank, IMF, and other multilateral donors to provision their claims and to write them off when needed, subject to a careful analysis of the underlying causes. This trust fund could then be granted a one-off endowment, out of the Monterrey commitments, to the benefit of multilateral agencies themselves.

Conclusion

To summarize the key ideas that we have developed in this report, what the international financial system needs is a set of new instruments—especially for the poorest countries; new rules of behavior—especially for the middle-income countries; and a new set of institutions geared towards a more cooperative outcome between creditors and debtors. This falls short of the kind of institutions that exist within a sovereign state, but it would be illusory to think that these could emerge from scratch. Time is needed to build new institutions, which is why one should not lose time in creating their premises.

References

Bazdarich, M. (1978). 'Optimal Growth and Stages in the Balance of Payments'. *Journal of International Economics*, 11: 425–43.

Berlage, L., Cassimon, D., Drēze, J., and Reding, P. (2000). 'Prospective Aid and Indebtedness Relief: A Proposal'. Paper presented at the interdisciplinary colloquium on 'Which Debt Relief for the Third World?', Louvain-la-Neuve, February 11–12. Available at: www.fundp.ac.be/eco/cahiers/filepdf/cr0005.pdf

Birdsall, N., Claessens, S., and Diwan, I. (2002). 'Policy Selectivity Foregone: Debt and Donor Behavior in Africa'. Working Paper, No. 17, Center for Global Development.

Borenzstein, E. (1991). 'The Debt Overhang: An Empirical Analysis of the Philippines'. Mimeo, International Monetary Fund.

Buiter, W. (1981). 'Time Preference and International Lending and Borrowing in an Overlapping Generations Model'. *Journal of Political Economy*, 89: 769–97.

Bulow, J. and Rogoff, K. (1988). 'The Buy-back Boondoggle'. *Brookings Papers on Economic Activity*, 2: 675–98.

—— —— (1989a). 'A Constant Recontracting Model of Sovereign Debt'. *Journal of Political Economy*, 97: 166–77.

—— —— (1989b). 'LDC: Is to Forgive to Forget?' *American Economic Review*, 79: 43–50.

—— —— (1991). 'Debt Buy-back: No Cure for Debt Overhang'. *Quarterly Journal of Economics*, 57: 1219–36.

Calvo, G. (1988). 'Servicing the Public Debt: The Role of Expectations'. *American Economic Review*, 78: 647–61.

Cantor, R. and Packer, F. (1995). 'Sovereign Credit Ratings'. *Current Issues in Economics and Finance*, 1: 3.

Causa, O. and Cohen, D. (2004). 'A New Approach to Competitiveness'. Mimeo, OECD Development Centre.

Cline, W. (1983). *International Debt and the Stability of the World Economy*. Washington, DC: Institute for International Economics.

Cohen, D. (1985). 'How to Evaluate the Solvency of an Indebted Nation?' *Economic Policy*, 1: 139–56.

—— (1991). *Private Lending to Sovereign States: A Theoretical Autopsy*. Cambridge, MA: MIT Press.

—— (1992). 'The Debt Crisis: A Post Mortem'. *NBER Macroeconomics Annual*, vol. 7. Cambridge, MA: MIT Press.

—— (1993a). 'A Valuation Formula for LDC Debt'. *Journal of International Economics*, 34: 167–80.

—— (1993b). 'Low Investment and Large LDC Debt in the Eighties: An Empirical Analysis'. *American Economic Review*, 83: 437–49.

—— (1995). 'Large External Debt and Slow Domestic Growth'. *Journal of Economic Dynamics and Control*, 19: 1141–63.

—— (2000). 'The HIPC Initiative: True and False Promises'. OECD Development Centre, Technical Paper, No. 166.

—— (2001). 'The HIPC Initiative: True and False Promises'. *International Finance*, 5.

—— and Portes, R. (2003). *Crise de la dette souveraine: entre prévention et résolution*, Rapport no. 43. Paris: Conseil d'Analyse Economique.

—— —— (2004). 'Towards a Lender of First Resort'. CEPR Discussion Paper No. 4615.

—— and Sachs, J. (1986). 'Growth and External Debt Under Risk of Debt Repudiation'. *European Economic Review*, 30: 529–60.

—— and Soto, M. (2002). 'Why are Poor Countries Poor?' OECD Development Centre Technical Paper.

—— and Verdier, T. (1995). '"Secret" Buy-backs of LDC Debt'. *Journal of International Economics*, 39: 317–34.

—— and Vellutini, C. (2003). 'Beyond the HIPC Initiative'. A report to the European Commission.

—— and Fally, T., and Villemot, S. (2007). 'In Favor of a Fund to Smooth Commodity Shocks'. OECD Development Centre, Policy Insight No. 50.

Cole, H. and Kehoe, T. (1996). 'A Self-fulfilling Model of Mexico's 1994–1995 Debt Crisis'. *Journal of International Economics*, 41: 309–30.

—— —— (2000). 'Self-fulfilling Debt Crises'. *Review of Economic Studies*, 67: 91–116.

Craig, R. (2004). *Treasonable Doubts: The Harry Dexter White Spy Case*. Kansas: University of Kansas.

Diwan, I. and Claessens, S. (1989). 'Market Based Debt Reductions', in M. Husain and I. Diwan (eds.), *Dealing with the Debt Crisis*. Washington, DC: World Bank.

—— and Kletzer, K. (1990). 'Voluntary Choices in Concerted Deal'. Working Paper, No. 527, World Bank, PPR.

Dooley, M. (1988). 'Buy-backs and the Market Valuation of External Debt'. *IMF Staff Papers*, 35/2: 215–29.

Dornbusch, R. and Fischer, S. (1985). 'The World Debt Problem: Origins and Prospects'. *Journal of Development Planning*, 16: 57–81.

Eaton, J. (1989). 'Debt Relief and the International Enforcement of Loan Contracts'. *Journal of Economic Perspectives*, 4: 43–56.

—— (1993). 'External Debt: A Primer'. *The World Bank Economic Review*, 7: 137–72.

—— Gersovitz, M. (1981). 'Debt with Potential Repudiation: Theoretical and Empirical Analysis'. *Review of Economic Studies*, 48: 289–309.

—— —— and Stiglitz, J. (1986). 'The Pure Theory of Country Risk'. *European Economic Review*, 30: 481–513.

Eichengreen, B. and Lindert, P. (eds.) (1989). *The International Debt Crisis in Historical Perspective*. Cambridge, MA: MIT Press.

—— and Portes, R. (1986). 'Debt and Default in the 1930s: Causes and Consequences'. *European Economic Review*, 30: 599–640.

—— —— (1995). *Crisis? What Crisis? Orderly Workouts for Sovereign Debtors*. London: Centre for Economic Policy Research.

Fischer, S. (1989). 'Resolving the International Debt Crisis', in J. Sachs (ed.), *Developing Country Debt and Economic Performance*. Chicago, IL: University of Chicago Press.

—— (1999). 'Reforming the International Financial System'. *Economic Journal*, 109: 557–76.

Frenkel, J. and Razin, A. (1989). *Fiscal Policy in an Interdependent World*. Cambridge, MA: MIT Press.

International Monetary Fund (IMF) (2003). 'Report of the Managing Director to the International Monetary and Financial Committee on a Statutory Debt Restructuring Mechanism'. Available at://www.imf.org/external/np/omd/203/040803.htm

Kenen, D. (1983). 'A Bailout Plan for Banks'. *New York Times*, March 6.

Kharas, H. (1984). 'The Long-run Creditworthiness of Developing Countries'. *Quarterly Journal of Economics*, 99/3: 415–39.

Kletzer, K. (1984). 'Asymmetries of Information and LDC Borrowing with Sovereign Risk'. *Economic Journal*, 94: 287–307.

Klingen, C., Weder, B., and Zettelmeyer, J. (2003). 'How Private Creditors Fared in Emerging Debt Markets 1970–2000'. Mimeo, IMF.

Krueger, A. (2001). *International Financial Architecture for 2002: A New Approach to Sovereign Debt Restructuring*. Washington, DC: American Enterprise Institute, (November 26).

—— (2002). *New Approaches to Sovereign Debt Restructuring*. Washington, DC: IMF.

Krugman, P. (1988). 'Financing vs. Forgiving a Debt Overhang: Some Analytical Notes'. *Journal of Development Economics*, 29: 253–68.

Lerrick, A. and Meltzer, A. (2001). 'Blueprint for an International Lender of Last Resort'. Mimeo.

Lindert, P. and Morton, P. (1990). 'How Sovereign Debt has Worked', in J. Sachs (ed.), *Developing Country Debt and Economic Performance*, vol. I. Chicago, IL: University of Chicago Press.

Lucas, R. (1988). 'On the Mechanics of Economic Development'. *Journal of Monetary Economics*, 22: 3–42.

—— (1990). 'Why Can't Capital Flow from Rich to Poor Countries?' *American Economic Review, Papers and Proceedings*, 83.

McDonald, C. (1982). 'Debt Capacity and Developing Country Borrowing: A Survey of the Literature'. *IMF Staff Papers*, 29: 603–46.

Meltzer, A. (2000). 'Report of the International Financial Institution Advisory Commission'. Available at: www.house.gov/jec/imf/meltzer.pdf

Powell, R. (2000). 'Debt Relief for Poor Countries'. *Finance and Development* (quarterly magazine of the IMF), 37/4 (December).

Razim, A. and Svensson, L. E. O. (1983). 'The Terms of Trade and the Current Account. The Harberger-Laursen-Metzler Effect'. *Journal of Political Economy*, 91: 97–125.

Reinhart, C. and Rogoff, K. S. (2004). 'Serial Default and the "Paradox" of Rich to Poor Capital Flow'. *American Economic Review*, 94/2: 52–8 (May).

Reisen, H. (1989). 'Public Debt, North and South', in M. Husain and I. Diwan (eds.), *Dealing with the Debt Crisis*. Paris: OECD.

—— (2003). 'Normes et codes de l'architecture financière internationale', in D. Cohen and R. Portes (eds.), *Crises de la dette souveraine*, Rapport no. 43. Paris: Conseil d'Analyse Economique.

Rogoff, K. and Zettelmeyer, J. (2003). 'Bankruptcy Procedures for Sovereigns: A History of Ideas, 1976–2001'. International Monetary Fund Staff Papers, No. 49, 471–507 (September).

Sachs, J. (1981). 'The Current Account and Macroeconomic Adjustment in the 1970s'. *Brookings Papers on Economic Activity*, 2: 201–82.

—— (1989a). 'The Debt Overhang of Developing Countries', in J. de Macedo and R. Findlay (eds.), *Debt, Growth and Stabilization: Essays in Memory of Carlos Dias Alejandro*. Oxford: Blackwell.

—— (ed.) (1989b). *Developing Country Debt and Macroeconomic Performance*. Chicago, IL: University of Chicago Press.

—— (1995). 'Do We Need an International Lender of Last Resort?' Graham Lecture, Princeton University.

—— and Cohen, D. (1985). 'LDC Borrowing with Default Risk'. *Kredit und Kapital, Special Issue on International Banking*, 8: 211–35.

—— and Huizinga, H. (1987). 'US Commercial Banks and the Developing Country Debt Crisis'. *Brooking Papers on Economic Activity*, 2: 555–606.

—— and Warner, A. (1996). 'Economic Reform and the Process of Global Integration'. *Brookings Papers on Economic Activity*, 1: 1–118.

Taylor, J. (2002). 'Sovereign Debt Restructuring: A US Perspective'. Available at: www.treas.gov/press/releases/po2056.htm

Uribe, M. and Yue, V. (2003). 'Country Spreads and Emerging Countries: Who Drives Whom?' Mimeo.

Warner, A. (1991). 'Did the Debt Crisis Cause the Investment Crisis?' *Quarterly Journal of Economics*, 67: 1161–86.

Van Wijnbergen, S. (1990a). 'Mexico's External Debt Restructuring in 1989/90: An Economic Analysis'. *Economic Policy*, 12: 13–56.

Williamson, J. (1988). *Voluntary Approach to Debt Relief*. Washington, DC: Institute for International Economics.

—— (2001). 'The Role of the IMF: A Guide to the Reports'. Institute for International Economics (May).

—— (2002). 'Is Brazil Next?' International Economics Policy Brief, Institute for International Economics.

World Debt Tables (1989). *External Debt of Developing Countries*. Washington, DC: World Bank.

Wyplosz, C. (2003). 'Un prêteur en dernier resort mondial?', in D. Cohen and R. Portes (2003) *Crises de la dette souveraine*, Rapport no. 13. Paris. Conseil d'Analyse Economique.

10

The World Trading System and Implications of External Opening[1]

Jeffrey A. Frankel

Introduction

The idea that it is more efficient for countries to engage in international trade than to produce everything they want domestically is virtually as old as the field of economics itself. During the first half of the 20th century, governments turned back the hands on the historical clock of international integration. The resulting decline in trade was implicated in world depression, political upheaval, and war. During the second half of the 20th century, the leadership of the Western alliance, in general, and at one time the United States, in particular, turned forward the hands of international integration. The resulting increase in trade has been accompanied by overall world prosperity and the spread of Western economic and political values to virtually all parts of the globe.

Nonetheless, critics are questioning the gains from further efforts to liberalize trade. Many are not convinced that historical correlation implies causation. Others might agree that the increase in trade has contributed to economic growth, but argue that concerns other than GDP—such as equality or the environment—point to a different judgment regarding the desirability of trade. Still others might agree with the characterization of the last half-century, but say that little more now remains to be done. After all, most tariffs are now close to zero, and international integration seems to be complete.

The chapter begins by pointing out that external opening, which here means reductions in barriers to international trade, still has a long way to

[1] The paper this chapter comes from was written for the forum 'From the Washington Consensus Towards a New Global Governance,' Fundacio CIDOB, Barcelona, Spain, held September 24–25, 2004. The author would like to thank Maral Shamloo for research assistance and the Kuwait Fund at Harvard University for research support.

go. It reviews the evidence on the economic benefits from integration. It reports an econometric attempt to address a major concern regarding simultaneous causality between growth and trade: does openness lead to growth, or does growth lead to openness? We remove the complication of simultaneous causality by isolating variation in trade patterns that could be clearly attributed to geographical influences. The result indicates that the observed effect of trade on growth—an estimated 0.3 percent increase in income over 20 years for each 0.01 increase in the ratio of trade to GDP—is not attributable to simultaneity.

Next the chapter considers non-economic effects, taking the case of the environment. The evidence suggests that for some pollutants (such as SO_2) trade can be on net beneficial, while for other environmental criteria (such as CO_2) the reverse is true. A ready explanation is that when externalities arise primarily at the national level as with local air and water pollution, an adequate level of income and effective national governance are sufficient to enact regulation to protect the environment, but that in the increasingly important case of global externalities such as emissions of greenhouse gases, the free-rider problem prevents individual countries from acting on their own in the absence of an effective international agreement.

What should be the priority areas for trade negotiations? A section of the chapter considers the form of negotiations (unilateral vs. reciprocal, regional vs. multilateral, the new role of developing countries, and the new role of NGOs). It then considers priority sectors (textiles, other manufactures, agriculture, and services), and other issues (anti-dumping abuse). The chapter suggests that admonitions to either rich countries or poor to liberalize unilaterally are not usually effective politically, and that economists ought instead to put their public voice in support of reciprocal multilateral negotiations. It concludes with a rough quantitative estimate of the economic benefits of a new World Trade Organization (WTO) round. Other authors, using static models, have estimated that a new round might raise trade by about US$300 billion, and that this might raise global welfare on the order of 1 percent of world income. But the implied increase in global trade volumes may have further benefits. The author's 'back of the envelope' attempt to also take into account dynamic gains says that the increase in welfare might be on the order of twice as large, over the subsequent two decades.

How Far Has External Opening Gone?

It is easy to get the impression that globalization is almost complete, that most trade barriers have already been dismantled, borders are irrelevant, and nation states are inconsequential. It is easy to imagine that citizens of each

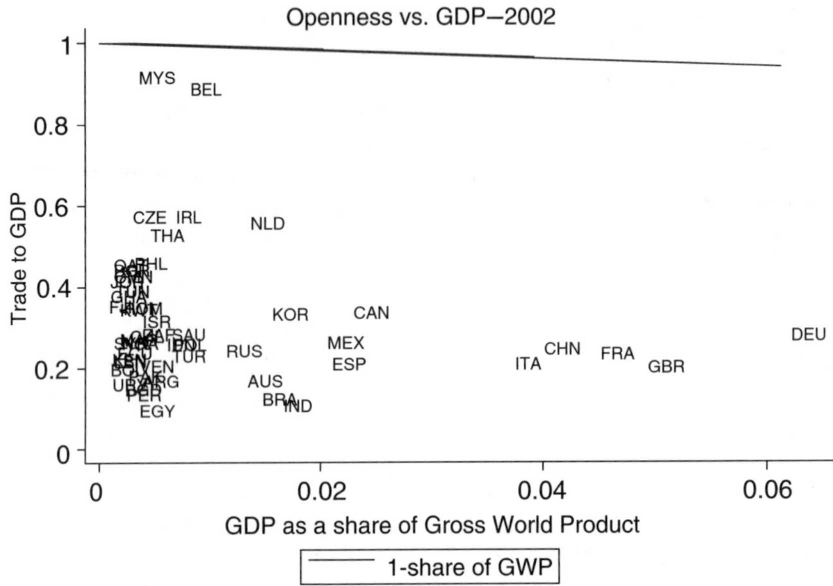

Figure 10.1. Countries' Openness vs. their Share of Gross World Product

country already trade with buyers or sellers on the other side of the globe as easily as the other side of town. But this is not the reality.

How Much Further Do We Have to Go?

Economic integration still has a lot further to go. Although trade as a share of the economy has increased virtually everywhere over the last half-century, the increase is less impressive viewed by the hypothetical standard of complete global integration. Figure 10.1 shows openness, measured as the average of exports and imports of goods and services as a fraction of GDP. Countries are arrayed along the horizontal axis according to their shares of world income. Large countries can be expected to have a lower ratio of trade to GDP; even in a perfectly integrated world, a typical US citizen would be probabilistically more likely to trade with another American than with the residents of a random country. Indeed, smaller countries tend to be naturally more open by this measure: notice that a regression line would slope downward. (Also relevant is that relatively remote countries like Australia tend to lie at the lower end of the openness range, and countries that are centrally located for trade, like Belgium, towards the top. Countries with a history of high trade barriers like India and Egypt tend to lie towards the bottom, whereas those that have followed more trade oriented policies such as Malaysia lie towards the top.) All countries have climbed upward in the openness graph over time, though with a big reversal in the first half of the 20th century. But despite this progress, most remain far from complete global integration, defined as the hypothetical condition that would hold if residents of a given country were truly no more likely to buy from, and sell to, each other than to trade with residents of other economies: they lie far below the line that slopes down from the 100 percent point on the vertical axis, which shows when countries' patterns with trading partners correspond only to the size of the trading partners.[2] We are still far from the day when we buy from across the globe as easily as across the country.

At any point in history, there are many powerful forces working to drive countries apart, at the same time as there are other powerful forces working to shrink the world. It is true that the shrinking forces have dominated over the last 50 years, but there is nothing inevitable about that. From 1914 to 1944, the fragmenting forces dominated (isolationism, tariff retaliation, rival blocs, war, and ideology), and it could happen again (after September 11, 2001 we saw tightened visa requirements, reasons for laborious searches of containerized cargo, and nationalist brand identification).

What Are the Barriers?

It is not difficult to identify some of the impediments to international economic integration that remain. Geographical, social, and policy factors all play a role. Their effect can be quantified in many ways. The following discussion of effects on bilateral trade draws on statistical estimates from the so-called gravity model.[3] Other approaches, such as inspection of the ability of cross-border arbitrage to narrow differentials in prices, give similar results.

Statistically, when two firms are located on opposite sides of a national border, operating for example under different legal systems, trade between them falls by an estimated two-thirds, that is, to one-third of what it would be if they were located in the same country. This estimate even allows that the two countries in question officially have free trade between them, speak the same language, and use the same currency. If the two countries use different currencies, trade falls by a further two-thirds, even if they fix the exchange rate between them. That is, the two border effects together reduce trade to

[2] For example, in the case of the US, even though the trade/output ratio has already tripled over the post-war period, it would have to rise from its current 12 percent to 70 or 75 percent before it fully reflected the share of non-US producers and consumers in the world economy. (Because of its size, the US appears off the chart, in the lower right corner.) Even this statistic of a six-fold gap is an understatement, because exports and imports are gross transactions, not net value-added. Singapore and Hong Kong, for example, export and import well over 100 percent of their GDPs (because of their extreme openness, they too appear off the chart, in the upper left corner).

[3] These estimates of the gravity model of bilateral trade are from Frankel (1997); Rose (2000); and Frankel and Rose (2002).

one-ninth of what it would be within the same country. In addition, when the exchange rate is as variable as it is for the average pair of currencies, currency risk and transactions costs may reduce trade by a further 13 percent. Such factors together explain why Canadians are ten times more likely to trade with other Canadians than with Americans, despite the physical and cultural proximity of the two countries,[4] and why price arbitrage is stronger between Vancouver and Montreal than it is just across the US border.[5] National borders still matter a great deal.

For most pairs of countries, the impediments to trade are much higher. If the two countries do not belong to a free trade area, but have tariffs and other trade barriers between them that are average in level, trade again falls by roughly two-thirds. It falls by even more if the trade barriers are at levels typically found in poor countries. If the two share no common historical or cultural links, the impediments are greater still. If they speak different languages, for example, trade falls by half.

Finally, notwithstanding the long-term historical decline in physical shipping costs, geography still matters. If two countries are not adjacent to each other, trade falls by half. In addition, for every 1 percent increase in the distance between them, trade falls by another 1 percent.

The increase in trade as a share of the economy over the last 50 years can be attributed in large part to declining trade barriers and declining transport costs. But neither of these sources of friction is yet close to zero. Differences in currencies and languages and the other factors mentioned above have diminished little. Globalization, though not in its infancy, has not yet reached full maturity. Unless we do something to screw it up, trade barriers and transport costs are likely to continue to fall during the 21st century. It follows that there are still large gains to be reaped from further reductions in trade barriers. That is, it follows provided integration is viewed as beneficial—the question to which we now turn.

The Economic Benefits from Trade

Why do economists consider free trade so important? What exactly are the benefits?

The Theoretical Case for Trade

Classical economic theory tells us that there are national gains from trade, associated with the concept of comparative advantage. Over the last two decades, scholars have developed an alternative new trade theory. Though

[4] For example, Helliwell (2000). [5] Engel and Rogers (1996).

often misinterpreted, it suggests the existence of possible additional benefits from trade, which are termed dynamic. Let us review each of these theories, very briefly, in turn.

The classical theory, of course, goes back to Adam Smith and David Ricardo. Adam Smith argued that specialization—the division of labor—enhances productivity. David Ricardo extended this concept to trade between countries. The notion is that trade allows each country to specialize in what it does best, thus maximizing the value of its output. If a government restricts trade, resources are wasted in the production of goods that could be imported more cheaply than they can be produced domestically.

What if one country is better than others at producing *every* good? The argument in favor of free trade still works. All that is required is for a country to be *relatively* less skilled than another in the production of some good in order for it to benefit from trade. This is the doctrine of comparative advantage—the fundamental (if perhaps counterintuitive) principle that underlies the theory of international trade. It makes sense for Tiger Woods to pay someone else to mow his lawn, even if Woods could do it better himself, because he has a comparative advantage at golf over lawn mowing. Similarly, it makes sense for each country to pay to import certain goods that can be produced with relatively greater efficiency abroad, because it has a comparative advantage in other goods. This is the classical view of the benefits of free trade in a nutshell.

A popular critique is that classic trade theory assumes an idealized world where: (a) others are not intervening; (b) there are no market failures; and (c) competition is perfect. The first objection misunderstands elementary trade theory (as do the comic claims that the classic theory of comparative advantage never envisioned trade based on unskilled labor, claims regarding information technology, or a world of mobile factors are not much better). The argument for accepting world prices is not necessarily changed just because those prices are affected by foreign subsidies or other interventions. The second argument is more important. Market failures such as environmental externalities, income inequality, and monopoly power can indeed justify government intervention. The example of the environment will be considered below. But in the first place, the optimal response to each is likely to be some intervention that is quite different from a trade barrier or subsidy, as Jagdish Bhagwati has long pointed out. In the second place, one must be as alert to government failures (rent seeking, ill-informed or ill-intentioned intervention, etc.) as to market failures. That leaves the third objection.

It is true that classical theory assumes perfect competition, constant returns to scale, and fixed technology, assumptions that are not very realistic. A second attribute of the classical theory worth highlighting is that the gains from trade are primarily static in nature—that is, they affect the *level* of real income. The elimination of trade barriers raises income, but this is essentially a one-time increase, rather than a permanent rise in the rate of growth. The 'new trade theory' associated with Elhanan Helpman and Paul Krugman is more realistic than the classical theory in that it takes into account imperfect competition, increasing returns to scale, and changing technology. It ultimately provides equally strong, or stronger, support for the sort of free trade policies that most countries have followed throughout the post-war period, that is, multilateral and bilateral negotiations to reduce trade barriers, than did the classical theory.[6]

Much has been made of the result from these theories (called 'strategic trade theory') that, under certain very special conditions, one country can get ahead by interventions (e.g., public subsidies to strategic sectors). Among the necessary conditions are that the government gets the intervention exactly right, and that other countries do not retaliate or emulate. But these theories also suggest that a world in which everyone is subsidizing at once is a world in which everyone is worse off—a classic 'prisoner's dilemma'—and that we are all better off if we can agree to limit subsidies or other interventions. An example would be the agreement between the United States and Europe to limit subsidies to our respective aircraft manufacturers. Assume for the sake of argument that the US government is knowledgeable enough to use aircraft subsidies in such a way as to reap extra profits for the American producer (Boeing) at the expense of the EU producer (Airbus) if the Europeans do not retaliate. But how does that help? The Europeans would in fact retaliate.

Furthermore, even when a government does not fear retaliation from abroad for trade barriers, intervention in practice is usually based on inadequate knowledge and is corrupted by interest groups. Special interests waste money lobbying to get the government to raise the price of whatever they are selling or lower the price of whatever they are buying. Ruling out all sector-specific intervention is the most effective way of discouraging such 'rent seeking' behavior. External opening also increases the number of competitors operating in the economy. Not only does this work to reduce distortionary monopoly power in the marketplace (which corporations exercise by raising prices); it can also reduce distortionary corporate power in the political arena (which they exercise by lobbying).

Most importantly, new trade theory offers a possible reason to believe that trade can have a permanent effect on a country's rate of growth, not just on the level of real GDP. Openness allows firms to keep in touch with global markets. A high rate of economic interaction with the rest of the world speeds the absorption of frontier technologies and global management best practices,

[6] The most important reference is probably Helpman and Krugman (1985).

spurs innovation and cost cutting, and competes away monopoly.[7] These arguments apply to imports as much as to exports.

The Empirical Case for Trade

Citing theory is not a complete answer to the question, 'How do we know that trade is good?' We need empirical evidence.

There are many studies of the static microeconomic costs of protection by tariffs, quotas, and other trade barriers, and the implied gains from liberalization. Economists have also undertaken macroeconomic statistical tests of the determinants of countries' growth rates. Investment in physical capital and education are the two factors that emerge the most strongly in these studies. But other determinants matter as well.

There has never been a shortage of empirical studies finding that trade is a significant determinant of growth across countries,[8] and often that it is an important explanation for East Asian success in particular.[9] A typical early specification began with the standard determinants of GDP suggested by neoclassical growth theory and added a variable for exports as a share of GDP. For example, Feder (1982) regressed growth rates for 31 semi-industrialized countries over the period 1964–73 against three variables: investment share, labor force growth, and growth of exports. The coefficient on the last variable was highly significant statistically. Contrary to popular intuition as well as to short-term Keynesian macroeconomics, theory suggests that imports can be as important as exports in stimulating long-term growth.[10] Thus the most standard measure of openness in growth studies is the sum of exports and imports as a share of GDP. Edwards (1993) regressed the rate of growth of total factor productivity on total trade as a percent of GDP, along with some other variables, and found that 'in every regression the proxies for trade distortions and openness are highly significant.'

Addressing Simultaneity

Simultaneity is always a concern, however. Rodrik (1994b), for example, argued that the standard view is 'quite misleading on the importance it attaches to the role of export-orientation in the growth performance. It also

[7] Important citations include Grossman and Helpman (1991a, b); Rivera-Batiz and Romer (1991); and Romer (1994).

[8] Examples include Michaely (1977); Krueger (1978); Feder (1982); Kohli and Singh (1989); Quah and Rauch (1990); de Melo and Robinson (1991); DeLong and Summers (1991); Dollar (1992); Edwards (1993a); Romer (1994); Sachs and Warner (1995); Harrison (1995); and Eusufzai (1996). Edwards (1993b), Rodrik (1993), and USITC (1997) survey the literature.

[9] Four examples for Asia are Helliwell (1995); Page (1994); Pack and Page (1994); and Fukuda and Toya (1995). Bradford (1994) surveys the literature.

[10] Empirical studies that emphasize imports include Lee (1995) and Wacziarg (2001).

has backward the causal relationship between exports, on the one hand, and investment and growth on the other.' The mechanism of reverse causality that Rodrik has in mind runs as follows: an exogenous increase in investment in a developing country with a comparative disadvantage in producing capital goods, such as Korea, will necessitate an increase in imports of such goods (and in turn an increase in exports to pay for the imports).[11] Similarly, Helpman (1988) asked, 'Does growth drive trade, or is there a reverse link from trade to growth?' Harrison (1995) concluded that 'existing literature is still unresolved on the issue of causality.'

Quite a few stories of reverse causality are possible. When the equation features a regression of GDP against exports (or the rates of change thereof), the simultaneity problem is clear: a correlation may emerge simply because exports are a component of GDP, rather than because of any extra contribution that trade makes to growth. In the case of imports, trade might rise with income because foreign goods are superior goods in consumption.

Many studies have sought to identify some direct measures of trade *policy*, hoping that they are exogenous. Probably the most influential has been Sachs and Warner (1995). But these have been subjected to two critiques. First, designing an aggregate measure of trade policy is difficult, and the measures that have been adopted have not escaped criticism.[12] Second, a fundamental conceptual problem of simultaneity remains (e.g., Sala-i-Martin 1991). What if free market trade policies are no more important to growth than free market domestic policies, but tend to be correlated with them? Then openness will be observed to be correlated with growth, even though trade does not cause growth. A final possible mechanism of reverse causality is a pattern whereby poor countries tend to depend fiscally on tariff revenue, and to reduce tariffs as they become more developed and income taxes or value-added taxes become administratively feasible.

A number of studies have tangled with the challenge posed by simultaneity.[13] What is needed are good instrumental variables, which are truly exogenous, and yet are highly correlated with trade. This chapter offers tests with such instruments: trade shares as predicted by the gravity model. The gravity model of bilateral trade, in its most basic form, says that trade between country *i* and country *j* is proportional to the product of GDP_i and GDP_j, and inversely related to the distance between them, by analogy to Newton's theory of gravitational attraction between two masses. Other explanatory variables

[11] Levine and Renelt (1992) reach similar conclusions.

[12] For example, Rodriguez and Rodrik (2001) argue that the Sachs-Warner measure is driven overwhelmingly, not by tariffs or quotas, but by the black market premium for foreign exchange, and a measure of state export monopoly. They argue that these largely reflect policies not related to trade.

[13] Jung and Marshall (1985), Hutchison and Singh (1987, 1992), and Bradford and Chakwin (1993) apply Granger-causality tests to the problem. Esfahani (1991) attempts a simultaneous equation approach.

often added include populations (or per capita GDPs), land areas, and dummy variables representing landlockedness, common borders, common languages, and common membership in regional trading arrangements. While the gravity model had long been an ugly duckling of international economics—obscure and allegedly lacking theoretical foundations—it has enjoyed a swan-like revival.[14]

Such variables as distances, populations, common borders, and common languages are as close to exogenous as we get in economics. From the viewpoint of a small individual country, the GDPs of trading partners are exogenous as well.[15] Yet these variables are highly correlated with trade. Thus they make good instrumental variables. An intuitive way to implement the idea is to use the values predicted by the gravity model to instrument for the trade variable in the growth equation. If trade still appears to be a significant determinant of growth with this correction (taking care, of course, to use the right standard errors), then we have some reason to believe that the effect is causal and not spurious.

Romer and I (1999) looked at a cross-section of 100 countries during the period from 1960 to 1985.[16] We found that the effect of openness on growth was even stronger when we correct for the simultaneity, as compared to standard estimates.

Table 10.1 reports a version of this equation on updated data.[17]

$$ln(Y/Pop)_{90,i} = \beta_0 + \alpha([X+M]/Y)_{90,i} + \beta_1\, ln(Pop)_i + \gamma\, ln(Y/Pop)_{70,i}$$
$$+ \delta_1(I/Y)_i + \delta_2 n_i + \delta_3(School_1)_i + \delta_4(School_2)_i + u_i$$

The dependent variable is the natural logarithm of real GDP (Y) divided by total population (Pop), measured in real PPP-adjusted dollars for country i. Aggregate exports, aggregate imports, and gross investment are denoted 'X', 'M', and 'I' respectively. The growth rate of population is denoted 'n'. '$School_1$'

[14] Perhaps the best theoretical rationale for the idea that bilateral trade depends on the product of GDPs comes from the model of trade in imperfect substitutes, e.g., Helpman and Krugman (1985). Frankel (1997) elaborates, applying the gravity model to issues of trade blocs, tests for trade blocs, and gives further references.

[15] For a study that seeks to explain growth for a cross-section of countries, one does not wish to treat GDPs of trading partners as exogenous, even if the domestic country is small. But if the standard factor accumulation terms in a growth regression (labor force growth, investment, and education) can be treated as exogenous in the domestic country, then they can also be considered exogenous in trading partners, as discussed below. An alternative is to omit income from the exogenous variables, and use population alone to represent country size.

[16] Estimates in Frankel and Rose (2002) contain updated data and a sample of 200 diverse countries, and added as variables in explaining bilateral trade: common languages, common borders, common colonizers, and FTA membership. Perhaps for this reason, the t-ratio on openness in the growth equation rose, from 2-3 in Frankel-Romer, to 3-5 in Frankel-Rose (and the correlation of the gravity-based instrument with actual trade/GDP rose from 0.62 to 0.72).

[17] Taken from the working paper version of Frankel and Rose (2005).

Table 10.1. Deep Determinants of Growth

	Determinant		
	1. Tropical conditions	2. Openness	3. Institutions
Measures commonly used	Malaria and other diseases; crop pests; length of growing season	Trade/GDP; Tariffs; FDI	Ratings regarding property rights; rule of law; corruption
Examples of endogeneity problems	Technological suppression of malaria or pests	Imported investment or luxury goods; tariffs for revenue in poor countries	Regulation systems develop with income; Ratings may be subjective
Exogenous instrumental variables	Distance from equator, tropical area; temperature; rainfall; frost days	Gravity model: including remoteness, landlockedness, linguistic & historical links	European settler mortality rates; extractive industries (plantation crops and mining)

Sources: Sachs and Warner (1995); Engerman and Sokoloff (1997, 2002); Gallup et al. (1998); Frankel and Romer (1999); Hall and Jones (1999); Acemoglu et al. (2001, 2002*a*); Rodríguez and Rodrik (2001); Acemoglu et al. (2002*b*); Easterly and Levine (2002); Bosworth and Collins (2003); Rodrik et al. (2002); Sachs (2003).

and '$School_2$' are estimates of human capital investment based, respectively, on primary and secondary schooling enrollment rates. Greek letters denote coefficients, and '*u*' denotes the residual impact of other, hopefully orthogonal influences. Variables that derive from neoclassical growth theory appear on the second line of the equation: initial income, investment rate, human capital, and population growth.[18] Variables other than GDP per capita and openness are computed as averages over the sample period.

The estimate of the effect of openness on income per capita is on the order of 0.3 over the span of 20 years, as it was in the earlier study, and is perhaps four-times that in the truly long run. That estimate means that when trade increases by one percentage point of GDP, income increases by about one-third of a percent over 20 years. By way of illustration, compare a stylized Burma (Myanmar), with a trade ratio close to zero, versus a stylized Singapore, with a ratio close to 200 percent. Our ballpark estimate, the coefficient of 0.3, implies that as a result of its openness Singapore's income is about 60 percent higher than Burma's over a 20-year period, or about 250 percent higher in the very long run.

[18] Frankel and Romer (1999) and Irwin and Terviö (2002) adopted a more stripped down specification by omitting these controls, following Hall and Jones (1999). They regress output per capita against distance from the equator and measures of country size, reasoning that the factor accumulation variables might be endogenous. Including the controls in the output equation might result in a downward biased estimate of α, if some of the effect of openness arrives via factor accumulation. But inappropriately excluding these variables would also produce biased results and could be expected improperly to attribute too *large* an effect to trade. My own preference is for the specification that includes the controls, in part because it is likely to avoid a possible upward bias in the openness coefficient.

One possible response to these claims is that this approach demonstrates only the growth benefits from geographically induced trade and need not necessarily extend to the effects of policy induced trade. But it is not obvious why the benefits of one impetus to trade should be so different from those of another. In any case, popular critics of globalization seem to think that increased international trade is the problem, regardless of whether it comes from technological progress or market opening negotiations. If the question is the broad brush phenomenon of globalization, the answer seems to be that the effect on incomes is clearly positive.

Needless to say, trade is far from the only important determinant of countries' economic performance. Other important factors are the accumulation of physical and human capital, increases in total factor productivity via technological and managerial innovation, a stable political and macroeconomic environment, and good institutional features such as the rule of law. Some of these factors are themselves favorably influenced by trade and other forms of international integration.

Institutions and Other Deep Determinants of Economic Performance

Perhaps the most interesting part of the current debate on growth is: *what are the deeper determinants*? Yes, policies regarding taxes, government spending, and tariffs help determine observed measures of investment, education, and trade. But what are the deeper determinants of those policies? A recent paper by Rodrik et al. (2002) poses the question well. The rendition that follows is very close to theirs. Three big theories of deep determinants seem to have emerged: tropical conditions, openness, and institutions. Each has been captured by some now standard measures. Although each may be more exogenous than macro policies, each has serious endogeneity problems of its own that must be addressed (Table 10.1 illustrates this.) Let us consider each in turn.

1. I would use the phrase *tropical conditions* for what some have taken to calling geography. By now 'geography' has (belatedly) made its way deep into the literatures on trade and growth in many different ways. So it is important to clarify here what sort of geography we mean. We are talking about the natural climate, biology, and geology—especially differences between the *tropics* and temporal zones, such as presence of malaria and other debilitating tropical diseases, agricultural pests, length of the growing season, and other climate effects.[19]
2. By *openness*, we mean international integration along several dimensions, but trade is the most important. A common measure is the simple ratio of trade to GDP.

[19] Diamond (1997); Gallup et al. (1998); Hall and Jones (1999); and Sachs (2001).

3. Finally, *institutions*. Measures of institutional quality are usually indicators of the rule of law, protection of property rights, and the extent of constraints on the executive.

As noted, each of the three has serious endogeneity problems. Fortunately, reasonable instruments have been proposed and implemented for each.

The presence of malaria can be partly endogenous: it was stamped out in Panama and Singapore, despite their tropical locations, by superior technology and social organization. The instrumental variables to capture the exogenous component of the tropical geography theory started out fairly crude and have been getting progressively better: moving from continental dummies to latitude, and from there to percent of land area in the tropics to average temperature or number of frost days.[20] The state of the art must be Jeff Sachs' latest (2003) measure of ecological predisposition to malaria.

Trade and trade policies are both endogenous. We have already discussed the gravity-based instrumental variable.

Institutions can also be endogenous. Many institutions—such as the structure of financial markets, mechanisms of income redistribution and social safety nets, and regulation and tax systems—tend to evolve in response to the level of income. But the problem is worse. Not only are institutions themselves likely to be endogenous, but the measures we are talking about are subjective evaluations of institutions. I submit that if you ask international businessmen to rate the quality of Switzerland's fire departments compared to Colombia's fire departments, the Swiss will come out on top even if they don't merit it, because of the halo effect of Switzerland's general reputation. The point, which Ricardo Hausmann has emphasized, is that reported evaluations of institutional quality are likely to be endogenous with respect to national economic performance.

What is a good instrumental variable for institutional quality? Acemoglu et al. (2001) proposed the mortality rate among European settlers (more precisely, among soldiers and clergymen) during the period of initial colonization. This is a better instrument than it sounds. In fact, it is probably the best we have. The theory is that, out of all the lands that Europeans colonized, only those where Europeans actually settled were given good European institutions. This theory is related to the idea of Engerman and Sokoloff (1997, 2002) that lands endowed with extractive industries and plantation crops (mining, sugar, cotton) developed institutions of slavery, inequality, dictatorship, and state control, whereas those climates suited to fishing and small farms developed institutions based on individualism, democracy, egalitarianism, and capitalism. Acemoglu et al. chose their instrument on the

[20] Bosworth and Collins (2003) use a composite of tropical area and frost days.

reasoning that initial settler mortality rates determined whether Europeans subsequently settled in large numbers.

A string of authors have found that the institutions variable tends to drive out the significance of policies, even when the Acemoglu et al. instrument is used for institutions: Hall and Jones (1999); Acemoglu et al. (2002); Easterly and Levine (2002); Bosworth and Collins (2003).[21] The conclusion has been phrased most aggressively by Rodrik et al. in their title as 'Institutions Rule.' Institutions trump everything else—the effects of both tropical geography and trade pale in the blinding light of institutions.

Sachs (2003), however, finds that tropical geography remains significant. Noguer and Siscart (2002) condition on country size, and implement the gravity instrument with a comprehensive set of bilateral trade data. They find that, yes, institutions have a statistically significant effect on income per capita, but openness and tropical location retain their significant effects as well. But they don't instrument for institutions. Alcalá and Ciccone (2002) instrument for both trade and institutions, and find that both significantly raise output per worker. Institutional quality works mainly via physical and human capital, while trade works through the efficiency of labor. Bosworth and Collins (2003), too, find that the geographically-based trade variable is statistically significant alongside the institutions and tropical geography variables.

My subjective ratings for the three sets of instruments in use for the three big categories of fundamental growth factors (tropical diseases and pests, trade, and institutions) are as follows: I still believe that the trade predictions of the gravity model are a relatively good instrument for a country's openness to trade. The instruments available for tropical diseases and pests are even better. The big challenge is institutions. I don't wish by any means to denigrate the importance of institutions. And, as I said, the settler mortality instrument is probably the best we have. But I am not convinced it is as good as the instruments for trade and tropics. For one thing, it is only available for former colonies. And there is another problem that I regard as more important. What are the big questions we are trying to answer? We already knew long ago that Australia, Canada, New Zealand, and the United States belonged with Europe in the list of countries that had industrialized. The big question is why they did and the Third World countries didn't.[22] Is it policies, institutions, culture...? In that light, to be told that the areas where Europeans settled

[21] Easterly and Levine just group openness together with other policies. Hall and Jones consider latitude a proxy for European institutions, and thus don't distinguish the independent effect of tropical conditions.

[22] There were exceptions to the rule: the failure of Argentina during the 20th century and the success of Japan, the failure of Eastern Europe during the last third of the century and the success of the East Asian Newly Industrialized Countries (NICs). But there is little agreement over what lessons to draw from these cases.

did well is not exactly news. It just repeats the big data point we already had. It doesn't help us all that much to choose among human capital, policies, institutions, and cultures to get our explanation.

In any case, external opening has more support in most countries now than it did 30 years ago. Trade has been a major component of the growth that has visibly lifted East Asia out of poverty over the last 40 years. The rest of the world now wants the same. Poor countries don't want to be protected from 'exploitation'—the exploitation of having the opportunity to sell their products abroad to willing buyers and thereby to raise their incomes.

The Non-economic Benefits or Costs of Trade

Many critics of globalization today do not dispute the claim that international trade has positive effects on GDP. Rather, they have other concerns in mind—non-economic goals such as the promotion of labor rights, equality of income, and protection of the environment. The most important lesson from the Seattle demonstrations of November 1999 was that these issues will increasingly dominate public debate regarding globalization and multilateral institutions. They cannot simply be shunted off to the side, with pure trade issues occupying alone the center stage of international negotiations.[23]

International trade and investment have implications, in such areas as income distribution or environmental quality, that are sometimes favorable and are in some cases unfavorable. Facile generalizations are likely to be wrong.

The Case of the Environment[24]

There is no question that the early stages of industrialization bring environmental damage. On the other hand, a clean environment is a 'superior good'—something that societies wish to purchase more of, even at some cost to income, as they grow rich enough to be able to afford to do so. If this effect is strong enough, then trade might be expected eventually to improve the environment, once the country gets past a certain level of per capita income. There is some empirical support for this pattern. Grossman and Kruger (1995) popularized what is called the environmental Kuznets curve: growth is bad for air and water pollution at the initial stages of industrialization, but later on

[23] Two references in this rapidly growing field are: Jagdish Bhagwati and Robert Hudec (1996) and Dani Rodrik (1997). Maskus (2002) argues that labor issues lack the international externalities of competition policy or cross-border environmental problems.

[24] Frankel (2004) surveys the effects of international trade and the WTO on the environment.

reduces some forms of pollution, as countries become rich enough to pay to clean up their environments.[25] A substantial literature has followed.

The idea that trade can be good for the environment is surprising to many. The pollution-haven hypothesis instead holds that trade and investment encourage firms to locate production of highly polluting sectors in low-regulation countries, and export their products to high-regulation countries. The race-to-the-bottom hypothesis holds that trade puts downward pressure on regulatory standards in *all* open countries, each seeking to 'stay competitive.' But research suggests that environmental regulation is not a major determinant of firms' decision where to locate internationally.[26] In a model that combines various effects of trade, including via the scale and composition of output, Antweiler et al. (1998) estimate that if openness raises GDP by 1 percent, then it reduces sulphur dioxide concentrations by 1 percent. The implication is that, because trade is good for growth, it is also generally good for the environment. Frankel and Rose (2005) find that even for a given level of income, countries that are more open to trade suffer lower concentrations of SO_2 and some other air pollutants.

It is important to note that government intervention is the most evident channel whereby people enact their desire for a cleaner environment as they grow richer. There is little reason to think that the market can take care of it by itself.

Most of the econometric studies of effects of trade and growth on the environment are limited, in that they examine only a few specific measures of pollution. There is a need to look at other environmental criteria as well. It is difficult to imagine, for example, that trade is anything but bad for the survival of tropical hardwood forests, absent substantial international efforts by governments to protect them.

The argument that richer countries will take steps to clean up their environments is likely to hold only for issues where the primary effects are felt domestically—where the primary 'bads,' such as smog or water pollution, though they may be external to the firm or household, are largely internal to the country. Two important environmental externalities are global, however: greenhouse gas emissions and depletion of stratospheric ozone. A ton of carbon dioxide has the same global warming effect regardless of where in the world it is emitted. In these cases, individual nations can do little to improve the environment on their own, no matter how concerned are their populations or how effective their governments. International cooperation is required, which inherently means a trade-off at the margin against national sovereignty. The same is true about those environmental concerns over

[25] An earlier reference is International Bank of Reconstruction and Development (IBRD) (1992). Frankel and Rose (2005) put the peak in concentrations at an income of about US$6,800 per capita, for the case of SO_2.

[26] Adam Jaffe et al. (1995).

so-called non-use values that are increasingly cross-border, such as the value placed on endangered species. Governments have negotiated international treaties in an attempt to deal with each of the three problems mentioned—ozone depletion, greenhouse gases, and biodiversity. Of the three, however, only the attempt to save the ozone layer, the Montreal Protocol, can be said as yet to have met with much success. The Kyoto Protocol on Global Climate Change faces hurdles that approach the insurmountable. Desire by countries to protect their national sovereignty is one of the most important hurdles.

Is the popular impression then correct that international trade exacerbates global environmental externalities? Perhaps, but only in the sense that trade promotes economic growth. Clearly, if mankind were still a population of a few million people living in pre-industrial poverty, greenhouse gas emissions would not be a big issue. Industrialization initially leads to environmental degradation, and trade is part of industrialization. But virtually everyone wants industrialization, at least for themselves. Deliberate self-impoverishment is not a promising option.[27] Once this point is recognized, there is nothing special about trade, as compared to the other sources of economic growth, such as capital accumulation, rural–urban migration, and technological progress.

The popular impression is that trade is somehow different. There are fears of pollution havens, a race to the bottom in regulation, and a powerful WTO trampling over countries' sovereign attempts to raise environmental standards. Some think there is a fundamental incompatibility among the three desideratums of international integration, regulation, and national sovereignty; this is the 'impossible trinity of global governance.'

Among the many misconceptions in this area is that countries could effectively address environmental problems if it were not for interference with their sovereignty. In fact, environmental problems are increasingly global, and therefore increasingly difficulty to address without multilateral institutions. For example, individual countries would have little effect on aggregate global emissions over the coming decades, even if they were willing to achieve the emission targets of the Kyoto Protocol and to bear the moderately high costs involved in gradually restructuring their domestic energy economies. This point has nothing to do with trade. It would be the same in a world where industrialization took place without external opening. International trade, whether in goods or in emission permits, actually offers a way of bringing down the economic cost of attaining any given reduction in global emissions, or a way of obtaining deeper cuts in emissions for any given economic cost. For example, elimination of such distortions as subsidies to

[27] In any case, indoor air pollution (particulate matter from cooking and heating fires) and lack of clean drinking water are larger environmental threats in poor countries, each claiming millions of premature deaths per year. Economic development is the best way to address them.

agriculture, logging, fishing, and coal mining would be pro-environment and pro-free trade at the same time. To make a concrete proposal, the G8 could lead a campaign, with help from the World Bank, to ban fossil fuel subsidies.

'Efficiency' as the Achievement of Objectives

Efficiency means maximizing one's objective, whatever it may be, subject to the constraints of nature and man. The objective is not limited to GDP, but includes such non-economic goals as the equality of income distribution and the quality of the environment. The principle remains that countries can better achieve their goals through free international exchange—subject to rules mutually agreed upon in international fora such as the WTO, International Monetary Fund (IMF), International Labor Organization (ILO), and United Nations Framework Convention on Climate Change (UNFCCC)—than they could if they hid behind barriers to trade and investment. Where global externalities are involved, as in global climate change and some other environmental problems an international agreement of some sort is necessary, due to the free-rider problem. If members of a multilateral institution like the UNFCCC or ILO are sufficiently committed to particular environmental or labor standards, then they should be prepared to sign on the appropriate international agreement. If they are serious about enforcement and willing to give up some sovereignty, then enforcement by means of trade penalties should not be ruled out. They should not be ruled out even if the penalties involve others' processes and production methods, where these are intrinsic to the problem at hand (e.g., coal-generated electric power, in the case of the Kyoto Climate Change convention). But if the members decline to negotiate such penalties multilaterally, individual countries should not be able on their own to adopt unilateral import barriers under the name of labor or the environment.

How Should Global Trade Liberalization Proceed?

Now that most tariffs have been reduced substantially, the remaining non-tariff barriers are more important, and merit more attention, even though they are inherently more complicated to negotiate. This was said at the time of each of the General Agreement of Tariffs and Trade (GATT) rounds of the last 40 years. But it has been true each time.

The challenge in proposing multilateral negotiations is not to identify sectors that remain to be liberalized. There are lots of those. Rather, it is to identify a set of liberalizations that is perceived by each major participant as a package that on net offers major benefits. Furthermore, under a well-known principle of political economy, which might be called reciprocal mercantilism, the benefits had better accrue to important producer interests in each country. The economist's argument that liberalization is beneficial to *consumers* in the importing country does not carry much weight in the political sphere.

There have been some exceptions to this rule of political economy in recent years. One type of exception is unilateral liberalizations in some countries that had become disenchanted with old import substitution policies. Another was a few post-Uruguay Round multilateral liberalizations in single sectors such as information technology, financial services, or telecommunications, in the late 1990s. These single sector negotiations succeeded despite the absence of scope for trading concessions across producers, because they involve sectors that firms in many countries see as *inputs* important to industrial development.[28] But it is unlikely that those single-sector negotiations can be repeated for many other industries.

The Form of Negotiations: Where and Who?

Should attempts at further liberalization be unilateral, regional, or multilateral? One possible, short answer is that we should take liberalization wherever we can get it. But this question is worth addressing at greater length, with an eye towards the political economy of what is possible.

Consider three alternative guiding principles or frameworks for thinking about trade negotiations:

1. *Mercantilist logic* tells each country that its goal should be to increase net exports. Even if this passed the tests of good economics, which it does not, it can't be achieved, since countries' trade balances have to add up. It is too stringent a criterion, in the sense that no global package of trade policies will satisfy it.
2. *Economists' logic* says the goal in international negotiations should be to leave each country better off economically in the aggregate. But this principle is not necessarily strong enough to get a deal politically. It is too easy a criterion in the sense that lots of packages satisfy the economics but not the politics. If income gains in the aggregate were a sufficient criterion, then unilateral liberalization would be easy, and international bargaining would not be necessary. The economists' logic applies to a country's aggregate real income; but in any real-world deal some gain (including consumers) and some lose (especially producers in uncompetitive sectors). Typically, although the gainers from trade liberalization outnumber the losers, the losers have more concentrated losses and tend to speak loudly, and are thereby able to block deals where the gains are

[28] Hufbauer and Wada (1997); Council of Economic Advisers (1999).

not large and easily identified. Thus, it is necessary to ask, 'Who are the key players and who must agree to the agenda?'

3. *Negotiators' logic*—each major group of countries needs to decide what some of the things it wants and what things it is willing to give up. Then there has to be enough of an overlap to get a deal. What should they want? Each country should want a package where the gains exceed the losses by a *sufficient* margin to make it through the domestic political process. Leaders, who understand the importance of the latter, know something that many economists do not.

Unilateral vs. Reciprocal

Bilateral or multilateral agreements where each country grants concessions in favor of its trading partners' products, in return for the concessions that its partners make, are the most common mechanism for achieving trade liberalization. Economists often urge countries to liberalize unilaterally. Although a few countries have pursued such a strategy (e.g., Chile, Mexico, Singapore), the typical country faces too much opposition from the import competing sectors that stand to lose from unilateral liberalization. Reciprocal liberalization is more workable politically. On top of the usual benefits of increased efficiency of production and gains to consumers from international trade, it adds a bonus, namely increased demand for the country's exports in the markets that are reciprocally liberalized. Adding the interests of specific identifiable exporters to the pro-liberalization side is more likely to make it possible to overcome the votes of those opposed:

> ... how can I convince a Tanzanian dairy farmer, who keeps a few cows but cannot sell his milk because the market is flooded with subsidized imported milk, that an open market is better than a closed or regulated one? ... If I cannot convince these people, from where will I draw a mandate for further deregulation and liberalization in my country? (Mkapa 2004)

The question of unilateral versus reciprocal liberalization is 'live' in the rhetorical debate regarding developing countries. Many advocates of poor countries demand that the rich countries remove their barriers to imports, such as on agricultural products and labor-intensive manufactures and their subsidies to cotton and other agricultural products that could be exported by developing countries. (In the case of NGOs such as Oxfam, this new position represents a substantial improvement over the preceding heavy emphasis on transfers to the exclusion of trade.) On the one hand, these advocates point out, correctly, the hypocrisy of the United States and other Western countries who lecture others on the virtues of free markets and 'pulling themselves up by their own bootstrap,' while simultaneously closing off their markets to products, in cases like cotton and sugar, for the benefit of a very small coddled domestic interest group. On the other hand, some Americans respond that developing countries could do much to help themselves unilaterally by removing their own import barriers, which tend to be high and are often especially high against the exports of their fellow developing countries. They argue that rich country protectionism may become the latest excuse that poor countries adopt to explain why they can't develop (which would be ironic, since the preceding excuse was imperialist exploitation in the form of fostering among poor countries excessive dependence on exports such as agricultural products), obscuring that the main policy levers for growth are in the hands of the developing countries themselves.

Both sides of the argument make correct points analytically. But this debate is an example of the generalization that unilateral liberalization—whether by rich or poor—is often infeasible politically. Indeed, if it is not possible politically to use economic arguments regarding domestic self-interest (gains to consumers, etc.) to achieve unilateral liberalization in rich countries, it is even less likely to be possible to use arguments about the interests of poor countries in order to persuade the rich to open up unilaterally. Multilateral liberalization is both more feasible politically and more beneficial economically, by creating identifiable winners among exporters. In this context, developing countries should agree to give up much of their high trade barriers in return for major concessions on the other side.

Regional vs. Multilateral

Given the difficulty of reaching agreements at the multilateral level, the question arises of whether more progress might be made at the regional level where fewer players are involved; political goals might help, and the countries might in any case be natural trading partners.[29] From 1982 to 1994, regionalism had a lot of momentum, in part because progress at the multilateral level was so slow (blocked largely by failure of the EU to agree to US demands to liberalize agriculture). But regional arrangements no longer look like such a promising alternative outside of Europe. On the one hand, the Uruguay Round was successfully concluded, while on the other hand regional clubs in the Western hemisphere have made no further progress, and in Asia have so far come to nothing. The current obstacles to liberalization (such as concerns about national sovereignty, the environment, inequality, and labor rights) exist as fully at the regional level as at the multilateral level. We might as well have the debate at the global level, where it really counts.

The general rule stands that packages must offer perceived benefits to producer interests in each major country. This means a package of market

[29] Frankel (1997) offers an analytical framework that evaluates whether regional trading arrangements are natural—more likely to be trade-creating than trade-diverting—and an extensive review of the literature, including the political economy of regional arrangements.

opening measures in a variety of well chosen areas. Even though progress in the Millennium Round (also called the Doha Round or Development Round) has been slow, it should remain the highest priority.[30]

The Developing Countries

Even though decisions in the GATT and WTO are technically made by consensus, with each country having an equal vote, it is inevitable that some players in practice count far more than others. The pattern in past GATT rounds has been that cut-and-thrust exchange between the United States and Europe has dominated the negotiations, and when those two powers had come to some agreement, the rest of the world generally fell into line. Other countries had little influence over the agenda. Little vote was given to the developing countries, largely because they had little in the way of lucrative concessions to offer the rich countries.

Increasingly, however, the developing countries are important players, at least collectively. Asia and Latin America now constitute major markets. Under the new rules agreed upon in the Uruguay Round they, like other WTO members, are generally no longer able to opt out of aspects of an agreement,[31] or to block decisions by panels under the dispute settlement mechanism. Furthermore, in the Uruguay Round developing countries were asked in the area of intellectual property rights to put energy into enforcement of a set of rules that, whatever their economic justification, benefit rich country corporations and not them. Next time their interests will have to be taken into account. This means liberalization of trade in textiles, apparel, and agriculture, as already noted. It also means protection against arbitrary anti-dumping measures. If a new round has nothing to offer the developing countries, they might this time try to block it. This was the message of the failed Cancun summit of September 2003.

Environment and Labor Standards

The other relevant set of players, who have gained a new seat at the table de facto if not de jure, are the NGOs in areas such as environmental and social policy. They are often confused and inconsistent about what they want. It was surprising at the time of the Seattle Ministerial to see demonstrators from the environmentalist and labor movements claim to share some beliefs about the

[30] Progress is unlikely to accelerate after the 2004 US presidential election, because the president will need to pass a farm bill and new fast-track authorization in 2006.

[31] Bhagwati (1998). The requirement that WTO members must adhere to all negotiated obligations as a 'single undertaking' still has exceptions for the poorest developing countries. Also, two areas, government procurement and civil aviation, remain under 'plurilateral accords' of the WTO (see Schott 1998).

proper role for multilateral institutions. (The former's complaint about the WTO is, for example, that they see it as an obstacle to enforcing regulations like the Kyoto Protocol on Global Climate Change. The latter are the strongest opponents to the Kyoto Protocol.) It was even more surprising to see them claim to share some interest with the populations of poor countries. (The labor and environmental groups want Western countries to import less from poor countries, the latter want them to import more.)

Nevertheless, the day has passed when those working to advance free trade can respond to environmental and labor concerns by simply explaining that the WTO deals only with trade. It is possible that some discussion of these issues will have to take place under the auspices of the WTO,[32] going beyond the step taken at the Singapore Ministerial of 1997 of mentioning the words 'labor and environment' in the agreement. Even if the discussion remains outside the WTO, some acceleration of effort towards international agreements on environmental and labor standards is necessary.

The ultimate goal should be international agreements voluntarily entered into. There is no alternative in a world of sovereign countries. The logical locus for most international agreements is designated multilateral institutions, such as the ILO in the case of labor standards, and the UN Framework Convention on Climate Change (UNFCCC) in the case of greenhouse gases, etc. In the meantime, one must recognize, as the NGOs point out, that the WTO is a more credible institution than the ILO or the UNFCCC, and that this is in part because withholding trade is one of the few powerful weapons that countries have, short of military action. The ILO, UNFCCC, and United Nations Environment Program (UNEP) have no teeth.

But the reason these institutions lack teeth is because the member countries, so far, want it that way. The failure to agree on binding international standards enforced by sanctions is attributable to the desire for retaining national sovereignty, to disagreements among countries, and to *internal* disagreements within each country on what priority to assign labor rights and the environment. It is the fault neither of globalization nor the international institutions themselves. Agreements should include sanctions if and only if members, acting through their chosen national governments, can agree that they want them to.

[32] In the past, the immediate legal obstacle to including most environmental and labor issues, beyond the more fundamental political obstacles, has been the key distinction between internationally traded goods, which are the proper subject of internationally agreed rules, and the processes by which the goods are produced within each country, which have not been considered an appropriate subject for the WTO. It might be argued that the inclusion of intellectual property rights in the Uruguay Round and the shrimp-turtle case in which the WTO panel and appellate body affirmed the right of the United States to seek to influence the methods used by shrimp fishermen in the Indian Ocean, have now shattered the distinction regarding processes. But environmentalists have failed to notice this trend or to capitalize on the precedent.

The anti-globalizers' choice of rhetoric is frequently perverse. They claim to want more decisions made more democratically in the WTO, even though a transfer of power from the United States to India, the world's largest democracy, would result in lower priority on labor and environmental standards, not more. They claim to want to assert national sovereignty against the trespasses of multilateral organizations like the WTO even though, again, national sovereignty is increasingly the obstacle to addressing environmental problems, not the means. Nevertheless, one can try to look past their choice of rhetoric, and to understand their frustration that they don't have an adequate vehicle for seeking to mobilize political support for international agreements with teeth.

One approach is to facilitate the desired ability of individuals to use their purchasing power as a signal to express their values and beliefs, and as a weapon to pressure corporations and countries to behave in particular ways. Such signals and weapons should help pressure the system to move in the direction of international agreements of the sort noted above. Multilateral institutions can play a major constructive role in the areas of:

- certification—monitoring multinational corporations that commit to particular codes of conduct, along the lines of the UN Global Compact;
- labeling—so that consumers can, if they choose to, exercise their right not to consume products that they view as environmentally or socially harmful or objectionable—for example, dolphin-unfriendly tuna or turtle-unfriendly shrimp.

But we should establish from the outset that countries must not make up their own rules for international trade, imposing trade penalties on other democratic countries in an attempt to bully them into changing their environmental or social policies, in violation of WTO rules. Without this assurance, developing countries will refuse altogether to discuss the whole subject of environmental and labor standards in the context of the WTO.

Priority Sectors for Negotiation

In what sectors are the prospects of efficiency gains from liberalization promising?

TEXTILES AND OTHER MANUFACTURES

The WTO has not finished lowering tariffs and quotas on manufactured products. This is especially true of manufactured imports into developing countries.

We have already mentioned textiles and apparel, the first rung of manufacturing exports for poor countries seeking to climb the ladder of development.

Rich countries agreed in 1995, under the Uruguay Round, to phase out over the subsequent 10 years the quotas that under the Multifibre Arrangement (MFA) had long kept the textile sector highly protected. The 10 years are now up, and little liberalization has occurred. The difficult time the administration had convincing the US Congress to support the elimination of barriers to apparel exports even from Africa and the Caribbean is revealing. China's accession to the WTO alarms some with the prospect of a huge increase in the global supply of inexpensive textiles and apparel. The United States and other rich countries should meet their obligation to keep their markets open. If rich countries fail fully to deliver on this promise, it is hard to see what incentive developing countries have to go along with a new round, or even to carry out their Uruguay Round commitments in the area of intellectual property rights.[33]

BUILT-IN AGENDA: AGRICULTURE AND SERVICES

Agriculture and services were both exempted from the original GATT rules. Both were formally brought under the WTO in the Uruguay Round that was completed in 1994. But in both cases, serious liberalization was postponed. Agriculture and services constitute the 'built-in agenda' of negotiations that was left for the future. Distortions in agriculture remain as high as ever—import barriers, export subsidies, and producer subsidies—especially in industrialized countries.[34] The Uruguay Round only got as far as expressing these distortions in terms of tariffs, with an eye towards facilitating future negotiated reductions. Anderson et al. (1999) estimate that one-third of the total worldwide gain from rich countries eliminating distortions in their goods markets is to be had in agriculture.[35] It is important in such discussions to disaggregate agriculture. If rich countries liberalized their markets in cotton, sugar, dairy, meat, peanuts, and tropical products, it would benefit developing countries that produce these products. But if they eliminated subsidies on some other major agricultural products, such as grains, it would actually be likely to hurt the developing countries that import these products.

Services constitute a diverse category of sectors, most of which have historically been less affected by trade than goods sectors, but many of which (e.g., business services) engage increasingly in trade, in part due to the Internet and other advances in telecommunications and computer technology.

[33] Wang and Winters (2000), Arvind Subramanian (1999).

[34] Less developed countries tend to tax agriculture rather than subsidizing it. In OECD countries, agricultural protection, measured as the rate of assistance, has risen to about 60 percent in 1998, from about 30 percent 30 years earlier, a period during which tariffs on industrial goods have fallen sharply (Hertel 1999; and Roberts et al. 1999).

[35] Anderson et al. (1999).

Within the large and diverse category of services, perhaps the greatest efficiency gains are to be had by liberalizing transportation services. Protection levels tend to be higher for transport services than for construction and business services.[36] The airline industry is heavily regulated internationally—passengers, air cargo, and express—with an overabundance of national champions and a lack of competition. The shipping industry is even more highly regulated and cartelized, and unevenly so around the globe. 'Liner conferences' operate as cartels. Thus the airline, shipping, and trucking sectors are prime candidates for liberalization. Their role as inputs into international trade makes them doubly important candidates: not only would liberalization reduce costs in the transport sector, but the enhanced ease of international trade would confer additional gains throughout the global economy.

Other Issues for Negotiation

An increasing number of issues cut across sectors of the economy.

ANTI-DUMPING

While trade distortions have been reduced in many areas, and are roughly unchanged in others, there is one kind of distortion that is on the upswing. That is anti-dumping (AD) measures. The name 'anti-dumping' sounds like it has something to do with anti-trust enforcement against predatory pricing; thus it gives the press and public the impression that these measures are a tool to combat trade distortions and increase competition. But they have nothing to do with predatory pricing, they suppress competition rather than defend it, and they are among the costliest of trade barriers.[37]

The use of AD measures has increased rapidly in the United States over the last two decades, because firms hit by increased imports have found it much easier to gain protection under the anti-dumping laws than under the safeguard laws. Their use has subsequently increased rapidly in other countries as they emulate and retaliate against the United States.[38] An attempt to rein in the indiscriminate use of anti-dumping would rank near the top of the economist's wish list of priorities for the next round of multilateral negotiations. (It could be coupled with some steps towards a multilateral competition policy, to reassure those who are under the illusion that the AD laws have some pro-competition value.) Unfortunately, the United States is reluctant to make concessions on this issue.

[36] Hoekman (1995, 1999).

[37] The enactment of anti-dumping duties means import quantities on average fall by almost 70 percent and import prices rise by more than 30 percent (Prusa 2000).

[38] e.g., China initiated 22 AD investigations in 2003, compared to six in 2000 (*FT*, June 7, 2004).

COMPETITION POLICY AND INVESTMENT

The Uruguay Round already included an agreement on trade-related investment measures, but its effects were minimal. Some hoped to generalize provisions in NAFTA to the multilateral level. But opposition from suspicious developing countries led to an attempt to begin by using the OECD as a venue for negotiating a multilateral agreement on investment (MAI) among industrial countries alone. Notwithstanding the inadequacy of the MAI, NGOs rallied opposition in a surprising first display of successful electronic populism that presaged Seattle. Some combination of that opposition and French intransigence killed the MAI in 1998. Investment may not now be the most promising issue with which to make progress in multilateral negotiations. If it is to be pursued, which would require more thought regarding environmental and labor standards, it should probably be moved back to the WTO.[39] But along with two other of the 'Singapore issues'—competition policy and procurement—only the EU wanted to pursue investment in the Doha Round that was launched in November 2001, and it has now agreed to drop it.

The world is probably even less ready for a comprehensive multilateral agreement in the related area of competition policy.[40] Countries vary widely in their conception of what sort of competition policy is desirable, even at the domestic level. History suggests that formation of a consensus world-view on an issue, even before horse-trading begins, is a prerequisite for international cooperation.[41]

GOVERNMENT PROCUREMENT

Potential gains from an agreement for enhanced market access in public procurement would be substantial, particularly covering such services as construction, maintenance, and repair services.[42] But this is yet another area where developing countries are in effect being asked to make larger concessions than industrialized countries, and that the EU has recently agreed to drop.

ENFORCEMENT OF DSM RULINGS

The Uruguay Round created in the WTO a dispute settlement mechanism (DSM) purged of the crippling limitation that the losing country could block a panel ruling. On the whole, it has worked well. But a mechanism to compel enforcement is still lacking. The EU has been very slow to comply with adverse panel rulings in the cases of bananas and hormone treated beef.[43] The US has been very slow to comply with adverse panel rulings in the cases of US foreign sales corporations, ruled a subsidy to exports in violation of WTO rules. The dispute settlement procedure could be strengthened in new

[39] Bhagwati (1998) and Graham (1998). [40] Richardson (1998).
[41] Cooper (1986). [42] Francois et al. (1996). [43] Jackson (2000).

negotiations, perhaps by adopting monetary penalties for non-compliance as Robert Lawrence has suggested, in place of the current system of approving retaliation in unrelated sectors.

Estimates of Welfare Gains from Further Multilateral Liberalization

Statistical estimates of the association between trade and growth, of the sort discussed earlier, cannot be used by themselves to put a number on the benefits of specific negotiations to liberalize trade. Too many other factors have contributed to the observed increase in trade in addition to past liberalization, such as technological reductions in the costs of transportation and communication. To assess the gains from multilateral negotiations aimed at further liberalization, we must turn to microeconomic models. Of the various possible econometric approaches to modeling trade, the computable general equilibrium (CGE) models are the most popular for evaluating multilateral negotiations, because they attempt to take into account interactions across sectors. An evaluation of the effects of lifting steel quotas, for example, would include not just the savings to firms that buy steel, but also the impact via the prices and sales of products made from steel, the impact on industries that produce other materials that might compete with steel, the diversion of resources out of the steel industry in steel importing countries and into other industries, the reverse movement within steel exporting countries, and so forth.

A number of researchers used versions of a global CGE model called the Global Trade Analysis Project, in advance of the Doha Ministerial, to evaluate the possible effects from a new WTO round. Hertel (1999) estimated that the gains from reducing trade barriers in manufacturing, services, and agriculture, to take effect in 2005, would be a global welfare gain of nearly US$350 billion. Other estimates were similar, depending particularly on the experiment in question.[44] Overall, the static gains were estimated on the order of 1 percent of world income. Welfare gains on this order are often described as disappointingly low. But an annual gain of US$300 billion is in fact a huge number,

[44] Nagarajan (1999) includes in his experiment a modest reduction in trade costs from a WTO agreement on trade facilitation, coupled together with a 50 percent across-the-board cut in worldwide protection in all agricultural, industrial, and services sectors. He estimates resulting annual welfare gains of around US$400 billion for the world economy, or about 1.4 percent of global income. In addition, a WTO agreement on competition is said to generate an annual welfare gain of approximately US$85 billion. Dee and Hanslow (2000) use a version of the model that has been modified to include the effects of foreign direct investment, so as to be able better to get at liberalization in services. They project an increase in world real income of more than US$260 billion in current dollars as a result of eliminating all post-Uruguay trade barriers (pp. 17–18). About US$50 billion of this would come from agricultural liberalization, US$80 billion from liberalization of manufactures, and US$130 billion from liberalizing services trade.

especially when one takes the (present discounted) sum over time. Perhaps it would sound more impressive as the numerator of a benefit/cost ratio, where the denominator is the budget of the WTO (a mere US$76 million per annum) and of national trade negotiators.

More recent estimates of the comparative static gains in economic welfare from a hypothetical full global liberalization of goods and services trade, surveyed by Anderson (2004), are similar. The more conservative estimates are: US$254 billion (1995 dollar, taking 2005 as the baseline year) according to ADFHHM (2002), US$355 billion (1997 dollar, on 2005 baseline year) according to WBGEP (2003), and US$367 billion (1997 dollar, on 1997 baseline year) according to FMT (2003).[45] In round numbers, again 1 percent of gross world product. Approximately half the gains accrue to OECD countries and half to poor countries. More specifically, according to the Anderson (2004) estimates of welfare gains to be had from removing all post-Uruguay Round barriers to goods trade, 57 percent of the gains accrue to developed countries and 43 percent to developing.

The more relevant policy question is what sorts of liberalization are most important. Liberalization by high-income countries is credited with 55 percent of world gains. The most important sector for liberalization is agriculture and food (responsible for 65 percent of global gains). Here the view that the emphasis should be on barriers in rich countries is true in that three times as much of the benefits of agricultural liberalization come from rich-country liberalization as poor; on the other hand three times as much of the benefits go to rich countries as well. Liberalization in manufactures also matters, and here it is the removal of the barriers kept by developing countries that is most important, responsible for three-quarters of the total. If one is choosing among priorities for liberalization by developing countries, in their own interests, the estimated returns to the agriculture and food sector are exactly the same as the return to manufactures (including textiles and clothing): each is equal to 12.3 percent of the aggregate global gains from removal of all remaining barriers to goods trade.

As estimates from the potential gains from the Doha Round, these CGE estimates are very optimistic in that trade negotiations usually in fact fall far short of goals such as cutting barriers in half, let alone eliminating them completely, as the authors know. On the other hand, they are conservative in two respects.

1. They build into the baseline full liberalization with respect to China, Taiwan, and textiles and apparel because it has already been agreed, though it might not be realistic to think it will be fully implemented.

[45] Anderson et al. (2002); Brown et al. (2003); Francois et al. (2003).

2. More importantly, they only attempt to capture static gains. The estimates of the CGE models are not generally designed to take into account the possible long-term effects on the growth rate, as opposed to a one-shot effect on the level of real income—the dynamic benefits mentioned earlier in this chapter.

As already noted, these potential dynamic gains include the benefits of technological improvements through increased contact with foreigners and their alternative production styles. Such interactions can come, for example, from direct investment by foreign firms with proprietary knowledge, or by the exposure to imported goods that embody technologies developed abroad. For a back of the envelope calculation that includes all growth effects, one approach is to return to the macro estimates of the effect of openness on growth. One of the CGE estimates entails a 20 percent increase in global trade volumes,[46] raising the global levels of merchandise exports plus imports as a share of income from a ratio of about 37 percent to 45 percent. Combining it with the 0.3 Frankel-Romer coefficient implies that global liberalization might raise global income per capita by 2 percent over a two decade period (and four times that in the truly long run). In other words, the dynamic gains over 20 years are roughly double the static estimates. Needless to say, such a calculation merits many qualifications. And some will say these effects are small. But to me they seem large. If trade can have long-term effects of this nature, it makes the case for further integration even more compelling.

References

Acemoglu, D., Johnson, S., and Robinson, J. (2001). 'Colonial Origins of Comparative Development: An Empirical Investigation'. *American Economic Review*, 91: 1369–401.

——— ——— ——— (2002*a*). 'Reversal of Fortune: Geography and Institutions in the Making of the Modern World Income Distribution', *Quarterly Journal of Economics*.

——— ——— ——— and Thaicharoen, Y. (2002*b*). 'Institutional Causes, Macroeconomic Symptoms: Volatility, Crises and Growth'. NBER Working Paper, No. 9124 (August).

Alcalá, F. and Ciccone, A. (2002). 'Trade and Productivity'. Working Paper (July), Universitat Pompeu Fabra.

Anderson, K. (2004). 'Subsidies and Trade Barriers'. Centre for International Economic Studies, University of Adelaide, Australia. (One of ten Challenge Papers prepared for the Copenhagen Consensus, roundtable May 24–8, 2004.)

——— and Hoekman, B., and Strutt, A. (1999). 'Agriculture and the WTO: Next Steps'. CEPR Workshop on New Issues in the World Trading System, London, February 19–20.

——— and Dimaranan, B., Francois, J., Hertel, T., and Martin, W. (2002). 'The Burden of Rich (and Poor) Country Protectionsim on Developing Countries'. *Journal of African Economies*, 10/3: 227–57 (September).

[46] Hertel (1999: 15–16).

Antweiler, W., Copeland, B., and Taylor, M. S. (1998). 'Is Free Trade Good for the Environment?' NBER Working Paper, No. 6707 (August).

Bhagwati, J. (1988). 'Export Promoting Trade Strategy: Issues and Evidence'. *World Bank Research Observer*, 3/1: 27–57 (January).

—— (1998). 'Fifty Years: Looking Back, Looking Forward'. Paper given at the Symposium on the World Trading System, WTO and Graduate Institute of International Studies, Geneva.

—— and Hudec, R. (eds.) (1996). *Fair Trade and Harmonization—Vol. 1: Economic Analysis*. Cambridge, MA: MIT Press.

Bosworth, B. and Collins, S. (2003). 'The Empirics of Growth: An Update'. *Brookings Papers on Economic Activity*, 2: 113–206.

Bradford, C., Jr. (1994). *From Trade-Driven Growth to Growth-Driven Trade: Reappraising the East Asian Development Experience*. Paris: Organisation for Economic Cooperation and Development.

—— and Chakwin, N. (1993). 'Alternative Explanation of the Trade–Output Correlation in the East Asian Economies'. OECD Development Centre Technical Papers, No. 87, Paris (August).

Brown, D., Deardorff, A., and Stern, R. (2003). 'Multilateral, Regional and Bilateral Trade-Policy Options for the United States and Japan'. *The World Economy*, 26/6: 803–28 (June).

Coe, D. and Helpman, E. (1993). 'International R&D Spillovers'. National Bureau of Economic Research Working Paper, No. 4444 (August).

Cooper, R. (1986). 'International Cooperation in Public Health as a Prologue to Macroeconomic Cooperation'. Brookings Discussion Papers in International Economics, No. 44, Brookings (March).

Council of Economic Advisers. (1999). *Economic Report of the President*, February, 224–6.

de Melo, J. and Robinson, S. (1991). 'Productivity and Externalities: Models of Export-Led Growth'. PRE Working Papers, No. PS 387. Washington, DC: World Bank.

Dee, P. and Hanslow, K. (2000). 'Multilateral Liberalisation of Services Trade'. *Productivity Commission Staff Research Paper*. Canberra: Ausinfo, 17–18.

DeLong, B. and Summers, L. (1991). 'Equipment Investment and Economic Growth'. *Quarterly Journal of Economics*, 56/2: 445–502.

Diamond, J. (1997). *Guns, Germs and Steel*. New York: W. W. Norton and Co.

Dollar, D. (1992). 'Outward-oriented Developing Economies Really Do Grow More Rapidly: Evidence from 95 LDCs: 1976–1985'. *Economic Development and Cultural Change*, 40: 523–44.

Easterly, W. and Levine, R. (2002). 'Tropics, Germs, and Endowments'. NBER Working Paper, No. 9106, Carnegie-Rochester Conference Series on Public Policy.

Edwards, S. (1992). 'Trade Orientation, Distortions, and Growth in Developing Countries'. *Journal of Development Economics*, 39/1: 31–57 (June).

—— (1993*a*). 'Openness, Trade Liberalization, and Growth in Developing Countries'. *Journal of Economic Literature* XXXI, 1358–93 (September).

—— (1993*b*). 'Trade Policy, Exchange Rates and Growth'. National Bureau of Economic Research Working Paper, No. 4511 (October).

Engel, C. and Rogers, J. (1996). 'How Wide is the Border?' *American Economic Review.*

Engerman, S. and Sokoloff, K. (1997). 'Factor Endowments, Institutions, and Differential Paths of Growth among New World Economies: A View From Economic Historians of the United States', in S. Haber (ed.) *How Latin America Fell Behind.* Stanford, CA: Stanford University Press, 260–304.

—— —— (2002). 'Factor Endowments, Inequality, and Paths of Development Among New World Economies'. Working Paper, No. 9259 (October).

Esfahani, H. (1991). 'Exports, Imports, and Economic Growth in Semi-Industrialized Countries'. *Journal of Development Economics*, 35/1: 93–116 (January).

Eusufzai, Z. (1996). 'Openness, Economic Growth, and Development: Some Further Results'. *Economic Development and Cultural Change*, 44/2: 333–50 (January).

Feder, G. (1982). 'On Exports and Economic Growth'. *Journal of Development Economics*, 12/1: 59–73 (Feb.–April).

Francois, J., Nelson, D., and Palmeter, N. D. (1996). 'Public Procurement: A Post-Uruguay Round Perspective'. CEPR Discussion Paper, No. 1412 (June).

Francois, J. F., Hertel, T., and van Tongeren, F. (2003). 'Trade Liberalization and Developing Countries Under the Doha Round'. CEPR Discussion Paper, No. 4032 (August).

Frankel, J. (1997). *Regional Trading Blocs.* Washington, DC: Institute for International Economics.

—— (2004). 'Globalization and the Environment', in M. Weinstein (ed.), *Globalization: What's New.* New York: Columbia University Press.

—— and Romer, D. (1999). 'Does Trade Cause Growth?' *American Economic Review*, 89/3: 379–99 (June).

—— Rose, A. (2002). 'An Estimate of the Effect of Currency Unions on Trade and Income'. *Quarterly Journal of Economics*, CXVII/2: 437–66 (May).

—— —— (2005). 'Is Trade Good or Bad for Pollution?' *Review of Economics and Statistics*, 87/1.

Fukuda, S. and Toya, H. (1995). 'Conditional Convergence in East Asian Countries: The Role of Exports for Economic Growth', in T. Ito and A. Krueger (eds.), *Growth Theories in Light of the East Asian Experience.* Chicago: University of Chicago Press.

Gallup, J., Sachs, J., and Messenger, A. (1998). 'Geography and Economic Development'. NBER Working Paper, No. 6849 (December).

Graham, E. (1998). 'Trade and Investment at the WTO: Just Do It', in J. Schott (ed.), *Launching New Global Trade Talks: An Action Agenda.* Washington, DC: Institute for International Economics.

Grossman, G. and Helpman, E. (1991*a*). *Innovation and Growth in the Global Economy.* Cambridge, MA: MIT Press.

—— —— (1991*b*). 'Trade, Knowledge Spillovers, and Growth'. *European Economic Review*, 35/2–3: 517–26 (April).

—— and Krueger, A. (1995). 'Economic Growth and the Environment'. *Quarterly Journal of Economics*, 353–77.

Hall, R. and Jones, C. (1999). 'Why do Some Countries Produce so Much More Output per Worker than Others?' *Quarterly Journal of Economics*, 114/1: 83–116 (February).

Harrison, A. (1995). 'Openness and Growth: A Time-Series, Cross-Country Analysis for Developing Countries'. NBER Working Paper, No. 5221 (August).

Helliwell, J. (1995). 'Asian Economic Growth', in W. Dobson and F. Flatters (eds.), *Pacific Trade and Investment: Options for the 90's*. Kingston, Ontario: International and Development Studies Institute, Queen's University.

—— (2000). *How Much Do National Borders Matter?* Washington, DC: Brookings Institution.

Helpman, E. (1987). 'Imperfect Competition and International Trade: Evidence from Fourteen Industrial Countries'. *Journal of the Japanese and International Economies*, 1: 62–81.

—— (1988). 'Growth, Technological Progress, and Trade'. National Bureau of Economic Research Working Paper, No. 1145.

—— and Krugman, P. (1985). *Market Structure and Foreign Trade*. Cambridge, MA: MIT Press.

Hertel, T. (1999). 'Potential Gains from Reducing Trade Barriers in Manufacturing, Services and Agriculture'. 24th Annual Economic Policy Conference, Federal Reserve Bank of St. Louis, October 21–2.

Hoekman, B. (1995, 1999). 'Assessing the General Agreement on Trade in Services', in W. Martin and L. A. Winters (eds.), *The Uruguay Round and the Developing Economies*, Discussion Paper, No. 307. Washington, DC: World Bank.

Hufbauer, G. and Elliott, K. (1994). *Measuring the Costs of Protection in the United States*. Washington, DC: Institute for International Economics (January).

—— and Wada, E. (1997). *Unfinished Business: Telecommunications After the Uruguay Round*. Washington, DC: Institute for International Economics.

Hutchison, M. and Singh, N. (1987). 'Exports and Growth in Developing Economies: Identifying Externality Effects'. Working Paper, University of California: Santa Cruz.

—— —— (1992). 'Exports, Non-exports, and Externalities: A Granger Causality Approach'. *International Economic Journal*, 6/2: 79–94.

International Bank for Reconstruction and Development (IBRD) (1992). *World Development Report 1992: Development and the Environment*. New York: Oxford University Press.

Irwin, D. and Terviö, M. (2002). 'Does Trade Raise Income? Evidence from the Twentieth Century'. *Journal of International Economics*, 58: 1–18 (October).

Jackson, J. (2000). 'The Role and Effectiveness of the WTO Dispute Settlement Mechanism', in S. Collins and D. Rodrik (eds.), *Brookings Trade Forum: Policy Challenges for the New Millennium*, (April 27–8): 13.

Jaffe, A. et al. (1995). 'Environmental Regulation and the Competitiveness of U.S. Manufacturing: What Does the Evidence Tell Us?' *Journal of Economic Literature*, 33: 132–63.

Jung, W. and Marshall, P. (1985). 'Exports, Growth, and Causality in Developing Countries'. *Journal of Development Economics*, 18: 1–12.

Kim, J. and Lau, L. (1994). 'The Sources of Growth of the East Asian Newly-Industrialized Countries'. *Journal of the Japanese and International Economies*.

Kohli, I. and Singh, N. (1989). 'Exports and Growth: Critical Minimum Effort and Diminishing Returns'. *Journal of Development Economics*, 30/2: 391–400 (April).

Krueger, A. (1978). *Foreign Trade Regimes and Economic Development: Liberalization Attempts and Consequences*. Washington, DC: Ballinger for National Bureau of Economic Research.

Krugman, P. (1994). 'The Myth of Asia's Miracle'. *Foreign Affairs*, 73/6: 62–78 (Nov.–Dec.).

Lee, J. W. (1995). 'Capital Goods Imports and Long-Run Growth'. *Journal of Development Economics*, 48: 91–110 (Oct.).

Levine, R. and Renelt, D. (1992). 'A Sensitivity Analysis of Cross-Country Growth Regressions'. *American Economic Review*, 82/4: 942–63.

Maskus, K. (2002). 'Regulatory Standards in the WTO: Comparing Intellectual Property Rights with Competition Policy, Environmental Protection, and Core Labor Standards'. *World Trade Review*, 1/2: 135–52 (July).

Michaely, M. (1977). 'Exports and Growth: An Empirical Investigation'. *Journal of Development Economics*, 4/1: 49–53 (March).

Mkapa, B. W. (2004). 'Cancun's False Promise: A View from the South'. *Foreign Affairs*, (May/June): 133–5.

Nagarajan, N. (1999). 'The Millennium Round: An Economic Appraisal'. Economic Papers, No. 139, European Commission, DG for Economic and Financial Affairs (November).

Noguer, M. and Siscart, M. (2002). *Trade Raises Income: A Precise and Robust Result.* New York: Department of Economics, New York University.

Pack, H. and Page, J. (1994). 'Accumulation, Exports, and Growth in the High-Performing Asian Economies'. *Carnegie-Rochester Series on Public Policy*, 40: 199–236.

Page, J. (1994). 'The East Asian Miracle: Four Lessons for Development Policy'. *NBER Macroeconomics Annual*. Cambridge, MA: MIT Press, 219–80.

Prusa, T. (2000). 'On the Spread and Impact of Antidumping'. NBER Working Paper, No. 7404.

Quah, D. and Rauch, J. (1990). 'Openness and the Rate of Economic Growth'. Working Paper. San Diego: University of California.

Richardson, J. D. (1998). 'The Coming Competition Policy Agenda in the WTO', in J. Schott (ed.), *Launching New Global Trade Talks: An Action Agenda*. Washington, DC: Institute for International Economics, 179–88.

Rivera-Batiz, L. and Romer, P. (1991). 'International Integration and Endogenous Growth'. *QJE*, 106: 531–56.

Roberts, I. et al. (1999). 'The Dynamics of Multilateral Agricultural Policy Reform'. 1999 Global Conference on Agriculture and the New Trade Agenda from a Development Perspective, World Bank and WTO, Geneva.

Rodríguez, F. and Rodrik, D. (2001). 'Trade Policy and Economic Growth: A Skeptic's Guide to the Cross-National Evidence'. *NBER Macroeconomics Annual 2001*. Cambridge, MA: MIT Press.

Rodrik, D. (1993). 'Trade and Industrial Policy Reform in Developing Countries: A Review of Recent Theory and Evidence'. National Bureau of Economic Research Working Paper, No. 4417 (August).

—— (1994*a*). 'King Kong Meets Godzilla: The World Bank and *The East Asian Miracle*'. CEPR Discussion Paper, No. 944 (April).

—— (1994*b*). 'Getting Interventions Right: How South Korea and Taiwan Grew Rich'. 20th Panel Meeting of Economic Policy, NBER Working Paper, No. 4964 (December).

—— (1997). *Has Globalization Gone Too Far?* Washington, DC: Institute for International Economics.

Rodrik, D., Subramanian, A., and Trebbi, F. (2002). 'Institutions Rule: The Primacy of Institutions over Geography and Integration in Economic Development'. CID Working Paper, No. 97 (October).

Romer P. (1994). 'New Goods, Old Theory and The Welfare Costs of Trade Restrictions'. *Journal of Development Economics*, 43/1: 5–38.

Rose, A. (2000). 'One Money, One Market? The Effect of Common Currencies on International Trade'. *Economic Policy*, 15/30: 8–45.

Sachs, J. (2001). 'Tropical Underdevelopment'. NBER Working Paper, No. 8119 (February).

—— (2003). 'Institutions Don't Rule: Direct Effects of Geography on Per Capita Income'. NBER Working Paper, No. 9490 (February).

—— Warner, A. (1995). 'Economic Reform and the Process of Global Integration'. *Brookings Papers on Economic Activity*, 1: 1–95.

Sala-i-Martin, X. (1991). 'Comment'. *NBER Macroeconomics Annual*, 6: 368–78.

Schott, J. (1998). 'The World Trade Organization: Progress to Date and the Road Ahead', in J. Schott (ed.), *Launching New Global Trade Talks: An Action Agenda*. Washington, DC: Institute for International Economics, 3.

Subramanian, A. (1999). 'Intellectual Property Rights'. Proceedings from Conference on Developing Countries and the New Round of Multilateral Trade Negotiations, Harvard University, November 5–6.

US International Trade Commission (USITC) (1997). *The Dynamic Effects of Trade Liberalization: An Empirical Analysis*, Investigation No. 332–75, Pub. 3069. Washington, DC: US International Trade Commission.

Van den Berg, H. (1994). 'Foreign Trade and Economic Growth: Time Series Evidence from Latin America'. *Journal of International Trade and Economic Development*, 3/3: 249–68 (November).

Wacziarg, R. (2001). 'Measuring the Dynamic Gains from Trade'. *World Bank Economic Review*, 15/3: 393–429 (October).

Wang, Z. K. and Winters, A. L. (2000). 'Putting "Humpty" Together Again: Including Developing Countries in a Consensus for the WTO'. CEPR Policy Paper, No. 4.

11

The World Trading System and Development Concerns

Martin Khor

Introduction

This chapter deals with trade policy and the world trading system from a development perspective. It starts with a review of the debate on trade liberalization, openness, and development in the next section, and makes some points on trade, development, and problems faced by developing countries in looking towards balancing the growth of their imports and exports in the third section. The problems facing developing countries in their commodity exports are examined in the fourth section, in particular the income losses experienced from falling commodity prices. While developing countries as a whole have increased the share of manufactures in their exports, and their share of world manufacturing exports, this picture is misleading as successful manufacturing exporting has been concentrated in relatively few countries, and the developing country share of world manufacturing value-added has actually decreased (covered in the fifth section).

The chapter then examines the global policy frameworks that influence developing countries' trade policy. It briefly reviews the role of loan conditionalities of the international financial institutions (IFIs) in the sixth section. A review is then made of the World Trade Organization (WTO), its objectives and principles, the problems arising from implementation of its rules, and specific agreements, including some recommendations on improving the situation in the seventh section. The effects of inappropriate import liberalization on industry and agriculture in developing countries are briefly looked at in the eighth section. Recent developments in the WTO, including the decision at its General Council meeting of July 2004, are analyzed in the ninth section. The chapter finally concludes with proposals on making the global trading system more oriented towards development needs.

Liberalization, Openness, and Development

The relationship between 'trade openness' and development has been one of the most contested issues in economic policy in recent times. The view from the 'Washington Consensus' is that trade openness is beneficial and indeed essential for the growth and development of a developing country. Countries that liberalize their imports and orientate production towards exports are assumed to have faster growth than those that do not, and the faster the rate of opening, the greater will be the prospect for development. This perspective underlies the policy conditionality of rapid or 'big bang' liberalization of the Bretton Woods institutions, under which many developing countries have lowered their applied tariffs on a wide range of products. This view is also the implicit assumption underlying the goal of import liberalization in the World Trade Organization.

Recently, the orthodox view has been augmented with the caveat that liberalization measures are not sufficient by themselves and should also be accompanied by sound macroeconomic policy, good governance, modern legal infrastructure, and other factors. However the basic approach, that liberalization has a direct positive link to growth and should be undertaken as fast as possible, remains intact.

In recent years, the orthodox view has been challenged by a number of empirical studies showing that there is a lack of relationship between the degree of trade liberalization and the rate of growth. These studies have raised doubts about the policy prescription of rapid trade liberalization. Empirical evidence is also growing on the negative consequences of rapid import liberalization on the industrial and agriculture sectors in many developing countries. There is an emerging paradigm that takes account of the complexities of the trade–development relationship, and stresses the importance of the context, sequencing, rate, and extent of trade liberalization if this process is to contribute to and not detract from development. Unlike the orthodox approach which implicitly assumes that there are only benefits to be derived from trade liberalization, the emerging paradigm accepts that there are possible costs as well as potential benefits of trade liberalization to a particular developing country, depending on the conditions in that country, and the type of liberalization undertaken. In this approach, it is thus crucial that the correct choices are made, with an appropriate blend between liberalization and protection, in a country's trade policy.

The orthodox assumption that countries that are poor are not sufficiently participating in world trade is not backed up by evidence. Many of the poorer countries are dependent on exports and may have higher export-to-GNP ratios than some industrialized countries or more advanced developing countries. However, they are dependent on their exports on primary commodities, the prices of which have declined over the past decades, especially when measured against the prices of manufactured products. The old colonial division of labor, in which the colonized territories exported raw materials and the colonial master countries exported manufactures, has continued to a significant extent. Although a number of developing countries have significant manufactured exports, a large number still depend on primary commodity exports. For them, the continuing decline in the terms of trade for their commodity exports vis-à-vis their imports of manufactures has resulted in the transfer of a huge volume of real resources through the mechanism of income losses arising from terms of trade changes. Thus it is not their lack of integration into world trade, but their integration in inappropriate ways in the world trading system, that has contributed to the persistence of poverty in these countries.

In the case of commodity exporters, there is a paradox that an expansion of export volume may bring about decreasing returns. A major cause of the decline in commodity prices is that there is a situation of oversupply in many commodities, as the growth of supply outstrips demand. Thus it is not correct that 'trade expansion' necessarily results in better income.

On the other hand, developing countries are advised to liberalize their imports in the expectation that this will result in welfare gain as consumers enjoy access to cheaper goods, and local producers are pressurized to become more efficient or to shift to more suitable activities in which they have a comparative advantage. In reality, many countries that rapidly liberalized their imports have experienced the collapse or reduced output of local industries, and the displacement of the market of local farmers. Moreover, as imports rose more than exports, many countries suffered wider trade deficits, making it more difficult for them to improve their external debt situation.

The United Nations Conference on Trade and Development's (UNCTAD) *Trade and Development Report 1999* found that for developing countries (excluding China) the average trade deficit in the 1990s was higher than in the 1970s by three percentage points of GDP, while the average growth rate was lower by two percentage points. In discussing why trade deficits have been increasing faster than income in developing countries, the report concludes: 'The evidence shows that a combination of declining terms of trade, slow growth in industrial countries and "big bang" liberalization of trade and of the capital account in developing countries has been a decisive factor' (UNCTAD 1999a: ch. VI).

On the role of rapid trade liberalization in generating the wider trade deficits, the report said:

> It [trade liberalization] led to a sharp increase in their import propensity, but exports failed to keep pace, particularly where liberalization was a response to the failure to establish competitive industries behind high barriers. With the notable exception of China, liberalization has resulted in a general widening of the gap between the annual

> growth of imports and exports in the 1990s, but the impact was particularly severe in Latin America, where the gap averaged about 4 percentage points.
>
> (UNCTAD 1999a: ch. VI)

One conclusion that can be drawn from the report is that if trade liberalization is carried out in an inappropriate manner in countries that are not ready or able to cope, or which face conditions that are unfavorable, it can contribute to a vicious cycle of trade and balance of payments deficits, financial instability, debt, and recession.

The UNCTAD report's findings correspond with some recent studies that show there is no automatic correlation between trade liberalization and growth. Countries that rapidly liberalized their imports did not necessarily grow faster than those that liberalized more gradually or in more strategic ways.

One of the earliest studies was by UNCTAD economist Mehdi Shafaeddin (1994), who surveyed 41 least developed countries (LDCs) and found

> no clear and systematic association since the early 1980s between trade liberalization and devaluation, on the one hand, and the growth and diversification of output and growth of output and exports of LDCs on the other. In fact, trade liberalization has been accompanied by deindustrialization in many LDCs, and where exports expanded it was not always accompanied by the expansion of supply capacity. (Shafaeddin 1994)

By contrast, the paper attributes success or failure of GDP and industrial growth to the volume of investment and availability of imports. 'The design of trade policy reforms has also been an important factor in performance failure.'

Dani Rodrik (1999) argued that developing nations must participate in the world economy on their own terms, not the terms 'dictated' by global markets and multilateral institutions. Noting the premise that reducing barriers to imports and opening to capital flows would increase growth and reduce poverty in developing countries, Rodrik concluded there is no convincing evidence that openness (low barriers to trade and capital flows) systematically produces these results.

> The lesson of history is that ultimately all successful countries develop their own brands of national capitalism. The States [sic] which have done best in the post-war period devised domestic investment plans to kick-start growth and established institutions of conflict management. An open trade regime, on its own, will not set an economy on a sustained growth path. (Rodrik 1999)

Rodrik (2001: 22) also found that

> cross-national comparison of the literature reveals no systematic relationship between a country's average level of tariff and non-tariff restrictions and its subsequent economic growth rate. If anything, the evidence for the 1990s indicates a positive (but statistically insignificant) relationship between tariffs and economic growth. The only

systematic relationship is that countries dismantle trade restrictions as they get richer. That accounts for the fact that today's rich countries, with few exceptions, embarked on modern economic growth behind protective barriers, but now have low trade barriers.

While few countries grew over long periods without having an increase in the share of their foreign trade in national product (and access to cheaper capital goods through imports is an important link between trade and growth), it is equally true that no country has developed simply by opening itself up to foreign trade and investment. The trick has been to combine the opportunities offered by world markets with a domestic investment and institution-building strategy, and almost all the outstanding cases (East Asia, China, and India since the early 1980s) involve partial and gradual opening up to imports and foreign investment (Rodrik 2001: 23–4).

The relation between trade policy and industrial policy is a crucial one. The orthodox Washington Consensus view is that a developing country should practice free trade and avoid an industrial policy targeted at developing selected sectors. The assumption is that if prices are right, there will be signals channeling resources to their most efficient use.

The poor record of such an approach led the orthodox thinkers to adopt what Rodrik calls the 'augmented Washington Consensus,' which recognizes that liberalization and privatization are not sufficient in themselves and need to be accompanied by creating institutional aspects that support the market, such as financial regulation, governance and anti-corruption, legal and administrative reform, labor market flexibility, and social safety nets. But these reforms have weaknesses. They are influenced by an Anglo-Saxon concept of desirable institutions, are driven by requirements for integrating into the world economy, and provide no sense of priorities among a list of institutional prerequisites, being at odds with practical realities and the historical experience of today's advanced economies (Rodrik 2001: 15–16).

Rodrik (2001: 16–21) outlines three types of investment strategies that have worked: import substituting industrialization (which was quite successfully practiced, with relatively high growth rates by many developing countries until they experienced a debt crisis in the mid-1970s), East Asian-style outward-oriented industrialization, and the Chinese style 'two-track strategy' (based on a combination of state and market, gradualism and experimentation).

Ha-Joon Chang and Ilene Grabel (2004) also show that both the present industrialized countries and the successful industrializing developing countries, with few exceptions, did not practice free trade during their development phase. They used a combination of policies, among which were high tariffs, tariff rebates on imported inputs used in the production of exports, export subsidies, restrictions on the export of raw materials used by key industries, government provision of information on export markets, and marketing assistance. These trade policies run counter to the present free trade orthodoxy. They counter the orthodox view that the state should not shape industrial development, and that selective industrial policy creates inefficiency, promotes corruption, compromises growth, and has not worked in developing countries. A large body of economic theory and empirical research provide a rationale for selective industrial policy, accompanied by a range of policies such as trade subsidies, licences, and the management of credit and capital allocation, prices, and investment. Selective industrial policies have been successfully used in both industrialized and developing countries. In Japan, South Korea, and Taiwan, governments used a mix of state intervention and market incentives to promote a range of domestic industries, and also used policy measures to modernize the industrial structure. These included infant industry protection, export and other business subsidies, directed credit (where state-controlled banks provided subsidized credit to designated industries), indicative investment planning, regulation, and coordination of industrial investment, research and development (R&D), and training. The automobile, steel, and electronics industries in Japan and Korea, and electronics and chemicals in Taiwan, would not have developed without industrial policy. Other developing countries also successfully used industrial policy, notably Brazil with its aerospace industry, and after World War II many European countries (including France, Austria, Norway, and Finland) aggressively used industrial policy (Chang and Grabel 2004: 53–80).

Most developing countries now face or potentially face the major problem that loan conditionalities and WTO principles and rules frown on and in many cases prohibit them from making use of the strategic trade policies or selective industrial policies that were utilized by the present industrialized countries and by the successfully industrializing developing countries. Moreover, their having to increasingly implement orthodox free trade policies has meant that the countries are open and vulnerable to their domestic industrial and agricultural sectors being damaged by competition from cheaper imports. The absence of industrial policy (as well as of an agriculture policy and a services policy) has also meant that they are unable to establish some of the crucial conditions and incentives required for development and growth, especially of the domestic economy.

Trade, Development, and the Need to Balance Imports and Exports

Trade is a means to and not a goal of development. To realize the potential of trade as a development instrument requires conditions tailored to the specific requirements of each country. These conditions for trade may differ from country to country, depending on such factors as the stage of development, resource endowment, and conditions relating to market access and prices of traded products. Thus, a one-size-fits-all approach will not work and, if enforced, might cause more harm than good. Each country has to make decisions on appropriate processes, degrees, and sequencing of trade and trade liberalization. The multilateral trading system should, therefore, be sensitive to the different needs of different countries, and allow them to have sufficient 'policy space' to choose from different options.

The two main components of trade are imports and exports, and a balance between the two is important. The factors determining imports and those that determine exports may differ. A country has more control over how fast it liberalizes its imports, but is much less able to influence the level and rate of growth of its exports.

Developing countries face two types of problems that hinder their effective and beneficial participation in international trade: pressures to liberalize their imports, affecting local production units in various sectors, including industry and agriculture; and the lack of adequate export earnings, export capacity, or opportunities. Under loan conditionalities of the international financial institutions, and under WTO rules, many developing countries have taken measures to rapidly liberalize their imports, and these have caused a rapid rise in imports. However, for many developing countries, the growth of export earnings has lagged, due to various factors, including a decline in commodity prices, continuing barriers to industrial exports, and supply constraints. As a result, there have been greater imbalances between imports and exports in many developing countries, adding to their trade deficits and external debt problem.

Pressures for Rapid Import Liberalization

Pressures on developing countries to rapidly open their economies to imports come from the Bretton Woods Institutions and the WTO (which set the global framework affecting trade policy) and the developed countries. According to orthodox theory, trade protection has negative effects, while trade liberalization brings benefits. While the negative effects of trade liberalization are sometimes recognized, they are seen as only temporary. According to the proponents of rapid liberalization, cheaper imports benefit the consumer, and generate greater efficiency in local firms, which are forced to compete to survive. Inefficient firms should close down, freeing resources to move to more efficient sectors, including for exports, and this is expected to generate new jobs and higher revenues. Overall, the economy is expected to gain.

However, this theory has been challenged by empirical evidence that indicates that there is no straightforward correlation between trade liberalization and overall economic growth (see the next sub-section).

Orthodox theory is also challenged by an emerging view that several other preconditions have to be present before trade openness can be of net benefit to developing countries. These include an adequate level of competitiveness of local firms or farms, the capacity to overcome supply-side constraints in producing for export, adequate levels of prices for the export products of developing countries, and the existence of export opportunities or adequate market access for their products. Other factors increasingly stressed by the international financial institutions (IFIs) include macroeconomic stability and good economic governance. In the absence of some or all of these prerequisites, import liberalization may not result in the projected benefits and may instead produce adverse results. It is thus critical to decide on the appropriate timing of liberalization in relation to the presence or absence of these prerequisites. It should be noted, however, that the IFIs and developed countries still insist on rapid liberalization in developing countries, even in those that do not have the conditions for successful liberalization. A more realistic and responsible approach would enable developing countries to first establish these conditions and integrate trade liberalization into their overall national development strategy when and where appropriate, rather than pressuring them to move towards an overly hasty liberalization of imports.

Constraints on Export Growth in Developing Countries

In many developing countries, the increase in imports was not matched by a corresponding expansion of export earnings. Many developing countries still depend on a few export commodities, and the continuous decline in their prices adversely affected export earnings. To realize its industrial export potential, a country must have the physical infrastructure and the human and enterprise capacity to produce competitively for both the local and export markets. This is a long and difficult process, making it unrealistic to expect that a developing country can quickly shift its resources from uncompetitive domestic industries threatened by the fast pace of import liberalization to globally competitive export industries.

It is rare for a developing country to be able to become a world-class exporter of modern industrial products based on its own locally-owned enterprises. Japan and South Korea developed their industries in a pre-WTO environment. Today, with WTO rules that severely constrain the use of subsidies for local industries, prohibit investment measures favoring the use of local components, and hinder local industries from using patented technology, it is far more difficult for developing countries to take a similar route.

A few developing countries have export industries based primarily on foreign direct investment (FDI). However, most of the industries are labor-intensive and the host countries are finding it difficult to prevent foreign companies from shifting operations to lower-cost countries. Moreover, developing countries cannot realistically base their growth primarily on FDI, as there is insufficient FDI, even if spread evenly throughout the developing world, for it to be the main basis for investment and job creation. Thus, developing countries have to develop their local industry and services, and rely on domestic capital and enterprises to generate jobs, livelihoods, growth, and exports, if they are to succeed as exporters. They also need mobilization and use of savings, and investment in health, education, and skills development and technology. To export, companies must establish regional and international marketing channels, brand development, or strategic alliances with bigger companies. It is not impossible for a country to succeed, but it is a difficult task with no guarantee of success.

Even then, successful export performance will also depend on market access. Currently, there are many barriers in the developed countries. As UNCTAD has pointed out, developing countries have been striving hard, often at considerable cost, to integrate more closely into the world economy. But protectionism in developed countries has prevented them from fully exploiting their existing or potential comparative advantage. The missed opportunities for them due to trade barriers are estimated at an additional US$700 billion in annual export earnings in low-tech industries alone (UNCTAD 1999a: 143).

The Consequences of Poorly Planned Trade Liberalization

To maintain a sustainable trade policy that also assists development, a developing country has to have a balance between imports and exports. Persistent trade deficits will have adverse consequences. It is thus important to re orient trade policy and the WTO operational principles away from the simplistic assumption that trade liberalization necessarily has a positive impact on developing countries. If the trading system is to meet the development needs and goals of developing countries, the criterion by which a policy should be judged should be whether it is development-consistent or development-distortive, rather than whether it is trade-consistent or trade-distortive.

Commodity Prices and Terms of Trade

A major problem in the world trading system is the decline in and volatility of prices of export commodities, and the resulting huge losses of income for exporting nations and their producers. The commodities crisis has been a longstanding problem since developing countries attained their independence, and even before that. It used to be perhaps the major economic issue on the international agenda, and was a major impetus for the establishment and initial work of UNCTAD when negotiations on commodities were the main item on the international trade agenda. However, from the mid-1980s, there has been a steady decline in the priority accorded to this issue in the international agenda. This has been unfortunate, as the decline in commodity prices in general has continued, with devastating effects on many developing countries. The commodities crisis has been a major cause of the persistence or even increase in poverty in the developing world. The low levels of and decline in commodity prices decrease the incomes of rural producers, place a constraint on export earnings, increase trade deficits, and keep many countries trapped in external debt. Resolving this problem is thus crucial.

From 1980 to 2000, world prices for 18 major export commodities fell by 25 percent in real terms. The decline was especially steep for cotton (47%), coffee (64%), rice (61%), cocoa (71%), and sugar (77%) (World Commission on the Social Dimension of Globalization 2004: 83).

The effects of falling commodity prices have been devastating for many countries. According to UN data, in Sub-Saharan Africa, a 28 percent fall in the terms of trade between 1980 and 1989 led to an income loss of US$16 billion in 1989 alone. In the four years 1986–89, Sub-Saharan Africa suffered a US$56 billion income loss, or 15–16 percent of GDP in 1987–89. For 15 middle-income highly-indebted countries, there was a combined terms of trade decline of 28 percent between 1980 and 1989, causing an average loss of US$45 billion per year in the 1986–89 period, or 5–6 percent of GDP (Khor 1993).

In the 1990s, the losses were higher. Non-oil primary commodity prices fell by 33.8 percent from the end of 1996 to February 1999, resulting in a cumulative terms of trade loss of more than 4.5 percent of income during 1997–98 for developing countries. 'Income losses were greater in the 1990s than in the 1980s not only because of larger terms-of-trade losses, but also because of the increased share of trade in GDP' (UNCTAD 1999a: 85). Moreover, the prices of some key manufactured products exported by developing countries have also declined. For example, the Republic of Korea experienced a 25 percent fall in the terms of trade of its manufactured exports between 1995 and 1997 due to a glut in the world market (UNCTAD 1999a: 87).

Among agricultural commodities exported by developing countries, some are in competition with the same commodities produced by developed countries. For such products, like cotton and sugar, the world prices are lower largely because of the high domestic and export subsidies attached to the developed countries' exports. The share of global export revenue accruing to developing countries has dropped in many cases, with the developed countries having an increased share. A large part of the problem facing developing countries is related to the subsidies of the rich countries, which give the latter an unfair advantage.

Besides competing with subsidized Northern products, developing countries face many problems, including their products being at the lower end of the value chain with the lack of capacity (or the lack of market access) to climb the value chain through processing and manufacturing. Another problem is a situation of global oversupply in the case of some commodities, which exerts a downward pressure on prices. This is partly the result of too many countries being advised by international agencies to expand the export of the same commodities. Yet another problem is that the developing countries have little bargaining power when selling their products to monopsonist buyers, which are usually transnational companies, and thus they get lower prices.

Following the collapse of the commodity agreements, there has been an absence of international institutions or mechanisms to tackle the key concerns of low level and volatility of commodity prices and the mismatch between supply and demand. Individual agencies such as the international financial institutions and UN organizations have suggested measures that individual producer countries can take to counter the fall in prices. However, as pointed out by Peter Robbins (2003), most of these suggested schemes have not worked, as they did not tackle the root problem of excess supply and the absence of a regulated framework.

> They have suggested a number of solutions, including niche marketing, risk management, quality improvement, fair trade, sales promotion, and so on, but these strategies have often only intensified competition between producers. Several major development agencies still support programmes to increase production of primary products using technical innovations to improve yields or implementing policy changes to offer incentives to farmers to grow a particular commodity. Side by side with the new doctrine of laissez-faire economics these agencies have been spending aid money to help some poor countries compete more aggressively with other poor countries... It has now become obvious that tropical commodity prices will continue to fall unless the root cause of oversupply is tackled head on. (Robbins 2003: 22–3)

In 2003, French President Jacques Chirac spoke of a 'conspiracy of silence' on the commodities crisis and attempted to have an initiative on it adopted at the Group of 8 Summit in Evian. It was not accepted due to objections from some major countries. However, there are recent initiatives to revive the commodities issue, including the report commissioned by the UN General Assembly of eminent persons on commodities, and the decision at the UNCTAD XI meeting in June 2004 to establish a task force on commodities. It remains to be seen whether interest and action on the problem can be generated at the international level.

Expecting the commodity problem to be solved by 'leaving it to the markets' is not realistic, as the experience of the past two decades shows. As oversupply is a major problem, there can be consideration of re-establishing producer–consumer commodity agreements, aimed at aligning supply with demand and at stabilizing prices. In the absence of political will to support such agreements, producer countries can consider cooperating with one another to plan their supply. The experience of the Organization of

Petroleum-Exporting Countries (OPEC) is useful in this regard. Recently, three leading rubber-producing countries (Indonesia, Thailand, and Malaysia) also formed an agreement that included a measure for each to slightly reduce production, and the price increased significantly.

Developing Countries and Trade in Manufactures

Although many developing countries remain dependent on a few commodity exports, others have significantly expanded their exports of manufactures. Indeed, manufactures today account for 70 percent of the total exports of developing countries overall (rising from 20 percent in the 1970s and early 1980s), and their share in world manufactured exports exceeds 25 percent compared to 10 percent in the 1970s. Some developing countries are involved in technology-intensive manufactured exports such as transistors and conductors, computers, and office machinery, through their participation in international production networks.

However, Akyuz (2004) points out that the gross statistics hide a less sanguine picture. First, many developing countries have not shared in the rise of manufactures in their export basket. Most countries that shifted from inward-oriented to outward-oriented development through rapid import liberalization did not succeed in increasing manufactured exports but experienced import surges and mounting trade deficits. Much of the expansion in manufactured exports was concentrated in East Asia. Second, with a few exceptions (e.g., Korea and Taiwan), the exports are still concentrated on products relying on natural resources and unskilled or semi-skilled labor, which have limited prospects for productivity growth and lack dynamism in world markets.

Third, Akyuz points out that statistics showing a rapid growth in technology-intensive exports from developing countries are misleading, as those countries are often involved only in the low-skill assembly stages of production, using technology-intensive parts and components imported from industrial countries; the imported parts are counted in the value of the exports. Thus, while the developing countries' share in world manufacturing exports appears to have risen rapidly, the incomes earned from such activities have not risen correspondingly. The developed countries' share in world manufactured exports fell from more than 80 percent to about 70 percent between 1980 and the end of the 1990s, but they actually increased their share in world manufacturing value-added. Developing countries had a steeply rising ratio of manufactured exports to GDP but without a significant upward trend in the ratio of manufactured value-added to GDP. Moreover, this relates only to value-added, which includes profits of the foreign firms in developing countries; when these profits are deducted, the income in developing countries arising from manufactures would be even smaller.

There is a diversity among developing countries, which are broken up into four categories by Akyuz: (1) the mature industrializers (first-tier newly industrializing economies (NIEs), notably Korea and Taiwan) which have rapid investment, growth in industrial employment, and productivity and exports; (2) the new generation of industrializers (second-tier NIEs like Malaysia, Thailand, and China) with a rising share of manufactures in total output, employment, and exports, upgrading from resource-based activities to labor-intensive manufactures and middle-range technology products; (3) enclave industrializers that moved away from dependence on commodity exports by linking to international production networks with a heavy reliance on imported inputs and machinery, and whose overall performance in investment, value-added, and productivity growth is poor; and (4) de-industrializers, including most middle-income countries in Latin America, which could not sustain structural change through growth and often have stagnant or falling shares of manufactured exports, employment, and output.

The developing countries also face the problem of competition and the fallacy of composition. Most of the industrial labor force is engaged in low-skill activity, and a simultaneous export drive by developing countries in labor-intensive manufacturing could flood the market and reduce their prices. The prices of manufactured exports from developing countries have been weakening vis-à-vis manufactures exported from developed countries in recent years. With more developing countries turning to export oriented strategies, the middle-income countries in Latin America and Southeast Asia are most vulnerable; greater price competition in electronics products has exposed the traditional exporters to competition from lower-cost countries. Unless they rapidly upgrade to high-skill, high value-added manufactures and compete with industrial countries, these exporters may be squeezed between the top and bottom ends of the markets for manufactures (Akyuz 2004: 12).

IFI Loan Conditionalities and Trade Policy

The trade policies of most developing countries are influenced by global frameworks, especially the loan conditionalities of the Bretton Woods Institutions (for those countries which rely on the institutions' loans) and the rules of the WTO (for those which are members).

Several of the loan conditionalities of the World Bank and International Monetary Fund (IMF) relate to trade. These have led many developing countries to sharply reduce their applied tariff rates for agricultural and industrial products. Due to these conditions, many of the countries have not been allowed to raise the applied rates even when cheaper imports adversely affect local products, and even though the WTO rules allow these countries to increase their applied rates up to the bound rates.

The unilateral policies taken under structural adjustment have then been reinforced or complemented by multilateral commitments that the countries are obliged to implement under the WTO rules. This combination of policies initiated under loan conditionality and then reinforced under multilateral rules has bound the developing countries in a web of commitments and policy constraints and measures and they find it difficult within this context to maneuver or to be able to choose those policy options that are suitable for their development.

Recent studies conducted by the UN Food and Agriculture Organization (FAO) have revealed that many developing countries significantly liberalized their agricultural imports as a result of IFI loan conditionality, rather than WTO rules. According to the FAO (2003: 75), structural adjustment programs over the past few decades resulted in radical agriculture reform in many developing countries, a period during which the majority of OECD agricultural sectors have continued to be heavily protected. The process adopted in many cases severely damaged the capacity of developing countries to increase levels of agricultural production and/or productivity. These unilateral reforms tend to have been reinforced by multilateral agreements.

The FAO adds that unilateral trade liberalization was undertaken in developing countries under pressure from the IFIs. By contrast, agricultural trade has only recently been impacted by multilateral agreements such as those under the WTO.

> This has resulted in a number of NGOs (non-governmental organizations) suggesting that the more negative aspects of unilateral liberalization in developing countries have been compounded by double standards in commitments to multilateral agreements, and maintaining the 'you liberalize, we subsidize' attitude is extremely damaging.
>
> (FAO 2003)

According to the FAO:

> The opening of markets in developing countries, in the context of a global agriculture still characterized by high levels of protection in developed countries, left the reforming developing countries less able to prevent (a) the flooding of their domestic market (import surges) with products sold on the world market at less than their cost of production; and (b) the displacement of local trading capacity which was intended to, and in some circumstances initially did, fill the void left following the deregulation of local markets and associated dismantling of parastatals. On point (a), the Washington institutions promoting structural adjustment did not take into account the existing imbalance in designing and proposing the reforms and therefore did not predict the resulting disincentive effects on local production in some regions. On point (b), rather than the emergence of sustained local private sector involvement, internal markets have often been overwhelmed by larger companies dominant in global value chains. The impact of the unilateral reforms preceding the first multilateral negotiations on agricultural trade (negotiations that essentially excluded developing countries) was to leave

developing countries potentially more vulnerable to greater openness, and to impose further constraints on policy intervention aimed at promoting agricultural growth.

(FAO 2003: 72–3)

An earlier study by the FAO (2001) on the effects on 14 developing countries of implementing the WTO Agriculture Agreement found that import liberalization had a significant adverse effect on small farmers and food security in many of the countries, and that the liberalization had been the result of loan conditionality of the IFIs, rather than the WTO rules. In fact the agricultural tariffs that were bound under the WTO were relatively high, but the applied rates were much lower as a result of the structural adjustment policies that formed the loan conditionality. The effects of import liberalization on the countries surveyed were thus mainly the result of World Bank-IMF policies.

Similarly, there are several cases of de-industrialization resulting from the loan conditionality of rapid tariff reduction in industrial products (see the eighth section of this chapter).

Many of the trade-related policies of the IFIs are not compatible with development, as they influence the loan recipient countries to sharply reduce their applied tariffs, often to levels which enable cheaper imports to damage the interests of local producers, which are unable to compete. Any review of the global framework influencing trade policy and performance in developing countries should therefore include a study and reform of the policies of the IFIs.

The WTO and the Multilateral Trading System

A large part (though not the whole part) of the multilateral trade system comes under the rubric and rules of the World Trade Organization. It sets principles and legally binding rules, and it houses a strong enforcement mechanism through its dispute settlement system. A systematic way of examining the WTO is the approach taken by Das (2003), in looking at its principles and structural aspects, instruments, rules, and enforcement.

Objectives, Principles, and Structure

The preamble to the Marrakesh Agreement establishing the WTO does contain the objective that trade and economic endeavor should be conducted

with a view to raising standards of living, ensuring full employment and a large and steadily growing volume of real income and effective demand, and expanding the production of and trade in goods and services, while allowing for the optimal use of the world's resources in accordance with the objective of sustainable development.

(Das 2003)

It also recognizes the need for positive efforts to ensure developing countries secure a share in the growth of international trade commensurate with the needs of economic development. The preamble also states the desire of 'contributing to these objectives by entering into reciprocal and mutually advantageous arrangements directed to the substantial reduction of tariffs and other barriers to trade and the elimination of discriminatory treatment in international trade relations.'

It can be argued that the main stated objectives of the WTO are raising living standards, full employment, and growth of real income, as well as ensuring that developing countries secure a fair share in global trade growth, while reduction of tariffs and non-tariff barriers and elimination of discriminatory treatment are the means or instruments. However, in practice, in their proposals and positions in the WTO, the developed members of the WTO have placed much more stress on the obligations of developing countries to reduce their tariffs and to counter 'discriminatory treatment.'

The scope of the WTO covers three main areas: trade in goods, services, and intellectual property. Rules for these are established respectively in the General Agreement on Tariffs and Trade (GATT) 1994, the General Agreement on Trade in Services (GATS) and the Agreement on Trade-Related Aspects of Intellectual Property Rights (TRIPS). The GATT and TRIPS agreements contain the two general principles of 'non-discrimination,' in other words, most-favored nation (MFN) and 'national treatment' (that imported goods must not be accorded treatment less favorable than that accorded to like domestic products), while GATS has the MFN as a general principle.

The directive of tariff reduction and the national treatment principle have been operationalized within the system in a way that pressurizes the developing countries to reduce their tariffs and non-tariff barriers, and to increasingly give up the policy options of giving preferences, subsidies, and other forms of promoting local products, services, and producers. This is often against the interests of development, which may require levels of tariff or non-tariff protection, and the provision of promotional measures for local producers that are not permitted by the system. Although growth, employment, and development may appear as the main objectives of the WTO, the driving forces in practice have been tariff reduction and trade liberalization, and the implementation of national treatment, to the extent that these have in effect become ends in themselves rather than the means.

Das (2003: 186–8) has also pointed out a structural defect, in that 'reciprocity' as the basis for exchange of concessions is inappropriate in a multilateral system which has a large membership at widely differing levels of development. Reciprocity implies that trading partners receive the same concessions as they give. 'This process of "give and get" implies get-more-if-give-more and get-less-if-give-less; it is thus a built-in mechanism for widening the gap between rich and poor countries, because those who can give go on getting more and more' (Das 2003: 186).

Das concludes that the fundamentals of the current GATT/WTO system are improper and inappropriate, and that the workings of the system since its inception in 1995 have given rise to ever-increasing discontent and frustration among the majority of the membership. In practice, in the areas of goods and services,

> the entire structure of the rules, disciplines and procedures is built around liberalization. This goal is very much incompatible with the basic objective of benefit-sharing which is essential for the viability and stability of the system. The direct beneficiaries of liberalization are those countries that possess a developed supply capacity. Those with poor supply capacity, i.e. the majority of developing countries, will not reap much benefit even if the trade is totally open and liberal in other countries. The system has naturally resulted in gross imbalance and this trend is continuing. (Das 2003: 186–7)

Thus, both liberalization as the goal and reciprocity as the tool for this goal are improper and inappropriate in the current multilateral trade system. Also, a basic pillar of the system, i.e. national treatment, can be a major handicap and its application needs to be modified.

Imbalances in the Rules and Problems Facing Developing Countries

The WTO and its predecessor, GATT, have contributed to the global trade system through the provision of a framework of rules within which member countries conduct trade and other commercial relations among themselves. This has contributed to a measure of stability and predictability as contrasted to an alternative scenario in which arrangements are dominated by unilateral policies and bilateral arrangements.

However, there are many problems that the developing countries face with the structural features, rules, and operations of the WTO system. First, some of the structural features of the system and many of the existing agreements are imbalanced against their interests. Second, the anticipated benefits to developing countries have not materialized, a major reason being that the developed countries have failed to fulfill their own commitments (e.g., in expanding market access in textiles and agriculture, or in providing special and differential treatment and assistance). Third, developing countries face mounting problems in attempting to implement their obligations under the rules. Fourth, there is increasing realization that many of the rules make it difficult or impossible for developing countries to choose policies required for their development process. Fifth, they face intense pressures to accept new obligations being proposed by developed countries under the Doha work program which began in 2001. Sixth, the decision-making process is not transparent or fair and makes it difficult for developing countries to adequately participate or to have their views reflected in the decisions of the organization, especially at ministerial conferences.

The old GATT system dealt with trade in goods. There were already some imbalances even in the GATT system. For example, sectors of export interest to developing countries remained highly protected, particularly agriculture and textiles. In effect, developing countries had made major concessions to the developed countries that had asked for time to adjust. The expansion of the GATT system under the Uruguay Round of negotiations which established the WTO, through the introduction of the then new issues (services, intellectual property, and investment measures), made the system even more imbalanced, as well as intrusive (as the system moved from its traditional concern with trade barriers at the border, to issues involving domestic economic and development structures and policies). The following are some of the major effects:

- Having to liberalize their industrial, services, and agriculture sectors may cause dislocation to the local sectors, firms, and farms as these are generally small or medium-sized and unable to compete with bigger foreign companies or cheaper imports.
- The Uruguay Round removed or severely curtailed the developing countries' space or ability to provide subsidies for local industries and to maintain some investment measures such as local content requirement.
- The developing countries are under tremendous pressure from the developed countries to commit to liberalizing a wide range of services under GATS. These pressures could lead to their committing to open up their services to foreign ownership before their local service providers have the capacity to compete; and to the host governments having to curtail measures that promote the local providers, if a commitment of national treatment is given to the foreign providers.
- The TRIPS Agreement will severely hinder or prevent local firms from absorbing some modern technologies over which other corporations (mainly foreign firms) have intellectual property rights (IPRs); this would curb the adoption of modern technology by domestic firms in developing countries. Also, the prices of medicines and other essential products are expected to rise significantly.

Thus, while a multilateral trading system can provide the benefits of predictability and stability, there is a danger that the WTO is also acting as a system that in many ways is making it difficult for appropriate policy measures for development to be taken.

Non-realization of Anticipated Benefits

When the Uruguay Round was concluded and the WTO established, developing countries had expected to benefit significantly from increased access to the markets of developed countries for products (especially in the textiles and agriculture sectors) for which they had a comparative advantage. However, there is now disillusionment as the expected benefits did not materialize.

It was expected that the two main sectors that the developed countries had heavily protected (agriculture and textiles) would be opened up. However, they have essentially remained closed. In agriculture, tariffs on many agricultural items of interest to developing countries are prohibitively high (some are over 200% and 300%). Domestic subsidies in OECD countries have risen from US$275 billion (annual average for base period 1986–88) to US$326 billion in 1999, according to OECD data (see OECD 2000), instead of declining as expected, as the increase in permitted subsidies more than offset the decrease in subsidy categories that are under discipline in the WTO Agriculture Agreement. There has been little expansion of access to developed country markets.

For decades, developing countries had made a major concession in agreeing that their textiles and clothing exports to developed countries be curtailed through a quota system. In the Uruguay Round, the developed countries agreed to progressively phase out their quotas over ten years to January 2005, but they have in fact retained most of their quotas even near the end of the implementation period. Genuine liberalization was avoided by the device of 'liberalizing' mainly products that were not actually restrained in the past. According to a submission at the WTO in June 2000 by the International Textiles and Clothing Bureau (see Hong Kong, China 2000), only a few quota restrictions (13 out of 750 by the US; 14 out of 219 by the EU; 29 out of 295 by Canada) had been eliminated by 2000 (the halfway point of the implementation period). There has also been little sign of 'structural adjustment' measures in the textiles sector in developed countries to prepare for the ending of the quotas. The end-loading of implementation and the absence of structural adjustment raise doubts as to whether there will be liberalization at the deadline, or whether other trade measures (such as anti-dumping and safeguard measures) will be taken, besides high tariffs, to continue the high protection. Recent reports indicate that the textile industry in the US is lobbying the US administration to organize action to have the textile quota system extended, or to take action such as safeguard measures to prevent the expected flood of textile imports, especially from China, when the quota system ends.

Tariff peaks and tariff escalation continue to be maintained by developed countries on other industrial products in which developing countries have manufacturing export capacity.

The supposed improvement of market access through tariff reductions has to some extent been also offset by non-tariff barriers in the rich countries, such as the use of anti-dumping measures and the application of food safety and environmental standards.

Problems for Developing Countries When Implementing Their Own Obligations

Although the major developed countries have not lived up to their own liberalization commitments, they have continued to advocate that it is beneficial for developing countries to liberalize their imports and investments as fast as possible. Developing countries are asked to bear for a little while the pain of rapid adjustment, which is said to surely be good for them after a few years.

Implementing their obligations under the WTO agreements has brought many problems for developing countries. These are dealt with in some detail in Third World Network (2001). These problems include: (1) the prohibition of trade-related investment measures and subsidies, making it harder for developing-country governments to encourage or promote domestic industry; (2) import liberalization in agriculture, threatening the viability and livelihoods of small farmers whose products face competition from cheaper imported foods, many of which are artificially cheapened through massive subsidies; (3) the effects of a high-standard intellectual property right regime that has led to exorbitant prices of medicines and other essentials, to the patenting by Northern corporations of biological materials originating in the South, and to higher cost for and lower access by developing countries to industrial technology; (4) increasing pressures on developing countries to open up their services sectors, which could result in local service providers being rendered non-viable; and (5) the recent negotiations (which began in 2001) for a new round of industrial tariff cuts are also likely to result in steep tariff reductions, which may unleash a level of import competition upon domestic industries that many may not be able to stand up to.

Thus, the issue is raised as to whether developing countries can still pursue development strategies and objectives, including technology upgrading, development of local industries, survival and growth of local farms and the agriculture sector, attainment of food security goals, and fulfillment of health and medicinal needs.

The problems arise from the structural imbalances and weaknesses of several of the WTO agreements. The developing countries have tabled in the WTO a list of the problems of implementation and proposals for addressing these, and summaries of these are contained in the WTO compilations on implementation issues (see WTO 1999, 2001d,e,f).

Requests by developing countries from 1999 to now that these problems be resolved first in the sequencing of the WTO's future activities have not been agreed to, and there has been little progress even though a set of these issues has been placed under the Doha negotiating agenda. The attitude of the developed countries seems to be that the developing countries had entered into legally binding commitments and must abide by them; any changes would require new concessions on their part. Such an attitude does not augur well for the WTO, for it implies that the state of imbalance will remain. At the WTO General Council meeting in July 2004, when a package of decisions was adopted in relation to the Doha work program, there were no concrete results in resolving the 'development issues' of implementation problems and special and differential treatment. The meeting merely agreed on a new timetable for further discussions on these issues (see the ninth section of this chapter).

Problems Arising from Specific Agreements or Sectors

INDUSTRIAL SECTOR

The GATT and WTO system until now has by and large allowed developing countries the flexibility to choose the scope of tariff bindings (the number of products whose tariffs are to be bound) and the levels at which to bind their tariffs. However, under the Doha work program, there are presently strong pressures from major developed countries to institute deep reductions in industrial tariffs of developing countries, through the application of a 'non-linear formula,' in which there will be sharper cuts the higher the tariffs. It is also proposed that developing countries will have to bind almost all their unbound tariffs, with the new bound rates to be set after multiplying the applied rates by two and then subjecting these to the formula cut. Since many developing countries have relatively high-bound tariffs (though their applied tariffs may be significantly lower), this may result in very sharp cuts to the existing bound tariffs, and also cuts to the presently unbound applied rates. It is also proposed that in several selected sectors, there will be accelerated tariff elimination on a fast track basis. If these proposals are accepted, the developing countries would be subjected to the shock of having to cope very quickly with cheap imports competing with local industrial products. Their prospects for industrialization involving domestic firms would be seriously darkened.

Thus, it would be more appropriate instead to retain the flexibility that developing countries enjoyed, to choose their own scope of tariff bindings and the rate of their bound tariffs. During the Uruguay Round, developing countries were obliged to decrease their bound tariffs by an overall average rate of 27 percent, but they could set different rates for different tariff lines. At least a similar degree of flexibility should be provided under the Doha work program, given that many developing countries are already experiencing a de-industrialization process.

On a more structural level, it should also be recognized that developing countries need to fine-tune their trade policy instruments to support the growth of specific sectors as a dynamic process, and thus require flexibility in raising and reducing tariffs. The current procedure for raising tariffs beyond the bound level is very cumbersome and should be made smoother and easier. For infant industry purposes, countries should be allowed to raise tariffs for a limited period to promote the establishment of an industry. The method of balancing the gains and losses in tariff negotiations should also be changed; the offer from a developing country should be evaluated not merely in terms of current trade but mainly in terms of future prospects for developed countries when the developing country's growth would enlarge its market (Third World Network 2001: 7, 80).

TRADE-RELATED INVESTMENT MEASURES (TRIMs)

Under the Trade-Related Investment Measures (TRIMs) Agreement, governments are constrained from adopting certain investment measures that oblige or encourage investors to use local materials or restrict imports, as this is counter to GATT's Article III (on national treatment) and Article XI (on quantitative restrictions). The illustrative list of prohibited measures includes local content policy (which developing countries had used to increase the use of local materials and improve linkages to the local economy) and some aspects of foreign exchange balancing (aimed at correcting balance of payments problems). The TRIMs Agreement is a notable example of a WTO rule that prevents developing countries from taking policy measures that promote domestic industrial development, and that had been used by the present industrial countries and by several developing countries previously.

Implementation of the TRIMs Agreement has already given rise to problems in several developing countries. Several cases have been brought to the WTO dispute settlement process against developing countries, including Indonesia, the Philippines, India, and Brazil (all in relation to the automobile sector) as well as against the Philippines (regarding pork and poultry), and Canada (regarding automobiles). In the Indonesia case, incentives under its national car program were found to violate the TRIMs Agreement, and they had to be withdrawn (Third World Network 2001: 63). Some developing countries have also requested extension of the transition period to give them more time to adjust.

To rectify these problems, developing countries should be given another opportunity to modify existing TRIMs, and the transition period should be extended for all developing countries in line with their development needs. Provisions should be introduced that allow developing countries flexibility to use investment measures for development objectives. The review process should consider exempting developing countries from the disciplines on local content and foreign exchange balancing policies. At the same time, there should not be an extension of the illustrative list or an attempt to extend the agreement to cover investment rules per se.

SUBSIDIES

There is an imbalance in the treatment of subsidies. Subsidies mostly used by developed countries (e.g., for R&D and environmental adaptation) have been made non-actionable (immune from counteraction) while subsidies normally used by developing countries (for industrial upgrading, diversification, technological development, etc.) have come under actionable disciplines, and countervailing duties could be imposed on the products enjoying such subsidies. The prohibition of these subsidies is another encroachment on the policy space needed by developing countries for their industrial development. Thus, these subsidies need to be recognized as an instrument of development rather than one of trade distortion, and should be exempt from countervailing duty and other forms of counteraction.

BALANCE OF PAYMENTS PROVISION

Article XVIIIB of GATT 1994 allows developing countries to restrict imports if they face balance of payments (BOP) problems. However, the method of operation and some new decisions have made this provision less effective, and an important instrument for reducing the imbalance in the system has thus been made almost non-operational. The WTO increasingly relies on IMF reports to determine whether or not a BOP problem exists. The IMF includes volatile and uncertain short-term flows (e.g., portfolio investments) and uncertain reserves in its assessment of a country's foreign reserves, thereby tending to overestimate them. The current criterion of deciding on whether a BOP problem exists thus appears faulty. Further, a recent decision in a dispute requires the developing country concerned to give priority to tariff type action over direct import control measures. This has reduced the capacity of developing countries to deal with the problem quickly and effectively. To correct these problems, the rules should specify that the existence of a BOP problem will be determined on the basis of long-term and stable reserves and flows only, and that developing countries' foreign exchange reserve requirements will be assessed on the basis of future development programs rather than on past trends. Also, the determination of the existence of a BOP problem should be made by the WTO General Council, based on the recommendation of the BOP Committee, using the IMF reports as inputs only. Current rules (designed to deal with temporary BOP problems) should be supplemented with new rules to provide relief for structural BOP problems (Third World Network 2001: 42–3).

AGRICULTURE

The WTO Agreement on Agriculture (AoA) established disciplines on three pillars—market access, domestic support, and export subsidies—and the developed countries were expected to reduce their protection. In reality, however, the developed countries have been able to continue to maintain high levels of protection. Many of them set very high tariffs on several products; thus, even after the required 36 percent reductions they remain prohibitively high. Domestic support has also remained very high; in fact, the total amount of domestic subsidies in OECD countries has actually risen as there was an increase in permitted types of subsidies, which more than offset the decrease in those subsidies that come under discipline. The export subsidies budget in developed countries is also to be reduced by only 36 percent under the agreement.

Of the three aspects above, worldwide public criticism has focused most on the expansion of domestic subsidies. The AoA has a loophole allowing developed countries to increase their total domestic support by shifting from one type of subsidy, the Amber Box (price-based, which is directly trade-distorting), to two other types, the Blue Box and Green Box (grants to farmers to set aside production and direct payments to farmers, and other 'indirect' subsidies), that are exempted from reduction discipline. In reality, the Blue and Green Box subsidies also have significant effects on the market and trade, and are thus also trade-distorting. For farmers, what is important is whether they can obtain sufficient revenue and make a profit. If a subsidy, in whatever form, is assisting farmers to obtain revenue and to be economically viable, then that subsidy is having a significant effect on production and on the market.

The effect of agriculture subsidies in developed countries is that their farm production levels are kept artificially high and their producers dispose of their surplus in other countries, often by 'dumping' on world markets at less than the production cost. Farmers in developing countries incur losses in three ways: they lose export opportunities and revenues from having their market access blocked in the developed countries using the subsidies; they lose export opportunities in third countries, because the subsidizing country is exporting to these countries at artificially low prices; and they lose their market share in their own domestic market—or even lose their livelihoods altogether, due to the inflow of artificially cheap subsidized imports.

High protection in developed countries and further liberalization in developing countries has resulted in surges of imports to many developing countries across the world. In many cases these imports were artificially cheapened by domestic and/or export subsidies. There are many cases of dumping in which the developed country products' export price is below the cost of production. Often, the poorer countries may have more efficient farmers, but their livelihoods are threatened by products of subsidized inefficient farmers in rich countries.

Thus, developing countries are facing serious implementation problems in agriculture. They have had to remove non-tariff controls and convert these to tariffs. With the exception of LDCs, they are expected to reduce the bound tariff rates progressively. They also have had low domestic subsidies (due to financial constraints) and are now not allowed to raise these subsidies beyond a *de minimis* level and have (excepting LDCs) to reduce them if they are above this level. Increased competition from imports has threatened the small farm sectors in many developing countries and increased fears of food insecurity. An FAO study in 14 developing countries concluded that liberalization in the agriculture sector has led, variously, to an increase in the food import bill, a decline of local production in products facing competition from cheaper imports, and a general trend towards consolidation of farms and displacement of farm labor. Promises to provide food aid to net food importing developing countries (NFIDCs) and LDCs have also not been fulfilled. Instead, food aid to these countries fell significantly and their ability to finance their increasing food bills deteriorated.

Proposals to rectify this situation have been given in Third World Network (2001: 8, 83–4). The domestic and export subsidies and tariff peaks in agriculture in developed countries should be drastically reduced. The loopholes that allow domestic subsidies to be maintained or increased by shifting subsidies from one box (or category) to another should be plugged. Meanwhile, developing countries should be allowed greater flexibility on the grounds of food security, protection of rural livelihoods, and poverty alleviation. Food production for domestic consumption in developing countries (as well as the products of their small and non-commercial farmers) should be exempt from the Agriculture Agreement's disciplines on import liberalization and domestic subsidy. At the least, developing countries should be allowed to self-designate 'special products' (on which they rely for food security, rural livelihoods, and rural development), which should be exempted from further tariff reduction. Also, developing countries should be able to use a special safeguard mechanism enabling them to raise their tariff above the bound rate when surges of imports affect local producers. However, the chances for many of these proposals to be accepted are slim, in light of the decision of the WTO General Council on a framework for agriculture modalities in July 2004 (see the ninth section of this chapter).

SERVICES

Services enterprises in developed countries have far greater capacity than those in developing countries, and thus the liberalization of services under GATS will mainly be to the benefit of the former. This is the source of a basic imbalance in GATS. Enterprises in developing countries generally lack the supply capacity to benefit from liberalization in developed country markets. In an area where developing countries do have an advantage, such as the movement of labor, developed countries have not yet been prepared to undertake liberalization. Although developing countries are allowed under GATS to liberalize fewer sectors and transactions, it is not specified how this is to be operationalized. Instead negotiations on financial services, for example, showed that developed countries insisted on high levels of commitments from developing countries.

There is a lack of adequate data on the services trade, making it difficult to assess the effects (in terms of gains and losses to a country and to developing countries as a whole) of GATS and services liberalization. Other problems for developing countries include supply constraints and barriers to services exports to developed markets, and challenges faced from attempts by developed countries to alter the basic architecture of GATS. There have also been concerns that GATS would affect the provision of and access by the public to social services.

Measures to deal with these problems are suggested in Third World Network (2001: 9–10, 84–5). The lack of data needs to be addressed, and until then, developing countries should not be expected to undertake further obligations. The special provisions for developing countries in GATS (articles IV and XIX.2) should be seriously implemented, and a mechanism set up to monitor the implementation. Developed countries should take concrete steps (such as providing incentives to domestic firms) to encourage the import of services from developing countries. There should be concrete measures and time frames for liberalizing the movement of labor from developing countries to developed countries. The GATS provisions for flexibility in the choice of sectors and pace of liberalization for developing countries should be preserved. In discussions on developing new rules (including on domestic regulation), care should be taken to ensure that governments have both the options and the flexibility to make their own domestic services regulations and that their policies are not adversely affected. Clarification of the nature and scope of exceptions to GATS commitments for government services should be made, along with an assessment of whether (and to what extent) countries can have adequate flexibility in making national policies for basic services.

INTELLECTUAL PROPERTY RIGHTS (IPRs)

Most of the world's registered intellectual property is owned by persons and enterprises in the developed countries. A strengthening of IPRs would thus benefit these countries more. A basic weakness of the TRIPS Agreement is that its benefits are inherently skewed to the rich countries, while the costs (in terms of royalties paid and high prices charged) are mainly borne by developing countries. Thus, there is no reciprocal benefit sharing under TRIPS.

TRIPS sets high minimum standards of IPR protection for all WTO members. This one-size-fits-all approach is heavily tilted in favor of holders of technology as opposed to its consumers and users. Many critics of TRIPS have pointed out that such a lopsided agreement on intellectual property (which is not a trade issue) which facilitates monopolization does not belong in the WTO, which is a trade organization that is supposed to be working against protectionism.

The share of developing countries in the ownership of patents worldwide is minuscule and thus almost all the benefits from owning IPRs (such as royalties and extra profits resulting from the ability to charge higher prices) accrue to the developed countries' firms and institutions. The granting of monopoly rights to IPR holders has curbed competition and enabled them to charge higher and often exorbitant prices.

Under TRIPS, members cannot exempt medicines from patentability, in contrast to the pre-TRIPS situation where many countries did not allow patents for the pharmaceutical sector. The high prices of some medicines that have been facilitated by TRIPS have caused a public outcry, especially in relation to drugs for treating HIV/AIDS. The Doha Declaration on the TRIPS Agreement and Public Health, adopted by the WTO's Doha Ministerial Conference in 2001, has only to a very limited extent softened the damage that is caused by TRIPS in this regard. The high-standard IPR regime is also making it more costly or difficult for local firms in developing countries to use patented technology. Further, TRIPS makes it mandatory for members to allow patenting of some life-forms and living processes, as well as IPR protection for plant varieties. This has facilitated the spread of 'biopiracy,' in which indigenous knowledge and biological wealth of developing countries are patented mainly by developed country firms. Promised technology transfer to poor countries has also not been forthcoming.

Many measures are required for TRIPS to become more balanced in its rules and implementation. Developing countries must be allowed to make maximum use of the flexibilities in the agreement. They should be allowed to choose between various options in devising intellectual property legislation, without being subjected to external pressure or influence. The mandated review of Article 27.3b of TRIPS should eliminate the artificial distinctions between those organisms and biological processes that can be excluded from patents and those that cannot. One way to do this, as proposed by the Africa Group of countries in the WTO, is to agree that all living organisms and their parts, and all living processes, cannot be patented. With the adoption of the Doha Declaration on the TRIPS Agreement and Public Health, developing countries should make full use of the flexibilities to take public health measures, including compulsory licensing and parallel importation, which can make medicines more accessible and affordable. Least developed countries should also make use of the extra flexibilities afforded to them under the same Declaration. The TRIPS objectives and transfer-of-technology provisions (including articles 7, 8, and 66.2) should be operationalized. Developing countries should also be given flexibility to exempt certain products and sectors on the grounds of public welfare and the need to meet development objectives.

Finally, WTO members should consider whether the WTO is the appropriate institution to house an agreement such as TRIPS, which is basically a protectionist device.

Attempts to Introduce New Issues and Agreements in the WTO

INVESTMENT, COMPETITION, AND GOVERNMENT PROCUREMENT

Proposals have been made (mainly by developed countries) to expand the WTO's mandate by negotiating agreements on several new issues. The first set of 'new issues' includes investment rules, competition policy, and government procurement. These three issues have a similar theme: to expand the rights and access of foreign firms and their products in developing countries' markets, and to curb or prohibit government policies that encourage or favor local firms and the domestic economy.

The proposed investment rules would place governments under greater pressure to grant the right of establishment to foreign investors, to liberalize foreign investments (defined broadly) and to bind the level of liberalization; prohibit or otherwise discipline 'performance requirements' imposed on investors (such as limits to foreign equity participation, obligations on technology transfer, geographical location of the investment, etc.); allow free inflows and outflows of funds; and protect investors' rights, for example through strict standards on compensation for 'expropriation.' The rules would also grant 'national treatment' to foreign firms, thus extending this GATT principle (which applies to goods) to the whole new domain of investment.

The proposed rules on competition would require members to establish national competition law and policy. Within that framework, it is proposed that the WTO non-discrimination principles be applied, so that foreign products and firms can compete freely in the local market on the basis of 'effective equality of opportunity.' Thus, policies and practices that give an advantage to local firms and products could be prohibited or otherwise disciplined.

Developed countries have also been advocating for government procurement policies (presently exempt from the WTO's multilateral disciplines) to be brought under the system, whereby the non-discrimination principles would apply with the effect that governments would have to open their procurement business to foreigners and the current practice of favoring locals would be curbed or prohibited. This serious step is unpopular with developing countries. Thus a two-step process was proposed by the developed countries. First, an agreement confined to transparency in government procurement would be established. Second, attempts would then be made to extend it to the market access dimension, whereby national treatment would have to be given to foreign firms and products. Local producers would lose their preference.

Developed countries have advocated that this set of new issues be taken up in a new round of negotiations. Many developing countries have objected to this. Their concerns include that: (1) the new obligations arising from these issues would further curtail their development options and prospects; (2) these are non-trade issues and bringing them into the WTO would be inappropriate and distort and overload the trading system; (3) the WTO should focus on resolving problems arising from existing agreements and the mandated agriculture and services negotiations instead of launching negotiations in new areas that would divert attention; (4) they have a serious lack of understanding of the issues and of resources to negotiate on them.

Despite these objections, the developed countries (particularly the EU) pushed hard for negotiations on these issues to be launched during the Doha Ministerial Conference in 2001. They partially succeeded, by having the adoption of a declaration that negotiations would begin on these issues at the next ministerial conference on the basis of an explicit consensus. However, at the following ministerial conference at Cancun in 2003, most developing countries opposed the launch of negotiations, and the meeting ended without any decision taken. In July 2004, the WTO General Council decided that no further work towards negotiations on these three issues would be undertaken during the period of the Doha work program. The issues are, however, expected to be revived, by the developed countries, after completion of the Doha program.

LABOR AND ENVIRONMENTAL STANDARDS

The second set of new issues relates to labor and environmental standards. Attempts to bring these issues for discussion (and possible rules) in the WTO have been strongly resisted by developing countries, which fear they are likely to be used as protectionist devices against their products. The argument of some proponents of these standards is that countries that have low social and environmental standards (or that do not adhere to some minimum standards) are practicing 'social dumping' or 'eco-dumping.' Their production costs are said to be artificially low because, unlike others, they are not recognizing labor standards or adhering to minimum wages, and are not spending on environmentally sound technology. There is a possibility that a next step in the argument is that countervailing duty can be placed on the products of these countries as an action against such 'dumping.' The developing countries fear that they would not be able to meet the standards that could be set, due to their lack of financial and technical resources, and would thus be punished. They therefore oppose a linkage between trade rules and these standards. These issues had figured prominently in 1995–96, up to the WTO ministerial meeting in Singapore in December 1996. Although it was agreed then that the issue of labor standards does not belong in the WTO, the issue keeps reappearing, especially at ministerial meetings. The issue of environmental standards also reappears often, usually in the form of proposals to incorporate 'processes and production methods' (PPMs), or the way in which a product is made, into discussions on trade and environment.

Transparency and Participation in the WTO

Unequal capacity has led to unequal degrees of participation by developing countries, a problem made worse by the relative lack of transparency in key WTO operations. To start with, developing countries are in general seriously understaffed both in capitals and in Geneva and are thus unable to adequately follow or take part in the WTO's deliberations. In addition, despite the 'one country one vote' rule, in practice, a few major countries have been able to dominate decision making in critical aspects, using informal meetings to make decisions among a small group of members that are then passed along to the other members. The so-called 'Green Room' process of exclusive decision-making is especially prevalent at and before ministerial conferences, where important decisions are taken. 'Consensus building' is also normally embarked on when proposed by the major players as opposed to the developing countries.

The WTO needs to evolve more inclusive, participatory, and transparent methods of discussion and decision-making, in which all members are fully enabled to participate and make proposals. Decision-making procedures and practices that are non-transparent and non-inclusive (including the 'Green Room' meetings), especially before and during ministerial conferences, should be discontinued. The WTO Secretariat should also be impartial and seen to be impartial. In particular, it should not be seen to be taking sides with the more powerful countries at the expense of the interests of developing countries. The system must reflect the fact that the majority of members are developing countries and must provide them with adequate means and with appropriate procedures to enable them to voice their interests and exercise their rights. Further, citizen groups must be allowed to follow developments in the WTO and channels opened to make their views better heard.

Effects of Import Liberalization on Developing Countries

Empirical evidence on the negative effects of inappropriate import liberalization has been increasing. Below are examples of effects in the industrial and agricultural sectors in developing countries.

In the industrial sector, disturbing evidence of post-1980 liberalization episodes in the African and Latin American regions has been described by

Buffie (2001: 190–1). For example, Senegal experienced large job losses following liberalization in the late 1980s; by the early 1990s, employment cuts had eliminated one-third of all manufacturing jobs. The chemical, textile, shoe, and automobile assembly industries virtually collapsed in Cote d'Ivoire after tariffs were abruptly lowered by 40 percent in 1986. Similar problems have plagued liberalization attempts in Nigeria. In Sierra Leone, Zambia, Zaire (now the Democratic Republic of Congo), Uganda, Tanzania, and the Sudan, liberalization in the 1980s brought a tremendous surge in consumer imports and sharp cutbacks in foreign exchange available for purchases of intermediate inputs and capital goods, with devastating effects on industrial output and employment. In Ghana, industrial sector employment plunged from 78,700 in 1987 to 28,000 in 1993 due mainly to the fact that 'large swathes of the manufacturing sector had been devastated by import competition' (Buffie 2001).

Adjustment in the 1990s has also been difficult for much of the manufacturing sector in Mozambique, Cameroon, Tanzania, Malawi, and Zambia. Import competition precipitated sharp contractions in output and employment in the short run, with many firms closing down operations entirely.

Some developing countries outside Africa have also experienced similar problems. According to Buffie (2001: 190),

> Liberalization in the early nineties seems to have resulted in large job losses in the formal sector and a substantial worsening in underemployment in Peru, Nicaragua, Ecuador and Brazil. Nor is the evidence from other parts of Latin America particularly encouraging.

The regional record suggests that the normal outcome is a sharp deterioration in income distribution, with no clear evidence that this shift is temporary in character.

In the agriculture sector, there are now many case studies of the incidence and damaging effects of import liberalization on local communities and rural producers in developing countries. These studies show how farmers in many sectors (staple crops like rice and wheat, milk and other dairy products, vegetables and fruits, poultry, and sugar) have had their incomes reduced and their livelihoods threatened by the influx of imports. The problems caused to small rural producers in developing countries are now very widespread. A compilation of such cases is found in Meenakshi (2004).

An FAO paper (FAO 2003) shows very high incidences of import surges in 1984–2000 for eight key products in 28 developing countries, with the incidence rising after 1994. For example, Kenya experienced 45 cases of import surges; the Philippines, 72 cases; Bangladesh, 43; Benin, 43; Botswana, 43; Burkina Faso, 50; Cote d'Ivoire, 41; Dominican Republic, 28; Haiti, 40; Honduras, 49; Jamaica, 32; Malawi, 50; Mauritius, 27; Morocco, 38; Peru, 43; Uganda, 41; Tanzania, 50; and Zambia, 41.

The import surges documented by the FAO were also accompanied in some cases by production shortfalls in some of the same products where there were import surges. For example, in Kenya, in wheat there were 11 cases of import surges and seven cases of production shortfall; in maize there were five cases of import surges and four cases of production shortfall. This indicates that the import surges were sometimes linked to declines in output by the farmers in the importing countries. The rise in imports led to declines in output and incomes of the farmers, affecting their livelihoods. As the FAO report concluded, 'Given the large number of cases of import surges and increasing reports of the phenomenon from around the world, this could be potentially a serious problem.'

The FAO study also cites several recent studies on import surges that trace the problem to unfair trade practices (e.g., dumping), export subsidies and domestic production subsidies. Import surges are more common for products where there are high subsidies (e.g., dairy/livestock products— such as milk powder and poultry parts—certain fruit and vegetable preparations, and sugar).

Recent Developments in the Trading System

The WTO system gives the appearance of being rather unstable, as the outcome of negotiations is often unpredictable, and often the result of intense pressures, horse trading, and untransparent methods of work. Of the last three ministerial meetings, two (Seattle 1999 and Cancun 2003) have ended in a state of some chaos without results, while the third (Doha 2001) was controversial for its last night exclusive Green Room meeting and the methods by which drafts of the Doha Declaration appeared without the participation or knowledge of most members. The most disputed parts of the Declaration involved the sections on the four so-called 'Singapore issues' (investment, competition, transparency in government procurement, and trade facilitation), which contained a decision to launch negotiations (for new agreements) at the next ministerial meeting on the basis of explicit consensus on the modalities of the negotiations. The Doha Declaration launched an ambitious work program that included negotiations on agriculture, non-agricultural market access (NAMA), services, intellectual property, environment, implementation issues, special and differential treatment, and rules; it also mandated focused discussions on the Singapore issues with a view to launching negotiations at the next ministerial meeting.

At the Cancun Ministerial meeting of 2003, there was strong opposition from a majority of developing countries to launching negotiations on the four Singapore issues. The meeting ended without a declaration when agreement could not be reached on this issue. The conference was also marked by intense negotiations on the agriculture issue, as well as on cotton, industrial tariffs, and proposals on special and differential treatment for developing countries.

The WTO went through a low point after the failure of the Cancun meeting. However, its confidence has picked up recently when a meeting of its General Council in Geneva at the end of July managed to conclude with a decision (dated July 31, 2004) incorporating frameworks for modalities of negotiations for agriculture, non-agricultural market access and trade facilitation, and guidelines for services, cotton, implementation issues, and special and differential treatment. It also notably decided not to proceed with work towards negotiations on three of the Singapore issues (investment, competition, and transparency in government procurement) during the period of the Doha work program, while launching negotiations on the remaining Singapore issue, trade facilitation. A preliminary analysis of the July decision is in Khor (2004).

From a development perspective, there were a few significant gains from the decision but also losses in some critical areas.

On the positive side, the developed countries agreed in principle to eliminate agricultural export subsidies and deal with export subsidy-like measures such as export credits. However, an end date for the elimination is still to be decided. It is expected that the eventual elimination of export subsidies will get rid of some of the most trade-distorting of the developed countries' subsidies that have unfairly kept out the developing countries' farm products.

Another positive development was the dropping of three of the unpopular Singapore issues (investment, competition, and transparency in government procurement) from the WTO's negotiating agenda, at least during the period of the Doha program. Most of the developing countries had opposed these issues, which they believed would interfere with their freedom to formulate national development policies, particularly those designed to encourage and promote local producers. The attempts by the rich countries to set up new agreements on these issues had generated heated controversy for years and were a major factor in derailing the Cancun meeting. The decision left it vague as to whether discussions (as contrasted to negotiations) would continue even now at the WTO, and left open the possibility of their making a comeback after the Doha program is finished. However, doing away with negotiations on these issues for the time being is a relief for developing countries.

Against these two positive developments were some setbacks. The most serious negative development was the adoption of a framework on trade in industrial goods, which could lead to the threat of cheap industrial imports overwhelming local goods and industries. The framework on NAMA, contained in Annex B of the July decision, advocates a non-linear formula for reducing tariffs sharply, with steeper cuts for higher tariffs. For example, under a variation of this formula, a 40 percent tariff on a product would have to be reduced to 7 percent. Many developing countries have relatively high-bound industrial tariffs to protect their local industries, and thus they will be much harder hit. In the history of GATT and the WTO, the developing countries have never had to come under a 'formula approach,' let alone an aggressive non-linear formula, not even during the Uruguay Round.

The NAMA framework also obliges developing countries to give up the WTO's present flexibilities for countries to choose how many of their industrial products' tariffs they would like to bind and at what rate. The July decision advocates that at least 95 percent of their tariff lines will have to be bound, many at very low rates. The reason is that to calculate the new bound rates, the applied tariff rates of the presently unbound products will be taken and multiplied by two (this figure is to be negotiated further) and then subjected to the harsh non-linear formula. The new bound rates could end up being significantly lower than the present applied rates. There would also, in these cases, no longer be a gap (as now exists) between applied and bound rates, thus eliminating or narrowing the 'safety zone.' As many developing countries have low applied rates for many products (as a result of structural adjustment loan conditionalities), the result of the NAMA exercise may be to depress the industrial tariffs (both bound and applied) of developing countries to unbearably low levels.

There is also a 'sectoral tariff component' in which many sectors (an earlier draft mentioned seven) would be slated for fast-track total elimination of tariffs. If sectors are selected that are important in a developing country's domestic production, then the risks to its domestic industries will be heightened.

If the negotiations that follow are not handled properly, and these measures are accepted, they could threaten the share and the very survival of many local firms and industries in developing countries. They may not be able to compete with imports if tariffs are brought down to low levels or to zero. Many developing countries (in Africa, Latin America, and the Caribbean) have already suffered from a de-industrialization process as cheap imports overwhelmed the local firms as a result of rapid liberalization under structural adjustment.

Most developing countries (especially from Africa and the Caribbean) had opposed the same draft on NAMA for many months, but the Chairman of the negotiations insisted on maintaining the text to the end, to the frustration of the opposing countries. The only concession was the insertion of a first paragraph indicating that the text on NAMA contains 'the initial elements' for future work, and that 'additional negotiations are required to reach agreement on the specifics of some of these elements.' This paragraph provides the developing countries a little space from which to continue to battle for a better framework.

On agriculture, there was a mixed result. As stated above, the commitment to eliminate export subsidies was a positive development. However, the decision on domestic subsidies is complex, with mixed results. While there is a commitment to further reduce the Amber Box subsidies, which are recognized as being trade-distorting, there is also a move to allow the criteria for the Blue Box subsidies to be altered, to enable the United States to maintain some types of subsidies under its Farm Bill that had been found to be trade-distorting. The expansion of the Blue Box is seen as a concession to the developed countries. Moreover, the Green Box subsidies, which are now permitted without disciplines, will continue to be allowed without a maximum limit, thus paving the way for the developed countries to shift the bulk of their domestic subsidies to this box, and continue legally to maintain high overall subsidies.

On market access for agricultural products, it was agreed that all countries (except the LDCs) would be subjected to a 'tiered formula' for tariff reductions, with 'deeper cuts in higher tariffs, with flexibilities for sensitive products.' There will be special and differential treatment for developing countries, which probably will be manifested in lower tariff cuts than for the developed countries. Though not mentioned in the Geneva decision, it is understood that the tiered approach will have a number of bands, with each band specifying the tariff range (e.g., 1–10%, 11–30%, 31–50%, etc.), and presumably the bands with higher tariffs will be subjected to deeper cuts. What kind of formula to use within each band is to be discussed. With this kind of tiered approach, there will be much less flexibility for developing countries than in the Uruguay Round approach (which had a guideline for developing countries of an overall average reduction of 24% and a minimum reduction of 10% in each tariff line). For developing countries generally, tariffs will have to be reduced and probably by more than during the Uruguay Round—especially affected would be the products with higher tariffs. There is thus ground for serious concern that further liberalization may increase the import surges and displacement of local products that have already been evident in recent years.

A concession to developing countries is that they would be able to designate some agricultural products as 'special products,' based on criteria of food security, livelihood security, and rural development needs, and these products are eligible for 'more flexible treatment.' The number, criteria, and treatment will be specified during further negotiations. A special safeguard mechanism will also be established, but further details are also to be negotiated. On the other hand, the developed countries also won a major concession, with the creation of a category of 'sensitive products' which would enjoy special treatment in relation to the standard tariff-cutting formula. There is concern that the developed countries will be able to place their high-tariff products in this category and thereby avoid having to significantly reduce tariffs on these key products, thus continuing to prevent or limit market access of developing country agricultural goods.

Another negative development was that the Geneva meeting again failed to agree on concrete measures on the 'development issues,' in other words, to provide special and differential treatment for developing countries, and to resolve their many problems of implementing the WTO rules. It merely set new deadlines (since the old deadlines have long expired) for the issues to be considered and for reports on these issues to be submitted. In fact, the Geneva meeting marked another sad step in the steady decline in status and action on these development issues. There have been hardly any concrete results for years on them.

When the Doha negotiations were launched in 2001, it was with a lot of rhetoric on the need to put developing countries' interests at the center. Sadly, the negative aspects far outweighed the positive developments at the Geneva meeting. Thus 'development' remains rhetoric, while some of the new decisions (especially on industrial tariffs) are potentially threatening to development prospects.

Rethinking Trade, Trade Policy, and the Trade System

Rethinking Trade Policy

This is an opportune moment to rethink the role of trade in development, trade policy, and the rules of the multilateral trading system. For many years, the basic assumption in the Washington Consensus and the GATT/WTO system has been that trade liberalization is a positive element for development and is even an essential prerequisite. The empirical evidence and new theories and approaches, however, point the way to another, emerging paradigm.

If import liberalization proceeds while the conditions for successful export growth are not yet in place, there are likely to be adverse results. Thus, trade liberalization should not be pursued automatically or rapidly as an end in itself. It is important to choose the appropriate timing, sequencing and scope of liberalization and to have other required factors present.

Developing countries must thus have adequate policy space and freedom to choose between different options in relation to their trade policies. They must have the scope and flexibility to make strategic choices in trade policies and related policies in the areas of finance, investment, and technology, in order to make decisions on the rate and scope of liberalization. This principle should be integrated into the WTO's principles and rules and in the policies of the IFIs.

Reorienting the WTO to Development

The preamble to the Marrakesh Agreement, establishing the WTO, recognizes the objective of sustainable development and also the need for positive efforts to ensure the developing countries secure a share in international trade growth commensurate with the needs of their economic development. However, in practice so far, development has not been seen as a primary WTO objective, neither was it a primary purpose of the Uruguay Round or the Marrakesh Agreement.

Although the substance of the Doha Declaration has not been development-friendly (and is in many ways contrary to the interests of development), the Declaration does make the following statement: 'The majority of WTO members are developing countries. We seek to place their needs and interests at the heart of the work programme adopted in this Declaration' (para. 2).

If the priority for the WTO is to promote the trade and development of developing countries, what would it take to orient the WTO to become such a pro-development organization?

Facilitating development should become the overriding principle guiding the work of the WTO, whose rules and operations should be designed to produce development as the outcome. The test of a rule, proposal, or policy being considered in the WTO should not be whether it is 'trade-distorting' but whether it is 'development-distorting.' Since development is the ultimate objective, while reduction of trade barriers is only a means, the need to avoid development distortions should have primacy over the avoidance of trade distortion. So-called 'trade distortions' could in some circumstances constitute a necessary condition for meeting development objectives. From this perspective, the prevention of development-distorting rules, measures, policies, and approaches should be the overriding concern of the WTO.

The re-orientation of the WTO towards this perspective and approach is essential if there is to be progress towards a fair and balanced multilateral trading system with more benefits rather than costs for developing countries. Such a re-orientation would make the rules and the judgment of future proposals more in line with empirical reality and practical necessities.

Taking this approach, the goal for developing countries would be to attain 'appropriate liberalization' rather than 'maximum liberalization.'

The rules of the WTO should be reviewed to screen out those that are 'development-distorting,' and a decision could be made that, at the least, developing countries be exempted from being obliged to follow rules or measures that prevent them from meeting their development objectives. These exemptions can be on the basis of special and differential treatment.

Improving the Basic Structure

As pointed out by Das (2003), many of the problems facing developing countries in the WTO arise from the basic structure which stresses trade liberalization, using reciprocity in the exchange of concessions as the main instrument (see the seventh section of this chapter). WTO member states have widely different levels of capacities and development. Reciprocity between members with different capacities leads to unequal outcomes. As the problem with this was recognized, the principle of special and differential (S&D) treatment for developing countries was incorporated in part IV of GATT. But the principle was not seriously implemented and it was further eroded in the Uruguay Round agreements (Third World Network 2001: 38).

Addressing these problems requires a system that effectively takes into account the different capacities of different categories of members at different stages of development, so that the outcome will be an equitable sharing of benefits. Given the inadequacy of the structure based on reciprocity, there should be some structural improvement to redress the problem of overall imbalance, and structural changes to compensate for the handicaps of developing countries in the WTO system.

Suggestions for improving this structural defect, including the following, have been provided in Das (2001) and Third World Network (2001: 79):

1. Differential and more favorable treatment for developing countries should not be considered as a concession, but rather as a way of redressing imbalances inherent in the system. Developing countries should not be treated as seekers of favors, nor called upon to make special concessions in order to get S&D treatment in any area.
2. Developing countries should be allowed under S&D treatment to undertake comparatively lesser levels of obligations than developed countries. S&D treatment should not be limited to a longer time frame for implementation, as is usually the case at present.
3. On the Doha program agenda is a review of how to enhance and strengthen the provisions on S&D treatment in the various agreements, and to create provisions where they are needed but absent. However, there has not been enough priority accorded to finding solutions so far, and this should be rectified.
4. Obligations of developed countries to provide benefits to developing countries should be made into binding commitments, rather than remaining as 'best endeavor' clauses.
5. Developing countries should not be called upon to give up or refrain from adopting policies and measures to support technological development and upgrading as well as diversification of their production and

exports. There should be a formal and enforceable waiver in this regard rather than merely a 'best endeavor' provision.

6. Developed countries should establish specific and concrete arrangements for encouraging imports of products of developing countries.

Enabling Developing Countries to have Policy Space for Development

In light of the above, some important principles and rules in the WTO should be modified to take into account the need for developing countries to have policy space to undertake measures required by their development needs. Among these are the following:

1. *National treatment.* The national treatment provision handicaps developing countries as it prohibits preferences to domestic products vis-à-vis like imported products. Since developing countries and their firms have less capacity than developed countries, the inability to provide advantages to local products would make these less viable, especially in an environment of tariff reductions. Many developing countries are thus likely to become more dependent on foreign goods. Therefore, there is a need for developing countries to adopt policies and measures to support and encourage the domestic production of goods and services. Thus, the national treatment principle should be relaxed, and developing countries be allowed to provide special facilities and preference to domestic products, at least in selected sectors (Das 2003: 191). The relevant rules in GATT, for example, provisions relating to national treatment and TRIMs, need to be suitably modified to enable developing countries to support domestic production and supply. In particular, developing countries should be allowed to apply the domestic-content requirement to their industries (Third World Network 2001: 80).
2. *Subsidies.* Subsidies in developing countries, in both industry and agriculture, should be recognized as an instrument of development, rather than as measures distorting trade. The rules should clearly say this, and they should contain enabling provisions for developing countries to use subsidies for technological development, upgrading of production, and diversification of production and trade. Such subsidies should be exempt from imposition of countervailing duty and other types of counteraction (Third World Network 2001: 81).
3. *Tariffs.* To pursue effective development strategies, developing countries have to modulate and fine-tune their trade policy instruments so as to support and encourage the growth of infant industries and specific sectors, the choice of which will vary with time depending on the need.

> As part of this dynamic process, developing countries need flexibility in the matter of raising and reducing tariffs. The current procedure of raising tariffs beyond the bound level is very cumbersome and should be made smoother and easier (Das 2001). If there were systemic assurance that countries could raise tariffs (under appropriate multilateral surveillance) for a limited period to promote infant industries to get established and become operational, it would be to the benefit of all (Third World Network 2001: 80).

Treatment of Proposals for 'New Issues' in the WTO

Before achieving the reorientation and reform of the WTO towards development objectives, it would be counterproductive to introduce yet more 'new issues' into the WTO that would further burden the developing countries with inappropriate obligations and make the system even more imbalanced. There should thus be a consideration of the proposed new issues from a development perspective.

The proposals for bringing in new issues (the Singapore issues, especially investment, competition, and transparency in government procurement, and environmental and social standards) are inappropriate. These are *non-trade* issues while the WTO as a multilateral trade organization should stick to its mandate for dealing with *trade* issues. Principles such as national treatment that were created for a regime dealing with trade issues may not be suitable when applied to non-trade issues. If the new issues are to be discussed internationally, other, more appropriate venues should be found for them. If they are nevertheless brought into the WTO, they will lead to a distortion and possibly to a destabilization of the multilateral trade system, to the detriment of world trade.

The major proponents are seeking to bring non-trade issues into the WTO not because this would strengthen the trade system, but because the WTO has a strong enforcement mechanism, in other words, its dispute settlement system, which means that developing countries would be more likely to comply with rules lodged in the WTO. However, the 'contamination' of a system created for trade issues with non-trade issues may cause serious damage to the WTO. Moreover, the fact that developing countries are likely to comply with binding rules backed by a strong enforcement mechanism does not necessarily mean that the outcome is appropriate. If the rules are inappropriate, then the fact that they are binding and complied with would actually worsen an inappropriate outcome.

If these non-trade issues are brought into the WTO, and WTO principles as interpreted by developed countries are applied to them, developing countries will be at a serious disadvantage, and would lose a great deal of their policy flexibility and the ability to make national policies of their own. During the Uruguay Round, the developed countries already brought in new issues: intellectual property, services, and investment measures. The agreements in these areas (TRIPS, GATS, and TRIMs respectively) are already causing many serious problems, giving rise to the implementation issues. Professor Jagdish Bhagwati, the renowned trade economist and advisor to the GATT Director-General, Arthur Dunkel, during the Uruguay Round, has commented in *The Financial Times* that it was a mistake to have introduced intellectual property into the WTO as it is not a trade issue, it has distorted the trade system, and it has been non-reciprocal (as most patents belong to developed countries and the developing countries have had to bear the high costs of royalty payment), and that the TRIPS Agreement should be taken out of the WTO. The lesson should be learnt from the inappropriate introduction of non-trade issues in the Uruguay Round, so that this is not repeated.

Even without the new issues, the present agenda of the WTO is overloaded. Introducing new issues into the WTO will make the overload much worse, and distract from the WTO's trade work. Developing countries do not have the manpower and financial resources to cope with negotiations on new issues as well as the other items on the agenda.

The WTO should therefore be limited in scope to dealing with trade issues that have a legitimate place within a system of multilateral trade rules, and these rules and the system must primarily be designed or redesigned to benefit developing countries, which form the majority of the WTO membership. There is at present no system for determining if or how new issues are brought into the WTO. Such a system should be established. Issues to be brought under the competence of the WTO should meet certain criteria, such as that: the issue is a trade issue appropriate for a system of multilateral trade rules; the WTO is the appropriate venue; the issue is sufficiently 'mature' in that members have an understanding of it and how it relates to the WTO and to their interests; if brought into the WTO, the issue (and how it will be interpreted) will clearly be in the interests of developing countries, which constitute the majority; there must be a consensus of all members that the issue should be brought in, and on how it should be brought in. And this should be a genuine consensus based on a full understanding by members, all of which should be allowed to participate fully in the decision-making process in Geneva and at the ministerial conference itself.

Rethinking the Scope of the WTO's Mandate and the Role of Other Agencies

It is not correct to equate the WTO with the 'multilateral trading system.' In fact the WTO is both less than and more than the global trade system.

There are key issues regarding world trade that the WTO is not seriously concerned with, including the trends and problems of the terms of trade of its members, and the commodity problem. There are other organizations, especially UNCTAD, that deal with aspects of international trade, including aspects that are not in the purview of the WTO. They should be considered vital parts of the multilateral trading system.

On the other hand, the WTO has become deeply involved in issues beyond trade, especially domestic policy issues such as intellectual property laws, domestic investment, and subsidy policies. There are also proposals to bring in other non-trade issues. Thus the WTO is more than a trade organization. The question is whether its mandate should have been extended beyond trade and whether it should be further extended.

GATT and the WTO evolved trade principles (such as non-discrimination, MFN, and national treatment) that were derived from the context of trade in goods. The application of the same principles to areas outside of trade may not be appropriate and could have negative outcomes. Moreover, incorporation of non-trade issues into the WTO system could distort the work of the WTO itself and the multilateral trading system.

Therefore, a fundamental rethinking of the mandate and scope of the WTO is required. First, issues that are not trade issues should not be introduced in the WTO as subjects for rules. This rule should apply at least until the question of the appropriateness and criteria of proposed issues is dealt with satisfactorily in a systemic manner.

Second, a review should be made of the issues that are currently in the WTO to determine whether the WTO is indeed the appropriate venue for them. Prominent orthodox trade economists such as Professors J. Bhagwati and T. N. Srinivasan have concluded that it was a mistake to have incorporated intellectual property as an issue in the Uruguay Round and in the WTO. There should be a serious consideration, starting with the mandated review process, of transferring the TRIPS Agreement from the WTO to a more suitable forum.

Within its traditional ambit of trade in goods, the WTO should reorient its primary operational objectives and principles towards development, as elaborated above. The imbalances in the agreements relating to goods should be ironed out, with the 'rebalancing' designed to meet the development needs of developing countries and to be more in line with the realities of the liberalization and development processes.

With these changes, the WTO could better play its role in the design and maintenance of fair rules for trade, and thus contribute towards a balanced, predictable international trading system which is designed to produce and promote development.

The WTO, reformed along the lines above, should then be seen as a key component of the international trading system, coexisting with, complementing and cooperating with other organizations, and together the WTO and these other organizations would operate within the framework of the trading system.

Other critical trade issues should be dealt with by other organizations, which should be given the mandate, support, and resources to carry out their tasks effectively. These other issues should include: (1) assisting developing countries to build their capacity for production, marketing, distribution, and trade; (2) the need for monitoring and stabilizing commodity markets, with a view to ensuring reasonable prices and earnings for commodity-producing developing countries; (3) addressing the restrictive business and trade practices of transnational corporations that hamper the ability of smaller firms to engage in production and trade; (4) addressing the problems of low commodity prices and developing countries' terms of trade. These issues can be dealt with by various UN bodies, especially a revitalized UNCTAD.

References

Akyuz, Y. (ed.) (2003). *Developing Countries and World Trade: Performance and Prospects.* London and Penang: Zed Books and Third World Network.

—— (2004). 'Challenges Facing Developing Countries in World Trade and Investment'. Public Lecture, Kuala Lumpur, February 24.

Buffie, E. (2001). *Trade Policy in Developing Countries.* Cambridge: Cambridge University Press.

Chang, H. J. and Grabel, I. (2004). *Reclaiming Development.* London: Zed Books.

Das, B.L. (1998). *The WTO Agreements: Deficiencies, Imbalances and Required Changes.* Penang: Third World Network.

—— (1999). *Some Suggestions for Improvements in the WTO Agreements.* Penang: Third World Network.

—— (2001). 'The Present Trading System, Opportunities and Problems'. Unpublished paper.

—— (2003). *The WTO and the Multilateral Trading System: Past, Present and Future.* London and Penang: Zed Books and Third World Network.

European Communities (1999). 'The Relevance of Fundamental WTO Principles of National Treatment, Transparency and Most Favored Nation Treatment to Competition Policy and Vice Versa'. Communication to the WTO, April 12.

FAO (1999). 'Experience with the Implementation of the Uruguay Round Agreement on Agriculture, Synthesis of Country Case Studies'. Paper prepared by Commodities and Trade Division.

—— (2000). *Agriculture, Trade and Food Security,* Vol. I. Rome: Food and Agriculture Organization.

—— (2001). *Agriculture, Trade and Food Security,* Vol. II. Rome: Food and Agriculture Organization.

FAO (2003). 'Some Trade Policy Issues Relating to Trends in Agricultural Imports in the Context of Food Security'. Paper prepared for the FAO Committee on Commodity Problems.

Hong Kong, China (2000). Statement by Hong Kong, China, at special session of the WTO General Council on June 22, on behalf of International Textiles and Clothing Bureau, WT/GC/W/405.

Khor, M. (1993). *South–North Resource Flows*. Penang: Third World Network.

—— (2000a). *Globalization and the South: Some Critical Issues*. Penang: Third World Network.

—— (2000b). 'Proposed New Issues in the WTO and the Interests of Developing Countries'. Paper presented at the Third World Network Seminar on Current Developments in the WTO, Geneva, September.

—— (2001). 'Present Problems and Future Shape of the WTO and Multilateral Trade System', Briefing Paper, No. 2. Penang: Third World Network.

—— (2002). *The WTO, the Post-Doha Agenda and the Future of the Trade System*. Penang: Third World Network.

—— (2004). 'Comments on the WTO's Geneva "July 2004 Package"', Briefing Paper, No. 22. Penang: Third World Network.

Meenakshi, R. (2004). 'Effects of Agricultural Liberalisation on Communities in Developing Countries'. Penang: Third World Network.

OECD (2000). *Agricultural Policies in OECD Countries: Monitoring and Evaluation 2000*. Paris: OECD Secretariat.

Robbins, P. (2003). *Stolen Fruit: The Tropical Commodities Disaster*. London: Zed Books.

Rodrik, D. (1999). *The New Global Economy and Developing Countries: Making Openness Work*. Washington, DC: Overseas Development Council.

—— (2001). *The Global Governance of Trade as if Development Really Mattered*. New York: UNDP.

SAPRIN (2004). *Structural Adjustment: The SAPRI Report*. London: Zed Books.

Shafaeddin, S. M. (1994). *The Impact of Trade Liberalisation on Export and GDP Growth in Least Developed Countries*. Discussion Paper, No. 85, UNCTAD, Geneva.

SUNS (South–North Development Monitor) (various years). *SUNS*, various issues (Geneva).

Third World Economics (various years). *Third World Economics*, various issues (Penang).

Third World Network (2001). *The Multilateral Trading System: A Development Perspective*. New York: UNDP.

UNCTAD (1999a). *Trade and Development Report 1999*. New York and Geneva: United Nations.

—— (1999b). 'Industrial Countries Must Work Harder for Development if Globalisation is to Deliver on its Promises'. Press release September 1, UNCTAD/INF/2816.

—— (2000). *Positive Agenda and Future Trade Negotiations*. Geneva: UNCTAD.

World Commission on the Social Dimension of Globalization (2004). *A Fair Globalization: Creating Opportunities for All*. Washington, DC: World Commission on the Social Dimension of Globalization.

WTO (World Trade Organization) (1999). 'Preparation for the 1999 Ministerial Conference: Ministerial Text'. Revised Draft, October 19.

—— (2001a). 'Preparation for the Fourth Session of the Ministerial Conference: Draft Ministerial Declaration'. Revision, October 27.

—— (2001b). 'Ministerial Declaration'. Adopted November 14.

—— (2001c). 'Declaration on the TRIPS Agreement and Public Health'. Adopted November 14.

—— (2001d). 'Implementation-Related Issues and Concerns'. General Council Decision, November 14.

—— (2001e). 'Compilation of Outstanding Implementation Issues Raised by Members'. General Council Document, JOB(01)152/Rev.1, October 27.

—— (2001f). 'Implementation-Related Issues and Concerns'. General Council Document, JOB(01)/14, February 20.

—— (2004). 'Doha Work Programme'. General Council Decision, July 31.

12

Reforming Labor Market Institutions: Unemployment Insurance and Employment Protection

Olivier Blanchard[1]

This chapter explores the characteristics of both optimal and actual unemployment insurance and employment protection. It then sketches potential paths for reforms in both rich and middle-income countries. It reaches three main conclusions:

1. There is a role for both state-provided unemployment insurance and employment protection.
2. In rich countries, one challenge is to combine unemployment insurance with strong incentives for the unemployed to take jobs. Financial incentives are unlikely to be enough at the low end of the wage scale. The other challenge is to redefine employment protection by reducing administrative constraints and judicial intervention, and by relying more on financial incentives.
3. In middle-income countries, the main challenge is to move from the current system of high severance payments and employment protection to a system of state-provided unemployment benefits and lower severance payments.

Modern economies are characterized by high levels of job creation and job destruction: such reallocation is central to productivity growth. However, with job destruction comes the risk of unemployment for workers. And based on both historical and cross-country evidence, there are good reasons to believe that private markets, left to themselves, do a poor job of

[1] Prepared for the Barcelona Conference on the 'Post-Washington Consensus', MIT and NBER, September 2004. I thank Hans Werner Sinn, Peter Diamond, Francesco Giavazzi, and Jean Tirole for comments.

protecting workers against unemployment risk. This suggests a potentially welfare-improving role for state intervention, through the joint design of unemployment insurance (which determines the pain of being unemployed), and employment protection (which determines the probability of becoming unemployed).

Designing and putting in place the right institutions, be it employment protection or unemployment insurance, is a complex task. The evidence is that many rich countries, particularly in Europe, have done a poor job. The mistakes they made have led both to poorly functioning labor markets and to high unemployment.

It is therefore essential to take a step back and think about the optimal design of labor market institutions, unencumbered by history or political economy considerations. Having taken that step, one can then attempt to sketch a path of reforms, a path to go from here to there. The 'here' and the 'there' vary across countries. European countries already have a complex set of labor market institutions; reforms mean transforming existing institutions. Poorer countries, such as those in Latin America, have more embryonic labor market institutions to start and more limited institutional capability; reforms mean putting in place new, potentially simpler, institutions.

The goal of this chapter is to explore these themes. The first section sets the stage and reviews the rationale for state intervention in the labor market. The second section offers an explanation of how, in Europe, desirable goals have led to flawed institutions and bad labor market outcomes. The third section turns to the optimal design of unemployment insurance and employment protection. The fourth section then explores paths for reforms in rich countries, i.e., Europe. The fifth section does the same for poorer countries, such as Latin America. The last section concludes.[2]

The Rationale for State Intervention

Few economists would argue against (at least some) state intervention in the labor market. One can think of a number of relevant dimensions here, where market outcomes may be either inefficient or socially unacceptable, or both. Collective bargaining may lead to both inefficient and socially unacceptable outcomes, implying the need for the state to define rules regulating bargaining. Low-skill workers may have a productivity lower than what society

[2] Two caveats: (1) As will be clear to the reader, what follows is a combination of conclusions based on formal work with Jean Tirole (see the second section of this chapter for some of the theory, and the first and third sections for applications to France and to the Netherlands respectively), of tentative conclusions from work in progress, and of more or less educated guesses. It is very much in the nature of a progress report; (2) I know French institutions much better than those of other countries. The conclusions of this chapter are likely to be particularly influenced by the French experience.

considers a 'living wage,' implying the need to provide additional income to those workers. Markets may do a poor job of insuring workers against unemployment, implying the need for the state to provide unemployment insurance and define rules regulating separations. In this chapter, I shall concentrate only on this last dimension. My excuse is that it is a central dimension, and I have not thought enough about the others.

The historical evidence (from rich countries before the provision of state-provided insurance), together with the cross country evidence (from poorer countries without state-provided unemployment insurance) strongly suggests that, left to itself, the labor market does a poor job of protecting workers against unemployment. To think about whether and how the state might do better, however, it is important to identify the sources of this failure.

Start with the workers themselves. The scope for self-insurance by workers, through accumulation and decumulation of savings to prepare for unemployment, is limited. Savings can do a good job in the case of high probability, small loss, events where the law of large numbers comes into play. They can also do a good job in the case of largely predictable events happening far off on the horizon, such as retirement. They can do at best a mediocre job for small probability events implying large losses, such as the loss of a job, and they do poorly against events happening early in working life, before workers have had time to build up savings. They do poorly against events happening late in working life, when workers may have a hard time getting another job, and, in any case, have little time to replenish their savings.

Firms are the next natural candidates for providing unemployment insurance to the workers they lay off. But they also face a number of constraints. Small, single owner firms are likely to inherit the risk aversion of their owners and are thus in a poor position to insure workers. Larger firms often face constraints in financial markets and may have shallow pockets. Even those firms which we can treat as risk-neutral face other obstacles: they are in a poor position to assess the labor market situation of the workers they have laid off, let alone to monitor their search behavior. Under those conditions, providing insurance directly is likely to be unattractive.

Third parties, say private insurance companies, are in a better position to diversify risk, and thus, at least on those grounds, they are in a better position than firms to insure workers. But, unless they have better monitoring capacity than firms, they face the same problems in checking the employment status and search behavior of the unemployed. And, unless they can monitor the productivity of jobs and workers (which they cannot), they face an additional problem relative to firms: the provision of unemployment insurance to workers affects the separation decision of firms. The more generous the insurance, and thus the payment to workers in case of separation, the higher the rate of separation and the more costly it is to provide insurance. This again makes provision of insurance unattractive.

All rich countries today have some form of state-provided unemployment insurance, so it is hard to know what private arrangements would emerge today in the absence of such insurance. (Before the state provision of insurance, unions and other worker organizations sometimes acted as third parties, providing limited insurance, typically with strong monitoring of their unemployed members.) One has to turn to poorer countries, where state-provided unemployment insurance is often absent. Leaving aside intra-family transfers—which clearly play an important role—arrangements typically take the form of severance payments by firms, either imposed by law or offered by the firms themselves. Severance payments eliminate the need to monitor the status and search effort of laid off workers. But they provide only mediocre unemployment insurance. In particular, being lump sum, severance payments provide no insurance against unemployment duration uncertainty.

The Mistakes of Europe

One can trace many of the labor market problems of Europe to flawed attempts at achieving a desirable goal, namely the protection of workers against unemployment.[3]

Employment Protection

1. Employment protection has been aimed at protecting existing jobs and at reducing job destruction.

   Protecting existing jobs sounds like a good idea, surely one with strong political support. Collective lay-offs, even if they account for a small proportion of total separations, are highly visible and often lead to long spells of unemployment. If unemployment is painful, why not try to reduce its incidence by reducing job destruction?

   Not surprisingly, however, the idea is not as good as it sounds: the anticipation of higher separation costs makes it less profitable to create new firms, to try new and risky ventures; it reduces job creation. Compared to the direct effect of employment protection on job destruction, this induced effect on job creation is nearly invisible: jobs destroyed (or saved) are easily identified; jobs not created are not. But it is present, and it has important implications:

[3] The usual and important caveats apply here. Europe is not a homogenous whole: today, while the large European countries still have high unemployment, many of the smaller ones have low unemployment. And, even in those countries with high unemployment, some reforms have taken place since the mid-1980s. What follows is a bit of a caricature, but a useful one.

- Employment protection may actually increase rather than decrease unemployment. The decrease in job destruction lowers unemployment; the decrease in job creation, however, increases it. In theory as well as in practice, the effect on unemployment appears ambiguous.
- Employment protection changes the nature of unemployment. Lower job destruction reduces the incidence of unemployment; lower job creation increases the average duration of unemployment. With the increase in unemployment duration comes an increase in long-term unemployment. And, with long-term unemployment, come high human costs, ranging from the loss of skills, the loss of self-confidence, to the loss of morale.
- Employment protection has an adverse impact on productivity. Much of the microeconomic evidence on productivity growth gives a central role to the process of job creation and job destruction. More productive firms replace less productive ones; more productive jobs replace less productive ones. Lower job creation and lower job destruction delay or slow this process, and thus have an adverse effect on the level of productivity, and perhaps even on the rate of productivity growth.[4]

2. Equally important is the form employment protection has taken in most European countries.

   In general, one should distinguish between three forms of employment protection: severance payments to the workers; direct payments to the state; and administrative and judicial constraints and costs, which go neither to the workers nor to the state.

   Much of the actual and perceived cost of employment protection in many European countries actually comes from the third form. In France, for example, firms that lay off more than a certain number of workers have to go through a series of time consuming steps. These include meetings with representatives of workers, the design of a plan aimed at finding jobs for workers in other firms, and so on. On the judicial side, the lay-off decision of the firm can be and often is challenged in court. For example, the economic rationale given by the firm for the lay-offs can be rejected by labor judges, and their decision can come after many years. Taken individually, many of the steps appear reasonable, and designed to alleviate the pain of unemployment. In effect, they introduce substantial uncertainty as to the final outcome and cost of lay-off decisions. This uncertainty, which benefits neither workers nor firms, appears to have a large impact on job creation decisions.

[4] To be fair, however, I feel that this last empirical connection has not yet been convincingly established.

Unemployment Insurance

Unemployment insurance has been aimed at helping the unemployed survive unemployment, rather than at getting them back into jobs. On the one hand, the nature of unemployment in Europe, and the large proportion of long-term unemployed, have created strong political pressure to extend more or less indefinite support to the unemployed, be it through social insurance or social assistance. On the other hand, state run unemployment agencies have been reluctant to condition unemployment benefits on search effort, and even more reluctant to condition benefits on a willingness to take an acceptable job if offered.

This combination of long-lasting and unconditional benefits has led many of the unemployed to exert low search effort, at least in the early stages of their unemployment spells. More visibly, it has led to unemployment traps at the low-wage end of the wage distribution. When account is taken of the various in-kind and cash benefit programs designed to help the non-employed, taking a job at the minimum wage, especially a part-time job, is often financially unattractive: the effective marginal tax rate sometimes exceeds one. Low search effort and unemployment traps have further contributed to increase long-term unemployment, and the overall unemployment rate.

Reforms at the Margin

Flawed as they are, existing labor market institutions form a coherent whole. High employment protection leads to long duration unemployment. Long duration unemployment in turn increases the demand for employment protection.

In that context, reforms have proven hard to achieve, and have sometimes turned out to be counterproductive.

The expansion of the scope for temporary contracts provides an interesting example. In order to decrease employment protection without running into the opposition of workers already protected, many European countries have attempted to reduce employment protection at the margin. They have allowed firms to offer, under certain conditions, temporary contracts to their new hires. At the end of such contracts, firms can lay off workers with small severance payments, few administrative steps, and limited judicial recourse by workers. In some countries, the conditions under which firms can offer such contracts have been fairly generous, and the proportion of temporary contracts is high. In Spain, for example, temporary contracts account for roughly 30 percent of employment, and 90 percent of new hires. In other countries, conditions have been more limited, and the proportion of temporary contracts is smaller. In France for example, temporary contracts account for 12 percent of employment and 75 percent of new hires.

Given the political constraints facing any across-the-board reform of employment protection, such reforms at the margin would appear to be a good idea. They have indeed increased the flexibility of firms in adjusting employment, at least at some margins such as seasonal movements. They have made it less risky for firms to hire new entrants, in other words, workers with no employment history. But this has come at two substantial costs. First, they have further insulated workers under permanent contracts from fluctuations in employment, increasing their bargaining power and decreasing the response of wages to unemployment. Second, they have made it very costly for firms to keep workers at the end of their temporary contracts: keeping a worker implies giving that worker a permanent contract, and the employment protection which comes with it. Unless the worker is exceptional, the firm has an incentive to let them go and hire another temporary worker. And, if the probability that the worker will not be retained is high, the incentives for the firm to give them training are limited. The result has been an increasingly dual labor market. In France, the evidence is that entrants typically go through a long succession of dead-end temporary jobs and unemployment spells before landing a regular job, and that the length of time to obtain a permanent job has actually increased since the introduction of temporary contracts.

Optimal Unemployment Insurance and Employment Protection

If one were free to design unemployment insurance and employment protection from scratch, what would one want to put in place? The question is obviously politically naive, but as our previous discussion suggests, reforms driven by political constraints may go in the wrong direction. It is essential to have a clear sense of the ultimate goal.

Unemployment Insurance

When, in the first section, we discussed the failure of private markets to provide adequate unemployment insurance, we identified a number of problems facing either firms or private third parties as providers of insurance. Is there any reason to think that the state can do better?

The answer is, yes. First, as a very large third-party insurer, the state is more likely to be able to diversify unemployment risk. Second, by having a ready administrative infrastructure, it is in a unique position to monitor the status of workers, for example to assess whether they are still unemployed or have found a job. It may also be better able than other third parties to monitor and condition benefits on search effort.

All this does not imply that unemployment insurance must be the exclusive domain of the state. The state may, for example, provide its administrative infrastructure to an agency jointly run by workers and firms, and one observes variations along these lines across different European countries. But it implies that the state must play an important role in the provision of unemployment insurance. So, for the rest of this discussion, I shall think of insurance as being state-provided.

The state still faces many of the problems that would be faced by firms and by private third parties:

1. It must monitor not only the status of workers, employed or unemployed (something which, in rich countries, is relatively easy to do), but also their search effort.

   Here one has to recognize the fact that, at the bottom of the wage distribution, financial incentives to take a job if unemployed are inevitably limited. Both the level of benefits and the lowest wage are likely to reflect what society considers as the minimum acceptable standard of living, and thus to be close to each other.

   If this is the case, the provision of benefits must be made conditional on the acceptance of a job if such an 'acceptable' job is available. The principle here is simple, but its implementation is not:

   - It requires in particular the definition of what an acceptable job is, and how this definition changes with the duration of unemployment. An interesting issue arises here from the possibility of on-the-job search. If searching while on a job is feasible (which it typically is), the class of 'acceptable jobs' should be larger. In other words, it may be better to force somebody who is unemployed into a mediocre job, from which they can search for a better one, than to allow them to stay unemployed.
   - It also involves giving the proper incentives for the employees of the unemployment agency. If the agency is run by the state, one might guess that state employees have few incentives to force the unemployed into jobs. This is indeed what one observes. If, instead, the agency is privately run, and its employees are rewarded according to their job placement record, the unemployed may be forced into jobs which are truly unacceptable.

2. It must address the distortion of the separation decision implied by the presence of unemployment insurance.

   Recall the nature of the distortion: the higher the unemployment benefits given to the worker if laid off, the higher the threshold level of productivity below which the firm will lay the worker off. The reason: if the worker is laid off, the firm and the worker taken together receive a transfer from the insurance agency, namely the unemployment benefits paid to the worker; this distorts the decision of the firm.

To take a simple example, suppose (counterfactually) that, if laid off, the worker remains unemployed forever, and derives no utility or disutility from being unemployed. Then the socially efficient decision would be to keep the worker employed so long as their productivity is positive. But, from the point of view of the worker and the firm, it is optimal for the firm to lay off the worker as soon as productivity is below unemployment benefits. The implication is that there will be too many lay-offs.

Can the state limit or undo this distortion? If firms are risk-neutral and have deep pockets, then the state can undo the distortion in a very simple way: by charging the firms for unemployment benefits paid to the workers they lay off. This can most easily be done ex post, by just sending the bills to the firms as workers go through their unemployment spell and collect unemployment benefits.

Under this arrangement, the state no longer provides insurance: firms do. The state only acts as an intermediary, better able than other third parties to solve some of the information problems associated with the provision of this insurance. Firms take into account the cost of unemployment insurance. As a result, they have incentives to lay off workers with the best chances of re-employment, and to help them find employment.

If firms are risk averse, or have shallow pockets—in other words, they face financial constraints, then fully charging firms for unemployment benefits may no longer be optimal. By their very nature, lay-offs are more likely to take place in relatively bad times for the firm. Asking firms for payment in bad times may increase the risk faced by the firm's owners, or may put the firm into more financial difficulty, or force the firm to make inefficient decisions.

One partial solution is to separate the timing of payments to the laid-off workers by the agency from the timing of payments by firms to the agency. Bonus malus systems, in which firms that lay off more face higher contribution rates in the future, are a standard way to combine the provision of insurance with better incentives. Accumulation of unemployment benefit balances by firms, and payments of these balances over time are another and closely related way to proceed.[5]

[5] This is the principle behind the 'reserve ratio' system used in many US states. Leaving aside the many complicated details, the principle is simple: each firm has a running balance with the state unemployment agency, with contributions by the firm to the fund on one side, and benefits paid by the agency to the workers laid off by the firm on the other. Once a year, the state computes the net outstanding balance, and requires the firm to pay some proportion of this outstanding balance over the following year. The factor of proportionality depends both on the net balance of the firm, and the net balance of the state fund as a whole. Ignoring discounting, and the various ceilings that limit contributions (all these considerations being very relevant in practice), firms eventually pay the full cost of unemployment benefits for the

This may, however, not be enough, in which case it may be optimal to charge firms less than the full amount of unemployment benefits, and to finance the rest in some other way, for example through payroll taxes. The distortions this creates at the separation margin may be more than offset by the reduction in risk or financial difficulties faced by firms.

Can one be more specific as to the relative role of 'lay-off taxes' (the contributions by firms to the agency, proportional to the benefits paid by the agency to the workers laid off by the firm) and, say, payroll taxes? Not easily, although my guess is that the proportion financed by lay-off taxes should be high. This is based on the notion that, while lay-offs associated with major financial difficulties for firms, including bankruptcy and firm closings, are the most visible, they account for a small fraction of all lay-offs. Most lay-offs take place in firms which are not in financial difficulty, where the assumption of risk neutrality and deep pockets may be quite reasonable.[6]

To summarize: there are good reasons to have the state provide unemployment insurance. This system must make unemployment benefits conditional on acceptance of jobs if available. And unemployment benefits must be financed, in part or in total, by proportional contributions from firms.

Employment Protection

1. The discussion of unemployment insurance we have just gone through has a straightforward and important implication for the design of employment protection: firms that lay off workers should pay a 'lay-off tax,' accounting in part or in total, for the unemployment benefits paid to the workers they lay off.

   Such a tax is clearly a form of employment protection. Although the payment does not go directly to the workers, it (optimally) deters firms from laying off workers. Put simply, employment protection (in this form) is part of the optimal set of labor institutions.
2. Should there be severance payments, that is, direct payments to workers, in addition to these layoff taxes? To answer this question, it is useful to distinguish between two costs, the cost associated with losing a job, and

workers they lay off. The factor of proportionality determines how the timing of payments depends on current and past lay-offs.

[6] There are other relevant dimensions here, some of which are discussed in the second section of the chapter. One of these is the extent to which different taxes affect the wage in different ways. Other things equal, a lay-off tax, which makes it more costly for firms to lay-off workers, increases the bargaining power of workers, and to the extent that wages are set ex post, may increase labor costs more than would a payroll tax. This provides an argument for relying more on payroll taxes, and less on lay-off taxes, in the financing of unemployment benefits.

the cost associated with becoming unemployed. (A worker who finds a job upon being laid off suffers the first, not the second.) So far, we have focused on the implications of the second. Let's now think about the implications of the first.

Losing a job often has a psychological cost: the loss of a long-held job, even if the loss is not followed by unemployment, can lead to the loss of a network of workplace friends, to health deterioration, and to a loss of self-esteem. However, this cost is not, per se, an argument for severance payments: financial payments cannot offset the psychological cost.[7] It is an argument instead for decreasing the incidence of lay-offs through a higher lay-off tax. If, as is plausible, the psychological cost is increasing with seniority in the firm, this suggests making the lay-off tax an increasing function of seniority.

Losing a job may also have a financial cost: there is substantial evidence that, in many jobs, the wage profile paid to the worker as a function of their seniority is steeper than their productivity profile. In other words, workers are relatively underpaid early in their tenure, overpaid later on. If this is the case, then losing a job can have a large financial cost for a worker with seniority. And, in contrast to the case of unemployment insurance, the firm is in a good position to insure workers against this financial cost: the cost is incurred at the time of separation, is relatively easy to assess, and payment can take the form of severance payments.

How should the schedule of severance payments look in this case? A tentative answer is that it should depend positively on seniority and negatively on distance from normal retirement age. The higher the seniority the higher the likely financial cost. The closer to retirement, the lower the cost (other benefits being equal, being laid off one year before retirement just anticipates an expected outcome by one year).[8] This suggests a schedule increasing, and then decreasing, in seniority.

It is not clear, however, why the level and schedule of severance payments and, in general, the many other dimensions of employment protection (advance notice, retraining) should not be left to contracting between firms and workers. Ex ante, firms have the incentives to offer the best separation package they can to the workers they hire. Advance notices will clearly be valued by workers, as will retraining. If so, they will be reflected in lower wages and lower labor costs. The role of the state in this case may simply be to put a number of basic minima in place, and then to make sure that whatever contracts are entered by firms and workers—in individual and collective bargaining—are enforced.

[7] More formally: insurance can only equalize the marginal utility of consumption; it cannot insure against psychological costs.

[8] This assumes that retirement and other benefits are fully vested, so the worker receives them even if laid off. If not, it may still be very costly to be laid off one year before retirement.

3. Suppose that unemployment contributions by firms are mostly financed by lay-off taxes (rather than payroll taxes). Should these lay-off taxes be applicable as soon as the worker is hired, or should they be phased in? Put another way, should the lay-off taxes paid by the firm be the same if it lays off a worker with six months seniority or if it lays off a worker with six years seniority (assuming both workers have the same labor market prospects after the lay-off)?

   One has a sense that there should be some phasing in—for at least two reasons: first, to reduce the problem of adverse selection arising from workers who intend to be hired and then force the firm into laying them off so they can receive unemployment insurance; second, to give some time for the firm and the worker to explore the quality of the match and to separate at little or no cost if the match reveals itself to be a bad one. Both reasons suggest making layoff taxes a function of seniority, with full lay-off taxes fully coming into play only after a certain number of years of seniority.

To summarize: employment protection, in the form of lay-off taxes covering part or all of the unemployment benefits paid to workers, is the natural counterpart of unemployment insurance. These lay-off taxes should increase with seniority, being low at the start of employment, and reaching their normal level after a few years of employment. Severance payments are also justified, to compensate for the financial costs associated with the loss of a job—as opposed to the financial costs associated with unemployment. For the most part, however, these payments and other aspects of separation should be left to bargaining between firms and workers, rather than imposed by the state.

Reforms in Rich Countries

Comparing optimal institutions to actual institutions in rich countries (i.e., Western Europe) suggests three main dimensions of reform:

1. A reform of unemployment insurance, to increase the incentives for the unemployed to take jobs, if available.

   Current systems rely for the most part on financial incentives. By necessity, these are likely to be weak at the low end of the wage distribution. There are two ways to force the unemployed back into jobs. The first is to decrease and eventually end benefits after some time. This, however, runs the risk of taking away unemployment insurance from those who need it most. The second is to force the unemployed to take jobs if those jobs are available and provide insurance otherwise. This is a much better option.

This reform is technically difficult. It requires defining what an acceptable job is and how this definition evolves with unemployment duration. It requires making sure that the unemployment agency has the proper incentives to get workers to take jobs. Here, however, a number of countries have been experimenting, and there is an increasing body of evidence on which to rely.

Is this reform politically feasible? It may be, because it provides in effect better insurance than the existing system. While forcing the unemployed into jobs, if such jobs are available, may be perceived as tough on the unemployed, the converse side of the reform is that, if no jobs are available, the unemployed receive unemployment benefits for as long as they need them. This implies, for example, that workers in distressed areas are likely to be better off than they are under the current system.

2. A reform of employment protection, with a larger role for financial incentives (in the form of lay-off taxes), and a reduction in the other dimensions of state imposed employment protection.

   In most European countries today, unemployment insurance is financed through payroll taxes. As we have seen, insurance should be financed, at least in part, through lay-off taxes.

   On the other hand, many aspects of the current system of employment protection should be eliminated or, more specifically, left to contracting and bargaining between workers and firms. For example, there is no obvious justification for letting judges assess whether lay-offs are economically justified. As long as firms respect the contracts signed with individual employees or with unions, firms should be free to adjust their level of employment.

   This reform is not technically difficult, although it involves major changes in labor law. Is it politically feasible? The potential trade-off between the increase in lay-off taxes—which obviously acts as a deterrent to lay-offs—and the decrease in the role of the judicial process in employment protection, may be attractive to both workers and firms. (The judicial uncertainty associated with the lay-off process is costly for both firms and workers. The decrease in uncertainty associated with such a shift suggests that both sides may benefit from the reform.) It is clear, however, that it may not be politically easy: the evidence suggests that the notion of shifting from judicial to financial employment protection is strongly at odds with the widely held notion that workers are stakeholders in the firm and should be involved in collective lay-off decisions.

3. A shift back to a single labor contract, with workers' rights increasing in seniority: as we have seen, the dual system of temporary and regular contracts introduced in many European countries is perverse, creating two classes of workers, and making it hard for entrants to obtain a

regular job. The source of the problem is the threshold effect coming from the large increase in employment protection the firm faces if it wants to keep a worker beyond the end of a temporary contract.

The natural solution is to eliminate this threshold effect by having a smoother transition in which workers' rights increase more smoothly with seniority in the firm. If, for example, the reform of employment protection discussed above is implemented and firms are subject to lay-off taxes, one can think of an increasing schedule of lay-off taxes, with a low tax rate in the first year after hiring, and the full tax rate after, say, five years of seniority. Under such a schedule, firms will be willing not only to hire, but to keep new entrants.

Is that reform politically feasible? The answer is that it may be. On the one hand, it increases employment protection and job prospects for those workers currently on temporary contracts. On the other, it decreases employment protection for those workers with permanent contracts and low seniority. These workers, however, can easily be grandfathered—protected by the old employment protection rules during a transition period. Thus, there may well be a majority in favor of reform.[9]

Reforms in Poorer Countries

Poorer countries find themselves in a very different starting position than does Western Europe. Most of them have either no or very limited state-provided unemployment insurance. They rely instead on high employment protection, with a combination of high severance payments and administrative and judicial constraints.

1. As their institutional capability improves, many of these countries should be and indeed are introducing state-provided unemployment insurance.

   It is unrealistic to expect them to be able to monitor search effort or to link benefits to job acceptance in the same way as richer countries.

[9] A related argument underlaid the introduction of temporary contracts in the 1980s. The argument was that, when the proportion of workers under temporary contracts became sufficiently high, there would be a constituency for a reform which reduced employment protection for workers under permanent contracts and increased it for workers under temporary contracts. Some have argued that this was indeed the case in Spain at the end of the 1990s when the number of unemployed workers and workers under temporary contracts exceeded the number of workers under permanent contracts. Whether or not this can happen depends on the rules under which temporary contracts can be offered. Under the rules currently in place in France, the proportion of temporary workers will remain too small to change the political equilibrium.

This suggests the desirability of a simpler system, with unemployment benefits decreasing with unemployment duration and eventually ending after some time. Such a system is still an improvement over severance payments in two ways: it provides some insurance against unemployment duration; and it eliminates one of the risks facing workers under severance payments, namely, that the firm is unwilling or unable to pay. This risk is transferred to the state, which is typically in a better position to go after the firm if needed.

For reasons we have already discussed, financing of unemployment benefits should be done, at least in part, through lay-off taxes. This suggests therefore a reform in which direct payments from firms to workers (severance payments) are replaced in from the unemployment agency to laid-off workers.

The previous paragraph points to one of the dangers facing such a reform—namely, that the unemployment insurance system is simply added on to the existing system of employment protection. It is important that, as state-provided insurance is put in place, severance payments be reduced: their role as unemployment benefits is no longer needed. Some recent experiences suggest that this risk is very much present and is one that governments must avoid as they introduce unemployment insurance.

2. A number of countries, worried about enacting a full-fledged unemployment insurance system with the distortions it entails, have explored self-insurance by workers as an alternative. While details vary, this typically has taken the form of mandatory unemployment saving accounts, to which the worker and the firm must contribute while the worker is employed, and from which the worker can withdraw if and when laid off.

   It is easy to see the appeal of such a solution. Recall that if workers can self-insure, then there is no need for state-provided unemployment insurance; no need to monitor search effort; no need for employment protection—fewer distortions all around. Unfortunately, for the reasons discussed in the first section of this chapter, the degree to which saving accumulation and decumulation by workers can insure them against unemployment risk is very limited. The probability is too small, the pain too large, for savings to easily absorb the risk. The use of interest rate subsidies does not substantially change this conclusion.[10]

   This is why, in practice, individual unemployment account systems typically include some additional state-provided insurance. This may

[10] Paradoxically, some of the mandatory saving schemes in place in Latin America actually pay below market or even zero interest rate.

take the form of allowing, for example, unemployed workers to borrow up to some ceiling either directly from the state or from financial institutions through a state guarantee. However, these additional provisions raise many of the same issues as does state-provided insurance. How much should the state provide or guarantee, and in what form? How do we make sure that firms internalize the cost of these guarantees to the state, and so take efficient lay-off decisions? It would appear that a system of state-provided insurance is a simpler and more transparent way to proceed.[11]

3. Poorer countries have a large informal sector. The decision by firms to operate in the formal or the informal sector is primarily an economic decision, based on the benefits and costs of informality. The issue in introducing any new regulation is whether and how this will affect the firms' choice and perhaps drive firms to the informal sector.

   If we think of the system of state-provided insurance as a more efficient replacement for the current system of severance payments, this should make it more appealing to be in the formal sector. Firms can now offer better insurance to their workers at the same cost. If state-provided unemployment insurance is only available to workers laid off from firms in the formal sector (firms that finance the unemployment insurance system through payment of payroll and lay-off taxes), then the incentive for firms to become formal must increase with the introduction of state-provided unemployment insurance.

   This argument suggests that the introduction of state-provided unemployment insurance—if accompanied by a corresponding reduction of severance payments—should lead to a decrease rather than an increase in the informal sector. I suspect the argument leaves out a number of other important considerations, but it provides, I feel, a useful starting point for a discussion.

Conclusion

This chapter has explored the nature and implications of actual and optimal unemployment insurance and employment protection. It has then sketched potential paths for reforms in both rich and poorer countries. A number of themes emerge:

1. When one moves away from slogans about 'labor market rigidities,' and looks at imperfections in the labor market, it is clear that there is a

[11] Some of the proponents of unemployment accounts appear to have another goal, increasing aggregate saving. Even if the goal is desirable, it is doubtful that such restricted saving accounts are the right instrument.

role for both state provided unemployment insurance and employment protection.

2. In rich countries, one challenge is to combine unemployment insurance with strong incentives for the unemployed to take jobs. Financial incentives are unlikely to be enough at the low end of the wage scale. Instead, unemployment benefits must be made conditional upon the acceptance of jobs if available. The other challenge is to redefine employment protection, by relying more heavily on financial incentives, in the form of lay-off taxes, while shifting most of the other dimensions to contracting between firms and workers.
3. In poorer countries, the challenge is to move from the current system of high severance payments and employment protection to a system of state-provided unemployment benefits and lower severance payments, while again shifting most of the other dimensions to contracting between firms and workers.

Can these reforms protect workers against unemployment risk while achieving low unemployment, high reallocation, and high productivity growth? One would be foolish to give an answer with much certainty. But the experience of successful European countries, such as the Netherlands and the Scandinavian countries, gives some ground for optimism.

References

Blanchard, O. and Tirole, J. (2003). 'Contours of Employment Protection Reform'. Report to the French Conseil d'Analyse Economique, December.

—— —— (2004a). 'The Design of Optimal Labor Market Institutions: A First Pass'. Report to the French Conseil d'Analyse Economique, January.

—— —— (2004b). 'Redesigning the Employment Protection System'. *De Economist*, 152: 1–20.

13

International Migration and Economic Development

Deepak Nayyar[1]

Introduction

The movement of people across national boundaries is a matter of interest and an issue of concern at the beginning of the twenty-first century. The attention is not just a function of the present conjuncture. It is attributable to the fact that the pressures for international migration are considerable and appear to be mounting despite restrictive immigration laws. This is not surprising in a world where income disparities and population imbalances between countries are vast, while the spread of education combined with the revolution in transport has led to a significant increase in the mobility of labor. Yet, this remains a relatively unexplored theme in the extensive literature on the world economy. The object of this chapter is to focus on international migration so as to outline the contours, examine the underlying factors, explore the implications of globalization, and analyze the consequences for development.

The structure of the chapter is as follows. The second section sketches a profile of international labor migration during the second half of the twentieth century and situates it in historical perspective. The third section examines the underlying factors with an emphasis on structural determinants at a macro level. The fourth section considers how globalization is creating conditions that are conducive to the movement of people across borders. The fifth section highlights some important asymmetries apropos migration in the contemporary world economy. The sixth section analyzes the impact of international migration on economic development. The last section sets out some conclusions.

[1] The author would like to thank José Antonio Ocampo, Dani Rodrik, and Joseph Stiglitz for comments and suggestions.

A Historical Perspective

In the second half of the twentieth century, it is possible to discern two phases of international labor migration: from the late 1940s to the early 1970s and from the early 1970s to the late 1990s. During the first phase, from the late 1940s to the early 1970s, there were two distinct streams of international migration. First, people migrated from Europe to the United States, Canada, Australia, and New Zealand. This movement was driven by a search for economic opportunities on the part of the migrants. It was also shaped by the nature of immigration laws in the countries of destination which, with the exception of the United States, restricted immigration largely to Europeans. In the period from 1951 to 1975, the total immigration was 7.8 million into the United States, 3.8 million into Canada, and 2.8 million into Australia.[2] Second, people moved from the developing world in Asia, North Africa, and the Caribbean to Western Europe where economic growth combined with full employment created labor shortages and led to labor imports. To begin with, this demand was met from the labor-surplus countries in southern Europe and Italy was perhaps the most important source of such labor. But these sources were not sufficient for long. And, by the late 1950s, the labor-scarce countries of Europe were searching elsewhere for labor, mostly unskilled or semi-skilled workers for employment in the manufacturing sector or the services sector. Britain imported workers from the Indian subcontinent and the Caribbean islands. France imported workers from North Africa. Germany imported workers from Yugoslavia and Turkey. Available evidence suggests that total immigration into Western Europe from 1951 to 1975 was about 10 million.[3]

During the second phase, from the early 1970s to the late 1990s, migration to Europe slowed down for a while. It was the end of the era of rapid economic growth combined with full employment. And immigration laws became restrictive almost everywhere in Western Europe. But this did not last long. Migration to Europe revived in the 1980s and gathered momentum in the 1990s. The destinations for the migrants, however, were different, as latecomers to the European Union began to import labor. The sources were also different, as a significant proportion of the migrants came first from Eastern Europe and then from the former USSR. There were, in addition, two different streams of migration. First, there was a permanent emigration of people not only from Europe but also from the developing world to the United States. These were mostly persons with professional qualifications or technical

[2] The figures cited here are obtained from immigration statistics published by the United States Immigration and Naturalization Service and the Canadian Employment and Immigration Centre. For details, see Nayyar (1994b).

[3] The evidence is not definitive and is possibly based on estimates. Stalker (1994) reports that between 1950 and 1973 net immigration into Western Europe was nearly ten million.

skills. This was made possible, in part, by a change in immigration laws in the United States, which meant that entry was related to skill levels rather than country of origin, thereby providing more access to people from developing countries.[4] And, in the period from 1976 to 2000, total immigration into the United States was 16.3 million, more than twice what it was in the preceding quarter-century, while total immigration into Canada at 4.2 million and into Australia at 2.4 million witnessed little change.[5] Second, there was a temporary migration of people from labor-surplus developing countries, mostly unskilled workers and semi-skilled, or skilled workers in manual or clerical occupations. There were three sets of destinations for such labor flows. Some went to the industrialized countries. Some went to the high-income, labor scarce, oil exporting countries.[6] Some went to the middle-income, newly industrializing countries which attained near full employment.[7] The guest workers in Western Europe, the seasonal import of Mexican labor in the United States, the export of workers from South Asia, Southeast Asia and north Africa to the oil exporting countries of the Middle East, and the more recent import of temporary workers by labor scarce countries in East Asia are all components of these temporary labor flows.

The second half of the twentieth century has also witnessed a movement of people, as refugees rather than migrants, across national boundaries. Refugees, as much as migrants, go back a long time. But such cross-border movements during the past 50 years are on a different, much larger, scale. This process began life in the late 1940s, at the end of the World War II, as displaced people, who could not or did not wish to return to their homes, sought

[4] The Immigration Act of 1965 abolished national origins quotas, fixed a ceiling on Western hemisphere immigration and devised a preference system that favored relatives of United States citizens and residents, those with needed occupational skills, abilities, or training, and refugees. Immigrant visas were allocated on a first-come, first-served basis, subject to seven categories of immigrants in order of preference and without any numerical limit on spouses, parents or children of US citizens. This led to a rapid shift in the countries of origin of immigrants. The Immigration Act was amended in 1990. It revised the numerical limits and the preference system. Re-unification of families continued to be the most important criterion, but the number of employment-based visas was almost tripled, from 54,000 to 140,000 per annum, and distributed among five main categories of preferences primarily for those with professional, managerial, or technical qualifications.

[5] The primary sources of data are the immigration statistics published by the United States and Canada. See also Nayyar (1994b) and *Trends in International Migration, SOPEMI 2003*, OECD, Paris.

[6] The estimated number of international migrants in the Gulf Cooperation Council countries (Bahrain, Kuwait, Oman, Qatar, Saudi Arabia, and United Arab Emirates) increased from one million in 1970 to 3.9 million in 1980, 8.3 million in 1990, and 9.6 million in 2000. See United Nations, *Trends in Total Migrant Stock: The 2003 Revision* (data in digital form).

[7] Malaysia has, for a long time, relied on workers from Indonesia for its agriculture and plantations. It had an estimated 1.4 million migrant workers in 2000. During the 1990s, Hong Kong, the Republic of Korea, Singapore, and Taiwan also emerged as destinations for migrant workers. In the early 2000s, China and Thailand are also beginning to seek foreign workers.

to resettle elsewhere. The onset of the Cold War was the next impetus for refugees as people, experiencing or claiming political persecution, fled from East to West seeking asylum. The de-colonization struggles in Africa during the 1960s were another new source of refugee flows. Such labor flows remained within manageable proportions until the early 1970s. During the last quarter of the twentieth century, however, the phenomenon of migration in distress was on an altogether different scale. The geographical spread was far greater, the number of people affected much larger, and the reasons were many more. The reasons for migration in distress ranged from the internationalization of liberation struggles, civil wars, ethnic strife, religious violence, political persecution, and xenophobic nationalism to famines and natural disasters. The geographical spread ranged from Angola, Mozambique, Ethiopia, Sudan, and Somalia through Afghanistan, Cambodia, and Laos to Central America and former Yugoslavia. It is estimated that the number of people seeking asylum went up from about 30,000 per annum in the early 1970s to more than 800,000 per annum in the early 1990s. And, over this period, the worldwide population of refugees, driven from their homes by natural disasters or the search for political asylum, rose from 4.3 million in 1970 to 19 million in 1990.[8]

It is clear that international migration during the second half of the twentieth century was significant despite stringent immigration laws and restrictive consular practices. The database on international migration is slender, particularly in the sphere of flows. The available evidence on the stock of international migrants and its distribution across regions in the world, during the period from 1960 to 2000, is presented in Table 13.1.

For a study of the trends, it is both necessary and appropriate to exclude the former USSR. Its inclusion distorts the picture, for comparisons over time, because its break-up into 15 independent countries, in 1991, instantly transformed internal migrants into international migrants. The table shows that the number of international migrants in the world, excluding the former USSR, rose from 72.9 million in 1960 to 145.4 million in 2000. Over this period, the share of developing countries in the stock of migrant population decreased from 60 percent to 45 percent while that of industrialized countries increased from 40 to 55 percent. In the span of four decades, the proportion of international migrants in the total population fell from 2.1 to 1.3 percent in developing countries and rose from 4 to 8.3 percent in industrialized countries. For the world as a whole, this proportion declined from 2.58 to 2.44 percent. In 1960, 1 in every 39 persons in the world was an international migrant, while in 2000, 1 in every 41 persons in the world was

[8] For evidence on, and a discussion of, the refugee problem, see Bohning and Schloeter-Paredes (1994) and Stalker (1994). See also, United Nations, *Trends in Total Migrant Stock: The 2003 Revision* (data in digital form). It is worth noting that the estimated number of refugees, worldwide, was about 17 million in 2000.

Table 13.1. International Migrants in the World: The Distribution of the Stock Across Country Groups, 1960–2000

Country group	Number of international migrants (in millions)				
	1960	1970	1980	1990	2000
Asia	29.3	28.1	32.3	41.8	43.8
Africa	9.0	9.8	14.1	16.1	16.3
Latin America-Caribbean	6.0	5.8	6.1	7.0	5.9
Developing countries	*44.3*	*43.7*	*52.5*	*64.9*	*66.0*
North America	12.5	13.0	18.1	27.6	40.8
Europe	14.0	18.7	22.2	26.3	32.8
Oceania	2.1	3.0	3.8	4.8	5.8
Industrialized Countries	*28.6*	*34.7*	*44.1*	*58.7*	*79.4*
Total	**72.9**	**78.4**	**96.6**	**123.6**	**145.4**
Former USSR	3.0	3.1	3.2	30.4	29.5
World	75.9	81.5	99.8	154.0	174.9

Note: The figures for Asia exclude the central Asian countries while those for Europe exclude the East European countries that were part of the USSR.

Source: United Nations, *Trends in Migrant Stock: The 2003 Revision*.

an international migrant. A comparison with the early twentieth century is revealing. It is estimated that in 1910, 33 million persons lived in countries other than their own and international migrants made up 2.1 percent of the world's population, so that 1 in every 48 persons in the world at that time was an international migrant.[9]

The aggregate statistics do not reveal changes in the nature of international migration. There are different forms of labor flows across national boundaries.[10] And new distinctions can be drawn between voluntary migration and distress migration, permanent emigration and temporary migration, or legal migration and illegal migration. Thus, in the contemporary world economy, it is possible to distinguish between five categories of labor flows, of which two are old and three are new.

The old labor flows are made up of emigrants and refugees. *Emigrants* are people who move to a country and settle there permanently. The principal destinations now are the United States, Canada, and Australia. Most such people are admitted for their professional qualifications or for reunification of families. Such emigration is estimated to be in the range of one million people per annum. *Refugees* are people who leave their homes because of famine, ethnic strife, civil war, or political persecution, to seek a home or asylum so as to take up permanent residence in other countries. It is estimated that such distress migration, which is involuntary, leads to the movement of about one million people across borders every year.

[9] See *World Statistics of Aliens: A Comparative Study of Census Returns 1910–1920–1930*, Studies and Reports, Series O (Migration), International Labor Office, Geneva, 1936.

[10] Cf. Stalker (1994).

The new forms of labor flows are guest workers, illegal migrants, and professionals. *Guest workers* are people who move to a country, on a temporary basis, for a specified purpose and a limited duration; most of them are unskilled or semi-skilled workers. The largest number, estimated at more than five million, is in the Middle East,[11] and there are now some in Malaysia, Singapore, and Western Europe. This category includes seasonal workers employed in agriculture or tourism, particularly in the United States and Canada. *Illegal migrants* are people who enter a country without a visa, take up employment on a tourist visa, or simply stay on after their visa has expired. The largest number of such persons are in the United States (about seven million), Western Europe (at least three million), and Japan (perhaps one million).[12] However, there is also a significant number in Latin America and East Asia. *Professionals* are people with high levels of education, experience, and qualifications, whose skills are in demand everywhere and can move from country to country, temporarily or permanently, as immigration laws are not restrictive for them. Most of them are employed by transnational corporations, but some of them circulate in their professional capacities or through systems of education and research.

It needs to be said that these categories are not mutually exclusive or exhaustive. Nor do they define a once -and-for-all status. After a time, it is difficult to distinguish between emigrants and refugees in their countries of settlement. Guest workers who acquire a right of residence are, in effect, not very different from emigrants. Illegal migrants who benefit from amnesties, which come from time to time, attain legal status. The distinction between professionals and emigrants is in any case somewhat diffused, for the former are often a subset of the latter in the industrialized countries. Yet, these categories serve an analytical purpose insofar as the distinctions are clear at the time that the cross-border movements of people take place.

The Underlying Factors

The available literature on the economics of international labor migration is rich in terms of microtheoretic analysis but somewhat sparse in terms of

[11] See Amjad (1989) and Abella (1994).

[12] It is exceedingly difficult to obtain reliable evidence on the number of illegal immigrants. Much of it is essentially conjecture or casual empiricism, often based on reports in newspapers. The figures cited here are more robust. For the United States, see *Estimates of the Unauthorized Immigrant Population residing in the United States: 1990 to 2000*, Office of Policy Planning, United States Immigration and Naturalization Service, 2003. Of the seven million, 4.8 million were Mexican. For Europe, see *Towards a Fair Deal for Migrant Workers in the World Economy*, Report VI, International Labor Conference, 92nd Session, International Labor Organization, Geneva, 2004. Europol estimates that about half a million illegal migrants enter the European Union every year. For estimates about Japan, which are more speculative, see Stalker (1994).

macroeconomic analysis. Some of the earlier literature was concerned with the effect of migration on economic welfare so that the focus was on costs and benefits for migrant workers or their families.[13] Subsequent contributions extended the analysis to factors underlying the decision to migrate.[14] Theoretical constructs sought to emphasize the sensitivity of migrant flows, both internal and international, to economic rewards. And, the more recent theoretical developments stress the importance of households as a decision-making unit in which it is argued that migration is a risk-reducing strategy for the household.[15] It is clear that migrant workers and migrant households have been the prime concern of theoretical analysis both in its normative aspects and in its positive aspects. This approach seeks to explain migration in terms of individual decisions. It is necessary but not sufficient[16]—movements of people are also shaped and influenced by structural determinants at a macro level. Therefore, the individual approach and structural explanations should be seen as complements rather than substitutes in attempting to understand the factors underlying migration. However, if we wish to analyze labor flows across national boundaries to understand patterns and determinants, it is essential to consider structural explanations of migration at a macro level.

The process of industrialization and development is associated with a structural transformation of economies. In a long-term perspective, the most important dimension of such transformations is a structural change in the composition of output and employment over time.[17] To begin with, the share of the agricultural sector in both output and employment is overwhelmingly large. As industrialization proceeds, the share of the manufacturing sector, and later the services sector, in output and employment rises, while that of the agricultural sectors falls. The absorption of surplus labor is reflected in the migration of unemployed or underemployed workers from rural hinterlands to urban settlements. Given the enormous differences in employment probabilities and wage levels, wherever possible, migration of workers across national boundaries also absorbs a part of the labor surplus. Over time, the process of economic development is associated with a migration transition. Rural–urban migration comes to an end when the surplus of labor in the subsistence sector is exhausted. Emigration flows are also significantly reduced in part because surplus labor is not readily available, and in part because economic development provides more employment, higher wages, and better

[13] See, for instance, Berry and Soligo (1969).

[14] For a survey of this literature, see Krugman and Bhagwati (1976).

[15] See Stark (1991).

[16] The macroeconomic implications and consequences of international labor migration, whether for labor-exporting countries or for labor importing countries, are also neglected in the extensive literature on the subject. There are some exceptions. See, for example, Paine (1974); Piore (1979); and Nayyar (1994b).

[17] Cf. Kuznets (1966).

living conditions at home, even if differences in the level of income or the quality of life persist vis-à-vis the world outside. In some economies, rapid industrialization and sustained growth, which create full employment, may open up the possibilities of a turnaround in migration flows as labor imports begin.[18] Late industrializers in southern Europe and East Asia have indeed experienced such a transition during the second half of the twentieth century.

During the early stages of industrialization, labor exports from surplus labor economies are a common occurrence. There are both push factors and pull factors underlying emigration pressures. On the supply side, demographic factors combined with unemployment and poverty obviously create pressures for internal migration, mostly rural–urban but also rural–rural, in surplus labor economies. The same push factors probably lead to a spill over of migration across national boundaries. The pull factor is also significant. It is attributable not only to the actual differences in wage levels and employment probabilities at a point in time, between labor-exporting countries and labor-importing countries, but also to the perceived differences in the stream of income and the quality of life over a period of time. In this context, it is worth noting that the emigration of educated people with professional qualifications, technical expertise, or managerial talents from poor countries to rich countries, described as the brain drain, is attributable almost entirely to this pull factor. It is not attributable to the push factor as these people are not only employed but also at the upper end of the income spectrum before emigration.

Given the massive differences in income levels and living conditions between countries, actual or perceived, international labor movements would be much larger in an unconstrained world. In fact, they are not. In labor-exporting countries, the desire to migrate, arising from both push and pull factors, is constrained by the ability to migrate, which depends on the endowments of skills, education, or savings among the potential migrants. There are, also, transaction costs of migration across borders which are significant. The ability to migrate is constrained further by the patterns of demand for labor in labor importing countries. And the story cannot be complete without considering the demand side. Emigration pressures surface, or emerge stronger, once destinations for migrants are opened up by a demand in labor scarce countries.

Labor shortages in economies are the fundamental reason for labor imports on the demand side. For analytical purposes, it would be instructive to consider the conditions under which industrialized countries seek to import labor from developing countries, or elsewhere, in the form of permanent emigration. As an economy reaches full employment, labor shortages surface

[18] For a discussion on migration transitions which, over time, transform labor-exporting countries into labor-importing countries, see Nayyar (1994a).

at the lower end of the spectrum of skills, whether in the agricultural sector, the manufacturing sector, or the services sector. Those who employ wage labor either face or anticipate a substantial increase in real wages as a consequence of the actual excess demand or the emerging scarcities. The response of producers or employers takes three forms. These responses are not, in general, simultaneous but often proceed in sequence. First, producers attempt to substitute capital for labor through technological choice, by acquiring technologies that economize on labor use or augment labor productivity. Second, firms endeavor to use trade flows as a substitute for labor, either by importing goods that embody scarce labor or by exporting capital which employs scarce labor abroad to provide such goods through an international relocation of production. Third, producers or firms seek to import labor, but this is a last resort in so far as immigration laws in most countries tend to be restrictive for social and political reasons.

It must be recognized that the possibilities of replacing labor by capital, within an economy through technological choice, are not unlimited. The possibilities of substituting trade flows for labor movements, across national boundaries, are much larger. Yet, there are reasons why it may not be possible to do without imports of labor altogether. In the manufacturing sector, trade flows and capital exports can be a substitute for labor imports for quite some time. However, the same is not true for the agricultural sector or the services sector. It is not true for the agricultural sector simply because, unlike capital, land cannot be exported, and once an economy reaches full employment it is exceedingly difficult, if not impossible, to reverse the initial flow of labor from the urban sector to the rural sector. It is not true for the services sector simply because services are not quite as tradable as goods, and even international trade in services often requires physical proximity between the producer and the consumer, for the service to be delivered, because these are services which cannot be stored and transported across national boundaries in the same way as goods.[19] It is not surprising, then, that labor imports often begin with unskilled or semi-skilled labor for employment in the agricultural sector or the services sector. In general, whenever such labor shortages surface, countries begin to import unskilled or semi-skilled workers for manual or clerical occupations. Until the early 1970s, such labor imports in the industrialized countries were possible within limits and consistent with immigration laws. Since then, however, such labor imports are in the form of either guest workers for a specified purpose and a limited duration or illegal migrants who enter in collusion with employers.

It should be obvious that the factors underlying international labor migration are manifold and complex. Nevertheless, it is possible and necessary to

[19] The distinction between goods and services, as also that between trade in goods and trade in services, is analyzed in Nayyar (1988).

highlight some structural explanations of migration at a macro level. The most important among them, of course, is disparities in income levels and employment opportunities between countries. The population imbalances between labor-scarce and labor-abundant countries also play an important role.[20] In this context, it is worth noting that a century earlier, differences in natural endowments between countries, particularly land, played a similar role as people moved from land-scarce to land-abundant countries. The process of economic development, too, exercises an important influence. Interestingly enough, it can both dampen and stimulate international migration. As economic development provides more employment, higher wages and better living conditions at home, it reduces the significance of the push factor even if differences in the level of income and the quality of life persist vis-à-vis the world outside. This is because people do not wish to leave their homes. Yet, even if economic development reduces the need to migrate, improved levels of education, and higher levels of aspiration increase both the desire and the ability to migrate.

Such structural factors at a macro level explain the fact of migration, but do not help us understand the link between the origin and the destination of international labor movements. For this purpose, we need to go beyond economics to history, geography, or even sociology. There are links between labor-exporting and labor-importing countries in each of these spheres. Post-colonial ties, a common language, or cultural similarities are often embedded in history and have shaped the direction of labor flows. The emigration from developing countries in Asia, Africa, or the Caribbean to Western Europe provides an example. The movement of people from the Indian subcontinent and the Caribbean islands to the United Kingdom, from Algeria to France, or from Indonesia to the Netherlands was shaped by such history embedded in post-colonial ties. Geographical proximity is another important determinant. The movement of people from Mexico to the United States, from Eastern Europe to Western Europe, or from Indonesia to Malaysia and Singapore provides examples. There is also a sociological dimension. Migrants follow trails charted by pioneers. And the notion of diaspora now extends much beyond Jews in exile. For the existence of an immigrant community, with which the migrant shares a language, nationality, or culture, in the country of destination, becomes a source of cumulative causation that continues to shape the direction of labor flows. The movement of people from Turkey to

[20] It is perhaps important to make the distinction between labor-scarce and labor-abundant countries clearer. The most plausible reference point, or denominator, is land. Historically, it is the land-labor ratio that has mattered. Even today, it is not irrelevant. Indeed, it is no coincidence that the United States, which is *inter alia* land-abundant, was for a long time (and still remains, possibly for different reasons) the single biggest destination for migrants. If the denominator has all other inputs (quality adjusted), rather than just land, then the distinction between labor-scarce and labor-surplus countries conforms closely to the distinction between high-wage and low-wage countries.

Germany, from India to the United States, or from China to Canada provides examples. Interestingly enough, the same sociological nexus explains why such migrants come from a particular region (rather than from anywhere else or, for that matter, everywhere) in the country of origin and move to a particular region, sometimes even specific cities in specific activities (instead of a more uniform distribution across geographical space) in the country of destination.[21]

It should be obvious why it is difficult to understand international migration in terms of economic analysis alone. There are two other important reasons. For one, non-economic factors are significant determinants of cross-border labor flows even where the underlying reasons are economic. For another, there are cross-border labor flows where the underlying factors are not economic. Consider each in turn.

International labor movements are, of course, influenced by forces of supply and demand but are also constrained by non-economic factors such as explicit immigration laws or implicit consular practices. Thus, in labor-importing countries, it is not only the pattern of demand for labor but also the barriers to entry that determine the magnitude and the composition of labor inflows. Such barriers to entry which constrain market-driven labor flows mean that actual outcomes are not shaped by economic factors alone.

There are also movements of people across national boundaries on a significant scale, almost as large as migration, which represent neither voluntary decisions nor economic decisions. To begin with, this was essentially a search for political asylum on the part of people who were driven from their homes by political persecution or just political repression. But things have changed with the passage of time. Migration in distress is now attributable to a much wider range of underlying factors. It is attributable, in large part, to man-made conflict situations such as civil war, ethnic strife, religious violence, or xenophobic nationalism often associated with the violation of human rights. It is also attributable to natural disasters such as recurring famines or environmental degradation. The relative importance of these factors, obviously, varies across space and over time.

Globalization and Migration

The world economy has experienced a progressive international economic integration since 1950. However, there has been a marked acceleration in this process of globalization during the last quarter of the twentieth century. This phenomenon has three manifestations—international trade, international

[21] There is an interesting example of this phenomenon at a micro level. A significant proportion of taxi drivers in New York City are migrants from a few districts of the state of Punjab in India.

investment, and international finance—which also constitute its cutting edge. An increasing proportion of world output is entering into world trade. There is a surge in international investment flows. The growth in international finance has been explosive. The economic factors underlying the process, which have enabled it to gather momentum, are the dismantling of barriers to international economic transactions and the development of enabling technologies. Globalization has followed the sequence of liberalization and deregulation in the world economy from trade flows through investment flows to financial flows. The technological revolution in transport and communications has pushed aside geographical barriers, as the time needed and the cost incurred are a tiny fraction of what they were earlier. But this is not new. There was a similar phase of globalization from 1870 to 1914. In many ways, the world economy in the late twentieth century resembles the world economy in the late nineteenth century.[22] The parallels between the two periods are striking in terms of the characteristics and underlying factors. And there is much that we can learn from history, for there is the past in our present. Yet, there is a fundamental difference between these two phases of globalization. It is in the sphere of labor flows. In the late nineteenth century, there were no restrictions on the movement of people across national boundaries—passports were seldom needed, migrants were granted citizenship with ease, and international labor migration was enormous. In sharp contrast, now, the cross-border movement of people is closely regulated and highly restricted. Yet, over the past 50 years, international labor movements have been significant in absolute terms, even if much less than in the nineteenth century and much smaller as a proportion of total populations.

There are both push factors and pull factors underlying international migration. But it is possible that globalization, in itself, may create conditions and unleash forces that could become an impetus for the movement of labor across national boundaries. The evidence is limited yet suggestive. And it leads me to set out two possible mechanisms which are plausible hypotheses. The first hypothesis is that there are some attributes of globalization which are conducive to, and helpful for, people who seek to cross borders in search of work. The second hypothesis is that globalization has set in motion forces which are creating a demand for labor mobility across borders, some old forms and some new forms, as also developing institutions on the supply side to meet this demand. Consider each in turn.

There are three migrant-friendly attributes of globalization which are supportive of cross-border labor flows.

First, the revolution in *transport and communications* has slashed geographical barriers in terms of time and cost, not only for the movement of goods,

[22] For an analysis of this historical parallel between globalization in the late nineteenth century and in the late twentieth century, see Nayyar (1995).

services, technology, and finance, but also for the movement of people across national boundaries. In the early 1990s, air transport costs per passenger mile were less than one-fifth what they were in the late 1930s. Similarly, international phone charges are less than 5 percent of what they were 50 years ago.[23] Thus, potential or actual migrants are no longer deterred by the cost of travel or the cost of speaking to their families, for it is now only a modest fraction of their incomes. And in most countries, airlines and telephone companies aggressively compete with each other in terms of prices to capture the large market for their services provided by migrants. The advent of the internet with its array of websites, combined with the remarkable speed and the negligible cost of e-mail, makes it that much easier for people to live away from their homes temporarily or even permanently.

Second, *market institutions* have developed which make it much easier for people to move across borders. For one, there are intermediaries in the labor-exporting countries, mostly brokers and agents who recruit and place people abroad for a price. For another, given the substantial demand for illegal migrants and the enormous profits associated with it, there are brokers in both labor-importing and labor-exporting countries who are engaged in illegal trafficking of people. In this milieu, the cross-border movement of people is no longer dependent upon the ability of individuals alone as it was until not so long ago. The process of migration is now facilitated by institutional arrangements that have emerged in response to needs perceived by the market. These market institutions are reinforced by *migrant networks* in the labor-importing countries. Such networks, which have evolved with the passage of time and become stronger with globalization, provide their compatriots with information on immigration procedures and employment possibilities. This help often extends to legal advice on visa procedures and immigration laws. But that is not all. The networks also find temporary homes and extend financial support to the new arrivals. The word diaspora has acquired a generic meaning.

Third, the reach of the *electronic media* is enormous, as is the power of television as a medium. For one, it has led to the global spread of cultural impulses. The culture and consumerism of the young in metropolitan cities everywhere—north or south, east or west—is globalized. Even corruption and crime have become similar everywhere, so that distant lands with an alien culture and a different language are neither strange nor unexpected for the potential migrant. For another, the same media creates a home away from home for the actual migrant. Immigrant communities have their own TV channels, their own newspapers, and their own entertainment.

The process of globalization is creating a demand for new forms and institutionalizing the demand for old forms of labor mobility. In this

[23] See World Bank (1995) and UNDP (1999).

process, there is an inherent coordination between the demand side and the supply side. There are three important manifestations that are worth noting.

First, the reach and the spread of *transnational corporations* are worldwide. In the past, such corporations moved goods, services, technology, capital, and finance across national boundaries. Increasingly, however, they have also become transnational employers of people.[24] They place expatriate managers in industrialized and developing host countries, and recruit professionals not only from industrialized countries but also from developing countries for placement in corporate headquarters or affiliates elsewhere. They engage local staff in developing countries who acquire skills and experience that make them employable abroad after a time. They move immigrant professionals of foreign origin, permanently settled in the industrialized world, to run subsidiaries or affiliates in their countries of origin. They engage professionals from low-income countries, particularly in software but also in engineering or health care, to work on a contract basis on special non-immigrant status visas, which has come to be known as 'body-shopping.' This intra-firm mobility across borders easily spills over into other forms of international labor mobility.

Second, the *mobility of professionals* has registered a phenomenal increase in the age of globalization. It began with the brain drain. This was facilitated by immigration laws in the United States, Canada, and Australia which encouraged people with high skills or professional qualifications to do what? This process has intensified and diversified. It is, of course, still possible for scientists, doctors, engineers, and academics to emigrate. But there are more and more professionals such as lawyers, architects, accountants, managers, bankers, or those specializing in computer software and information technology, who can emigrate permanently, live abroad temporarily, or stay at home and travel frequently for business. These people are almost as mobile across borders as capital.

Third, the *globalization of education* has gathered momentum. This has two dimensions. The proportion of foreign students studying for professional degrees or doctorates in the university system of the major industrialized countries, in particular the United States, is large and more than two-thirds simply stay on.[25] The situation is similar in Europe albeit on a smaller scale. At the same time, centers of excellence in higher education in labor-exporting developing countries are increasingly adopting curricula that conform to

[24] In 1992, for example, total employment in transnational corporations was 73 million, of which 44 million were employed in the home countries while 17 million were employed in affiliates in industrialized countries and 12 million were employed in affiliates in developing countries. The share of developing countries in such employment rose from one-tenth in 1985 to one-sixth in 1992. See UNCTAD (1994).

[25] See Bhagwati and Rao (1996).

international patterns and standards. Given the facility of language, such people are employable almost anywhere.

It is thus plausible to argue that globalization, in itself, has set in motion forces which are creating a demand for labor mobility across borders and is, at the same time, developing institutions on the supply side to meet this demand. The basic reason is simple. The factors which make it easier to move goods, services, capital, technology, and information across borders, but for explicit immigration laws and implicit consular practices that are barriers to entry, also make it easier to move people across borders. Earlier, I made a distinction between five categories of labor flows across national boundaries. It would seem that the process of globalization is going to increase labor mobility in three categories. The professionals, at the top of the ladder of skills, will be almost as mobile as capital. Indeed, we can think of them as globalized people who are employable almost anywhere in the world. Similarly, where it is not feasible to import goods or export capital as a substitute for labor imports, or is less profitable, the use of guest workers who move across borders on a temporary basis, for a specified purpose and a limited duration, is bound to increase.[26] And, despite the political reality of immigration laws, the market-driven conditions and institutions being created by globalization will sustain, perhaps even increase, illegal immigration and the associated cross-border labor flows.

In sum, it would be reasonable to infer that there is a potential conflict between the laws of nations that restrict the movement of people across borders and the economics of globalization that induces the movement of people across borders. And, within limits, markets are adept at circumventing regulations.

In the first quarter of the twenty-first century, this process may be reinforced by demographic change and population imbalances.[27] It is expected that, between 2000 and 2025, the population of industrialized countries will remain almost unchanged at about 1.25 billion while the population of developing countries will increase from four billion to 7.5 billion. But that is not all. The zero population growth in the industrialized world, combined with increased life expectancy, is expected to lead to a rapid ageing of the population in these countries. Consequently, dependency ratios (the proportion of the population aged 65 years or more) are projected to rise sharply from about one-fifth to more than one-third. This means that a shrinking

[26] During the 1990s, there was a rapid increase in the number of temporary workers admitted under the skill-based categories into the industrialized countries. In the United States, for example, the number of admissions under H-IB visas increased from 143,000 in 1992 to 343,000 in 1998 and 505,000 in 2000 (see United States Immigration and Naturalization Service, *Statistical Yearbooks*). The number of such skilled workers, admitted on a temporary basis into the United Kingdom, Australia, and Canada, taken together, rose from 165,000 in 1992 to 334,000 in 2000 (see *Trends in International Migration SOPEMI 2003*, OECD, Paris).

[27] For a more detailed discussion, see Nayyar (2002).

working population, made up of producers and earners, would have to support an expanding elderly population, made up of consumers and pensioners. Notwithstanding technical progress, labor shortages are inevitable. This, in itself, will create a demand for migrants. The ageing of industrial societies, however, will also generate a demand for labor imports to provide services, such as health care and home care, so as to maintain the quality of life among the aged or the elderly in the population. Such service providers, whether permanent emigrants, guest workers, or illegal migrants, would have come from the developing world. Therefore, even if globalization creates more employment and better living conditions in surplus labor countries, the demographic factor may accentuate both emigration pressures and immigration needs to shape labor flows in the future. If such movements of labor become an economic necessity, it could even lead to selective relaxation of immigration laws and consular practices. History, probably, will not repeat itself. But it would be wise to learn from history.

Some Important Asymmetries

In this context, a fundamental question arises from the asymmetry between the free movement of capital and the unfree movement of labor across national boundaries. In the contemporary world economy, economic openness is not simply confined to trade flows, investment flows, and financial flows. It also extends to flows of services, technology, information, and ideas across borders. But the cross-border movement of people is closely regulated and highly restricted. A perfect symmetry between labor and capital may not be a plausible idea in the context of political reality. In the abstract world of orthodox economic theory, however, the symmetry between labor and capital, as factors of production, is only logical. After all, international labor movements create efficiency gains in a neoclassical sense, as much as international capital movements, when workers move to where they are more productive. Indeed, it is clear that the efficiency gains from labor mobility are much greater than the efficiency gains from capital mobility, given the differences in marginal productivity across countries. In this mode, the case for unrestricted labor mobility is as compelling as the case for unrestricted capital mobility or the case for free trade. It would contribute as much to optimizing resource allocation and maximizing economic welfare for the world as a whole. Yet, this is not part of conventional wisdom. Economic theory, it would seem, is also shaped by political reality.

Nevertheless, it is plausible to suggest that if there is almost complete freedom of capital mobility across national boundaries, the draconian restrictions on labor mobility across national boundaries should at least be reduced if not eliminated. In fact, there would be enormous benefits even from a marginal relaxation of such restrictions on the mobility of labor. In this context, it is important to recognize that the significance of the temporary movement of people across borders is even greater. Similarly, it is reasonable to argue that any provisions for commercial presence of corporate entities (capital) should correspond to provisions for temporary migration of workers (labor), just as the right of establishment for corporate entities (capital) has an analog in the right of residence for persons (labor).[28] Indeed, if such a perspective is carried to its logical conclusion, the movement of labor across borders must be just as free as the movement of capital. It is not surprising that the two views on this matter are polar opposites.[29] On the one hand, there is a rights-based argument that the freedom of movement within countries is a basic human right and there is no reason why it should not extend across countries. What is more, insofar as the citizenship of industrialized countries is the modern equivalent of feudal privilege, such freedom of movement would reduce international economic inequalities.[30] On the other hand, there is a community-based argument that nations have a right to self-determination in terms of social cohesion and cultural solidarity. What is more, unrestricted immigration is bound to have serious economic and social implications for citizens. It is worth noting that the United Nations charter incorporates both perspectives. For one, it accepts the human right of freedom of movement as a universal principle. For another, it recognizes that sovereign states have a right of self-determination. There is clearly an inherent tension between these perspectives which can readily turn into a contradiction.

Irrespective of how any person chooses between these two extreme positions, the political reality is clear: a significant relaxation of immigration laws is simply not in the realm of feasibility. An international acceptance of universal moral obligations is perhaps out of the question, at least for the present. There is, of course, a strong concern about mounting pressures for international migration which surface almost everywhere. National interests and liberal concerns appear to coincide in the response that has gathered momentum as an idea in recent times. The prescription is to somehow reduce emigration pressures.[31] In the economic sphere, it is believed that economic development that improves the material living conditions of people in poor countries would dampen the pressures for voluntary migration that is motivated by economic factors. Development assistance from the rich to the poor countries is meant to facilitate this process. In the political sphere, it is believed that the spread of political democracy which protects the human rights of people in poor countries with authoritarian regimes would dampen the surge of distress migration that is driven by political repression or

[28] This argument is developed, at some length, in Nayyar (1989).

[29] Cf. Lee (1998).

[30] See Carens (1996).

[31] This is the central theme in Bohning and Schloeter-Paredes (1994).

social exclusion. Humanitarian assistance from rich to poor countries, which seeks to assist in rehabilitation and reconstruction, is meant to facilitate this process. These are statements of good intentions which are sometimes long on words and short on substance, and there is often a mismatch between what is said and what is done. Even without such problems, it must be recognized that the reach of economic development and the spread of political democracy require much more than development assistance or humanitarian assistance. Thus such endeavors, which are most desirable, may or may not reduce pressures for labor exports, for even if the need to migrate decreases, the ability to migrate increases.

But this is not all. There are other important asymmetries related to the rights of migrants in the contemporary world economy that need to be recognized and corrected. In this context, it is necessary to make a distinction between legal migrants and illegal migrants.

There are some genuine causes for concern even about the working and living conditions of legal migrants.[32] In the industrialized countries, the problems of immigrant workers are accentuated by: (a) high levels of unemployment among unskilled workers; (b) flexibility in labor markets with much weaker trade unions; and (c) reforms in social security systems associated with the retreat of the welfare state. Even without xenophobic attitudes, which are beginning to surface in many countries, each of these developments has a more pronounced effect on migrants than on nationals. In the high-income or middle-income developing countries, which import labor, the problems of immigrant workers are much more acute and are exacerbated by: (a) the distinctly inferior status of contract workers who have no legal claim to permanent settlement, let alone citizenship; (b) rudimentary or minimal systems of social protection; and (c) the near absence of trade union movements or mandated labor standards. It is not surprising that the living conditions of immigrant workers in developing countries are discernibly worse, while their rights are much weaker, than in the industrialized countries. What needs to be done is clear. First, there must be social protection for migrants which is at par with that for nationals. Second, employers who exploit migrant workers in terms of wages paid or hours worked must be disciplined. Third, everything must be done to combat the physical and sexual abuse of migrants, particularly women migrant workers. In other words, there must be some equivalent of the concept of 'national treatment' for migrant workers who have been admitted to their countries of destination in accordance with the laws of the land. The importance of such 'national treatment' cannot be stressed enough.

In this context, it is essential to draw attention to a striking asymmetry. There is so much emphasis on labor standards, which are sought to be lodged

[32] For a more detailed discussion, see Lee (1998); see also Amjad (1996).

in the WTO. There is so little concern about the rights of migrant workers, which are written into obscure ILO conventions that have been ratified mostly by labor-exporting countries rather than by labor-importing countries. Yet, it should be clear that labor standards and migrants' rights are two sides of the same coin. The former is the focus of attention because labor standards are to be imposed mostly on poor countries, while the latter is the object of neglect because migrants' rights are to be implemented in large part by rich countries. There is an obvious need to redress the balance. The rights of migrant workers can only be protected through an understanding between, and a commitment on the part of, sovereign nation states. This, in turn, requires a universal acceptance and ratification of ILO conventions on migrant workers.[33] The issue of labor standards, of course, is simply not in the domain of the WTO and should remain in the ILO where the rights of workers are a fundamental concern.

The labor flows associated with illegal migration, attributable to market forces despite immigration laws, are also a reality.[34] And it is possible that such labor flows may increase in the future. Yet, the plight of illegal migrants, everywhere, is a cause for serious concern. The working conditions are exploitative, the living conditions are abysmal, the risk of capture and repatriation is ever present, and the stranglehold of international criminal syndicates is common enough. This is not simply a matter of enforcing the law. In many countries that experience labor shortages in selected occupations, sectors, or activities, intermediaries who act in collusion with employers are responsible for the illegal immigration while governments turn a blind eye to this reality. This neglect is not without purpose. For one, it means that labor shortages can be met without relaxing immigration laws and providing such workers with a legal right of residence. For another, governments have no obligation to provide social security for such illegal immigrant workers. There is a clear need for transparency rather than ambivalence in the attitude of governments towards illegal immigrants. Such tacit approval of illegal migration to meet labor shortages must be replaced by an explicit recognition of the need for labor imports which should be met through legal channels even if such imports are seasonal or temporary. At the same time, there is clear need for concerted action to curb the trafficking in people that is organized by international criminal and smuggling syndicates. In the hope of reaching new havens, migrants often provide such syndicates with large sums of money. They are passed down a chain of agents, smugglers, ships, safe houses, and corrupt officials. There

33 In this context, it is worth noting that the International Convention on the Protection of the Rights of all Migrants and their Families, which was formulated with the technical assistance of the ILO and adopted by the United Nations General Assembly in 1990, has so far been ratified by less than ten countries, all of which are labor-exporting economies.

34 For a discussion on the causes and consequences of what is described as undocumented migration, see United Nations (1998).

are risks at most points in transit. Sometimes, however, the aspiring migrants are simply abandoned in transit to fend for themselves in countries where they do not speak the language, and they are without money or passports, to end up in prison and await repatriation. Such trafficking in people is a gross violation of human rights. It is a telling example of international 'public bads' which need to be regulated through concerted joint action by labor-exporting and labor-importing countries both at a regional level and at the global level.

Migration and Development

Migration has significant implications and consequences for development in home countries at a macro level: migration has an impact on output and employment, influences growth and development, and shapes distributional outcomes. Consider each in turn.

The impact of migration on output and employment at a macroeconomic level depends on the magnitude of the outflow of people, their employment status before migration and the skills composition of the migrants. If the magnitude of international migration is small as a proportion of the increments in the workforce, or as a proportion of the existing surplus labor, its impact on output would be negligible, whether at the micro level or at the macro level. But this impact would be significant, leading to output foregone, if migration absorbs a large proportion of increments in the workforce or if surplus labor is limited. If the emigrants are unemployed or underemployed before their departure, it would lead to a direct reduction in the level of open or disguised unemployment. The migration of employed workers, on the other hand, may also lead to an indirect reduction in unemployment if they can be readily replaced from a pool of surplus labor. The extent of the reduction in unemployment or underemployment would, of course, depend on the size of the outflow. The impact on output may not be negligible and the impact on employment may not be favorable, if labor markets are segmented either due to geographical factors and regional specificities or due to labor force attributes such as profession, skill, and unionization. The skill composition of migrants is important in this context. The migration of unskilled workers should have little or no impact on output and should reduce unemployment. However, the migration of skilled workers or high skill professionals is likely to have a negative impact on both output and employment, particularly if the migrants cannot be replaced without training, which absorbs not only resources but also time.

The focus of the literature on the brain drain is somewhat different, for it is concerned with the costs for the country of emigration and the benefits for the country of immigration at a macroeconomic level.[35] The costs and benefits to the respective societies are considered at two levels. First, the loss of skilled personnel embedded in the brain drain represents income foregone for the home country and income created for the host country, so that the emphasis is on income rather than output or employment.[36] Second, the cost of education or training is incurred by the country of origin while the benefits accrue to the country of destination, so that there is an unrequited transfer of human capital from the former to the latter.[37]

This analysis of the impact of migration on output and employment assumes that the emigration is permanent. But if such migration is temporary, or if migrants choose to return home after a time, it becomes necessary to analyze not only the initial impact of the withdrawal but also the subsequent impact of the re-entry on output and employment. Once again, if the return migration is small as a proportion of the increments in the workforce, or of the surplus labor, the impact of re-entry on output and employment is likely to be marginal if not negligible in a macro sense. The acquisition of skills by migrants while abroad and the utilization of such skills on return may, of course, positively influence productivity and output.

From the perspective of home countries, international migration has both positive and negative consequences for economic growth and development. In such analysis, it is important to make a distinction between the short and long term.

The most obvious positive consequence of international migration for economic growth, in the short or medium term, is the remittances from migrants. The importance of this phenomenon is widely recognized.[38] Some available evidence on remittances from migrants and the distribution of these inflows across regions in the world, during the period from 1980 to 2000, is presented in Table 13.2. It shows that remittances to developing countries increased rapidly from US$24.3 billion in 1980 to US$66 billion in 2000, as did remittances to industrialized countries from US$16.8 billion in 1980 to US$44.7 billion in 2000. Over this period, about 60 percent of remittances

[35] There is an extensive literature on the brain drain. See, for example, Watanabe (1969); Sen (1973); UNCTAD (1975), and Bhagwati (1976).

[36] Clearly, the income foregone in the home country where wage levels are low would be significantly less than the income created in the host country where wage levels are high. This does not, however, mean that such international migration leads to an increase in world welfare insofar as the gain for industrialized countries, so measured, is greater than the loss for developing countries. It has been argued by Sen (1973) that such welfare comparisons cannot be made for the simple reason that a dollar of income foregone in a poor country may cause much more hardship than the comfort that would come from a dollar of income created in a rich country.

[37] See Grubel and Scott (1966). The implications for developing countries, in terms of a significant loss of human capital and a substantial diminution of technological capability, are highlighted in UNCTAD (1975).

[38] See, for example, Nayyar (1994b); Ratha (2003); and Solimano (2004).

Table 13.2. Remittances from Migrants: The Distribution of the Flows Across Regions, 1980–2000

Region/Country group	In US$ billion			In percentages		
	1980	1990	2000	1980	1990	2000
East and South Asia	6.6	9.5	23.2	16.0	12.6	21.5
West Asia	5.8	6.6	8.4	14.1	8.7	7.5
North Africa	4.5	7.2	5.8	10.9	9.5	5.2
Sub-Saharan Africa	1.4	1.6	1.9	3.4	2.2	1.7
Latin America-Caribbean	1.9	5.7	19.5	4.7	7.6	17.6
Transition economies	4.1	9.5	7.2	10.0	12.5	6.5
Developing countries	24.3	40.1	66.0	59.0	53.1	59.6
Industrialized countries	16.8	35.5	44.7	41.0	46.9	40.4
Total						
World total	**41.1**	**75.6**	**110.8**	**100.0**	**100.0**	**100.0**

Note: The IMF separates remittances into three categories: (a) workers' remittances recorded under 'current transfers' in the current account on the balance of payments; (b) compensation of employees which includes wages, salaries, and other benefits of border, seasonal, and other non-resident workers recorded under 'income' in the current account; and (c) migrants' transfers which are reported under 'capital transfers' in the capital account. The figures in this table are the sum of all three categories.

Source: United Nations, Department of Economic and Social Affairs, New York, based on IMF *Balance of Payments Statistics*.

went to developing countries while about 40 percent of remittances went to industrialized countries. For developing countries, taken together, remittances have become the second largest source of external finance, less than direct foreign investment but more than official development assistance. What is more, remittances are a more stable source of external finance and are more evenly distributed among countries.[39] On an average, remittances are the equivalent of a little more than 1 percent of GDP for developing countries. Of course, their significance differs across countries. For some developing countries, remittances are an important source of foreign exchange earnings, compared with exports, and an important source of financing debt servicing or current account deficits.

The macroeconomic impact of remittances, which is not the focus of attention, is perhaps even more important. In a situation where the departure of migrants does not reduce domestic output, remittances should increase national income. Alternatively, as long as the value of remittances exceeds income foregone as a consequence of migration, which is a plausible

[39] It is worth noting that the distribution of remittances among developing countries is far from equal. In 2001, for instance, the five largest recipient countries (India, Mexico, Philippines, Morocco, and Egypt) accounted for 45 percent of total remittances to developing countries. The top ten countries (including Turkey, Lebanon, Bangladesh, Jordan, and the Dominican Republic) accounted for 60 percent, while the top 20 countries (including El Salvador, Columbia, Yemen, Pakistan, Brazil, Ecuador, former Yugoslavia, Thailand, China, and Sri Lanka) accounted for 80 percent (these proportions have been calculated from IMF Balance of Payments Statistics).

assumption, the migration of workers should lead to some increase in national income. In order to analyze the impact of such an increase in national income on macroeconomic aggregates, it is useful to begin with the simple national income accounting identity: $Y = C + I + X - M$. An increase in income (Y) would lead to a consequent increase in consumption expenditure (C), investment (I), and imports (M). In absolute terms, all these components would register an increase. In proportional terms, the mix would depend on how the propensities to consume, invest, or import out of income received from abroad differs from the propensities to consume, invest, or import out of domestic income. The macroeconomic consequences of changes in income and expenditure can be traced through the impact on the major components of the identity.

An increase in aggregate consumption expenditure can have the following consequences: in a demand-constrained situation, it may lead to an increase in output; in a supply-constrained situation, it may stimulate a price rise or it may spill over into imports—the distribution of consumption expenditure between non-traded goods and traded goods would determine the relevant importance of inflation and imports as a consequence.

The difference between the increase in income and the increase in consumption attributable to remittances would be saved. The rate of saving may rise or fall depending on the propensities to save out of domestic income and foreign income. The use of savings would influence not only the level but also the mix of investment. The consequent increase in investment may lead to a further increase in output and income through the multiplier effect.

Given that $Y - C = S$, the identity can be rewritten as $I - S = M - X$. Therefore, an increase in income attributable to remittances may enable the economy to realize an excess of investment over savings, through a corresponding excess of imports over exports, with a smaller draw on external resources than would otherwise be the case.[40] Therefore, remittances from migrants can alleviate either the saving constraint or the foreign exchange constraint, thus enabling the economy to attain a higher rate of growth, which is somewhat akin to the role of foreign aid in two-gap models.[41] In this context, it is worth noting two important attributes of remittances. For one, remittances appear to be a more stable source of external finance, which are not characterized by the instability or volatility of foreign capital flows whether direct investment or portfolio investment. For another, remittances appear to be countercyclical with respect to growth in home countries. This is because remittances may

[40] This proposition may appear paradoxical at first sight because, in an accounting sense, it follows from the identity that there would be a corresponding increase in savings. But it is gross national saving rather than gross domestic saving that would rise and the economy would be able to realize an excess of investment over the latter.

[41] See Chenery and Strout (1966).

increase during economic crises to support consumption, or an economic downturn at home may induce migration and increase remittances.

The most obvious negative consequence of international migration for economic growth, in the long term, is the brain drain. This has been both recognized and emphasized for a long time. The brain drain represents an unrequited transfer of human capital which is bound to constrain growth. The problem may be accentuated in economies where international migration absorbs a large proportion of increments in the workforce or where the labor surplus is small and the skills are scarce. The export of workers in these circumstances may lead not only to a qualitative but also to a quantitative depletion of the labor force with serious repercussions for growth and development.

In a labor-exporting country, the depletion of human capital constrains economic growth for several reasons. First, there is a loss of scarce skills that are not easy to replenish. Second, the education or training of professional or skilled workers absorbs scarce investible resources, but the returns to public investment in education do not accrue to society. Third, the training of workers to replace emigrants imposes additional costs in terms of both resources and time. Fourth, the migration of people at the higher end of the spectrum of incomes means revenue foregone by the government, particularly in the sphere of direct taxes.

But that is not all. The brain drain may also be associated with negative externalities which could have an adverse effect on economic growth. New growth theory suggests that the knowledge embedded in a person has a positive effect on the productivity of another person, whose knowledge, in turn, has a positive effect on the productivity of this person. Therefore, the emigration of highly educated workers is not simply a once and for all knowledge loss to the home country. It also restrains the productivity of those left behind. Such negative externalities in productivity can only impede economic growth in the long term.

There are some other, longer-term consequences of international migration which could have positive implications for development. In the sphere of trade, a migrant population may induce an export expansion by creating a demand for exports, particularly in the realm of taste-specific or culture-specific consumer goods, the most important example of which is ethnic foods. In the sphere of investment, migrants could be an important source of capital inflows, whether in the form of repatriable deposits, portfolio investment, or direct investment. For the home country, the benefits and costs of such capital flows associated with international migration depends on the composition and the nature of these inflows.[42] In the sphere of technology, international migration may, after a time lag, yield benefits to home countries in the form of a brain gain by providing persons with professional

[42] For an analysis of this issue, see Nayyar (1994b).

qualifications or technical expertise through return migration or placement by transnational corporations. In the sphere of tourism, migration could stimulate tourism, to begin with, through the interest it arouses in host country nationals and subsequently through the interest in the home country that surfaces among non-resident migrants in search of their roots.

International migration leads to significant distributional consequences over time not only within countries but also between countries. These consequences are, of course, inter-related but are analytically separable.

Remittances are the most important channel of transmission and outcomes within countries depend on the skill composition of migrants. There is considerable evidence to suggest that remittances, in the aggregate as well as per capita, from unskilled and semi-skilled migrants are significantly higher than remittances from other migrants.[43] These migrants are generally persons who are at the lower end of the spectrum of skills, and also of incomes, before departure from their home countries. Remittances from such migrants are essentially meant to support consumption of their households or extended families at home. Remittances of this sort almost always reduce poverty and improve distribution. In fact, if these remittances provide resources for investment in the rural sector, particularly agriculture, or help acquire assets for self-employment in the urban sector, they create income opportunities for the less well endowed to improve the distribution of income. But when migrants are better educated, drawn from the upper end of the spectrum of incomes or skills at home, the distributional consequences are different. For one, remittances, in the aggregate as also per capita, are lower for such migrants, not only because they do not need to support the consumption of their extended families at home but also because they would much rather support the consumption of their households, or use their savings for investment, in the host country. For another, insofar as such migrants send remittances to their home countries, these inflows accrue not to poor households but to well endowed or higher income families, which tends to worsen income distribution. In this context, it is important to recognize that there is a selection principle, which sometimes borders on a systematic bias, which shapes the skills composition of migrants from developing countries to industrial societies. It is partly attributable to the initial endowments of migrants which provide them with the ability to migrate. It is also partly attributable to immigration laws in industrialized countries which are liberal for those with professional qualifications or technical skills. This underlying principle of self-selectivity among migrants could reinforce negative distributional consequences.

The impact of international migration on income distribution between countries also depends, to a significant extent, on the skills composition

43 See, for example, Nayyar (1994b).

of migrants. It is clear that international migration, in the form of a brain drain, tends to worsen income distribution between countries. It means a privatization of benefits for migrants in the host country, and a socialization of costs for those left behind in the home country. It also means an internalization of benefits and an externalization of costs for the host countries in the industrialized world and vice versa for home countries in the developing world. This phenomenon of the brain drain can, and often does, worsen income distribution between countries. It is just as clear that the mobility of professionals, which has registered a phenomenal increase with the gathering momentum of globalization, would also tend to worsen income distribution between countries. The reason is simple. These people, who are almost as mobile as capital, tend to move from low-income countries in the developing world to high-income countries in the industrialized world. Obviously, a brain gain, through transnational corporations or return migration, could improve income distribution between countries but, given the globalization of incomes for such people, it would at the same time worsen income distribution within countries. There are, however, new forms of cross-border movements of people, which could improve income distribution between countries. The increase in the number of guest workers and illegal immigrants, associated with markets and globalization, could make the distribution of income between countries less unequal than would otherwise be the case. Guest workers and illegal immigrants not only send remittances to their families while abroad but also return home with their savings.

In sum, it needs to be said that there is a maturity mismatch between costs and benefits of international migration in the wider context of economic development. The costs are certain while the benefits are uncertain. The costs are immediate, while the benefits accrue later. Most important, perhaps, the costs and benefits are asymmetrical between countries and between people. What is more, even if there is an increase in economic welfare for the world as a whole, the gainers cannot compensate the losers.

Conclusion

The cross-border movements of people are governed entirely by national immigration laws and consular practices. There are hardly any international rules or international institutions in this sphere. Yet, international migration is a reality. It cannot be wished away. Thus, it is essential to work towards an institutional framework that would govern movements of people across borders.

In this context, it is necessary to make a distinction between actual migrants and potential migrants. Actual migrants are made up of legal immigrants and illegal immigrants. For the former, the essential objective should be to ensure a respect for their rights. For the latter, the fundamental objective should be to eliminate exploitation and abuse. For potential migrants, it is necessary to develop institutions, or rules, that govern the cross-border movement of guest workers, who move temporarily for a limited duration, as well as professionals or service providers who move temporarily for a specified purpose. The temporary migration associated with guest workers is market-driven. It is often based on an ad hoc relaxation of, or accommodation in, immigration laws. Similarly, for service providers other than professionals, the cross-border movement of people is largely subject to discretionary regimes. It is often based on an ad hoc modification of consular practices to grant visas more easily, say, for body-shopping. These are unilateral acts on the part of the labor-importing countries. It is, therefore, important to develop a set of transparent and uniform rules for the temporary movement of guest workers or service providers across national boundaries. In doing so, the equivalent of the 'most favored nation principle,' which makes for unconditional non-discrimination, could provide a basic foundation.

Sooner rather than later, therefore, it is worth contemplating a multilateral framework for immigration laws and consular practices that governs the cross-border movement of people, similar to multilateral frameworks that exist, or are sought to be created, for the governance of national laws, or rules, about the movement of goods, services, technology, investment, finance, and information across national boundaries. This may seem far-fetched at present and perhaps not in the realm of the feasible. But it is no more implausible than the thought of a general agreement on trade in services, an international regime of discipline for the protection of intellectual property rights, or a multilateral agreement on investment, would have appeared a quarter of a century earlier.

References

Abella, M. (1994). 'International Migration in the Middle East: Patterns and Implications for Sending Countries'. *International Migration: Regional Processes and Responses*. Geneva: UN Economic Commission for Europe.

Amjad, R. (ed.) (1989). *To the Gulf and Back: Studies on the Economic Impact of Asian Labour Migration*. New Delhi: ILO-ARTEP.

—— (1996). 'International Labour Migration and its Implications in the APEC Region'. *Journal of Philippine Development*, XXIII: 45–78.

Berry, R. A. and Soligo, R. (1969). 'Some Welfare Effects of International Migration'. *Journal of Political Economy*, 77: 778–94.

Bhagwati, J. (ed.) (1976). *The Brain Drain and Taxation: Theory and Empirical Analysis*. Amsterdam: North Holland.

Bhagwati, J. and Rao, M. (1996). 'The US Brain Gain: At the Expense of Blacks?' *Challenge* (March).

Bohning, W. R. and Schloeter-Paredes, M. L. (eds.). (1994). *Aid in Place of Migration*. Geneva: International Labour Office.

Carens, J. H. (1996). 'Aliens and Citizens: The Case for Open Borders', in R. Cohen (ed.), *Theories of Migration*. Cheltenham: Edward Elgar.

Chenery, H. B. and Strout, A. (1966). 'Foreign Assistance and Economic Development'. *American Economic Review*, 56: 679–733.

Grubel, H. G. and Scott, A. D. (1966). 'The International Flow of Human Capital'. *American Economic Review*, 56: 268–74.

Krugman, P. and Bhagwati, J. (1976). 'The Decision to Migrate: A Survey', in J. Bhagwati (ed.), *The Brain Drain and Taxation*. Amsterdam: North Holland.

Kuznets, S. (1966). *Modern Economic Growth: Rate, Structure and Spread*. New Haven: Yale University Press.

Lee, E. (1998). 'The Migrant in an Era of Globalisation'. Paper presented at the World Congress on the Pastoral Care of Migrants and Refugees, Vatican City (October) 5–10, mimeo.

Massey, D. (1988). 'Economic Development and International Migration in Comparative Perspective'. *Population and Development Review*, 14/2.

Nayyar, D. (1988). 'The Political Economy of International Trade in Services'. *Cambridge Journal of Economics*, 12/2: 279–98.

—— (1989). 'Towards a Possible Multilateral Framework for Trade in Services: Some Issues and Concepts'. *Technology, Trade Policy and the Uruguay Round*. New York: United Nations.

—— (1994a). 'International Labour Movements, Trade Flows and Migration Transitions: A Theoretical Perspective'. *Asian and Pacific Migration Journal*, 3: 31–47.

—— (1994b). *Migration, Remittances and Capital Flows*. Delhi: Oxford University Press.

—— (1995). 'Globalization: The Past in Our Present'. Presidential Address to the Indian Economic Association, Chandigarh, December 28 (reprinted in *Indian Economic Journal*, 43/3: 1–18).

—— (2002). 'Cross Border Movements of People', in D. Nayyar (ed.), *Governing Globalization: Issues and Institutions*. Oxford: Oxford University Press.

Paine, S. (1974). *Exporting Workers: The Turkish Case*. Cambridge: Cambridge University Press.

Piore, M. J. (1979). *Birds of Passage: Migrant Workers in Industrial Societies*. Cambridge: Cambridge University Press.

Ratha, D. (2003). 'Workers' Remittances: An Important and Stable Source of External Finance'. *Global Development Finance 2003*. Washington, DC: World Bank.

Sen, A. K. (1973). 'Brain Drain: Causes and Effects', in B. R. Williams (ed.), *Science and Technology in Economic Growth*. London: Macmillan.

Solimano, A. (2004). 'Remittances by Emigrants: Issues and Evidence'. Mimeo.

Stalker, P. (1994). *The Work of Strangers: A Survey of International Labour Migration*. Geneva: International Labour Office.

Stark, O. (1991). *The Migration of Labour*. Oxford: Basil Blackwell.

United Nations (1998). *International Migration Policies*. New York: United Nations.

UNCTAD (1975). *The Reverse Transfer of Technology: Economic Effects of the Outflow of Trained Personnel from Developing Countries*. New York: United Nations.
UNCTAD (1994). *World Investment Report 1994*. New York: United Nations.
UNDP (1999). *Human Development Report 1999*. New York: Oxford University Press.
Watanabe, S. (1969). 'The Brain Drain from Developing to Developed Countries'. *International Labour Review*, 99: 401–33.
World Bank (1995). *World Development Report 1995*. New York: Oxford University Press.

Part III

Towards a New Global Governance

14

The Future of Global Governance

Joseph E. Stiglitz[1]

Today, the problems with global governance and the consequences of these problems are becoming better understood. The closer integration of the countries of the world—globalization—has given rise to a greater need for collective action. Unfortunately, economic globalization has outpaced political globalization. We are just beginning to develop an international rule of law, and much of the 'law' that has developed—for instance, the WTO rules governing international trade—is grossly unfair; it has been designed to benefit the developed countries, partly at the expense of the developing countries.

We approach international issues in an ad hoc, piecemeal manner. Because international institutions are few and limited in scope, special treaties designed to address particular problems must complement these institutions. For instance, global warming is a global environmental problem with potential immense economic consequences; there is an international scientific consensus on its causes, as well as an international consensus that something should be done. An international treaty, the United Nations Framework Convention on Climate Change signed in 1992, and the Kyoto Protocol signed in 1997 provided the beginnings of an answer. However, the world's largest polluter refuses to sign the latter or to alter its behavior, regardless of the consequences for others.

The international institutions that do exist have undemocratic governance and suffer from 'smokestack syndrome.' A single country, for instance, has effective veto power at the International Monetary Fund (IMF). Votes are allocated on the basis of economic power not even based on current economic standing.[2] Today, few democracies limit voting to

[1] This chapter is based on a paper prepared for the conference in Barcelona, September 24–5, 2004 on 'From The Washington Consensus Towards A New Global Governance.' Financial support from the Ford Foundation, the Macarthur Foundation, and the Mott Foundation is gratefully acknowledged.

[2] The argument sometimes put forward, that votes are related to member-states' 'contributions' to the capital of the organizations, is disingenuous. China would have been willing and able to increase its capital contribution were it allowed to do so.

those with property or apportion voting rights on the basis of economic wealth.

Even though the policies of the IMF and other international economic institutions have enormous implications for many aspects of society, including on issues of education, health, or the environment; only the finance ministers and central bank governors have a direct say. By contrast, within Western democracies, when important economic issues are being discussed, all of those who are affected usually have a voice in the decision, even if some voices are stronger than others.

The underlying democratic deficiencies are reflected in both the outcomes and the procedures—for instance, the lack of transparency or accountability, and the absence of some of the basic regulations that democracies typically impose to prevent conflicts of interest, such as on revolving doors.

The weaknesses in the democratic underpinnings have a further consequence: they undermine the legitimacy of the global public institutions. This has become of particular concern with the strengthening of democracies all over the world: why, it is asked, should a country accede to demands or advice of international institutions that are seen as reflecting the interests of the advanced industrial countries, many of them former colonial masters? This has become especially true as the IMF and the World Bank have argued that problems of development are related to inadequacies in governance *in developing countries*: what standing do these international institutions have to speak on issues of governance, when their own governance is so flawed?[3] We have seen these consequences unfold—the discontent with globalization is at least partly related to these failures, to the unfair trade agreements, and to the economic policies by the IMF that often do more to advance the interests and ideology of financial markets than they do to promote growth, stability, or equity in developing countries. Today, few would defend asymmetric trade agreements, especially those that allow for continued huge subsidies for agriculture; few would defend the intellectual property provisions of the Uruguay Round, which deprived the poorest countries of the world of access to life saving drugs for diseases like AIDS. Today, even the IMF (Prasad et al. 2003) recognizes that though it tried to change its charter to promote capital market liberalization a scant six years ago, for many countries capital market liberalization has led to more instability—without faster growth. It has been risk without reward (see Stiglitz 2000, 2002b, 2004b).

There is also a recognition that the international community has yet to address effectively some of the most important economic problems it faces, including: huge instability in exchange rates; festering problems with the

[3] These problems were highlighted by the appointment of Paul Wolfowitz—widely seen as one of the principal architects of the failed war in Iraq, a war that was in violation of International Law—to be President of the World Bank by President Bush. His subsequent conduct was consistent with fears expressed at the time of his appointment.

global reserve system; the fact that, in spite of seeming advances in the ability of the market to transfer risk from those less able to those more able to bear it, developing countries still bear the brunt of exchange rate and interest rate risks in their loans; and the absence of a mechanism to handle sovereign defaults.

Even as we move away from the deficiencies of the *formal* institutions, there is a growing awareness of the inadequacies of the informal institutions. Why, when the leaders of the world get together to discuss future economic reforms, are China, India, Brazil, or representatives of poorer countries, not at the table? What is the selection principle, other than historical accident, that would leave out some of the most populous and largest economies in the world?

In spite of the recognition of the problems with globalization, change has been slow. In this brief chapter, I want to focus my attention on the forces that may actually lead to meaningful reform of global government. I shall also discuss a few of the elements of the system of governance that may or should eventually evolve.

Some Forces for Change

Change is needed, but change is slow to come. This is not surprising, as there are those who benefit from the current arrangements. Indeed, one of the central criticisms of globalization—that rules and institutions serve some interests and some countries at the expense of others—gives rise to a natural question: why would those in power give up that power? What are the underlying forces for change? In this chapter, I will explore two sets of motivations for change.[4]

Self-interested Motives for Change

The first set of motives is premised on the self-interest of the powerful. The powerful sometimes find it desirable or necessary to give up some power to get what they want, or to prevent even worse things from happening. Of course, the powerful within a country have not been the strongest advocates of the rule of law; they do better in closed door proceedings where they can use their economic muscle to achieve their objectives. So too in the international arena. America, the sole remaining superpower, often pursues a policy of unilateralism. It does not want to have its hands tied by any international rule of law and has walked away from the International Criminal Court and the agreement on global warming.

[4] There is a parallel question—what gave rise to a democratic rule of law *within* various Western countries? In some cases, there were explicit revolutions, but in others, there was a more evolutionary process.

THE NEED FOR COOPERATION

However, even the most powerful countries need cooperation from others; and they cannot force cooperation. The 'bargaining equilibrium' requires important concessions.

Today, in the context of the war in Iraq, it has become increasingly clear that the United States by itself cannot suppress the insurgency, and that most of the rest of the world is increasingly unwilling to provide assistance unless a governance framework that greatly circumscribes US power is adopted. There is a lack of confidence in the decisions of the US, and others are naturally unwilling to allow those in whom they have little confidence to determine the way in which their resources (including their troops) are used. When there is meaningful participation in the decision-making, there is greater willingness to go along with decisions, even if these decisions are viewed to be ill-advised.

In addition, the reconstruction of Iraq will require enormous amounts of money. Iraq's immense oil wealth was effectively encumbered by equally immense foreign debts. If there were to be successful reconstruction without large foreign assistance, it would require debt forgiveness. However, most of the debts are owed not to the United States, but to other countries. Without successful reconstruction, America's Iraq 'project' is almost surely doomed to failure. Again, the United States needed the cooperation of others.

In the international trade arena, the developing countries walked away from a new agreement, as they recognized that no agreement was better than another agreement as unfair as previous agreements. The United States and Europe had made no significant concessions in the pivotal area of agriculture; indeed, since 1994 there had been considerable backsliding, with the US doubling its subsidies. Since the failure of Cancun, the United States has been using its economic muscle to induce a few, relatively small, countries to sign bilateral agreements; as a percentage of American or global trade, however, these bilateral agreements are of little significance. The United States has failed to achieve a bilateral agreement with any major economy, and American unilateralism makes it unlikely that it will do so.

LEVERAGING LIMITED POWER

While current international agreements may have been unfair to the developing countries—not surprisingly, those with power have used that power to advance their interests—a modest 'rule of law' has begun to develop, albeit an unfair one. However, once created, these institutions can assume a life of their own, and the developing countries can use them to advance some of their interests.

For instance, the United States did not want Brazil to bring to the WTO a case against the United States' use of cotton subsidies. The ruling against the United States is of enormous import because it can potentially force the United States and Europe to scale back their subsidies well beyond the levels that they had previously 'offered' to do in the so-called development round.

Another possibility of even greater significance involves using trade policy to achieve environmental objectives. The United States tried to force Thailand to use turtle-friendly nets in catching shrimp, threatening to ban from the United States shrimp caught without such nets—a position sustained by the WTO appellate body. When the United States brought the case, it did not consider fully the import of its actions (though at least some on the WTO appellate body were aware of the far-reaching consequences of their decision)—that other countries could presumably *keep out* goods produced by energy intensive technologies that contribute to global warming. International trade law might be able to fill in the gap left by the United States' rejection of the Kyoto agreement. American firms *are* effectively subsidized, in the sense that they do not pay for the full costs of what they produce: the full costs should include the social cost of pollution. International law precludes such hidden subsidies and allows countries to take actions to address global environmental problems, particularly when other mechanisms to do so have failed.

Thus, the threat to use what limited international law exists may become an important instrument for reform, not only to address the specific problems—agricultural subsidies or environmental pollution—but to achieve broader reforms in governance.

INCREASING RECOGNITION OF THE NEED FOR THE RULE OF LAW

This brings me to another basis for optimism about improvements in global governance. Not only does the United States need cooperation from other nations, but other nations (and many within the United States) have increasingly recognized that their well-being—the well-being of the world—depends on the establishment of a stronger rule of law at the international level. One of the arguments for democracy is based on the dangers of a lack of checks and balances. It is evident that the current arrangements do not provide for a check on the power of the United States. The United States is willing to consult with others and to use international institutions, as long as those institutions agree with what it wants; when they do not, the United States walks away. This demonstrates a lack of commitment to democratic processes. Meaningful democracy means that actions cannot reflect the beliefs of a single individual, or in democratic decision-making among countries, of a single country (see Arrow 1951). Making matters even worse is the evident lack of *internal* controls. In one interpretation, at the time the United States Constitution was written, there was little need to provide for an effective check on the president with respect to foreign relations: the United States' limited power meant that foreign nations would provide that check. Now, with the United States as the only superpower, foreign nations have not provided an effective check, and Congress and the courts have increasingly ceded power to the president.

Not surprisingly, American unilateralism often leads to decisions that are not in the interests of other countries. This, by itself, would not necessarily lead to reforms; but the lack of effective democratic international institutions with legitimacy is such an impediment to taking effective actions in areas where such actions appear increasingly essential that citizens in both the United States and abroad are likely to demand changes in the rules of global governance.

Issues of legitimacy of political institutions and decisions become most intense when the decisions appear to fail. When IMF policies led to increasing immiseration of the poor in many developing countries and did not bring about promised growth, the IMF lost much of its political legitimacy in the developing world. When the IMF policies, including the mega billion dollar bailouts, failed in East Asia, Russia, and Argentina, the IMF lost much of its political legitimacy in financial markets and in the developed world. When trade liberalization did not bring about promised benefits and many countries saw their incomes fall, seemingly because of *asymmetric* liberalization, or when thousands faced the threat of death because of a lack of access to lifesaving drugs because of the Uruguay Round Trade Agreement, the WTO lost much of its political legitimacy.

To many, the consequences of economic failures that resulted from deficiencies in global governance pale in comparison to the consequences of deficiencies in the area of 'security'—in particular, to those that have been associated with the war in Iraq. American unilateralism has not made the world safer; many have already suffered due to the increased instability engendered by American actions, and more are likely to suffer in the future.

Iraq has thus brought home the risks of unilateralism, but it has also undermined the confidence in the credibility of the statements of leaders. Why should one believe that, say, the United States is really committed to creating a fair trading system? Or why should one believe that its policies in other spheres represent anything other than ideology or its interests or special interests within the United States?

Such skepticism is exacerbated by the United States' actions, which are widely seen as self-serving and hypocritical. For instance, there was a general understanding as the countries signed the Uruguay Round agreement that agricultural subsidies would not increase, and would actually be cut. The United States instead doubled its subsidies, claiming that it was entitled to do so because of technical loopholes that it had inserted. But these claims further exacerbated the skepticism: the United States went so far as to claim that cotton subsidies were not trade distorting, when they plainly were (and the WTO panel found so, not surprisingly).

Even when there might be justifications for the seeming hypocrisy, the glaring contrast between US policies and the policies expected of other nations has undermined American credibility. Though the US government has defended its policy of running huge deficits, arguing that tax cuts stimulate the economy, the IMF (where the US has veto power) forces other nations to cut back their expenditures and raise taxes, even when facing far smaller deficits. The United States' central bank focuses on jobs, growth and inflation, while abroad, the IMF demands that central banks focus only on inflation. In the United States, privatization of social security is hotly contested, with one of the two parties staunchly defending the public old-age pension system; abroad, the IMF encourages countries to privatize their social security systems, suggesting that privatization is the only economically sound way to proceed.

Such hypocrisy is enough to undermine the legitimacy of the international economic institutions; however, it has also become increasingly clear that while the international economic institutions are not supposed to be 'political,' in fact at least the IMF pursues an economic agenda that is closely associated with the conservative political agenda. This too undermines the IMF's legitimacy, especially in the eyes of those who do not subscribe to that political agenda. That the countries that have followed the IMF's advice have not fared as well as those countries that have not (as in East Asia) has made matters even worse.

Democratic Forces for Change

These failures naturally lead to a closer look at the governance of the international economic institutions and their decision-making processes. Protests at virtually every meeting of international economic leaders have called attention to the deficiencies in governance to which I alluded earlier—the allocation of voting rights, the smokestack structure, and the problems of representation (who represents each country), transparency, and accountability.

The international institutions are *supposed* to reflect democratic principles, and however such principles are formulated, the decision-making structures are a far cry from principles that govern democratic decision-making *within* countries. No government allocates voting rights—even on economic matters—on the basis of economic 'power.' It would be unacceptable for Bill Gates to cast, say, 100,000 votes, or even 10,000 votes, simply because he has 100,000 or 10,000 times the income or wealth of the average American. Similarly, it would be unacceptable to deny voting rights to those without wealth. No democratic government allows only the finance minister and central bank governor to make decisions about economic policy on their own: others must be brought to the table.

The problems of governance are reflected in the *actions, processes,* and *choices* of leadership. For instance, the head of the IMF is always a European.

Traditional democratic principles would suggest that the institution look for the most qualified person, regardless of race, gender, or nationality, but these principles have been pushed aside. The agreement among the majority shareholders, the G8, is that the head of the IMF is always to be a European. The Europeans in turn decide whose turn it is. Seemingly, little weight is given to whether the person chosen has any detailed knowledge of developing countries, where most of the work of the IMF has been located for the past 30 years. Thus when a new managing director was chosen in 2000, the Europeans decided it was Germany's turn; next it was Spain's turn; then France's. The US continued to have veto power, however, and the US Treasury vetoed Germany's first choice. The uproar led many to hope that the *next* selection of a new Managing Director would be more open and transparent, but this was not to be the case.

The processes through which decisions are made reflect the same lack of openness and transparency. At the WTO, the green room process—whereby the US and the EU meet with several other rich countries and the Director General behind closed doors[5]—has been widely criticized. Though there have been some reforms, the developed countries have been reluctant to respond adequately to the demands of the developing countries.[6] At the IMF, greater transparency has often meant little more than a better website.

It is not surprising, given these problems in governance, that the decisions and actions made by the international economic institutions conform so much to the ideology and interests of the advanced industrial countries, or more accurately, to the interests of the multinational corporations and financial institutions in those countries.

The problems in governance help us understand better some of the 'biases,' deficiencies, and seeming inconsistencies in the decision-making. These 'biases' include the lack of balance concerning intellectual property rights at the WTO (where the concerns of users and even those in the scientific community were given short shrift),[7] and the availability of billions of dollars to finance bailouts for Western banks, while there were seemingly no funds for even modest food subsidies for the poor who were often unemployed due to depressions or recessions that accompanied IMF programs. Further deficiencies range from beggar-thy-self policies, which were even worse than the beggar-thy-neighbor policies,[8] to the peculiarity of an institution—the

[5] Because all of this goes behind closed doors, it is never fully clear how the developing countries are 'strong-armed,' for example, are there explicit threats to cut off aid or to curtail some set of preferences or are the threats simply implicit?

[6] See for instance Stiglitz and Charlton (2005). Even reforms in the last few years that have given developing countries *more* voice have not given them *adequate* voice, and thus have not gained the WTO the legitimacy that it had hoped.

[7] See Stiglitz (2004a).

[8] In the 'beggar-thy-neighbor' policies that were often employed in the Great Depression, countries would impose tariffs to deflect consumption from their neighbors towards their own producers; increases in domestic aggregate demand occurred at the expense of one's

IMF—founded to correct a market failure, but that at the same time preached market fundamentalism, arguing that markets by themselves solve all economic problems and yet itself, in seeming contradiction to these pronouncements, endorsing intervention in exchange rate markets.[9] It explains too why there is a greater focus on 'efficiency' and less on equity.

It also helps explain what is on the agenda, as well as what is off the agenda. Capital and financial market liberalization have been on the agenda, even though there is little evidence that they are good for developing countries and considerable evidence that they are bad. High tax rates are on the agenda, but land reform is not, despite huge inequalities in land ownership that force many peasants to work under sharecropping arrangements that impose on them effectively a 50 or even 67 percent tax rate.

Inside most developed countries, democratic forces have tempered capitalism; they have, to use a cliché, put a human face on it. These countries have recognized that there are market failures and that even when markets yield *efficient* outcomes, they do not generally lead to a socially acceptable distribution of income. Governments must provide a safety net and engage in some redistribution. There are also non-material values that may trump economic concerns. For example, firms have no incentive *not* to pollute, and thus governments have a responsibility to limit the damage to the environment.

In the international arena, too often this tempering process is absent or greatly attenuated. For instance, *abroad*, drug companies can limit generic drugs through international agreements in ways that the United States Congress would not likely have enacted *at home* (assuming that there was an open debate on the issue). The Clinton Administration opposed 'takings provisions' (providing compensation to firms for reductions in profits resulting from regulations, including those protecting the environment), but chapter 11 of NAFTA effectively introduced such a provision.

The absence of 'tempering' in the international arena is only partially a consequence of the democratic deficit. It also arises because of the limitations in social conscience—that attitudes towards social justice or social solidarity often change markedly at national borders. Politicians naturally worry far more about inequality or poverty within their own country than inequality or poverty beyond their borders; but the perspective of politicians reflects those of most of those they represent.

To make matters worse, international institutions are not directly accountable to anyone.[10] Citizens of countries affected by IMF programs, for instance,

neighbors. In the new IMF 'beggar thyself' policies, countries are advised to increase taxes and interest rates and cut expenditures, to reduce fiscal and trade deficits—policies that have the effect of depressing incomes at home (hence the term 'beggar thyself') in order to restore 'external balance,' in other words, to help repay foreign debts. See Stiglitz (1999).

[9] See, e.g., Stiglitz (2002a).

[10] For more extensive discussion of accountability, see Stiglitz (2003).

do not vote on the head of the IMF or even on their representative to the IMF. In addition, we have seen how weak the system of *indirect* accountability is: even abject failure is not remedied by the firing of the head of the IMF. The absence of direct democratic accountability perhaps also accounts for why there is not greater concern about public perceptions—why, for instance, strong revolving door policies have yet to be introduced. Were these institutions worried about their political legitimacy, the lack of *direct* accountability would have led them to be particularly sensitive about such matters, and to be especially concerned to be open and transparent.

While the failures in governance have most affected those in the developing world, even those in the developed world have felt the impact. For instance, chapter 11 of NAFTA threatens environmental legislation even in the United States. Many in the scientific community in the United States worry that the Agreement on Trade-Related Aspects of Intellectual Property Rights (TRIPS) will adversely affect scientific progress. Equally important, many in the developed world have felt sympathy for those in the developing world, as they see them deprived, for instance, of lifesaving drugs.

We have already noted that citizens in both the developed and developing world have become increasingly concerned about the lack of political legitimacy of the international economic institutions, about the democratic deficit, and about unfair outcomes. They are uncomfortable with the imposition of a particular ideology—especially those who (like me) spend much of their time fighting such ideologies at home (including, for instance, the privatization of social security). But even those who might agree with the policies being advocated often feel uncomfortable with the 'colonial' overtones of the advanced industrial countries that impose their views on others and in doing so, undermine democratic processes in the developing world.

In short, many in the developed countries take seriously democratic processes in their own country, in other countries, and in international economic institutions. They see the ability of special interests to dominate American international economic policy (or the international economic policy of other advanced industrial countries) as a reflection of a shortfall in the democracies in *their* countries.

Ideas matter: I see the growing concern about this democratic deficit both in developing and developed countries as the final pillar for change in the system of international governance.

Reforms

In the preceding section, I have outlined some of the forces that should help bring about change in global governance. In this section, I want to outline several directions that such reforms might, or should, take.

1. *Changes in the governance of the World Bank and the IMF*. Changes in the governance of the World Bank and the IMF have been extensively discussed elsewhere. The most important are changes in voting structure and representation.[11] Even if, or especially if, these changes do not occur quickly, it is important to have improvements in transparency and accountability, and in conflict of interest rules. There are also *informal* procedural and *institutional* changes that would give developing countries a more effective voice, for example, the creation of a think tank to help developing countries formulate positions that more effectively reflect their interests.
2. *Changes in the governance of the WTO*. Changes in the governance of the WTO include greater transparency, the elimination of the green room processes,[12] the creation of more representative processes for decision-making, and the creation of an independent body to evaluate alternative proposals—in particular, their impact on developing countries, to assess whether bilateral and regional trade agreements are more trade diverting than trade creating, and to determine *before* dumping or countervailing duties are imposed whether there is a prima facie case.[13]
3. *Moving from the G8 to the G24*. The informal institutions in which world leaders meet to discuss global economic policies are as flawed and out of date as the formal institutions. China, as one of the largest economies and one of the world's major traders, should be at the table. *Being invited for lunch is not good enough*. One cannot just be a guest: one has to be an integral part of the process. The voices of the emerging markets, such as India and Brazil, should be there too, as should representatives of the least developed countries.
4. *A strengthened Economic and Social Council*. At Monterey, it was finally recognized that development is too *important*—and too *complex*—to be

[11] It is likely that more than just a change in voting power, however, will be required. Africa has such a small fraction of global economic power that, no matter what formula one uses, its voting power will be limited. What almost surely will be required is some system of double majority—for example, a majority of votes by 'economic' power (appropriately defined), and a majority of countries; or a majority of borrowing countries, and a majority of lending countries.

The argument that the lending countries should dominate because, after all, they finance the whole operation, is not totally convincing. Under current financial arrangements, the lending countries get a return on their capital roughly commensurate with market rates. The operations of the IMF are really financed by the borrowing countries. By 2007, this was presenting serious problems for the institution, since most countries had repaid their loans, and the world had fortunately gone several years without a crisis. Over half the IMF's revenue came from one country, Turkey.

[12] In which a select group of countries engage in behind the scenes, secret negotiations; pressure is then put on others to go along with whatever has been agreed to by this small group of countries.

[13] These issues are discussed more fully in Stiglitz and Charleton (2005).

left just to finance ministers. This is true of other aspects of global economic policy, which touch on every facet of modern life. Worse still, finance ministers and central bank governors bring a particular perspective to the discussion—an important perspective, but not the only one. Consider, for instance, the issue of sovereign debt restructuring. No government would entrust legislation setting forth the framework for bankruptcy to a committee dominated by creditor and creditor interests. However, putting the IMF in charge—which is what the IMF wanted—would have done this. Such decisions must be approached with greater balance. Initially, such a strengthened Economic and Social Security Council might have to rely more on moral suasion. Today, however, it is such moral suasion that in any case largely determines whether a country repays its loans. A strengthened Economic and Social Security Council could provide some oversight over the other international economic institutions, to make sure that they were not captured by special interests (as many people think has in fact happened both at the WTO and the IMF). It could also help set the overall economic agenda, and help integrate the economic agenda with other agendas, for example on the environment.

5. *Financing for global public goods*. Increasing global integration has resulted in global public goods taking on increasing importance, but we rely mostly on moral suasion to generate the funding for such global public goods. Not surprisingly, there has been underfunding; moral suasion has been only partially effective. For instance, while the advanced industrial countries have agreed to provide 0.7 percent of their GDP for funding assistance to developing countries, and a few European countries have exceeded that target, the world's richest country has fallen woefully short. Elsewhere, I have outlined a set of proposals for global funding.[14]

   - *Revenues from the management of global natural resources*. There are a number of global natural resources—international fisheries, the sea bed, Antarctica, the global atmosphere, satellite slots. The efficient management of these global natural resources can give rise to substantial revenues, for example auctioning off fishing rights, charging for greenhouse gas emissions, etc.
   - *Revenues from the issuance of Special Drawing Rights (SDRs)*—global greenbacks. The deficiencies in the global reserve system are being recognized more and more—its inefficiencies, its instability, and its inequity. Every year, some US$200 to US$400 billion are effectively buried in the ground in the form of reserves. The US benefits—the fact that the dollar is the reserve currency helps enable the US to consume

[14] See Stiglitz (2004c).

well beyond its means; and it helps enable the US to borrow trillions of dollars abroad at low interest rates. However, as the US becomes increasingly in debt, questions are being raised about the viability of the system. The revenues from the issuance of SDRs could be used to finance global public goods, including development assistance.[15]

- *Taxation of global (negative) externalities,* like arms sales to developing countries, pollution,[16] and destabilizing cross border financial flows.

6. *Management of global natural resources and the environment,* including the world's oceans and atmosphere. Even if the international community does not seize the opportunity of revenue generation afforded by the management of global natural resources, the efficient, sustainable, and equitable management of resources is important. There needs to be a more effective Global Environmental Agency.
7. *Production and protection of global knowledge.* Among the more important global public goods is knowledge. TRIPs can be viewed as having recognized this—incentives to produce knowledge depend on the ability to capture rents globally. However, TRIPs demonstrates forcefully the flaws in current global governance—it provided a set of rules that did not reflect a balance of concerns (between producers of knowledge and users of knowledge, between developed and developing countries, between academics and profit-making firms), but rather the concerns of American drug and media industries. We need to recognize that since knowledge is a global public good, it is important to finance knowledge in an equitable manner. This may not entail imposing on the poorest countries taxes so high as to deprive people of access to lifesaving medicines.
8. *A global legal infrastructure.* One of the most important functions of government *within countries* is to provide a legal infrastructure, for example, the enforcement of contracts, the protection of competition, and bankruptcy. Today, economic relations are increasingly transnational. In the United States a century ago, states provided most of the legal infrastructure, even though the similarity across states was sufficiently great that the legal structures adopted were broadly similar. The differences gave rise to a multiplicity of problems, however. Great efforts have been put into providing more uniform legislation and harmonization. Today, as globalization proceeds, a similar process needs to occur across countries. We recognize that each country on its own may not be able to ensure competition, e.g. in the software market or the market for operating systems. It is important in creating a global legal infrastructure that it not be

[15] A modest version of this proposal is contained in Soros (2002). (More recently, I have elaborated on this proposal in ch. 9 of *Making Globalization Work,* New York: W.W. Norton, 2006.)

[16] A few countries have recently agreed to impose an airline fuel tax for these purposes.

based on the lowest common denominator, for example the least protective of competition. Moreover, it may be desirable to retain some duplication: for instance, the overlap in securities legislation and enforcement in the United States proved extremely important when political pressures and incompetence led to inadequate enforcement at the national level, and New York State assumed the mantel of responsibility.

Concluding Remarks

I began this chapter by arguing that in recent years, we have come to understand better, not only why there is such discontent with globalization, but why globalization has not worked as well as it can for so many of the people around the world. The international rules of the game are often unfair, and the international institutions have pushed a particular ideology—an ideology that has resulted in economic policies particularly ill-suited to many of the developing countries. However, that only pushes the question back further: why have the rules been so unfair, and why has this particular ideology been pushed? Underlying these failures is a failure of governance.

I have suggested that while those who benefit from current arrangements will work hard to maintain them, there are forces for change. The pace of globalization makes the need for change all the greater. It will be difficult to maintain increasing *economic* globalization[17] unless there are reforms in *governance*, particularly in the institutions that govern globalization and in the rules and regulations that define how globalization proceeds are adopted and evolve.

Perhaps the strongest force for change is a change in mindset that globalization itself engenders: improvements in communication and the reduction of transportation costs have brought with them an increasing familiarity with the mindsets of other countries. There is a growing recognition that we live on a single planet, that we are increasingly interdependent.

In my mind, the question is not so much whether there will be change, but whether it will come fast enough. Globalization is not an inevitable

[17] I have had little to say in this essay about the benefits and costs of increasing economic globalization. It is clear that the advanced developed countries have benefited greatly from globalization and, increasingly, political leaders of both the left and right have taken the extent to which they have been able to advance the globalization agenda as a mark of their success. But even within developed countries, there is discontent with globalization. Even if the country as a whole gains, there are winners and losers. Increasingly, there is a concern that the benefits may be distributed very inequitably—a few gain a great deal, and many may lose. Without some form of compensation, support for globalization even in the developed countries may wane. But globalization may impede the ability to provide the requisite compensation, as increased mobility of capital and highly skilled workers makes imposing redistributive taxes more difficult. However, these are issues that take us beyond the scope of this chapter.

process. Capital flows today have yet to recover fully from their peaks before the global financial crisis. Capital and trade integration were weaker in the interwar period than they were before World War I. Unless changes are made, the already palpable disillusionment with globalization will spread, with untold consequences, both for those in the developed and the less-developed countries.

References

Arrow, K. (1951). *Social Choice and Individual Values*. New York: John Wiley.

International Monetary Fund Technical Group. 'Report of the Technical Group on Innovative Financing Mechanisms: Action Against Hunger and Poverty'. IMF (September).

Prasad, E., Rogoff, K., Wei, S., and Kose, A. M. (2003). 'Effects of Financial Globalization on Developing Countries: Some Empirical Evidence'. IMF Occasional Paper, No. 220 (September).

Soros, G. (2002). *George Soros on Globalization*. New York: Public Affairs.

Stiglitz, J. E. (1999). 'Beggar-Thyself vs. Beggar-Thy-Neighbor Policies: The Dangers of Intellectual Incoherence in Addressing the Global Financial Crisis'. *Southern Economic Journal*, 66/1: 1–38 (July).

—— (2000). 'Capital Market Liberalization, Economic Growth, and Instability'. *World Development*, 28/6: 1075–86.

—— (2002a). *Globalization and its Discontents*. New York: W. W. Norton & Company, ch. 4.

—— (2002b). 'Capital Market Liberalization and Exchange Rate Regimes: Risk without Reward'. *The Annals of the American Academy of Political and Social Science*, 579: 219–48 (January).

—— (2003). 'Democratizing the International Monetary Fund and the World Bank: Governance and Accountability'. *Governance*, 16/1: 111–39 (January).

—— (2004a). 'Towards a Pro-development and Balanced Intellectual Property Regime'. Keynote address presented at the Ministerial Conference on Intellectual Property for Least Developed Countries, World Intellectual Property Organization (WIPO), Seol, October 25. Available at: www.policydialogue.org

—— (2004b). 'Capital Market Liberalization, Globalization, and the IMF'. *Oxford Review of Economic Policy*, 20: 57–71 (March).

—— and Charlton, A. (2005). *Fair Trade for All*. Oxford: Oxford University Press.

Van Houtven, Leo. 'Governance of the International Monetary Fund: Decision Making, Institutional Oversight, Transparency and Accountability'. IMF Pamphlet Series, No. 53, August 9.

15

Growth Diagnostics*

Ricardo Hausmann, Dani Rodrik, and Andrés Velasco

Introduction

Most well-trained economists would agree that the standard policy reforms included in the Washington Consensus have the potential to be growth promoting. What the experience of the last 15 years has shown, however, is that the impact of these reforms is heavily dependent on circumstances. Policies that work wonders in some places may have weak, unintended, or negative effects in others.[1] We argue in this chapter that this calls for an approach to reform that is much more contingent on the economic environment, but one that also avoids an 'anything goes' attitude of nihilism. We show it is possible to develop a unified framework for analyzing and formulating growth strategies that is both operational and based on solid economic reasoning. The key step is to develop a better understanding of how the binding constraints on economic activity differ from setting to setting. This understanding can then be used to derive policy priorities accordingly, in a way that uses efficiently the scarce political capital of reformers.

Our approach is motivated by three considerations. First, while development is a broad concept entailing the raising of human capabilities in general, we believe increasing economic growth rates is the central challenge that developing nations face. Higher levels of living standards are the most direct route to achieving improvements in social and human indicators. Reform

* We owe thanks to Eduardo Engel, Robert Lawrence, Lant Pritchett, Andrés Rodríguez-Clare, and Arvind Subramanian, our collaborators on a number of related projects, as well as other participants in the Kennedy School Lunch Group on International Economic Policy (LIEP) for many discussions over the years that led to the development of the ideas reported here.

[1] This is well-reflected in the view expressed recently by Al Harberger (2003: 15): 'when you get right down to business, there aren't too many policies that we can say with certainty deeply and positively affect growth.'

strategies should be principally targeted at raising rates of growth—that is, they should be growth strategies.

Second, trying to come up with an identical growth strategy for all countries, regardless of their circumstances, is unlikely to prove productive. Growth strategies are likely to differ according to domestic opportunities and constraints. There are of course some general, abstract principles—such as property rights, the rule of law, market oriented incentives, sound money, and sustainable public finances—which are desirable everywhere. But turning these general principles into operational policies requires considerable knowledge of local specificities.

Third, it is seldom helpful to provide governments with a long list of reforms, many of which may not be targeted at the most binding constraints on economic growth. Governments face administrative and political limitations, and their policymaking capital is better deployed in alleviating binding constraints than in going after too many targets all at once. So growth strategies require a sense of priorities.

What we propose to do in this chapter is to develop a framework for *growth diagnostics*—that is, a strategy for figuring out the policy priorities. The strategy is aimed at identifying the most binding constraints on economic activity, and hence the set of policies that, once targeted on these constraints at any point in time, is likely to provide the biggest bang for the reform buck.

The methodology that we propose for this can be conceptualized as a decision tree (see Figure 15.1, discussed below). We start by asking what keeps growth low. Is it inadequate returns to investment, inadequate private appropriability of the returns, or inadequate access to finance? If it is a case of low returns, is that due to insufficient investment in complementary factors of production (such as human capital or infrastructure)? Or is it due to poor access to imported technologies? If it is a case of poor appropriability, is it due to high taxation, poor property rights and contract enforcement, labor–capital conflicts, or learning and coordination externalities? If it is a case of poor finance, are the problems with domestic financial markets or external ones? And so on.

Then we discuss the kind of evidence that would help answer these questions one way or another. We also illustrate the practical implications of this approach by drawing on examples from specific countries.

Aside from providing a useful manual for policymakers, our approach has the advantage that it is broad enough to embed all existing development strategies as special cases. It can therefore unify the literature and help settle prevailing controversies. For example, our framework will clarify that doctrinal differences on development policy—between proponents of the Washington Consensus and of state led strategies, or between pro-globalizers and cautious globalizers—are grounded in divergent evaluations about the nature of the binding constraints on growth. Making these differences

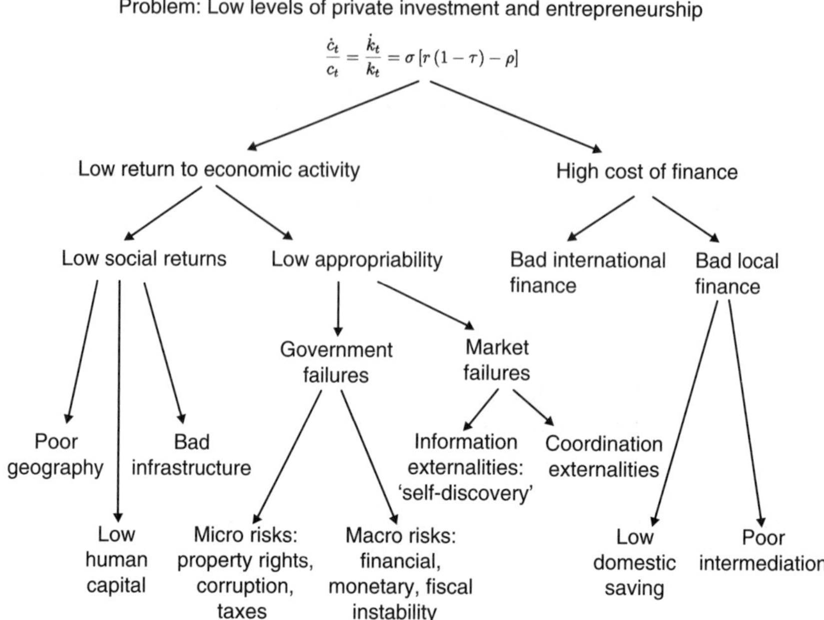

Figure 15.1. Growth Diagnostics

explicit, and clarifying the nature of the evidence that can resolve them, can move us forward to a more productive policy agenda.

The outline of the chapter is as follows. We first lay out the conceptual framework, linking our terminology of 'binding constraints' to standard economic models. In particular, we relate our framework to theories of second-best and partial reform, and of endogenous growth. We next cast the framework in the form of a decision tree, and discuss the nature of the evidence that is required to move along the nodes of the tree. In the final section we carry out an empirical analysis for several 'archetypal' cases, each representing a different syndrome, or combination of binding constraints.

Thinking About Reform and Growth: A Framework

We begin with a formal treatment of our approach. This should help clarify how our discussion of 'binding constraints' and 'growth diagnostics' relates to conventional economic theory. We show that our approach is grounded on the standard theories of second-best and partial reform. These conceptual foundations provide structure to our framework, even though we naturally have to take a number of short cuts when we make it operational. We begin with a general treatment, and then provide a more stylized model that allows us to discuss a number of illustrations.

An economy that is underperforming and in need of reform is by definition one where market imperfections and distortions are rampant. These distortions can be government imposed (e.g., taxes on production) or inherent to the functioning of certain markets (e.g., human capital externalities, information spillovers, and so on). They prevent the best use of the economy's resources and, in particular, keep the economy far below its attainable productivity frontier. At this level of generality, we need not take a position on the nature of these distortions, although we will later do so. At this point it suffices to note that, regardless of how they arise, such distortions drive a wedge between private and social valuations of specific economic activities.

Let us denote these wedges by $\tau = \{\tau_1, \tau_2, \ldots, \tau_k\}$ with τ_i representing the distortion in activity i. Let us focus also on the problem of a policymaker bent on maximizing social welfare subject to the standard resource constraints, but also constrained by these pre-existing distortions or wedges in the economy. The distortions can be modeled as constraints on the policy-making problem that take the general form:

$$\mu_i^{\mathrm{s}}(\tau, \ldots) - \mu_i^{\mathrm{p}}(\tau, \ldots) - \tau_i = 0, \tag{1}$$

where $\mu_i^{\mathrm{s}}(\tau, \ldots)$ and $\mu_i^{\mathrm{p}}(\tau, \ldots)$ represent net marginal valuations of activity i by society and by private agents, respectively. Of course they depend not just on the set τ of distortions, but on levels of consumption, labor supply, asset-holdings, etc. Equations of this type are nothing other than restatements of the first order conditions for the private sector. For example, a tax on investment (or a learning externality) keeps the private return on capital accumulation below the social return, with the result that the economy under invests. Note that the private and social valuation functions for each activity will depend in general equilibrium on all the wedges in the system. What this means is that the distortion in any one activity also affects the first order condition for other activities. That is the essence of the second-best problems that we will explore below.

How does welfare depend on these distortions? If u is welfare of the average member of society, then the gain in welfare from reducing one of the distortions marginally is:

$$\frac{du}{d\tau_j} = -\lambda_j + \sum_i \lambda_i \frac{\partial\left[\mu_i^{s}(\tau, \ldots) - \mu_i^{p}(\tau, \ldots)\right]}{\partial \tau_j} \tag{2}$$

and $\lambda_i \geq 0$, $i = \{1, 2, \ldots, k\}$ are the Lagrange multipliers corresponding to the constraints associated with each of the distortions.

The interpretation of this expression is as follows. Assume, without loss of generality, that the initial value of τ_j is strictly positive. The wedge created by the distortion in market j can be thought of as a tax that reduces the equilibrium level of activity in that market by keeping the net private return below the social return. The first term on the right-hand side of (2) captures the direct effect of a small change in τ_j: a small reduction in τ_j increases aggregate welfare by an amount given by the multiplier associated with the jth constraint, λ_j. In other words, λ_j is the marginal welfare benefit from reducing the distortion in market j, disregarding the effect on other distorted activities. The more costly is the distortion, the higher the magnitude of λ_j. At the other end of the spectrum, when activity j is undistorted ($\tau_j = 0$), the constraint ceases to bind, since the planner's first order conditions coincide with those of private agents, and $\lambda_j = 0$.

Turn now to the second term on the right-hand side of equation (2). When activity j is the sole distorted activity, this term vanishes since $\lambda_i = 0$ for all $i \neq j$. In this case, only the direct effect matters. But when there are other distorted activities in the economy, which is the typical case in a reforming economy, we need to track the interaction effects across distorted margins, which is what the term with the summation does. This second term captures the effect of changing τ_j on the weighted sum of the gaps between social and private valuations, with the weights corresponding to each distorted activity's own Lagrange multiplier. If on balance the effect is to reduce these gaps, holding everything else constant, then the reduction in τ_j produces an additional welfare benefit. If, on the other hand, these interactions tend to increase the gap between private and social valuations at the margin, the welfare gain is reduced.[2] Conceivably, the reduction in τ_j could even produce a welfare loss. This is a typical second-best complication.

Consider an illustration with two activities: j = intermediate input production; and ℓ = final good production. Suppose both activities are protected by import tariffs, given by τ_j and τ_ℓ respectively. Let us consider the partial effect of reducing τ_j while keeping τ_ℓ constant. A reduction in τ_j produces a direct welfare gain that would be captured by its own multiplier. But it also produces an indirect effect downstream in the production of the final good. Since the final good is protected, private valuations of producing the good exceed social valuations. A reduction in the intermediate-good tariff, τ_j, aggravates this distortion by increasing private profitability further. The increased gap between private and social valuations reduces the welfare gain from the reduction in τ_j. Indeed, if λ_ℓ is sufficiently high relative to λ_j, implying that the distortion

[2] Note that in equilibrium, the gaps between social and private valuations for the non-i activities have to revert back to their original values, since the wedges for these activities have not changed. What restores the equilibrium is the (privately optimal) adjustments in the consumption, production, or accumulation levels—i.e., changes in c, y, v—that enter the valuation functions. So, for example, an increase in the private valuation of producing a good would normally result in an increase in the quantity supplied, with a corresponding decline in the marginal valuation.

in the final good activity is particularly severe, the tariff reform could even result in a welfare loss.

As a second macroeconomic illustration, consider the case of a single good economy with two periods (today and tomorrow). Let j = goods today; and ℓ = goods tomorrow. Suppose the government maintains a restriction on international borrowing, which means that the social marginal valuation of expenditure today exceeds its private marginal valuation: $\lambda_j > 0$. Relaxation of the borrowing restriction would normally enhance domestic welfare. But suppose that for moral hazard reasons households and firms discount tomorrow's expenditure at a heavier rate than is socially optimal ($\mu_i^s(.) - \mu_i^p(.) > 0$, with corresponding $\lambda_\ell > 0$). In this case, relaxing today's borrowing restriction would aggravate the latter distortion. As before, if λ_ℓ is sufficiently high relative to λ_j, removing the borrowing restriction could make the economy worse off.

With this broad framework as a background, consider now several archetypal reform strategies.

Wholesale Reform

One way to eliminate all ambiguities and uncertainties with regard to the consequences of reform strategies is to simultaneously eliminate all distortions. If all the wedges are tackled and eliminated simultaneously, the multipliers associated with each of them go to zero, and none of the second-best issues we have highlighted above remains relevant. Wholesale reform is guaranteed to improve welfare. The best possible economic growth rate is achieved by eliminating all obstacles that stand in its way.

But notice what this strategy requires. It requires us not only to have complete knowledge of all prevailing distortions, it also necessitates that we have the capacity to remove them all in their entirety. This is the technically correct, but practically impossible strategy.

Do as Much Reform as You Can, as Best You Can

The second strategy, which seems to us to characterize the prevailing approach today, is to ignore the basic economics of the framework outlined above and to simply go for whatever reforms seem to be feasible, practical, politically doable, or enforceable through conditionality. This is a laundry list approach to reform that implicitly relies on the notions that (1) any reform is good; (2) the more areas reformed, the better; and (3) the deeper the reform in any area, the better.

Our framework shows why this approach, even if practical, is faulty in its economic logic. First, the principle of the second-best indicates that we cannot be assured that any given reform taken on its own can be guaranteed to be welfare promoting, in the presence of multitudes of economic distortions. Second, welfare need not be increasing in the number of areas that are reformed—except in the limiting case of wholesale reform, as discussed above. Third, in the presence of second-best interactions, more extensive reform in any given area is as likely to fall prey to adverse interactions as an incremental approach.

Second-best Reform

A more sophisticated version of the previous strategy is one that explicitly takes into account the second-best interactions discussed above. Thus, one could envisage a reform strategy that is less ambitious than the wholesale approach, but that recognizes the presence of the second term in equation (2), namely the possibility that interactions across distorted markets have the potential to both augment and counter the direct welfare effects. Under this strategy, one would give priority to reforms that engender positive second-best effects, and downplay or avoid altogether those that cause adverse effects. As the examples given above show, partial trade reform or capital account liberalization may reduce welfare unless more extensive reforms in trade and in financial markets are carried out at the same time.

The difficulty with a second-best reform strategy is that many, if not, most of these second-best interactions are very difficult to figure out and quantify ex ante. The strategy requires having a very good sense of the behavioral consequences of policy changes across different markets and activities. The state of the art (based largely on static computable general equilibrium models) is not very encouraging in this respect. In practice, most of the second-best interactions remain obscure, and tend to be revealed after the fact rather than ex ante.

Target the Biggest Distortions

If second-best interactions cannot be fully figured out and it is impractical to remove all distortions at once, reformers may instead focus on eliminating or reducing the biggest distortions in the economy—in other words, the largest wedges (τ_j) between private and social valuations. This would be an application of what is known as the concertina method in the literature on trade theory: order distortions from largest to smallest in proportional terms, start by reducing the largest of these to the level of the next largest, and proceed similarly in the next round. Under certain (fairly restrictive) conditions,[3] this strategy can be shown to be welfare improving.

[3] The (sufficient) condition is that the activity whose tax is being reduced be a net substitute (in general equilibrium) to all the other goods. See Hatta (1997).

However, even leaving aside its limited theoretical applicability, this approach has two severe shortcomings. First, it does require us to have a complete list of distortions, even those that do not take the form of explicit taxes or government interventions. Distortions that arise from market failures or imperfect credibility, for example, are unlikely to show up on our radar screen unless we have reason to look for them. Second, the concertina method does not guarantee that the reforms with the biggest impacts on economic welfare and growth will be the ones undertaken first. It may well turn out that the highest 'tax' is on some activity with very limited impact on growth. For example, there may be very high taxes on international borrowing, yet their removal could have miniscule effect on growth if the economy is constrained not by savings but by investment demand. For these reasons, this strategy is of uncertain benefits, especially in the short run.

Focus on the Most Binding Constraints

The approach we advocate in this chapter is to design reform priorities according to the magnitude of the direct effects—in other words, the size of the λ_j. This is the strategy that we think is the most practical, as well as the most promising with regard to the likely bang from reform. The idea behind the strategy is simple: if (a) for whatever reason the full list of requisite reforms is unknowable or impractical, and (b) figuring out the second-best interactions across markets is a near impossible task, the best approach is to focus on the reforms where the direct effects can be reasonably guessed to be large. As equation (2) indicates, as long as reform focuses on the relaxation of the distortions with the largest λ's associated with them, we have less to worry that second-best interactions will greatly diminish or possibly reverse the welfare effects. The principle to follow is simple: go for the reforms that alleviate the most binding constraints, and hence produce the biggest bang for the reform buck. Rather than utilize a spray gun approach, in the hope that we will somehow hit the target, focus on the bottlenecks directly.

Whether these binding constraints can be effectively identified is a practical and empirical matter, and we will spend considerable time below arguing that this can be done in a reasonable manner. In practice, the approach we take starts by focusing not on specific distortions (the full list of which is unknowable, as we argued above), but on the proximate determinants of economic growth (saving, investment, education, productivity, infrastructure, and so on). Once we know where to focus, we then look for associated economic distortions whose removal would make the largest contribution to alleviating the constraints on growth.

Moving from Theory to Practice

How can one apply the results of this rather abstract analysis of policy reform and its pitfalls? How do we locate the distortion(s) with the largest potential impact on economic growth?

Our strategy is to start with some of the proximate determinants of economic growth. As we discuss below, economic growth depends on the returns to accumulation (broadly construed), their private appropriability, and on the cost of financing accumulation. The first stage of the diagnostic analysis aims to uncover which of these three factors pose the greatest impediment to higher growth. In some economies, the 'constraint' may lie in low returns, in others it may be poor appropriability, and in yet others too high a cost of finance.

The next stage of the diagnostic analysis is to uncover the specific distortions that lie behind the most severe of these constraints. If the problem seems to be poor appropriability, is that due to high taxes, corruption, or macro instability? If the problem is with the high cost of finance, is that due to fiscal deficits or poor intermediation? This approach enables the design of remedies that are as closely targeted as possible.

To begin putting together a list of possible candidates, consider the determinants of growth and the role of distortions in a standard model. In the appendix we sketch the simplest possible endogenous growth model with a number of distortions. In that model the representative domestic household can borrow abroad, but subject to a collateral constraint. This is the first distortion, or wedge. The household can accumulate capital, used to produce productive inputs that are sold to the firm. There is an externality in the production of productive inputs from capital. This is the second distortion. There is a public subsidy to the hiring of productive inputs, which may partially offset the effects of the externality.

Government provides services to firms, for which it charges a price. This price need not reflect production costs fully. This is the third potential wedge. To fund public services and other activities, the government imposes a tax on firm income. This is the fourth wedge. Finally, government bureaucrats waste resources in ways that give citizens no utility. This is the fifth and last wedge.

The standard model yields the result that along a (constrained) balanced growth path consumption and capital grow according to:

$$\frac{\dot{c}_t}{c_t} = \frac{\dot{k}_t}{k_t} = \sigma\,[r\,(1-\tau) - \rho] \tag{3}$$

where a dot over a variable denotes the rate of change over time, and where other definitions are as follows:

- c = consumption;
- k = capital;
- r = the rate of return on capital;
- τ = the tax rate on capital, actual or expected, formal or informal;
- ρ = the world rate of interest;
- σ = elasticity of intertemporal elasticity in consumption.

In addition, the private return on capital r is given by:

$$r = r(a, \theta, x) \tag{4}$$

where:

- a = indicator of total factor productivity;
- x = availability of complementary factors of production, such as infrastructure or human capital;
- θ = index of externality (a higher θ means a larger distortion).

These two equations summarize the possible factors that can affect growth performance. An exercise of *growth diagnostics* simply consists of reviewing and analyzing these factors to ascertain which of these are the most binding constraints on growth. As the analysis above reveals, all factors (including market distortions and policy wedges) are likely to matter for growth and welfare. The challenge is to identify the one that provides the largest positive direct effect, so that even after taking into account second-best interactions and indirect effects, the net impact of a policy change is beneficial (and hopefully sizeable).

It helps to divide the factors affecting growth into two categories.

High Cost of Financing Domestic Investment

This is a case in which growth is low because, for any return on investment, accumulation is kept down by a high ρ. Stretching definitions slightly, we can interpret ρ as the rate of interest relevant for investment decisions in the economy in question. In turn, this could be connected to two kinds of policy problems:

- *Bad international finance*: country risk is still too high, foreign direct investment conditions unattractive, debt maturity and denomination increase macro risk, there remain excessive regulations on the capital account, etc.
- *Bad local finance*: when domestic capital markets work badly, collateral cannot be aggregated properly among domestic borrowers (Caballero and

Krishnamurty 2003) and the risk of banking crises and non-payment rises. Both of these increase the cost of capital, especially foreign capital.

Low Private Return to Domestic Investment

The other component of the growth equation is given by the private expected return on domestic investment, given $r\ (1 - \tau)$. A low such return can be due to:

- *High* τ: high tax rates and/or inefficient tax structure and/or high expected expropriation risk.
- *High* θ: large externalities, spillovers, coordination failures.
- *Low* α: low productivity, too little technology adoption or 'self-discovery,' weak public incentives.
- *Low* x: insufficient human capital, inadequate infrastructure, high transport, telecommunications, or shipping costs.

Moving Down the Multilemma

The tree then naturally organizes the policy questions, which can be asked in logical order. Is the problem one of inadequate returns to investment, inadequate private appropriability of the returns, or inadequate access to finance?

If it is a case of low returns to investment, is that due to insufficient supply of complementary factors of production (such as human capital or infrastructure)? Or is it due to poor access to appropriate technologies? If it is a case of poor appropriability, is it due to high taxation, poor property rights and contract enforcement, labor–capital conflicts, or learning externalities?

Or alternatively: if it is a case of poor finance, are the problems with domestic or external financial markets?

Moving down the branches of the decision tree is tantamount to discarding candidates for the most binding constraint on growth. The overarching lesson from our theoretical analysis is that it is this constraint, once identified, that deserves the most attention from policymakers.

Country Experiences: Identifying the Binding Constraints

We now have a framework to think of growth diagnostics. In this section we apply our approach to three countries with three very different growth experiences: Brazil, El Salvador, and the Dominican Republic.

The first two countries have had lackluster growth in spite of quite impressive reforms. The last had a sustained period of very rapid growth triggered by

Table 15.1. GDP Growth Rates

Country	Average GDP (% real change pa)			
	1998–2003	1993–2003	1990–2000	1980–2000
Brazil	1.4	2.7	2.7	2.7
Dominican Republic	4.8	5.1	4.8	4.3
EL Salvador	2.6	3.7	4.6	1.5
OECD (Agg.)	2.3	2.4	2.7	2.9
United States	3.0	3.2	3.2	3.3

Source: Economist Intelligence Unit.

rather modest reforms, but more recently has stumbled into a financial crisis from which it has yet to extricate itself fully.

Both Brazil and El Salvador made major efforts at dealing with their perceived problems during the 1990s. Brazil returned to democracy in the 1980s, started opening up its economy in the early 1990s, stopped mega inflation in the mid-1990s through exchange rate based stabilization, implemented privatization and financial reform, and after 1999 was able to maintain price stability while floating the currency and improving its fiscal surplus. El Salvador stopped its civil war, negotiated successful peace agreements, reformed its judiciary and police, stabilized prices, opened up the economy, privatized utilities and social security, and improved social services. Both countries underwent a brief period of decent growth—or should we say recovery—but in the last five years growth has been quite lackluster. As Table 15.1 indicates, in spite of the improvements in the political and policy framework over the 1993–2003 decade, Brazil grew more slowly than the US and barely 0.3 percentage points faster than the OECD average, in spite of the fact that its rate of demographic growth—and the rate at which its working age population expands—is over 1 percentage point per year higher. In other words, there was no catch-up or convergence. Moreover, both economies slowed down quite significantly in the 1998–2003 period. And future prospects look modest. In the context of a very favorable external environment and coming back from three years of stagnant GDP per capita, which should have left underutilized resources, Brazil was barely able to grow at 5.1 percent in 2004, a rate which was clearly above its sustainable level, as it involved a reduction in the rate of unemployment by over 1.2 percentage points (see Table 15.2). In 2005 and 2006, it slowed down to less than 3 percent growth. El Salvador grew at 2 percent in 2003–4 and barely averaged 3 percent in 2005–2007. The obvious question is, why? What is keeping these economies from converging towards higher levels of income in spite of its policy improvements? What is the growth diagnostic? What should the authorities focus on in each country?

Table 15.2. Brazil: Basic Macroeconomic Indicators

	1998	1999	2000	2001	2002	2003	2004e	2005f
GDP (real annual %-chg)	0.1	0.8	4.4	1.3	1.9	0.5	5.1	3.2
Inflation (CPI, annual var. in %)	1.7	8.9	6	7.7	12.5	9.3	7.6	6
Exchange rate (real/US$)	1.208	1.789	1.955	2.32	3.533	2.889	2.650	2.850
	–	–	–	–				
Current account (US$ m)	33,416	25,335	24,225	23,215	−7,637	4,177	11,700	−400
Trade balance (US$ m)	−6,606	−1,252	−751	2,651	13,121	24,793	33,700	24,500
Capital account (US$ m)	29,702	17,319	19,326	27,052	8,004	5,111		
CA/GDP	−4.2	−4.7	−4.0	−4.6	−1.7	0.8		
Unemployment (%)	6.3	6.3	4.8	10.6	10.5	10.9	9.7	9.1
Fiscal balance (% of GDP)	−7.5	−5.8	−3.6	−3.6	−4.6	−5.1	−2.8	−3.3
Bond market (EMBI over UST)	1,226	632	746	896	1,446	463	583	
BOVESPA (% in US$)	−44.1	61.6	−14.2	−21.8	−33.8	102.9		
BOVESPA (% nominal Reais)	−33.5	151.9	−10.7	−11.0	−17.0	97.3		
Interest rate (SELIC rate in %)	33.0	21.0	15.4	18.1	25	16.5	17.75	17
Real ex post interest rate (SELIC)	30.8	11.1	8.9	9.7	11.1	6.6	9.4	10.4
Multilateral real exchange rate[1]	77.6	106.6	106.1	123.4	170.7	146.1	140.8	
Investment rate	21.1	20.2	21.5	21.2	19.8			
Savings rate	16.8	15.4	17.3	16.8	18.5			
GDP in US$	787.9	536.6	602.2	509.8	459.4	506.8		

Notes: [1] Media rate of the Brazilian currency in relation to the currencies of 15 countries, corrected for consumer price inflation in each country and weighted by the participation of these countries in total Brazilian exports to this group of countries. The Brazilian CPI is by FIPE. June 1994 = 100, i.e., just before the adoption of the Real, which happened on July 1, 1994.

It will be useful to contrast El Salvador and Brazil with the Dominican Republic, a country with a much less impressive reform effort and with significantly weaker institutions. Its reform history starts with a currency crisis in the late 1980s addressed with an effective stabilization policy and some trade liberalization, but the reforms were nowhere as significant as in the other two countries. Nonetheless, the Dominican Republic achieved more than a decade of very fast growth interrupted only in 2002 by a banking crisis.

We will argue that Brazil and El Salvador look like a case of wholesale reform that eliminate some distortions but not necessarily the binding constraint. The Dominican Republic, by contrast, found a way around that binding constraint with minor reform effort. Its eventual crash indicates that as growth proceeds, the shadow prices of other constraints—such as that of weak institutions—increase and these may become eventually the binding constraint on growth.

Brazil versus El Salvador

Brazil and El Salvador are obviously very different countries in terms of size, history and structure. But they share one feature: lackluster growth in spite of significant reform. The case of El Salvador is particularly puzzling: broad ranging reforms were associated with a short lived growth spurt and then relative stagnation since 1996.[4] Let us apply our framework to see if Brazil and El Salvador share a similar diagnostic.

For a long time, promoting saving and capital accumulation was the dominant idea in development policy. Under this view, low growth could be explained by an insufficient increase in the supply of factors of production, physical capital in particular. While 'capital fundamentalism' has long been discarded (along with Soviet style planning), it has been replaced more recently with a focus on human capital. Increasing the supply of human capital—through a greater health and education effort—is expected to lead to a faster accumulation of these assets and hence to a higher level of income. Can the poor growth performance in Brazil and El Salvador be explained by

[4] A recent World Bank study (Loayza et al. 2002) implicitly finds that the decline in the rate of growth in El Salvador after 1996 is difficult to explain. In their model, improvements in secondary school enrollment, availability of private domestic credit, the increase in openness and in phone lines, the low inflation rate, and the absence of banking crises should have compensated for the increase in the initial level of income, the declining output gap, the increased real appreciation of the currency, and the adverse terms of trade shifts. This should have left growth unchanged in the second half of the 1990s relative to the first half. Instead, growth declined by 2.8 percent. Hence, they are unable to account for the growth decline. In line with this, López (2003) attributes the growth decline to 'temporary,' business cycle related factors—an unsustainable boom in the early 1990s followed by a pricking of the bubble in the second half. This leaves open the question of why the economy has not performed better in the first decade of the new century and why prospects are not more encouraging.

Table 15.3. Savings, Investment, and the Current Account (as percent of GDP, average 1990–2000)

Country	Gross national savings	Gross fixed capital formation	Current account balance
Brazil	18.7	20.8	−2.2
Dominican Republic	18.9	22.2	−3.2
EL Salvador	15.6	17.4	−1.8

Note: Remittances are counted as part of national income.
Source: World Penn Tables.

low saving and education effort? Can these variables explain the difference with the Dominican Republic?

On the face of it, there are two elements that make this argument compelling for El Salvador and Brazil. Both countries have low savings and investment rates (Table 15.3). Second, both countries have relatively low educational attainment. The investment rate has averaged around 20.8 percent and 17.4 percent for Brazil and El Salvador respectively, during the decade of the 1990s. The saving rate in the 1990s (including the remittances as part of national income) was even lower as both countries ran current account deficits which averaged 2.2 percent in Brazil and 1.8 percent in El Salvador.

A similar comment can be made about human capital. The supply of education in both countries—measured as the average years of schooling of the labor force—is at the bottom of Latin American countries (Figure 15.2),

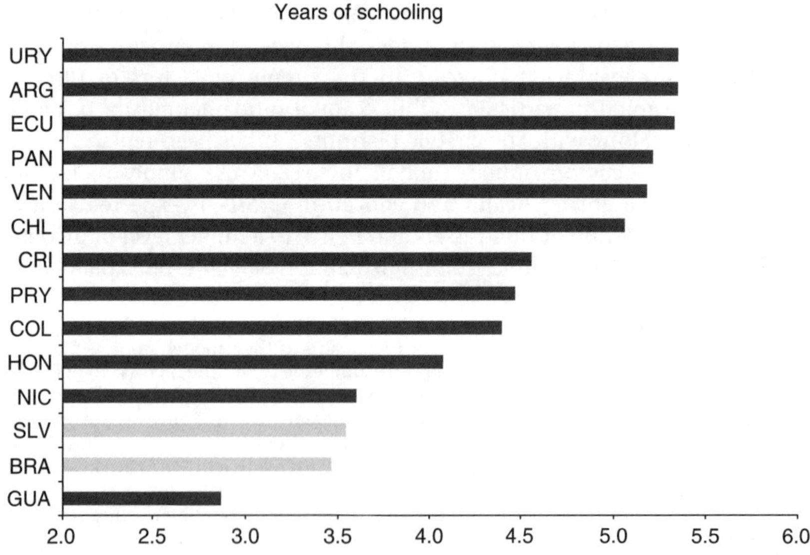

Figure 15.2. Average Years of Schooling of 12-Year-old Children (circa 1998)
Source: IDB.

although it has been growing in both countries at over one year per decade in the 1990s.

When is lack of an adequate saving and educational effort a basic reason for the country's stagnant growth performance? For this story to be plausible, one should be able to observe high returns to both capital and schooling. The economy must be willing to gobble up additional resources, but be prevented from doing so because these are just not adequately provided. Hence, we should observe the tightness of the constraint in the price society is willing to pay for the scarce resource.

Let us deal first with savings. If savings were scarce, one would observe a high foreign debt or a high current account deficit—a signal that the country is using or has already used up its access to foreign savings to the hilt, given the paucity of domestic savings. Alternatively, one would observe a high willingness to remunerate savings through high interest rates to depositors or government bondholders.

Here Brazil and El Salvador provide completely different stories. Time and again, Brazil has had serious difficulties with its balance of payments. As Table 15.2 shows, the country was running a current account deficit in 1998 of US$33.4 billion or 4.2 percent of a rather overvalued GDP. However, with a debt already at 460 percent of exports, the scarcity of savings was reflected in a spread on external bonds of 1,226 basis points and in a real ex post overnight (SELIC) interest rate of over 30 percent. In January 1999 the country was forced to devalue: the real multilateral exchange rate depreciated by 37.4 percent in 1999. The current account deficit was reduced in dollars to an average of US$24 billion per annum for the following three years (1999–2001). The spread on external bonds averaged a still hefty but lower 758 basis points and the domestic real ex post overnight interest rate declined to a still high 10 percent. This amount of foreign borrowing also proved unsustainable, and a new balance of payments crisis ensued in 2002. The spread on external bonds averaged 2,160 basis points during a three week period in August of 2002 and averaged 1,446 for the year, in spite of massive international official support lead by the International Monetary Fund. The real exchange rate depreciated by an additional 38.3 percent in 2002. Lack of external financing, a domestic recession, and real depreciation forced the current account to finally turn around, moving to surplus in 2003.

In short, the country has been trying to cope with the paucity of domestic savings by both attempting to attract foreign savings and by remunerating domestic savings at very high real rates. Over time, the country has borrowed so much from abroad that it has been perceived as being on the brink of bankruptcy, (as indicated by the spread on its foreign debt). In addition, Brazil's growth performance has moved pari passu with the tightness of the external constraint. When the external constraint is relaxed—say, because of an increase in the general appetite for emerging market risk or because of higher commodity prices, as in recent months—the economy is able to grow. But when the external constraint tightens real interest rates increase, the currency depreciates, and growth declines. This suggests that growth is limited by the availability of savings.

The situation in El Salvador is very different. In the past the country has not used up its access to foreign savings: its total gross external debt stands at less than 30 percent of GDP and it enjoys an investment grade credit rating. Nor is the country currently using foreign savings rapidly: the current account deficit has averaged 2 percent of GDP in the past five years. Nor is the country willing to remunerate savings at high rates: it needs to pay among the lowest interest rates in the region to attract demand for deposits or government bonds. Its banks have more liquidity than domestic credit demand can soak up, and are actively lending to enterprises in the neighboring countries in the region. Figure 15.3 shows the average real lending rate for 16 Latin American countries for October 2001, as reported by FELABAN. Brazil and El Salvador are at the opposite extremes: with El Salvador exhibiting the lowest lending rates while Brazil exhibits the highest. And perhaps the most telling indicator that El Salvador is not saving constrained is that the external savings that the dramatic boost in remittances has enabled have not been converted into investment. As Figure 15.4 shows, the decline in domestic savings has substituted almost one-for-one for the increase in remittances, with no discernible effect on the total investment effort. So there are no symptoms that El Salvador's growth is constrained by lack of savings.

In fact, Brazil and El Salvador are also at opposite extremes in terms of the cost of domestic financial intermediation. In a comparative study by Barth et al. (2001) the net interest margin was reported to be 11.5 percent in Brazil and 3.7 percent in El Salvador while the overhead costs were 9.8 in Brazil and 3.2 percent in El Salvador. In spite of this, credit to the private sector was almost the same in both countries (25.8 in Brazil and 27.5 in El Salvador).

All this suggests that El Salvador is a country where investment is constrained by low returns to capital, not by low availability of savings. The country invests little not because it cannot mobilize the resources to invest—although savings are low—but because the country does not find productive investments in which to deploy the resources. There is ample access to foreign borrowing, deposit rates are low and intermediation costs are among the lowest in Latin America. In terms of our decision tree in Figure 15.1, it seems clear that El Salvador is a low return country.

Brazil, by contrast, is a high return country. In spite of very high overnight real interests and very high intermediation costs, investment has outstripped domestic savings and the country has used its capacity to borrow abroad from the rest of the world to the hilt. Clearly, the investment rate in Brazil and credit to the private sector would be dramatically higher if the prevailing cost of capital were that of El Salvador.

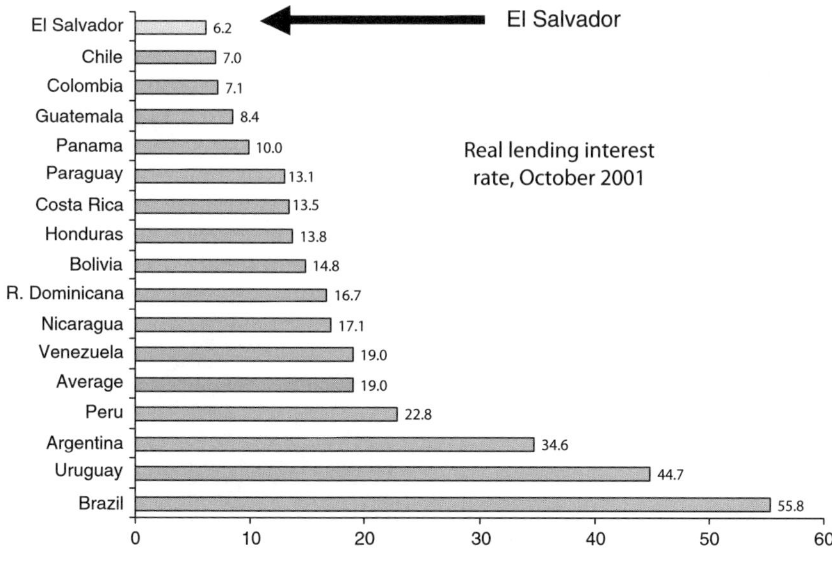

Source: FELABAN

Figure 15.3. Lending Rates in Latin America (October 2001)

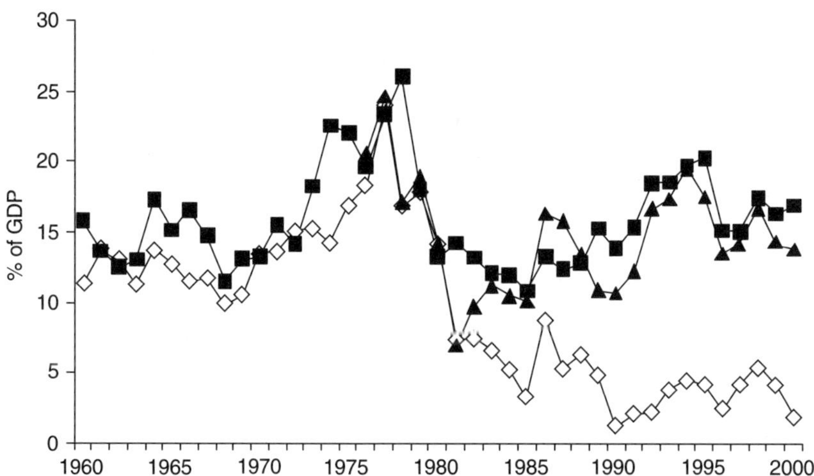

Figure 15.4. Domestic Savings, National Savings (including remittances), and Investment (as % of GDP)

Notes: National savings equals gross fixed capital formation plus the current account surplus. —◇— Gross domestic savings, —■— Gross capital formation, —▲— I + CA.

Source: World Penn Tables.

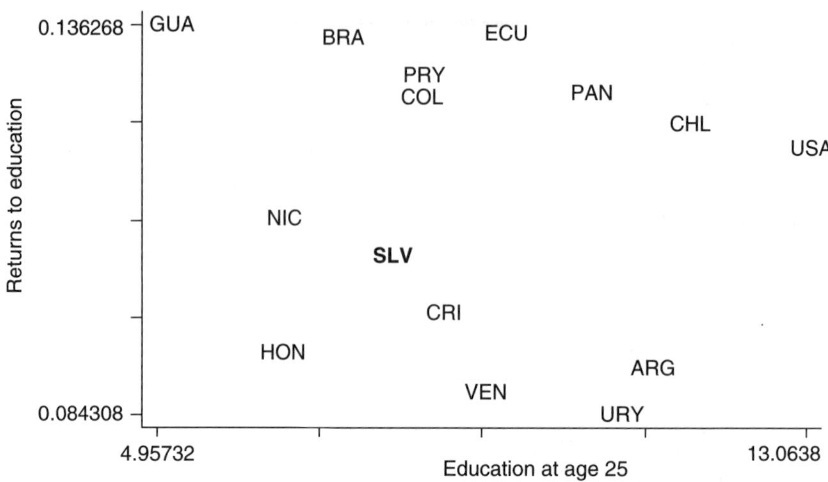

Figure 15.5. Returns to Education and Years of Schooling

Source: Calculations based on surveys collected by the Inter-American Development Bank.

A similar contrast between the two countries emerges when looking at education. If education were the constraint on growth one would expect to see high returns to the few who get educated. Figure 15.5 shows a scattergram of returns to education and years of schooling for a sample of 14 Latin American countries and the US. The picture that emerges is clear: while the years of schooling of the labor force are low both in El Salvador and in Brazil, the returns are quite different. Brazil has just about the highest returns in Latin America while El Salvador is below the regional average. Hence, the evidence suggests that lack of educational effort is not at present a principal source of low growth in El Salvador, while it may well be part of the story in Brazil.

What is at stake here is whether a sudden increase in the supply of more educated citizens is likely to unleash significantly faster growth at the present time. If growth is being constrained by other factors, other things equal, more education is likely to lead mainly to lower returns to human capital, not to higher incomes. In this respect, Brazil and El Salvador look quite different.

Hence, the challenge in El Salvador is to identify what constraints may be behind the low returns to investment while the challenge in Brazil is to explain why the country is constrained in external markets and why domestic savings do not rise to exploit the large returns to investment.

Misdiagnoses in El Salvador

As Figure 15.1 indicates, the low investment in El Salvador may be the consequence of many potential distortions that keep private returns low, even if social returns may be high. One possibility is that the social returns are not privately appropriable. Appropriability problems can emerge from many fronts. We can group these into four major areas:

- High taxes: actual or expected explicit taxes make private returns low and hence investment unattractive, although social returns may be high.
- Macroeconomic imbalances: unsustainable fiscal or external accounts usually presage the need for implicit taxation or expropriation through surprise inflation, depreciation, default, or banking crises. In anticipation, country risk and interest rates rise, further depressing investment.
- Poor definition and protection of property rights: productive investments may be limited by the expectation that investors will not be able to appropriate the returns because their claims are ill-defined or poorly protected, through corruption, judicial manipulation, or outright crime. Measures to avoid these problems create additional high transaction costs, which may render investment unattractive.
- Uncertainty: doubts—deriving from political or other factors—regarding the commitment to the current rules of the game create excessive risks about the environment in which projects will evolve.

The issues involved here are multiple and complex. We will review them quickly and assess their relative importance in El Salvador.

CONCERNS ABOUT EXCESSIVELY HIGH TAXATION

This is not a problem that can explain low growth in El Salvador. The country has a very moderate income tax with a marginal rate at 25 percent, well below the rate that global corporations pay in their home country. Moreover, the country has eliminated the double taxation of capital. The value-added tax, at 13 percent, is moderate by regional standard and a fraction of that applied in Western Europe. Tariffs are low and the economy is one of the most open in the region.

In fact, it is easier to argue that El Salvador may be suffering from the opposite problem. Tax revenue may be so low that the government lacks the resources to provide an adequate supply of public goods needed to make economic activity productive. The *Global Competitiveness Report* of 2002–03, which views smaller government spending as a virtue, ranks El Salvador in 14th place in a sample of 80 countries in terms of low government spending. Unfortunately, the world leader in this indicator is Haiti. Even within Latin American countries, El Salvador's public spending appears low. This may be a reason why the country ranks poorly in measures of the quality of infrastructure (especially in roads, rail, and ports) and public education.

We conclude that excessive current or expected explicit taxation is not a sensible explanation of El Salvador's development challenge.

CONCERNS ABOUT MACRO STABILITY

When the economy is on an unsustainable path—for example, when the country as a whole or the government are accumulating obligations at a rate that will compromise their ability to abide by them—participants in the economy know that the current rules of the game will need to be abandoned and act to protect themselves from the expected changes rather than engage in productive investments. Problems of macro stability can be generated by imbalances arising from different areas. The fiscal accounts may be in deficit and public debt may be increasing faster than the capacity to service it. Longer-term fiscal commitments, in particular the actuarial liabilities of the government vis-à-vis the pension system, may bankrupt an otherwise solvent government. Monetary policy may be too loose causing a loss of international reserves and an eventual large depreciation. Banks may be taking excessive risk, which can end up in a disruptive crisis that often weakens both fiscal and monetary stability. The country may be running large external imbalances that translate into reserve loss or a rapidly rising external debt and signal the need for eventual currency depreciation. The real exchange rate may be misaligned, limiting the profitability and growth of export and import competing sectors.

The question is to what extent the relatively disappointing growth of the last few years can be interpreted mainly as the outcome of limitations on these fronts. It is worth noting that the *Global Competitiveness Report* 2002–03 ranked El Salvador as number 33 out of 80 countries in the world in terms of its macro environment, well ahead of all Central American countries and most Latin American countries, except for Chile. Underpinning this ranking was the country's low inflation rate, low bank spreads, good access to credit, moderate fiscal deficit, small government, and good credit rating. While macro problems may appear in the future, especially if not enough attention is paid to them, it seems reasonable to argue that El Salvador's low growth in the past five to six years cannot be easily explained in terms of macroeconomic imbalances. More likely, the puzzle is precisely why is it that a relatively good macro environment has not generated faster growth.

CONCERNS ABOUT CONTRACT ENFORCEMENT AND PROPERTY RIGHTS

The role of institutions in development has received increasing attention in recent years. Could it be that El Salvador is being held back by an inadequate institutional environment?

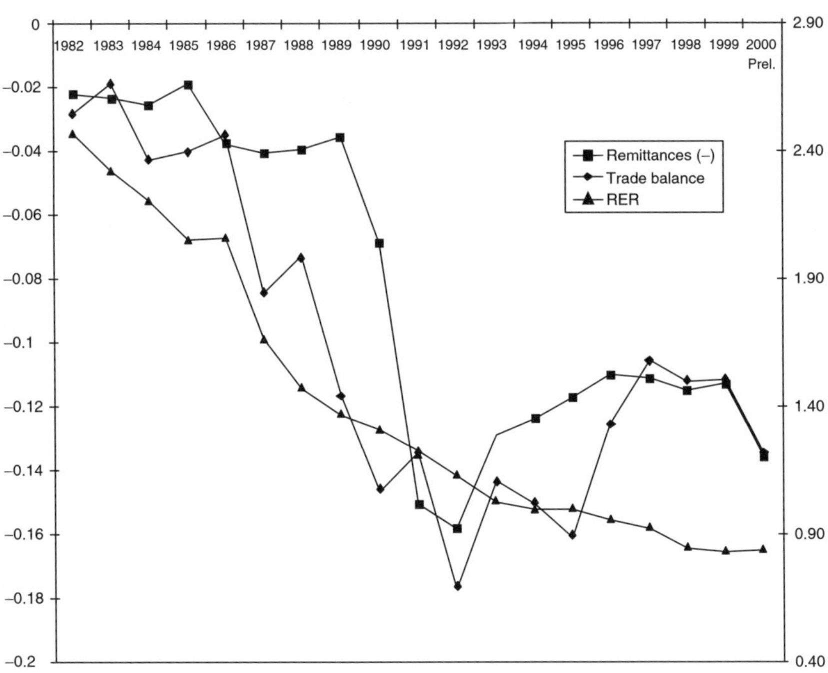

Figure 15.6. Real Exchange Rate, Remittances, and the Trade Balance

Our answer is negative. The Heritage Foundation ranked El Salvador 17th in the world in 2002 in terms of 'economic freedom' and third in Latin America (behind only Chile and the Bahamas). According to Lopez (2003: 2), El Salvador 'always [ranks] near the top in terms of the World Bank's Country Policy and Institutional Assessment ratings.' On the financial front, El Salvador ranks very favorably in indicators associated with credit availability and cost. This is telling because financial markets are particularly sensitive to problems of contract enforcement. Moreover, in 2003 the World Economic Forum ranked El Salvador third among Latin American countries in terms of low corruption and low tax evasion (after much wealthier Chile and Uruguay) and second in the efficiency with which it uses its public funds (after Chile)—see Figure 15.6.

If anything, El Salvador looks like a country with very good institutions for its low level of income. In fact, it ranks better than Brazil in most indicators in spite of the fact that it has a level of per capita income, which at US$3,530 for 2003 is less than half that of Brazil (US$7,720). It is hard to argue that it is the bad institutional framework that is keeping returns to capital low.

INFRASTRUCTURE, LABOR, AND REAL EXCHANGE RATE MISALIGNMENT

Other stories in our decision tree involve rigid labor markets and bad infrastructure. Here again, it is hard to make the case that these factors are critical to the growth story. Electricity and telecommunications have been privatized and have undergone a major expansion. While the country ranks low in the *Global Competitiveness Report* in terms of roads, ports, and rail infrastructure, there have also been important recent improvements in these areas with scant impact on the investment rate of other sectors.

The same can be said of labor institutions. The country has relatively low restriction to hiring and firing, and low payroll taxes. These limited sources of rigidity cannot account for low investment returns.

However, the country does have a high minimum wage in relation to the average wage. In addition, the country is dollarized, which means that the exchange rate cannot move to clear the labor market. The real exchange rate appreciated quite dramatically between 1974 and 1994 but has remained stable in the decade since then (Figure 15.6). Such a long-term stable level in the context of low current account deficits cannot be anything other than an equilibrium phenomenon (as the labor market should clear in less than a decade!). In part the appreciation reflects the rise in remittances, which represented 17.6 percent of GDP in 2002. These external flows increase the supply of foreign exchange and in addition are caused by a contraction in the domestic supply of labor. Both effects tend to appreciate the real exchange rate. Hence, even if the exchange rate is misaligned by some measures, it does not seem to be unsustainable or to be generating fears of a currency crisis down the road. In this sense it does not seem like a central explanation for the mediocre growth of recent years.

INNOVATION AND THE DEMAND FOR INVESTMENT

The third element in our growth framework is productivity and innovation. What we have in mind here is not innovation and R&D in the sense that these terms are used in the advanced economies, but the ability to identify and generate higher productivity activities within the Salvadoran context. These are new, non-traditional products that could be profitably produced in El Salvador, but which do not currently attract investment because of various market shortcomings (see Hausmann and Rodrik (2003) for a general discussion).

El Salvador is facing bad news in its traditional sectors, and the speed at which it comes up with new ideas in other areas has not been able to compensate. The country has lost its cotton industry completely. Coffee is in crisis. Nobody has been able to make a decent living in the international sugar market. These 'ideas,' after creating hundreds of thousands of jobs in

El Salvador, are in some sense dying. To achieve growth, new productive ideas must take their place. The speed at which these ideas appear and their economic significance are critical. The only important new sector has been the maquila industry and this barely represents US$480 million (slightly more than 3 percent of GDP) in net exports. The absence of new ideas explains why the expected return to current investment ideas is low, and why investment and growth are low. It is not because of lack of savings. It is not mainly because of fear of taxation, expropriation, or fraud. It is because the actual real returns to investment are low given the absence of profitable investment opportunities.

El Salvador has opened up to the world, stimulated foreign investment, and endeavored to protect property rights. Is that not the way to encourage innovation and secure sufficiently rapid technological advances? The Salvadoran experience suggests that the answer may well be negative. This may be due to the fact that the innovation that matters to countries such as El Salvador—identifying and operating profitable new activities—is substantially more problematic than this simple picture assumes.

The problem with innovation is that it is hard to create but easy to copy or imitate. This means that part (or most) of the returns to innovation spill over to other people. This reduces the expected private return to innovation and hence may cause it to be inadequately supplied. In response to this, the world has opted to consider the output of innovators as an item of property that needs protection: hence the development of patents, copyrights, and other forms of intellectual property rights protection. These grant monopoly power over an idea to its creator.

The development process in less advanced countries is largely about structural change: it can be characterized as one in which an economy finds out—'self-discovers'—what it can be good at, out of the many products and processes that already exist. The problem is that the ideas that are valuable at low levels of development are typically not patentable. For example, the idea that an Ethiopian seed—coffee—could be planted in the hills of Central America was of historic importance, leading to a dramatic transformation of the fabric of society, but yet not patentable.

New ideas that lead to new sectors may require specific public capital or changes in rules and regulations that were designed in ignorance of their negative consequences to the sector. Coffee requires, not education, research, and training in general, but rather in the *specifics* of coffee. Road and infrastructure networks need to take account of the areas where the new activities can expand. New forms of contracting, transacting, and financing may be required. The whole maquila industry requires a specific form of custom treatment.

The problems of self-discovery in tradable activities are likely to be potentially more important and the payoffs to addressing them much larger. They are more important because, contrary to non-tradable activities, in which the first domestic supplier is by definition a monopolist, in the tradable sector, any new firm in a given country will start operating in a market where foreign suppliers already exist, limiting the rents of discovery. The payoffs can be larger in the tradable sector because the productive ideas can be scaled up to supply the world market, not just the more limited local market to which non-tradable activities are restricted by definition. In conclusion, problems with self-discovery seem to be the binding restriction on growth in El Salvador. That may well be the appropriate focus of policy in a development strategy for this country.[5]

Explaining Slow Growth in Brazil

As opposed to El Salvador, Brazil is not in such dire need of ideas on where to invest. It has more ideas than investable funds. That is why the balance between supply and demand for these funds occurs at such a high interest rate.

Misdiagnosis in Brazil

This first analysis clearly eliminates a set of potential diagnoses and policies from the list of priorities. Brazil suffers from an inadequate business environment, high taxes, high prices for public services, low supply of infrastructure, insecure property rights and judicial enforcement, and inadequate education relative to some best practice benchmark. But our framework would discard them as priority areas for policy reform. This is because all these factors should depress private investment by keeping private returns low. But in spite of the sub-par atmosphere, private returns are very high and investment is constrained by the inability of the country to mobilize enough domestic and foreign savings to finance the existing investment demand at reasonable interest rates. If the country were to embark on a campaign to improve the business environment it would make investment even more attractive and consequently would increase investment demand. In addition, it may improve the productivity of the projects that get undertaken (although this is not necessarily so). However, in the first instance, this would not relax the constraint on savings, which is where the binding constraint resides. In fact, some reforms that could improve the business environment, such as lowering taxes, reducing public sector prices, and improving infrastructure

[5] What policies can be designed to promote self-discovery in El Salvador is beyond the scope of this chapter, but is addressed in Fusades (2003) 'Oportunidades, seguridad, legitimidad: bases para el desarrollo.' See also Hausmann (2003) 'In Search of The Road Ahead: Identifying a Development Strategy for El Salvador Social Goals and Development Strategy', at: http://ksghome.harvard.edu/~rhausma/publication.htm and (2003) 'Discovering El Salvador's Production Potential', at: http://ksghome.harvard.edu/~rhausma/publication.htm

and education may in fact lower public savings and thus reduce total savings. In addition, the increased demand for investment will translate mostly into a higher real interest rate, which will complicate public debt dynamics and generate more adverse selection in private financial markets (and hence, potentially worse investments). The overall health of the economy may show little improvement or could even deteriorate. This is a case in which doing reforms that are apparently good may cause overall negative effects given the way these policies interact with other existing distortions, through the second-best logic described above.[6]

THE PROBLEM WITH EXTERNAL SAVINGS

As argued above, Brazil has often been rationed in international capital markets, to which it has been paying a hefty premium to access funds. These markets have been concerned by the fact that the country already owes an uncomfortably large amount of money and hence asset prices tend to go up when markets hear about positive innovations to the current account, implying that the country will stop its borrowing binge. Hence, the recent large reduction in country risk that took place between 2002 and 2005 (Table 15.2) did not coincide with an increase in external savings (i.e., an increase in the current account deficit) as would be the case if the dominant change was an increase in the supply of external savings. Instead, the decline in country risk coincided with a rapid decline in foreign savings, indicating that it was the demand curve for external savings that did most of the work. Hence, country risk seems to move in tandem with the demand for external savings as would be the case when there is a highly inelastic supply of external savings.

Models of sovereign risk assume that what makes international lending enforceable is some punishment technology for opportunistic behavior by the borrower. Since Eaton and Gersovitz (1981), a typical assumption is that trade sanctions are the typical penalty that lenders can impose and hence the volume of international trade is related to the credit ceiling lenders would like to avoid breaching.

In this context, Brazil has been a very closed economy with almost twice the population of Mexico but less than half of its exports. This means that its credit ceiling should be limited by this fact. While the export to GDP ratio has risen in recent years this has been due more to the decline in the dollar value of GDP at market prices than to the increase in exports, especially until 2002. If we take GDP at its purchasing power parity, exports are below 10 percent of output. Hence, while the external debt looks high as a share of GDP, it looks astronomical as a share of exports.

[6] Interestingly, the World Bank in its 2002 *New Growth Agenda for Brazil* came to the opposite view stressing the importance of improving the investment climate in Brazil in order to trigger higher growth.

One can imagine a policy to make foreign investors even more eager to lend by raising the credit ceiling. However, ceteris paribus this is bound to lead to a short lived acceleration of growth until the economy reaches its new credit ceiling. Hence, we conclude that while the external constraint clearly binds, it is a reflection of the fact that the country has already used its borrowing capacity to the hilt. Some relaxation of that borrowing capacity would lead to faster growth in the transition to the new credit ceiling. But clearly, the underlying problem must be the conflict between the relatively healthy demand for investment in the context of inadequate domestic savings.

EXPLAINING INADEQUATE DOMESTIC SAVINGS

A more sustained relaxation of the constraint on growth would involve an increase in the domestic savings rate. This opens the question about what is keeping it low at present, in spite of high real interest rates.

To search for an answer it is useful to note some fiscal characteristics of Brazil.

- At 34 percent of GDP, the country has by far the highest public revenue share in Latin America and one of the highest in the developing world.
- In spite of this, public savings have been negative by more than 2 percent of GDP: public investment has averaged less than 2 percent of GDP between 1999 and 2002, while the fiscal deficit averaged 4.4 percent.
- To achieve its high level of taxation the country is forced into using quite distortionary levies at very high rates, such as a cascading sales tax, a tax on financial transactions, and very hefty payroll taxes, which Heckman and Pages (2002) estimate at 37.6 percent of wages.
- In spite of the extraordinary level of taxation, fiscal balance is precarious. According to the IMF, general government debt as a share of GDP stood at 95.1 percent in 2002, while the overall deficit averaged 4.3 percent of GDP between 1999 and 2004.
- The high taxes and low savings reflect a very high level of current spending and transfers. For example, social security expenditures stand at 8.5 percent of GDP, which is unusually high given the country's relatively young demography. They reflect the country's low retirement age and generous terms for its mostly middle class public and formal sector employees.

The high taxation and negative public savings must have an adverse effect on aggregate savings: it reduces the disposable income of the formal private sector and the resources are not used to increase public savings. This may be an important part of the explanation of the low saving equilibrium. In addition, since the equilibrium happens at a high real interest rate, the positive effect high interest rates may have on stimulating private savings is offset by the negative effect it has on public savings as the cost of servicing the inherited stock of public debt is increased.

High taxation and negative savings reflects the existence of a very high level of entitlements and/or waste, and a high level of inherited debt. In the context of the model presented in the previous section, this forces the country to choose among a very high tax rate, high public sector prices, low investment in infrastructure, and low subsidies for human capital. All these things are bad for growth because they depress the private return to capital. But returns are already very high and investment is constrained by lack of loanable funds. If high taxation and the paucity of public goods were in themselves the binding constraint, the private return to investment would be low and equilibrium between savings and investment would be established at a lower return to capital. This is an important distinction because it goes to the heart of the policy question about what elements to emphasize in the reform process: should it be the impact of the reform on aggregate savings (such as fiscal consolidation) or should it be on the implications for private returns to capital (such as lower taxation)? In this interpretation, the problem of Brazil is that too heavy a burden of transfers and too high an inherited stock of public debt mean that a very large part of national income gets taxed away, depressing national savings.

Two factors may amplify or multiply this distortion. First, consider the cost of financial intermediation. As the deposit interest rate goes up, intermediation margins tend to increase for several reasons. This is caused in part by the cost of bank reserves, since the cost of holding reserves goes up with the deposit interest rate and must be recouped through a higher lending spread. This is further aggravated by the fact that a country with a high fiscal burden will optimally use a higher level of reserve requirement in its optimal tax strategy. Hence, the reserve requirements would tend to be higher. As the loan rates go up, so does the probability of default, causing a further rise in lending rates. This is exacerbated by adverse selection. So the fact that Brazil has high intermediation margins, as previously noted, may be related to its fundamental distortion.

Second, fiscal stress may limit external savings as foreign investors may fear expropriation. This limits access to foreign savings for the whole society and thus will aggravate the scarcity of aggregate savings.

What should the focus of policy be in this case? The goal is to improve national savings. One alternative would be to lower government entitlements and waste with the resources used to increase public savings. The direct effect would be a higher level of aggregate savings, a lower interest rate, better public debt dynamics, lower intermediation margins, and could potentially have a positive effect on foreign savings if it is related or affected by fears of fiscal insolvency. Lowering the burden of pensions through a social security reform may be an effective way to achieve this.

In the absence of this first-best policy, the question is whether a pro-growth strategy can be based on an apparently anti-growth set of policy measures such as increases in taxation and public prices, and cuts in infrastructure and human capital subsidies. The analysis above would suggest a positive response. The microeconomic inefficiencies of taxation and sub-optimal spending structures are not binding because reducing them would increase the returns to capital but would not generate the means to exploit those returns.

If the country can get into a more accelerated growth path and if 'waste' does not grow with GDP, the economy may outgrow its burdens and be able to gradually improve its tax and spending system as fiscal resources become more abundant. In this respect, the fiscal strategy followed by the country until now, in spite of the microeconomic inefficiencies it generates, may perhaps be the best way to go.

The Dominican Republic: Growth and Then Crash

The Caribbean is an unlikely place to find a success story. The region once seemed naturally destined to produce sugar cane, the source of its wealth since the seventeenth century. With the heavy protection of sugar in Europe and the US, the Caribbean lost its obvious export crop. States in the region are too small to embark on import substitution industrialization although some tried with disastrous consequences. The Dominican Republic had been lucky because in addition to sugar it had a gold mine. However, this resource became exhausted in the 1980s. The country had to reinvent itself and it was not obvious how.

The country had quite precarious political and bureaucratic institutions. The difficulties of the 1980s had wreaked havoc with its macro balance. A balance of payments crisis erupted in 1991 and the country dealt with it swiftly and accompanied it with modest structural reforms: a unification of its exchange rate regime and some trade liberalization. This triggered a sustained period of high growth that essentially lasted a decade until it was quickly brought to an end in the 2002 banking crisis. Yet even in a period of extreme financial turmoil in 2002–04, the economy did not contract, as happened in most other places in the region, namely, Argentina, Colombia, Ecuador, Uruguay, and Venezuela.

What explains its success and its current problems? Why did the achievement of macro balance and some reform lead to such fast growth in the Dominican Republic and not in other places? Ex post, the answer seems to be in the importance of three main drivers of growth: tourism, maquila, and remittances.

Remittances tripled in the last decade to a level of US$2.1 billion in 2002 or 9.9 percent of GDP. Tourism did even better. It increased from US$0.7 billion in 1991 to US$2.5 billion in 2000 (11.8 percent of GDP). Net maquila exports per capita doubled to a level of about US$200 per capita in 2000–01, the highest in the Americas including NAFTA member, Mexico.

Now, these three engines of growth are dependent on some institutional setup. Tourism requires some level of investor, personal, and environmental security. While it would be ideal to assure these three elements for all sectors of the economy, relatively closed all-inclusive resorts can do with a more targeted provision of these public goods, using private security and infrastructure. So the country created an adequate environment for that industry to take off.

By the same token, maquila is an exception to the general laws that apply to other activities. With a sufficiently effective institutional framework for this sector, it can take off even if the rest of the economy is stranded with ineffective institutions and regulations.

In this sense, the Dominican Republic is a good example of an alternative path to institutional development. Such a path would involve listening to the institutional and public good requirements of sectors that see high potential returns and that can be scaled up significantly to become important. In other words, the reforms are geared at solving the specific institutional problems that potentially important new sectors face so as to increase their expected rate of return and allow an investment boom to start there.

As these 'enclave' sectors grow and generate employment and income, they contribute directly or indirectly to the tax base and to domestic intermediate demand. This is the time to try fixing up the bottlenecks in the rest of the economy. It resembles a game of curling that as the puck slides on the ice, the players work feverishly to polish the ice so that the puck keeps sliding forward. Trade liberalization will make the rest of the economy more like the maquila sector. Personal security and environmental standards can be upgraded in the rest of the country. This will bring benefits to all, including those tourists who might actually venture beyond the grounds of the resort.

Clearly, the problem with this strategy is that the economy might outgrow its relatively weak institutional setting. It is hard to know which institution will crack. It could be that economic success makes foreign lending available to the government without the budget institutions to keep fiscal discipline, as happened in many Latin American countries in the 1970s when they were showered for the first time with syndicated foreign loans. It could be that the stakes of the political game become so high that the political process gets disrupted.

None of this happened in the Dominican Republic. Fiscal balance was maintained and the political process became, if anything, more institutionalized. However, the financial system did grow very fast with the economic expansion and became more integrated to the rest of the world. Imposing prudential regulatory standard on rapidly expanding banks proved institutionally and politically difficult. Some banks were politically influential and as a group they were capable of blocking legislation and administrative actions by a technically and politically weak regulator. When September 11, 2001 brought a sudden stop to the flow of international tourism, a Ponzi scheme in the banking system was uncovered. Through some mix of limited institutional competence and inadequate political independence, managing this crisis involved converting over 20 percent of GDP in bank losses into the public debt.

As usual, these bank rescues involve drastic expansions of domestic credit by the central bank, which in the Dominican Republic had no international reserves with which to sterilize money creation. The exchange rate quickly depreciated from 17.8 R$/US$ in January 2003 to 34.9 R$/US$ in July of 2003 and 48.6 R$/US$ by June 2004. This massive depreciation caused an acceleration of inflation of over 65 percent in the year to June 2004.

These changes wreaked havoc with the fiscal accounts. The new debt issued by the central bank raised the quasi-fiscal deficit by over 2 percent of GDP. The depreciation increased the domestic resource cost of the foreign currency public debt. The domestic value of the public debt almost tripled from less than 20 percent of GDP to over 50 percent of GDP. In addition, a system of indirect subsidies for liquefied petroleum gas (LPG) and for electricity, which had prices fixed in pesos, became much more expensive to sustain. Unable to impose harsher adjustment measures in an already difficult situation, the government decided to limit price increases for these goods but this meant a level of fiscal subsidy that it was unable to pay. Massive shortages of electricity and gas ensued.

The country is still in the midst of this crisis, although there are some indications it may be pulling itself out. But the moral of the story is clear. Re-igniting growth may not require the infinite laundry list of reforms that have become the current consensus on best practices. But once the economy is on the path of growth, the onus is on policymakers to solve the institutional and other constraints that will inevitably become more binding.

Conclusions

Across the board reform packages have often failed to get countries growing again. The method for growth diagnostics we provide in this paper should help target reform on the most binding constraints that impede growth.

An important advantage of our framework is that it encompasses all major strategies of development and clarifies the circumstances under which each is likely to be effective. Strategies that focus on resource mobilization through foreign assistance and increased domestic national saving pay off when domestic returns are both high and privately appropriable. Strategies that focus on market liberalization and opening up work best when social returns are high and the most serious obstacle to their private appropriation is government imposed taxes and restrictions. Strategies that emphasize industrial policy are appropriate when private returns are depressed not by the government's errors of commission (what it does), but its errors of omission (what it fails to do).

As our discussion of El Salvador, Brazil, and the Dominican Republic illustrates, each of these circumstances throws out different diagnostic signals. An approach to development that determines the action agenda on the basis of these signals is likely to be considerably more effective than a laundry list approach with a long list of institutional and governance reforms that may or may not be well-targeted on the most binding constraints to growth.

References

Barth, G. C. and Levine, S. (2001). 'The Regulation and Supervision of Banks Around the World: A New Database'. World Bank Working Paper Series, No. 2588.

Caballero, R. J. and Krishnamurthy, A. (2003). 'Emerging Market Crises: An Asset Markets Perspective'. NBER Working Paper, No. 6843.

Eaton, J. and Gersovitz, M. (1981). 'Debt with Potential Repudiation: Theoretical and Empirical Analysis'. *Review of Economic Studies.*

Edwards, S. (1984). 'The Order of Liberalization of the External Sector in Developing Countries'. *Princeton Essays in International Finance,* 56.

Harberger, A. C. (2003). 'Interview with Arnold Harberger: Sound Policies Can Free Up Natural Forces of Growth'. *IMF Survey,* International Monetary Fund, Washington, DC, July 14, 213–16.

Hatta, T. (1997). 'A Theory of Piecemeal Policy Recommendations'. *Review of Economic Studies,* 44: 1–21.

Hausmann, R. and Rodrik, D. (2003). 'Economic Development as Self-Discovery'. *Journal of Development Economics,* 72 (December).

Hausmann, R., Pritchett, L., and Rodrik, D. (2004). 'Growth Accelerations'. Harvard University, May.

Loayza, N., Fajnzylber, P., and Calderón, C. (2002). '"Economic Growth in Latin America and the Caribbean" Stylized Facts, Explanations, and Forecasts'. World Bank Working Paper.

López, E. (2003). 'El Salvador: Growing in the Millennium'. World Bank, May 21.

16

A Practical Approach to Formulating Growth Strategies

Dani Rodrik[1]

Introduction

The central economic paradox of our time is that 'development' is working while 'development policy' is not. What I mean by this is the following: on the one hand, the last quarter-century has witnessed a tremendous and historically unprecedented improvement in the material conditions of hundreds of millions of people living in some of the poorest parts of the world; on the other hand, 'development policy' as it is commonly understood and advocated by multilateral organizations, aid agencies, Northern academics, and Northern-trained technocrats has largely failed to live up to its promise. Hence we are faced with the confluence of two seemingly contradictory trends.

Let us start with the successes. According to the latest World Bank estimates, there were roughly 400 million fewer 'poor' people in the world in 2001 compared to two decades earlier, when poverty is measured by the US$1 a day standard.[2] That represents a striking decline in the absolute number of the poor, not just in the relative incidence of poverty. What has made these gains possible is the sharp increase in economic growth in some of the poorest and most populous countries of the world—China and India in particular. China's growth rate since 1978 has been nothing short of spectacular, bringing considerable poverty reduction in its wake. In fact, the reduction in poverty in China alone accounts for the full 400 million global reduction, with the gains and losses in the rest of the world canceling each other out. The number of people below the US$1 a day line has fallen somewhat in South

[1] I thank Ricardo Hausmann, Lant Pritchett, Andres Rodriguez-Clare, Arvind Subramanian, and Andres Velasco, my co-authors on various research projects who contributed to the development of these ideas.

[2] Chen, S. and Ravallion, M. (n.d.) 'How Have the World's Poor Fared since the Early 1980s'. Working Paper, World Bank.

Asia, but increased sharply in Sub-Saharan Africa. In Latin America, poverty incidence has remained roughly constant, while the number of poor people has increased.

These regional disparities in performance match up very poorly against reform effort, when the latter is judged by the standard yardsticks of stabilization, liberalization, and privatization. The high performing economies have bucked conventional wisdom on what makes for good economic reform. China and Vietnam liberalized their economies in a partial, two track manner, did not undertake ownership reform, and protected themselves from GATT/WTO rules (in the case of China until very recently). India reformed very gradually, and only after a decade of strong economic growth. By any conventional measure of structural reform, these economies would be considered laggards. Given the policies in place in China, Vietnam, and India, it is hardly an exaggeration to say that it would have been easier to explain their performance if these countries had failed abysmally instead of succeeding the way that they did.

Meanwhile, Latin America, which adopted the standard agenda with great enthusiasm and undertook a considerable amount of 'structural reform', ended up growing slower not only relative to Asian countries but also relative to its own historical benchmarks. Reform in Sub-Saharan Africa may have been more halting than in Latin America, but still few can deny that this region now has much greater price stability than in the 1970s, is considerably more open to international trade, and gives much smaller role to parastatals and much greater role to markets. Yet the African successes have remained few, fleeting, and far between. It is apparent that reform efforts have not directly targeted the public health, governance, and resource mobilization challenges to which the continent has fallen prey.

To downplay the importance of these disappointments requires us to go through a number of contortions, none of which is particularly convincing. One counterargument is that countries in Latin America and Africa have simply not undertaken enough reform. What is 'enough' is obviously in the eyes of the beholder, but this claim seems to me to be grossly unfair to the scores of leaders in Latin America and Africa who have spent considerable political capital in pursuit of Washington Consensus style reforms. The weakness of the claim is also evident from the ease with which temporary successes in these countries have been ascribed to the reforms being implemented. Remember, for example, Argentina in the first half of the 1990s and how the growth spurt there was broadcast as evidence that 'reform pays off.'

A second counterargument is that 'the check is in the mail' (to use my colleague Ricardo Hausmann's caricature of this position). That is, the payoffs from reform have yet to appear, but will surely do so if we do not give up. The trouble is that this is entirely inconsistent with everything we know about the empirics of reform and growth. Growth follows rather immediately when the right things are done; there is no evidence to suggest that the returns to reform tend to be delayed. A third, somewhat related counterargument is that the first and second generation reforms were not enough, and that much more needs to be done to ensure growth will follow. Once again, this position is inconsistent with the evidence. As I have pointed out above, the countries that performed well are not those that undertook ambitious reform agendas—quite to the contrary. A fourth counterargument is that the poor performance in the reforming countries was due to external circumstances, for example, the overall slowdown in industrial country growth. This is not convincing because other developing countries managed rapid growth in the same economic environment. In any case, economic convergence ought to be a function of the convergence gap—the difference with the level of income prevailing in rich countries—which actually was larger in the case of Latin America and Africa in the 1990s compared to the 1970s.

Finally, there is the counterargument that the contrast I have drawn above is false insofar as countries that did well were those in fact that did follow conventional advice. China did turn to markets and sought to integrate itself with the world economy. India did liberalize. Both of these countries, the argument goes, reformed at the maximum speed that their complicated politics allowed, and reaped the benefits. So what is the problem? For one thing, this line of thought overlooks the unconventional elements in these countries' successes (just as the focus on Korea's and Taiwan's outward orientation often obscured their active use of industrial policy). China did not simply liberalize and open up; it did so by grafting a market track on top of plan track, by relying on Township and Village Enterprise (TVEs) rather than private enterprise, and through special economic zones rather than across the board trade liberalization. Moreover, implicit (and sometimes explicit) in this line of argument is that the partial, heterodox reform efforts in these countries would have yielded even more fruit had they been more by the book. One commonly hears that India, for example, would in fact have grown faster had its government been able to reform more comprehensively and rapidly. The trouble is that one looks in vain for countries that did in fact reform more comprehensively and rapidly than India did and ended up with higher growth. Nonetheless, the fact that there is enough in the successful heterodox approaches to give some comfort to the adherents of the orthodox agenda does indicate something. What it indicates is that there are indeed some broad principles which all successful countries have adhered to. Hence, all high performing economies have managed to maintain macroeconomic stability; they have relied on market forces to varying extents and sought to integrate into the world economy; they have protected property rights of investors and entrepreneurs to some extent and enforced contracts; they have maintained a semblance of social cohesion and political stability; they have ensured adequate standards of prudential regulation and avoided financial crises; they have maintained productive dynamism and encouraged economic diversification; and perhaps a few others. Note however that these commonalities can be articulated only at a sufficiently high level of generality, and in a manner that yields scant guidelines for operationalization. Take, for example, the objective of integration into the world economy. What is missing from the list is the specification of what specific policies would best serve that objective. It is tempting to say that the requisite policies are low policy barriers to foreign trade and investment, but then again the evidence hardly points to a straightforward relationship between trade and/or capital account liberalization and economic growth. The countries that most successfully integrated into the world economy (Korea and Taiwan in the 1960s and 1970s; China and Vietnam in the 1980s and 1990s) had highly protected home markets, and achieved integration through other means (export subsidies in the former and special economic zones in the latter). The bottom line is that these common elements do not map into unique, well-defined policy recommendations.

One conclusion one could take from this is that our ability as economists to design and recommend growth strategies is extremely limited. Basically, anything goes, and it is up to imaginative politicians to come up with recipes that will work. We have very limited advice to give them ex ante, even though we are in the possession of many tools to evaluate the consequences of their policy decisions ex post.

I think we can do better than adopt this kind of nihilistic attitude towards policy advice. If the original Washington Consensus erred in being too detailed and specific, and in assuming that the same set of policies work the same everywhere, policy nihilism goes too far in undervaluing the benefit of economic reasoning. I would like to outline here a way of thinking about growth strategies that avoids these two extremes. This approach consists of three elements. First, we need to undertake a diagnostic analysis to figure out where the most significant constraints on economic growth are. Second, we need creative and imaginative policy design to target the identified constraints appropriately. Third, we need to institutionalize the process of diagnosis and policy response to ensure that the economy remains dynamic and growth does not peter out. I will say a few words about each of these in what follows.

Step 1: Growth Diagnostics

An important reason why the Washington Consensus, and its subsequent variant, second generation reforms have failed to produce the desired outcome is that they were never targeted on what may have been the most important constraints blocking economic growth. The fact that poor economies are poor indicates that they suffer from a variety of afflictions: they are poorly endowed with human capital, make ineffective use of capital and other resources, have poor institutions, have unstable fiscal and monetary policies, provide inadequate private incentives for investment and technology adoption, have poor access to credit, are cut off from world markets, and so on. To say that one has to overcome all these disadvantages in order to develop is at once a tautology and quite unhelpful. If Chad did not have these problems, it would look like Sweden, and then it would not need to know the answer to the question: how can a country rise out of poverty? The trick is to find those areas where reform will yield the greatest return, or where we can get the biggest bang for the reform buck. What we need to know, in other words, is where the most binding constraint on growth lies. Otherwise, we are condemned to a spray gun approach: we shoot our reform gun on as many potential targets as possible, hoping that some will turn out to be the real live ones. That is in effect what the augmented Washington Consensus does. While there is nothing wrong in principle with any of the recommendations on this laundry list of reforms, there is also no guarantee that the really serious constraints are targeted in a priority fashion. A successful growth strategy, by contrast, begins by identifying the most binding constraints.

But can this be done? Is it possible to figure out where the most binding constraints are? In a longer paper that is summarized elsewhere in this volume, my co-authors Ricardo Hausmann, Andres Velasco, and I develop a framework that we believe suggests a positive answer.

We begin with a basic but powerful taxonomy. In a low-income economy, economic activity must be constrained by at least one of the following three factors: the cost of financing economic activity may be too high, the economic (social) return to economic activity may be too low, or the private appropriability of the (social) returns may be too low. The first step in the diagnostic analysis is to figure out which of these conditions more accurately characterizes the economy in question. At first sight, this may seem like a hopeless task. But fortunately, it is possible to make progress because each of these syndromes throws out different sets of diagnostic signals or generate different patterns of co-movements in economic variables. For example, in an economy that is constrained by cost of finance we would expect real interest rates to be high, borrowers to be chasing lenders, the current account deficit to be as high as foreign borrowing constraints will allow, and for entrepreneurs to be full of investment ideas. In such an economy, an exogenous increase in investable funds, such as foreign aid and remittances, will spur primarily investment and other productive economic activities rather than consumption or investment in real estate. This description comes pretty close to capturing the situation of Brazil, for example. By contrast, in an economy where economic activity is constrained by low private returns, interest rates will be low, banks will be flush in liquidity, lenders will be chasing after borrowers, the current account will be near balance or in surplus, and entrepreneurs will be more interested in putting their money in Miami or Geneva than in investing it at home. An increase in foreign aid or remittances will finance consumption, housing, or capital flight. These in turn are the circumstances of El Salvador, for example.

When we identify low private returns as the culprit, we will next want to know whether the source is low social returns or low private appropriability. Low social returns can be due to poor human capital, lousy infrastructure, or bad geography. Once again, we need to be on the lookout for diagnostic signals. If human capital (either because of low levels of education or the disease environment) is a serious constraint, we would expect the returns to education or the skill premium to be comparatively high. If infrastructure is the problem, we would observe the bottlenecks in transport or energy, private firms stepping in to supply the needed services, and so on. In the case of El Salvador, none of these seem to pose serious problems. Hence we infer that the constraint lies on the side of private appropriability. Appropriability problems can in turn arise under two sets of circumstances. One possibility has to do with the policy/institutional environment: taxes may be too high, property rights may be protected poorly, high inflation may generate macro risk, or labor–capital conflicts may depress production incentives. Alternatively, the fault may lie with the operation of markets insofar as markets cannot deal adequately with technological spillovers, coordination failures, and problems of economic 'self-discovery.'[3] As usual, we look for the tell-tale signs of each of these. Sometimes, the diagnostic analysis proceeds down a particular path not because of direct evidence but because the other paths have been ruled out. So in the case of El Salvador we concluded that lack of self-discovery was an important and binding constraint in part because there was little evidence in favor of the other traditional explanations.

It is possible to carry out this kind of analysis at a much finer level of disaggregation, and indeed any real world application has to be considerably more detailed than the one I have offered here. What I hope I have been able to provide is a glimpse of a type of analysis that is both doable and potentially much more productive than the conventional approach, which lacks any diagnostic component.

Step 2: Policy Design

Once the key problem(s) have been identified, we need to think about the appropriate policy response. Here, conventional welfare economics becomes invaluable. The key in this step is to focus on the market failures and distortions associated with the constraint identified in the previous step. The

[3] Hausmann, R. and Rodrik, D. (2003). 'Economic Development as Self-Discovery'. *Journal of Development Economics*, December.

principle of policy targeting offers a simple message: target the policy response as closely as possible on the source of the distortion. Hence if credit constraints are the main constraint, and the problem is the result of lack of competition and large bank spreads, the appropriate response is to reduce impediments to competition in the banking sector. If economic activity is held back because of high taxes at the margin, the solution is to lower them. If coordination or self-discovery externalities are at the root of stagnation, the solution would be to internalize those through government programs or private sector coordination. Simple as it may be, this first-best logic often does not work, and indeed can be even counterproductive. The reason is that we are necessarily operating in a second-best environment, due to other distortions or administrative and political constraints. In designing policy, we have to be on the lookout for unforeseen complications and unexpected consequences.

Let me illustrate this point with a few examples from China and elsewhere. Any economist visiting China in 1978 would have guessed that the most significant constraint holding the economy back was the lack of incentives in agriculture, due to the state purchase system and the communal ownership of land. The recommendation to abolish obligatory deliveries to the state at controlled prices and to privatize land would have followed naturally. After all, these are the first-best solutions to the problems at hand. However, a more detailed consideration of the situation reveals that these policies would have been fraught with danger. Abolishing the state purchase system would have wiped out a significant source of fiscal revenue for the central government, since the difference between the purchase and sale prices of crops constituted part of the government's tax base. Since the government used its crop supply to subsidize food prices in urban areas, it would also have implied a rise in food prices in urban areas, leading to demands for higher wages. Privatization of land in turn would have brought in its wake severe legal and administrative difficulties. Therefore, agricultural price liberalization and land privatization look considerably less desirable once their attendant costs in the form of macro instability, social strife in urban areas, and legal/administrative chaos are factored in.

Of course, this is not an argument for not undertaking reform. It is instead an argument for being creative and imaginative in designing policy responses that are sensitive to these second-best interactions. That in any case is the lesson of the Chinese reforms. For China neither abolished the state purchase system nor privatized land. The incentive problems were solved instead through the two-track pricing system—which involved grafting a market system on top of the state order system, and the household responsibility system—which effectively made households the residual claimants of output without giving them ownership rights. Under these reforms, households were required to deliver their quotas to the state at controlled prices, but were free to sell any of their surplus produce at free market prices. As long as the state quotas remain infra-marginal, efficiency in agriculture is obtained. The beauty of this arrangement, easier to appreciate in hindsight than with foresight at the time, is that it de-links the provision of supply incentives from its fiscal and distributive consequences. Therefore it avoids the second-best minefields that the more direct reforms would have stepped on.

A second illustration comes from another Chinese institutional innovation: township and village enterprises (TVEs). The TVEs were the growth engine of China until the mid-1990s, with their share in industrial value added rising to more than 50 percent by the early 1990s. Formal ownership rights in TVEs were vested not in private hands or in the central government, but in local communities (townships or villages). From the lens of first-best reform, these enterprises are problematic, since if our objective is to spur private investment and entrepreneurship, it would have been far preferable to institute private property rights (as Russia and other East European transition economies did). Here again, the first-best logic runs into trouble. A private property system relies on an effective judiciary for the enforcement of property rights and contracts. In the absence of such a legal system, formal property rights are not worth much—as minority shareholders in Russia soon discovered to their chagrin. And it takes time to establish honest, competent courts. In the meantime, perhaps it makes more sense to make virtue out of necessity and force entrepreneurs into partnership with their most likely expropriators, the local state authorities. That is exactly what the TVEs did. Local governments were keen to ensure the prosperity of these enterprises as their equity stake generated revenues directly for them. In the environment characteristic of China, property rights were effectively more secure under direct local government ownership than under a private property rights legal regime. The efficiency loss incurred due to the absence of private control rights was probably outweighed by the implicit security guaranteed by local government control. It is difficult to explain otherwise the remarkable boom in investment and entrepreneurship generated by such enterprises.

Or consider the case of achieving integration into the world economy. Policy leaders in countries such as South Korea and Taiwan in the early 1960s and China in the late 1970s had decided that enhancing their countries' participation in world markets was a key objective. For a Western economist, the most direct route would have been to reduce or eliminate barriers to imports and foreign investment. Instead, these countries achieved the same ends (i.e., they reduced the anti-trade bias of their economic policies) through unconventional means. South Korea and Taiwan employed export targets and export subsidies for their firms. China carved out special economic zones where foreign investors had access to a free-trade regime. These and other countries that opened up successfully but in an unconventional manner—for example, Malaysia and Mauritius—presumably did so because their approach created fewer adjustment costs and put less stress on established social bargains.

Let me offer as a final illustration the case of a saving constrained economy. Saving constraints can arise because households are in some sense short-sighted or do not fully internalize the high rate of returns that prevail in the real sector, in which case the first-best response would be to subsidize saving (say by offering favorable tax treatment of saving). Or they could arise because financial intermediation is not working properly, in which case the first-best response is to enhance the legal and supervisory apparatus that governs the financial markets.

These solutions are impractical and/or take a long time to implement in low-income economies. A second-best solution is a moderate amount of financial repression—what Hellman et al. call 'financial restraint.'[4] This entails controls on bank entry and ceilings on deposit rates, which generate rents for incumbent banks. Paradoxically, these rents induce banks to expand effort to mobilize deposits (since there are rents to be earned on them). The quality and level of financial intermediation can both be higher than under financial liberalization.

The bottom line is that while the first-best is an obvious place to start, the lesson of successful countries is that desired objectives—supply incentives, effective property rights, integration into the world economy, saving mobilization—can be achieved in a variety of ways, often taking unconventional forms. Functions that institutions perform do not map into unique institutional forms. We need to be imaginative, look for home grown solutions, and be prepared to experiment.

Step 3: Institutionalizing Reform

It is in the very nature of the growth diagnostics approach that I outlined above that the identity of the binding constraint will change over time. Schooling may not be a binding constraint at present in a country, but if the strategy works and investment and entrepreneurship is stimulated, it is likely to become one unless the quality and quantity of schools increase over time. The poor quality of the judiciary may not have high cost at present, but legal shortcomings are likely to loom larger when the economy develops and becomes more sophisticated. Poor financial regulation may not be an issue when financial intermediation is rudimentary, but can prove to be explosive when the economy begins to boom.

[4] Hellmann, T., Murdock, K., and Stiglitz, J. (1997). 'Financial Restraint: Towards a New Paradigm', in M. Aoki et al. (eds.), *The Role of Government in East Asian Economic Development: Comparative Institutional Analysis*. Oxford: Clarendon Press.

In Chapter 15 on growth diagnostics, Hausmann, Velasco, and I illustrate this with the example of the Dominican Republic. This country was able to spur growth with a number of sector specific reforms that stimulated investment in tourism and maquilas. But it neglected making the institutional investments required to lend resilience and robustness to economic growth—especially in the area of financial market regulation and supervision. When September 11 led to the drying up of tourist inflows, the country paid a big price. A Ponzi scheme that had developed in the banking sector collapsed, and cleaning up the mess cost the government 20 percentage points of GDP and led the economy into a downward spiral. It turned out that the economy had outgrown its weak institutional underpinnings. The same can be said of Indonesia, where the financial crisis of 1997–98 led to total economic and political collapse. It may yet turn out to be the case also of China, unless this country manages to strengthen the rule of law and enhance democratic participation.

Sustaining economic growth may be even harder than stimulating it. This was the clear message of the research that Ricardo Hausmann, Lant Pritchett, and I undertook on 'Growth Accelerations.' We found in this research that growth accelerations—our criterion was an increase in growth of two percentage points that was maintained for at least eight years—are a fairly frequent occurrence. On average a country has a one in four chance of experiencing a growth acceleration in any given decade. Sustained growth, by contrast, is rare. Very few of the 83 accelerations we uncovered had turned into sustained convergence with the living standards of the rich countries.

What is needed to sustain growth? I would emphasize two forms of institutional reforms in particular. First, there is the need to maintain productive dynamism over time. Natural resource discoveries, garment exports from maquilas, or a free-trade agreement may spur growth for a limited time. Policy needs to ensure that this momentum is maintained with ongoing diversification into new areas of tradables. Otherwise, growth will simply peter out. What stands out in the performance of East Asian countries is their continued focus on the needs of the real economy and the ongoing encouragement of technology adoption and diversification. Market forces are not necessarily enough to generate this dynamism, and need to be complemented with proactive public strategies.[5]

The second area that needs attention is the strengthening of domestic institutions of conflict management. The most frequent cause for the collapse in growth is the inability to deal with the consequences of external shocks—in other words, terms of trade declines or reversals in capital flows. Endowing the economy with resilience against such shocks requires strengthening the rule

[5] See Rodrik, D. (2004). 'Industrial Policy for the Twenty-First Century'. Unpublished paper for UNIDO, Harvard University, for an elaboration of this thesis.

of law, solidifying (or putting in place) democratic institutions, establishing participatory mechanisms, and erecting social safety nets. When such institutions are in place, the macroeconomic and other adjustments needed to deal with adverse shocks can be undertaken relatively smoothly. When they are not, the result is distributive conflict and economic collapse. The contrasting experiences of South Korea and Indonesia in the immediate aftermath of the Asian financial crisis are quite instructive in this regard.

Concluding Remarks

I have offered here not a policy reform agenda, but a way of thinking about such an agenda that I think has considerably more potential than the Washington Consensus in any of its variants. I have tried to show that the diagnostic approach I advocate can be implemented, that it has the advantage that it provides country specific solutions, and that it is by its very nature sensitive to political and administrative constraints. This approach is inherently bottom-up: it empowers countries to do their own diagnostic analyses; it warns multilateral organizations against uniformity and excessive restrictions on 'policy space'; even when it does not yield clearcut results on what the binding constraint is, it provides a useful framework for discussing what should be done and why.

Furthermore the diagnostic approach embeds all major existing strategic approaches to growth, and serves to clarify the conditions under which they are relevant. Hence, a substantial rise in foreign aid will work in settings where a country is saving constrained. Industrial policy will work when private returns are low due to informational and coordination failures. Reducing trade barriers will work when such barriers are the main determinant of the gap between private and social returns to entrepreneurial activity. And so on.

Finally, the diagnostic approach has the advantage that it employs economists in their proper capacity: as evaluators of trade-offs instead of as advocates. Carlos Diaz-Alejandro once quipped, paraphrasing Oscar Wilde, that an economist is someone who knows the shadow price of everything but the value of nothing. The diagnostic approach makes virtue of this occupational hazard: it asks economists for estimates of shadow prices (of various constraints associated with economic growth) and not for their value judgments.

Index

Index